Politics of the Womb

Politics of the Womb

Women, Reproduction, and the State in Kenya

LYNN M. THOMAS

University of California Press

BERKELEY   LOS ANGELES   LONDON

An earlier version of chapter 1 appeared as Lynn M. Thomas, "Imperial Concerns and 'Women's Affairs': State Efforts to Regulate Clitoridectomy and Eradicate Abortion in Meru, Kenya, c. 1910–1950," *Journal of African History* 39 (1998): 121–45. Reprinted courtesty of Cambridge University Press.

An earlier version of chapter 3 appeared as Lynn M. Thomas, "'Ngaitana (I will circumcise myself)': The Gender and Generational Politics of the 1956 Ban on Clitoridectomy in Meru, Kenya," *Gender and History* 8, 3 (1996): 338–63. Reprinted courtesy of Blackwell Publishers.

An earlier version of chapter 5 appeared as Lynn M. Thomas, "The Politics of the Womb: Kenyan Debates of the Affiliation Act," *Africa Today* 47: 151–76. Reprinted courtesy of Indiana University Press.

University of California Press
Berkeley and Los Angeles, California

University of California Press, Ltd.
London, England

Library of Congress Cataloging-in-Publication Data

Thomas, Lynn M.
    Politics of the womb : women, reproduction, and the state in Kenya / Lynn M. Thomas.
        p.   cm.
    Includes bibliographical references and index.
    ISBN 0–520–22450–7 (Cloth : alk. paper) — ISBN 0–520–23540–1 (Paper : alk. paper)
    1. Women—Kenya—History.   2. Female circumcision—Kenya—History.   3. Women—Kenya—Social conditions.   4. Kenya—Social conditions.   5. Sex role—Kenya.   I. Title.
HQ1796.5 .T48 2003
305.4'096762—dc21   2002012586

Manufactured in the United States of America
12   11   10   09   08   07   06   05   04   03
10   9   8   7   6   5   4   3   2   1

The paper used in this publication is both acid-free and totally chlorine-free (TCF). It meets the minimum requirements of ANSI/NISO Z39.48–1992 (R 1997) *(Permanence of Paper).*⊗

For my mother and in memory of my father

Contents

Acknowledgments

The roots of this book lie in an honors thesis on marriage law in postcolonial Kenya. When I was a second-year undergraduate, David William Cohen agreed to be my academic advisor. He continued in that role over the next ten years and at three different universities. In freely sharing his scholarship and ideas, he encouraged me to develop my own and convinced me that I had something significant to contribute. I would also like to thank a remarkable group of students at Johns Hopkins University—Keith Breckenridge, Timothy Burke, Catherine Burns, Clifton Crais, Garrey Dennie, Carolyn Hamilton, George Martin, and Jonathon Sadowsky—who first showed me the intellectual and political excitement of studying African history.

I am grateful to the Thomas J. Watson Foundation for granting me a fellowship to study women and customary law in Kenya during 1989–90. The generosity of Gitobu and Florence Imanyara, their families, and the staff of the *Nairobi Law Monthly* made that year a tremendous experience. The Imanyaras introduced me to Meru by inviting me to accompany them on a visit "home." And when I expressed an interest to return, they arranged for me to stay with relatives. In Meru, Sara Ayub, Zipporah and Kiautha Arithi, Charity Nduru, and Grace Kirimi extended unending hospitality and taught me much about life in Meru town and its surrounding environs. In Nairobi, Martin Fischer, Mary McVay, and Pauline Njuki similarly offered hospitality and friendship. During that first visit to Kenya, I also met Luise White. Her innovative scholarship, generous advice, and enthusiasm for this project have strongly influenced its development. I thank them all.

As a graduate student at Northwestern University and the University of Michigan, I had the privilege to study with a number of gifted scholars and teachers. Frederick Cooper provided me with orienting questions and working chronologies. Each chapter of this book bears the mark of his judicious advice and astute criticism. Nancy Rose Hunt's imaginative and rigorous approach to the study of gender and medicine in Africa nurtured this project from its earliest stages. I am also grateful to several other teachers who shaped my intellectual path: Keletso Atkins, Joseph Barton, Caroline Bledsoe, James Campbell, Kathleen Canning, Nicholas Dirks, Jonathon Glassman, Ivan Karp, Micaela di Leonardo, Richard Lepine, James Oakes, and Ann Laura Stoler. Fellow graduate students Lisa Lindsay, Stephan Miescher, Steven Pierce, Orit Schwartz, Rebecca Shereikis, Kerry Ward, and especially Keith Shear offered comradery and constructive criticism.

I am grateful to the History Department at the University of Nairobi and its then chair, Henry Mutoro, for granting me affiliation status, providing advice, and inviting me to present a paper during my dissertation research in 1994–95. I thank Ntai wa Nkararu for tutoring me in the Meru language and sharing his insightful perspective on my research interests and politics in contemporary Kenya. I deeply regret that his untimely death means that I cannot hear what he thinks of this book. Other friends and fellow researchers in Nairobi and Meru who provided valuable support and feedback during 1994–95 or during a shorter trip in 1999 include: Lucy Arithi, Judith Brown, Ashley Cruce, Catherine Dolan, Margaret Gachihi, Joseph Heathcott, Tove Jensen, Paul Goldsmith, Juliet Kireru, James Laiboni, Maureen Malowany, Mwiti Manyara, Kenda Mutongi, Agnes Odinga, and David Sandgren. In particular, I learned much from countless conversations with Kenda Mutongi about research findings and African historiography. Mary McVay and Shirin Walji offered gracious hospitality and assistance in Nairobi.

My greatest debt is to the people who assisted me in conducting oral history research in Meru and to those who agreed to be interviewed. Carol Gatwiri, Doreen Kathure, Richard Kirimi, Rosemary Kithiira, Thomas Mutethia, Nkatha Mworoa, and Diana Rigiri made this part of my research possible by providing logistical and translation assistance during interviews, and by transcribing and translating interview tapes afterwards. In the process of spending many hours waiting for public transportation, hiking to the homes of interviewees, conducting interviews, and reviewing transcripts, I shared the thrills and frustrations of research with them. To the several dozen men and women in Meru who agreed to spend a couple of hours or more answering our queries and telling stories, I am deeply grateful. Many of the arguments in this book depend upon their contributions. I would also like to thank a retired colonial officer and three retired missionaries in England who shared their memories of Meru with me.

I cannot imagine a more pleasant and collegial environment in which to teach, research, and write than the History Department at the University of Washington. As chair of the Department, Robert Stacey provided advice and understanding at key moments. The History Research Group, "Daughter of HRG," and the members of my writing group—Madeleine Yue Dong, Ranji Khanna, Uta G. Poiger, Priti Ramamurthy, and Alys Eve Weinbaum— helped to clarify and strengthen my analysis. Stephanie Camp, Lucy Jarosz, and Sarah Stein similarly offered encouragement and insightful commentary. Uta G. Poiger deserves special acknowledgment for reading and discussing each chapter more than once and helping me to see the arguments that connected them. My students, particularly those in my health and healing course during spring 2001, taught me much about what is most interesting and important in the study of African history.

At various stages of writing, David Anderson, E. S. Atieno-Odhiambo, Angelique Haugerud, Gillian Feeley-Harnik, Steven Feierman, Andy Ivaska, Corinne Kratz, Paul Landau, John Lonsdale, Agnes Odinga, Bethwell A. Ogot, Randall Packard, Derek Peterson, Richard Roberts, Pamela Scully, Brett Shadle, Kearsley Stewart, Susan Cotts Watkins, and Justin Willis provided useful commentary and research leads. I thank Caroline Morris for cleaning up my footnotes and bibliography and Jessica Powers for suggesting ways to make my prose more readable. I am also grateful to Monica McCormick of the University of California Press for her interest in this project and her patience throughout the revision process.

Financial support during coursework, research, and writing was generously provided by a Jacob K. Javits Fellowship; a Social Science Research Council Pre-Dissertation Africa Fellowship; a Hans E. Panofsky Pre-Dissertation Fellowship, Northwestern University; a Fulbright–Institute of International Education Scholarship for Kenya; an International Doctoral Research fellowship sponsored by the Joint Committee on African Studies of the Social Science Research Council and the American Council of Learned Societies; a Charlotte W. Newcombe Doctoral Dissertation Fellowship; a tuition waiver from the Rackham Graduate School and grant from the History Department at the University of Michigan; and the Royalty Research Fund, the Keller Fund, and the Simpson Center for the Humanities at the University of Washington. This book would not have been possible without research clearance from the Office of the President, Government of Kenya. I am also grateful to the staff at the various archives, libraries, and offices in Kenya, England, Scotland, and the United States where I did documentary research. A special thanks to Stephen M'Mugambi of Nairobi for granting me access to the personal papers of his grandfather, Philip M'Inoti.

The support of my own family has also been essential. My brothers and especially my sister's words and acts of kindness have meant much to me. Even when I was thousands of miles away, my mother's love has been a source of strength and comfort. The memory of my father and his passion for learning has been an inspiration. Finally, I would like to thank Michael Sanderson. From that first trip to Kenya to the final book revisions, with humor and affection, he has expressed an unfailing confidence in my work while continually reminding me of the world beyond it.

List of Abbreviations

ADC   African District Council (previously, LNC)
AR   Annual Report
CSM   Church of Scotland Mission (Presbyterian)
DC   District Commissioner
EAMJ   *East Africa Medical Journal*
EARC   East African Royal Commission
FGM   Female genital mutilation
KATU   Kenya African Teachers' Union
KCA   Kikuyu Central Association
Ksh   Kenyan shillings
LNC   Local Native Council (later, ADC)
MMS   Methodist Missionary Society
PC   Provincial Commissioner
Shs   shillings

For abbreviations used in archival citations, see Bibliography.

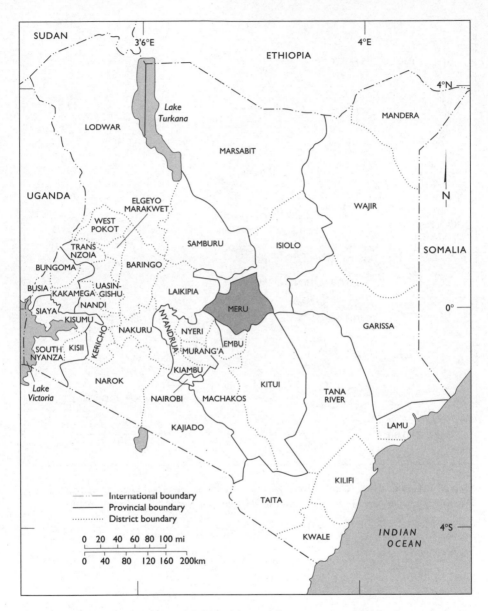

Map 1.   Meru District in Kenya. Adapted from Gideon S. Were, ed. *Meru District, Socio-Cultural Profile.* Nairobi: Ministry of Planning and National Development and Institute of African Studies, University of Nairobi, 1988, p. 2.

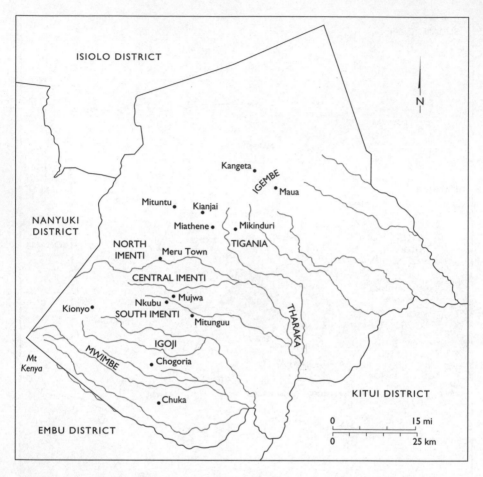

ISIOLO DISTRICT

N

Kangeta
IGEMBE
Maua

Mituntu   Kianjai
Miathene   Mikinduri

NANYUKI
DISTRICT

TIGANIA

NORTH
IMENTI   Meru Town

CENTRAL IMENTI

Kionyo   Nkubu   Mujwa
SOUTH IMENTI   Mitunguu

THARAKA

IGOJI
Chogoria

Mt
Kenya   MWIMBE

KITUI DISTRICT

Chuka

EMBU DISTRICT

0   15 mi
0   25 km

Map 2.   Meru District. Adapted from Jeffrey A. Fadiman, *An Oral History of Tribal Warfare: The Meru of Mt. Kenya*. Athens, OH: Ohio University Press, 1982, p. iii.

Introduction

Elder of the Church, your uncircumcised daughter
is pregnant and she will give birth to dogs.[1]

During the last few months of 1929, thousands of African young men and women gathered on mission stations and school grounds in colonial central Kenya to perform a dance-song called the *Muthirigu*. This dance-song protested colonial interference in female "circumcision" or excision, a part of adolescent initiation.[2] It chastised white Protestant missionaries, British colonial officers, and local leaders who supported efforts to end the practice. The above *Muthirigu* verse mocked a black church elder by proclaiming that his uninitiated daughter was ill-mannered and incapable of giving birth to proper human beings. According to this central Kenyan perspective, girls who had reached puberty but were not initiated represented reproductive aberrations; they were physically able but not socially consecrated to conceive and give birth. Through performing the *Muthirigu* dance-song, young people defended excision as a reproductive necessity.

Missionaries, government officials, and their local allies perceived the *Muthirigu* dance-song as a direct threat to political stability. In early 1930 the colonial government banned it as seditious. Those caught performing the *Muthirigu* dance-song were ordered to pay heavy fines or serve jail terms of several months. These severe penalties quickly curtailed its performance. But by the time this ban came into effect, young men and women had already made their point. The vigor and scale of their performances had demonstrated to colonial officials the depth of local commitment to female excision. Officials realized the political difficulties, if not impossibilities, of enforcing a prohibition on the practice.

Within Kenyan history the *Muthirigu* dance-song and the 1928–31 "female circumcision controversy" of which it was part have been identified as crucial events in the development of nationalist politics. In fact, historians have viewed these events as the most significant period of anticolonial resis-

1

tance in central Kenya prior to the Mau Mau rebellion of the 1950s.[3] The Kikuyu Central Association (KCA), a black political organization demanding the return of Kikuyu land given to white settlers, played a key role in the controversy. Recognizing an opportunity to increase popular support for their organization, KCA leaders denounced all colonial interference with female excision. In turn, verses of the *Muthirigu* dance-song were devoted to praising KCA leaders, including Johnstone (later, Jomo) Kenyatta, the organization's representative in London and future first president of an independent Kenya. In addition to increasing support for the KCA, the "female circumcision controversy" prompted black teachers, parents, and students to leave Protestant mission stations and found their own churches and schools. The establishment of these independent churches and schools further demonstrated to government officials and missionaries the political difficulties of interfering with female excision.

The "female circumcision controversy" encompassed all of central Kenya, including Meru, an administrative district occupying the northeast reaches of the region. As in the other five districts of central Kenya, in Meru, missionary efforts to discourage female excision and rumors of an imminent government ban provoked local Christians to renounce their church memberships and young people to perform the *Muthirigu* dance-song. At the Methodist mission station near Meru town, church membership suddenly dropped from 70 members to 6, while at Chogoria, a Presbyterian station in the southern part of the district, membership plummeted from 120 to 16.[4]

Unlike in most other districts, however, colonial interference in female initiation in Meru did not end in 1930. Rather, in the years following the "female circumcision controversy", British officers in conjunction with government-appointed black headmen and police undertook a series of campaigns to enforce female excision at a younger age. These campaigns were a profound contradiction of the colonial government's stated opposition to the practice. While colonial officials in Nairobi and London continued to denounce female excision, their subordinates in Meru actually enforced it. As will be explored and explained in chapter 1, officials undertook these campaigns as a pro-natalist measure. They believed that by initiating girls at a younger age they would be able to combat local practices of abortion and prevent the demographic decline of the Meru people.

In situating this extraordinary history of colonial enforcement of female initiation as a starting point, this book seeks to deepen our understanding of the "female circumcision controversy" and others concerning black Kenyan women and their reproductive capacities. Previous scholarship has identified such controversies as key episodes in the development of anticolonial resistance. Like so many other topics in twentieth-century African history, reproductive controversies have been folded into narratives of nationalist triumph. While such an approach rightfully insists on the political importance of such episodes, it reduces a complex array of political struggles and positions to the stark dichotomy of colonial oppression versus anticolonial resistance. Moreover, it fails to explain why reproduction was such a fraught realm of state intervention in colonial and, after 1963, postcolonial Kenya. This book, by contrast, analyzes specific reproductive interventions and debates to elucidate the shifting relations and ideologies of gender, generation, and governance that animated them. It asks a new set of questions. What motivated white missionaries' and colonial officers' uneven efforts to remake and control reproduction? Why did some black Kenyans participate in these interventions and debates while others defied or simply ignored them? And how did these reproductive events contribute to the reworking of political and moral order?

POLITICS OF THE WOMB

To answer these questions, this book develops the analytical concept of the politics of the womb. My formulation of the politics of the womb draws inspiration from Jean-François Bayart's concept of the politics of the belly. In his far-reaching and influential interpretation of African politics, *The State in Africa*, Bayart takes the Cameroonian idiom, *la politique du ventre* (the politics of the belly), and deploys it as an analytic for understanding the political history of Africa.[5] According to Bayart, the politics of the belly connotes several key realities. First, this bodily idiom speaks to the fact that in many African contexts hunger has been and continues to be a pervasive problem, while being well-fed or corpulent is considered a sign of wealth and power. Bayart argues that sub-Saharan Africans have often described politics through the imagery of how much and what different people eat. The politics of the belly points to the propensity of politicians to hoard and greedily consume resources in things and people. In addition to highlighting the significance of idioms of eating and the belly to African conceptions of power, Bayart's analysis insists on the importance of vertical relationships—those between social unequals such as parents and children or patrons and clients—to understanding African political history. It is these hierarchical relationships rather than ones based in lateral connections such as class solidarity, Bayart argues, that structure state politics.

Building on these insights, this book insists that struggles centered on another, specifically gendered, part of the abdomen—the womb—have also been important to the political history of Africa. In fact, in older forms of Swahili, the lingua franca spoken throughout much of East and Central Africa, the same word—*tumbo*—referred to both the belly and the womb.[6] Assuming a male belly as the universal belly, Bayart's analysis reveals how hierarchies of wealth and power are enacted and symbolized through eating and consumption. Alternatively, this study examines the particular capacities and powers attached to the female belly or the womb to demonstrate the centrality of reproductive struggles to African history.[7]

The politics of the womb makes three main contributions to African historiography. First, it elucidates how reproductive struggles have been a crucial part of intertwined efforts to gain material resources and fulfill moral ambitions. Material resources have encompassed things that satisfy bodily needs and desires, while moral ambitions have included efforts to act in ways valued by the living and the dead. Through examining the politics of the womb, we can see how questions of who should conceive and carry a pregnancy to term and who should assist in childbirth and childrearing have repeatedly been framed as pressing material and moral issues. Second, the politics of the womb highlights how reproductive concerns have structured old hierarchies based in gender, generation, and kinship, and contributed to the construction of new ones grounded in racial difference and "civilized" status. Relations of inequality have long entailed struggles over who should control women's sexuality and who should reap the rewards of and bear the responsibility for their fertility. The politics of the womb draws attention to elites' persistent efforts to regulate reproduction and the continual challenges that they faced from juniors and dependents, subjects and citizens. Finally, it reveals that the political history of Africa and elsewhere must be explored through relations that stretch from the local to the global. Reproduction, perhaps more so than any other realm of social life, demonstrates how the most intimate actions and desires are connected to debates and interventions that flow from community, colonial, and international regimes. By drawing these various regimes into a single frame of analysis, the politics of the womb elucidates how African political history must encompass the study of households, initiation, and marriage as well as overseas trade, imperialism, and international aid.

Focusing on twentieth-century Kenya, this book argues that reproduction became the subject of colonial and postcolonial debate and intervention because so many people viewed its regulation as fundamental to the construction of political and moral order, and proper gender and generational relations. During the female circumcision controversy, for instance, white missionaries, British colonial officers, black leaders, and those who organized and underwent excision vehemently contested the best ways to prepare female bodies and minds for pregnancy and childbirth. Yet they all agreed that reproductive processes were essential to the well-being of individuals and communities and to the formation of respectful and respectable men and women. During such colonial and postcolonial controversies, women's status, their health, and intimate relations between men and women became subjects of widespread discussion and targets of new policies. Through these episodes, people also defined and contested men's and women's relative powers, and the just content and scope of state power. The politics of the womb provides a framework for elucidating the importance of reproductive struggles to African political history and exploring the mutually constitutive relationship between gender, generation, and governance in twentieth-century Kenya.

Reproductive controversies are especially illuminating sites through which to analyze state power because they reveal how officials and politicians have simultaneously sought to juggle the material and moral obligations of rule. They also reveal how women's bodies and reputations have often provided the link between these two realms. As Ann Stoler and Frederick Cooper have argued, studies of colonialism need to attend to the connections between colonial states' efforts to promote "specific relations of production and exchange" and the "cultural work" these states performed in gaining consent from metropolitan and local constituencies.[8] Few colonial officers were ever simply interested in securing profits for imperial coffers or their compatriots. They sought to balance colonial demands for African land and labor against the need to maintain political control and to fulfill the "white man's burden" of civilizing the "barbaric" and improving women's status. Whether prompted by metropolitan critics, local exigencies, or their own consciences, colonial officials undertook moralizing projects. In rural Kenya, they staged campaigns against "repugnant" practices, including excision and abortion, established maternity clinics, and instituted laws to deter pregnancy prior to marriage. But rather than viewing such projects as detracting from the colonial objectives of extracting wealth and securing political control, officials often framed them as furthering such objectives. Pronatalist initiatives such as anti-abortion campaigns and maternity clinics asserted the superiority of white ways and sought to foster the development of larger and stronger pools of black labor. Similarly, officials justified efforts to curb premarital pregnancies as shoring up the authority of African patriarchs upon whom they depended to keep unruly young men and women in check.

Through the politics of the womb, competing reproductive concerns and domains of power intersected and, eventually, became entangled. People, things, and ideas moved back and forth, between households and hospitals in rural areas; government offices and medical training centers in Nairobi; the Colonial Office and the House of Commons in London; and, later, between international aid offices and conferences in New York and Beijing. Attention to such connections necessarily engages what Steven Feierman and John M. Janzen have identified as a core challenge in the study of reproduction and health in Africa: tracing "the relationship between the most intimate sphere of people's everyday lives and overarching political and economic power."[9] Unpacking the politics of the womb allows us to see how the colonial and postcolonial Kenyan state has consistently operated at the nexus of forces from below, above, inside, and outside the colony and nation. It also suggests that reproductive debates and interventions have been particularly tenacious in their ability to engage concerns emanating from various domains of power—local, colonial, national, and global—and strikingly different cultural frameworks. Few participants in twentieth-century Kenyan politics were ever able to neatly separate issues of land, labor, and political control from those of gender, sexuality, and reproduction. For colonial rulers and subjects as well as their postcolonial successors, managing the politics of the womb has been crucial to ensuring material prosperity and constructing moral persons and communities.

CRITICAL EVENTS

This book explores the politics of the womb by analyzing a series of "critical events." As defined by Veena Das, critical events are those that rework "traditional categories," prompting "new modes of action" to come into being. Moreover, they are events that leave their mark on a variety of institutions, including "family, community, bureaucracy, courts of law, the medical profession, the state, and multi-national corporations."[10] The following chapters analyze critical events that contributed to redefining reproduction in twentieth-century Kenya.

Chapter 1 examines efforts during the 1920s and 1930s to regulate the severity and alter the timing of female excision and to prevent abortion. Chapter 2 explores how colonial rulers and subjects linked female initiation to childbirth. While missionaries and colonial officers believed that excision led to complications in childbirth and hence promoted hospital births for some excised parturients, many central-Kenyan women viewed excision as facilitating childbirth and were suspicious of those who assisted with hospital births. Chapter 3 examines the colonial government's wildly unsuccessful attempt to ban female excision during the Mau Mau rebellion of the 1950s. Chapters 4 and 5 explore the development and use of laws relating to premarital pregnancy in the late colonial and early postcolonial periods.[11] These laws, which aimed to hold men responsible for the reproductive consequences of sexual encounters, were the subject of intense debates among government officials, nationalist politicians, women's and welfare organizations, and young people and their parents. While chapter 4 focuses on struggles over the customary law of pregnancy compensation in a rural area, chapter 5 examines national debates over the Affiliation Act, a statutory law that granted single women the right to sue for paternity. The Conclusion further considers the postcolonial politics of the womb by discussing ongoing struggles surrounding population control, family planning, HIV/AIDS, and "female genital mutilation."

These critical events were chosen because of the reproductive themes that they share. Nancy Rose Hunt has observed that while much scholarship on women and gender in African history has been framed through the Marxist-feminist analytic of production and reproduction, historians have generally shied away from exploring the conventional meaning of reproduction—procreation.[12] This book challenges that reluctance by taking female initiation, pregnancy, and childbirth as starting points. It explores how these procreative processes became the subject of political controversy in twentieth-century Kenya and, in turn, how these controversies shaped and were shaped by broader debates over how best to produce families, communities, states, and nations. Female initiation, pregnancy, and childbirth were such contentious matters because they were important to parents' and elders' efforts to create respectful and successful descendants and juniors, and the colonial and postcolonial state's efforts to cultivate loyal and productive subjects and citizens. The critical events examined in this book also share a tendency to conflate heterosexuality with reproduction. This conflation is at odds with much current thinking within the academy and beyond that insists that sex and reproduction be considered as distinct conceptual categories.[13] While recognizing that these categories are not coterminous, this book explores how and why various people in colonial and postcolonial Kenya framed heterosexual relations as reproductive concerns.

Analyzing these critical events required collecting and connecting a wide range of sources. The following chapters draw upon documentary sources gathered at archives and libraries in Kenya, Britain, and the United States.

Relevant holdings included government and missionary reports and correspondence, ethnographies, personal papers and letters, court records, parliamentary debates, and newspapers. The following chapters also draw upon interviews conducted with a few former colonial officers and missionaries in Britain and dozens of men and women in central Kenya.[14] The combination of sources used in each chapter varies, reflecting the shifting types of evidence generated by each critical event. Whereas the first three chapters draw heavily on the published writings of government officials and missionaries, and interviews with older people in Meru, the latter two chapters make extensive use of the contending viewpoints presented in court records, legislative proceedings, and the press. The most compelling arguments of this book emerge from bringing a range of sources into dialogue to reveal the disjunctures, contradictions, and at times continuities between them. This approach recognizes the analytic challenges and potential political pitfalls of "speaking for" historical subjects living in worlds quite distinct from one's own.[15] But it is grounded in the supposition that historical scholarship derives much of its critical edge from reconstructing and juxtaposing the very different ways in which historical subjects have understood and engaged the events and processes that shaped their lives.

Much of the action in the following chapters takes place in Meru. Demarcated as an administrative district by colonial officials in 1910, it covered over 9,900 square kilometers, including the eastern slopes of Mt. Kenya, the equally verdant Nyambene hills, and the drier surrounding plains. By 1948, over 320,000 people lived in this area. The most recent census figures put the total population for the area, now subdivided into four districts (Meru Central, Meru North, Tharaka, and Nithi), at 1.4 million.[16] Kikuyu intellectuals and politicians, including the late Jomo Kenyatta, have often considered Meru to be the northeastern reaches of Kikuyuland.[17] People in Meru do share strong cultural and linguistic similarities, along with an uneven history of political alliance with Kikuyus as well as Embus, their neighbors to the south. They speak closely related Bantu languages, and in the precolonial period they lived in small, similarly organized agricultural communities that interacted with each other through trade and marriage as well as cattle raiding and warfare.[18] Over the course of colonial rule, however, Meru intellectuals and leaders, together with British officials and missionaries, worked to establish Meru as a distinct language and "tribe."[19] As we shall see, these architects of Meru ethnicity placed varying practices of female initiation, courtship, and child custody alongside differences in language, historical origins, and political institutions when distinguishing Merus from Kikuyus.

Due to its great distance from Nairobi and any railway lines, Meru was the last section of the central highlands to come under colonial rule. The area's remoteness similarly discouraged all but a few white farmers from appropriating land and settling there. Early colonial officials viewed Meru as a source of male migrant labor for building roads and railway lines, and for working on settler farms elsewhere in central Kenya. Geographically marginal, Meru remained at the fringe of colonial economics and high politics. This peripheral status encouraged administrative officers to attempt interventions rarely contemplated elsewhere in central Kenya. During the 1930s Meru became the first district in which black Kenyans were permitted to cultivate coffee, as well as the site of unparalleled efforts to rework customary institutions like female initiation.[20]

Attention to a single (albeit large) rural area enables a thorough exploration of reproductive politics at the local level. Meru became the geographical focus of this study because of its extraordinary and largely unexamined history of colonial interventions targeting excision and abortion. Meru proved to be a particularly productive site for exploring the politics of the womb because of its position within the colonial imagination, initially as an exceptionally remote and "backward" area and, later, as an area in which "traditional" institutions remained intact. Although some of the critical events explored in this book occurred only in Meru, the issues that animated these interventions and debates often existed elsewhere and always embodied more widely shared concerns about who should conceive, bear, and rear children.[21] The following chapters reveal how the politics of the womb, even at the local level, involved complex meanings and intersecting hierarchies. As the twentieth century unfolded, these local reproductive meanings and hierarchies became increasingly entangled with those emanating from Nairobi, London, and New York.

COMPETING REPRODUCTIVE CONCERNS

This book provides a history to contemporary interest in African reproduction. Over the past three decades, policymakers and politicians have repeatedly linked the health and prosperity of African peoples and nations to fertility and sexuality. Since the 1960s population specialists have offered dire predictions for African countries that fail to institute large-scale family planning programs aimed at curbing African women's high rates of fertility. The AIDS epidemic of the past twenty years and recent debates over practices of female genital cutting in Africa and among African immigrant communities abroad have only strengthened this international perspective tying Africa's future to issues of sexuality.

In focusing attention on these issues, social scientists, politicians, and the press have located the roots of many of Africa's postcolonial problems in "traditional" reproductive practices. This book casts these contemporary concerns and campaigns in critical perspective by revealing that such concerns are not new and that present-day reproductive practices cannot be simply understood as "natural" or "traditional" relics from an unchanging past. Rather, female initiation, pregnancy, and childbirth have long been important sites through which men and women of various ages and positions have constructed and contested power.

For a number of reasons, postcolonial Kenya has attracted a disproportionate share of international attention and resources directed at African reproductive practices. During the 1960s and 1970s demographers estimated that the average number of children born alive to a Kenyan woman over the course of her life was between 6.6 and 8.0. These high fertility rates, coupled with a relatively well-developed infrastructure, stable government, and a heavy dependence on foreign aid, made Kenya a favored target of population-control advocates. International demographers and funders were also probably attracted to Kenya by Nairobi's good weather, the widespread use of English, and the chance to go on "safari" while working in the country. During the 1990s, population experts and agencies refocused international attention on Kenya, touting the drop in national fertility rates to 4.7 live births per woman as a family planning success story.[22] As the regional base for countless foreign journalists and international organizations, Kenya and its capital city of Nairobi also stood at center stage during the emergence of the AIDS epidemic. During the mid-1980s, stories of HIV infection among Nairobi's sex workers featured prominently in the international news coverage of AIDS in Africa.[23] Over the past decade, funds from the growing international anti–"female genital mutilation" (FGM) movement have been directed toward Kenya. With its numerous women's and health organizations, many with their roots in the family planning movement, Kenya continued in the late 1990s to be a comparatively attractive place for intervening and attempting to alter African reproductive practices.

Of course, the troubled history of Euro-American interest in and anxiety over African reproduction extends back beyond the twentieth century. Since as early as the sixteenth century, accounts of African men's virility and African women's licentiousness and fecundity had been a staple of European representations of African "barbarity." These images cast black women as less moral, and more sexually independent and reproductively able, than white women. During the era of the Atlantic slave trade, Euro-American slave traders and slave owners raped African women and subjected them to work as mistresses and wet nurses.[24] While abolitionists protested such brutalization and exploitation of black women, they were unable to subvert Euro-American stereotypes of African women as oversexed. Instead, abolitionist efforts to end the slave trade within Africa contributed to the construction of an alternative image of African women as victims of African men. Just as defenders of New World slavery perceived black men as a sexual threat to white women, opponents of the slave trade within Africa often portrayed African men as abusing African women. Building upon this abolitionist rhetoric, European powers justified imperialism throughout Africa in the late nineteenth century by claiming that the spread of Christianity and "civilization" would curb African "immorality" and eradicate practices that reduced African women to the status of slaves.[25] Through the duration of the Atlantic and Indian Ocean slave trades, Euro-Americans constructed an image of African men as sexual predators and a paradoxical set of images of African women as licentious and reproductively able, as well as vulnerable and sexually oppressed.

With the onset of formal colonialism, these sexualized stereotypes about Africans shaped European strategies for ruling and reforming African societies. Late-nineteenth- and early-twentieth-century imperialism coincided with European states' heightened interest in regulating sexual behavior and promoting the growth and health of national populations. This period saw the rise of sexology and eugenics as scientific pursuits, the expansion of maternalist campaigns to improve children's health and welfare, and heated debates over degeneracy and population decline.[26] Colonial rule in Asia and Africa fueled these reproductive concerns by situating the definition and maintenance of racial, cultural, and sexual boundaries as important state projects. Pro-natalist political agendas and racial purity initiatives circulated between colonies and metropoles via official, missionary, and reformist channels.[27] Through colonial concerns about race and sexuality, reproduction was cast as a crucial site of state intervention and popular debate.

In the first decades following the declaration of the East African Protectorate in 1895 (renamed Kenya Colony and Protectorate in 1920), British reproductive concerns focused on population decline and degeneration. Early officials defended British imperialism in East Africa by arguing that the Pax Brittanica would enable African populations to increase by putting an end to the slave trade, "inter-tribal" warfare, and "barbaric" practices. Viewing population growth as a measure of peace and prosperity, these men portrayed the precolonial period as a time of demographic stagnation and even decline, and situated population increase as one of the "philan-thropic" objectives of British rule.[28] Such officials, not surprisingly, failed to mention how much of the death and destruction that they witnessed in turn-of-the-century East Africa was tied to colonialism. Colonial rule exac-erbated mortality in the region by introducing new human and cattle dis-eases including smallpox, sleeping sickness, influenza, and rinderpest, and by causing Africans to suffer fatalities in anticolonial uprisings and through military service during World War I.[29]

The Colonial Office's decision in 1902 to encourage white immigration to the East African Protectorate cast colonial reproductive concerns in a new light. Motivated by a desire to develop commercial agriculture in the area and recoup some of the costs of building a railway from the coast to Uganda, the policy of white settlement raised a number of demographic issues. On the one hand, officials used arguments about African population decline to explain why the Protectorate needed white settlers and why there was land available for them. On the other, they recognized that the success of settler agriculture depended upon the existence, not to mention exploitation, of a substantial pool of black labor. These labor concerns came to dominate colo-nial discussions of population. As one colonial medical officer declared in 1925, "The man-power available for the development of the country is in-adequate."[30] Between 1905–06 and 1926, the white population increased from less than 2,000 to more than 12,000, leading to louder settler com-plaints about inadequate labor supplies and more coercive state policies aimed at compelling black Kenyans to work for white settlers.[31]

As the white population grew, so did a desire among some settlers and of-ficials to clarify racial boundaries and prohibit social and sexual intercourse across them. In 1907 the Protectorate experienced its first "black peril" scare. Such periods of heightened fear over the possibility of black men rap-ing white women occurred periodically in British settler colonies. The 1907 episode in Nairobi, prompted by the purported insulting of two white women by three African rickshaw drivers, culminated in the public flogging of the African men and the arming of settlers in anticipation of a rumored African uprising.[32] Black peril scares enacted a colonial logic that situated black men as sexually aggressive and white women as the virtuous and vulnerable vessels of the ruling race.

Similar fears of miscegenation informed the organization of colonial households. Seeking to prevent intimate liaisons between white men and black women, most settlers preferred to employ African men rather than women as domestic servants. This preference was a direct response to the practice, common among the single men who pioneered British imperialism, of taking local women as housekeepers and concubines. As the white population expanded to include women and families, such practices came under attack. In 1908 a white couple complained to the governor of the Protectorate about a colonial officer who kept three local girls, two of whom were around the age of twelve years, as concubines. Their complaints eventually caused the Colonial Office to issue a circular prohibiting such relations between officers and indigenous women in the East African Protectorate and throughout most of the British empire. This condemnation of a long-standing colonial practice reflected a newly emergent consensus in the Colonial Office that concubinage both jeopardized "the honour of the ruling race" and compromised imperialism's commitment to elevating the status of colonized women.[33] The official prohibition on concubinage, like the black peril scares, worked to construct and maintain racial boundaries by defining appropriate sexual and social relations.

The colonial politics of the womb emerged in earnest during the 1920s. By this decade, Protestant missionaries had established black congregations in many parts of the colony and had learned enough about female initiation in central Kenya to begin calling for a government ban on excision. They argued that it debased women and produced scar tissue that lead to complications and deaths in childbirth. At the same time, Protestant missionaries started to encourage some black women to give birth in hospitals. Such efforts were supported by metropolitan-based feminists and social reformers who viewed the improvement of women's status and the promotion of better maternal practices as important to the moral mission of British imperialism.[34] British colonial officials, by contrast, were generally more skeptical of efforts to transform African social life. By the 1920s, however, their concerns about black labor and their desire to demonstrate some commitment to the moral obligations of colonial rule caused them to offer tentative support to mission campaigns aimed at combating female excision and encouraging hospital births. The colonial politics of the womb conflated concerns about improving women's status with efforts to encourage population growth and expand the availability of cheap labor. It also conflated sexuality with reproduction. More so than either the black peril scares or efforts to stop concubinage, campaigns aimed at ending female excision and promoting hospital births left little room for considering sex as something distinct from procreation.

These campaigns located intimate relations as key to the survival and prosperity of "tribes," the Kenya colony, and the British empire. High-level officials argued that in some areas like Meru, "tribal customs and practices," namely excision and abortion, were leading to "the progressive sterility of the female population." The Director of Medical Services justified the provision of biomedical maternal and child health services to African women in terms of labor limitations: "We must reduce the present infantile mortality even if only because it represents a waste of labor."[35] Medical personnel further reasoned that the establishment of midwifery training programs in Kenya would contribute to the emergence of a class of enlightened black women. Prior to World War II, the resources devoted by the Kenya colonial government to improving maternal and child health rarely matched the rhetoric. Pro-natalist ideals and a desire to elevate women's status, however, did provide an important impetus for the colonial campaigns targeting female initiation and childbirth that did take place.

The colonial politics of the womb did not simply emerge from the importance assigned to such reproductive matters by white officials, settlers, and missionaries. Female initiation, pregnancy, and childbirth became contentious sites of colonial debate and intervention because they encompassed issues of long-standing concern for blacks in central Kenya. Archaeological and comparative linguistic evidence suggests that early Bantu-speaking agriculturists, like those who settled in central Kenya at the beginning of the second millenium A.D., viewed the proper regulation of procreation as crucial to constructing a moral society and controlling transformative power. A politics of the womb operated in precolonial times. For instance, reproductive idioms informed the language and organization of ironworking, a technology important to the success of agricultural communities. Bantu-speakers likened the transformation of ore into iron to procreation, and often adorned smelting furnaces with female sexual characteristics. Moreover, leaders' and healers' strategies for ensuring prosperity and well-being entailed promoting the fecundity of the land and the fertility of women.[36]

Oral traditions told by the descendants of central Kenyan pioneers often describe the local social order as having emerged from the taming of reproductive and sexual chaos. One legend recounted in twentieth-century Meru speaks of a distant time when women chose their husbands, children belonged to mothers, bridewealth did not exist, and incest and divorce were rampant. This state of affairs, according to the legend, was only corrected through the introduction of female initiation and bridewealth, practices that disciplined women, made husbands into household heads, and strengthened marriage as an exchange between families.[37] Similar legends from other areas of central Kenya locate the origins of contemporary societies in an original act of incest or the overthrow of matriarchal authority.[38] These stories link social turmoil to unruly women and aberrant sexual acts, suggesting that people in central Kenya have long associated social harmony and success with a patriarchal order that can effectively manage sexuality and reproduction.

Ethnographic evidence from the late nineteenth century onward further clarifies how central Kenyans tied health and prosperity to procreative relations. The formation and growth of households, lineages, and clans, the basic units of social organization in the region, centered on the axiom that "people are wealth" *(antu ni utonga)*. In equating people with wealth, central Kenyans spoke of intertwined material and moral imperatives. As in much of precolonial Africa where land was plentiful and free, access to and control over knowledgeable dependents determined who prospered and who lived in poverty.[39] The richest people, usually men, were, as Charles Ambler has written, "those who could command the resources of labor necessary to open new fields for cultivation, watch over large herds, protect their settlements, and engage in trading, hunting, and raids."[40] To secure dependents who could perform these tasks, people pursued a range of strategies. They hired laborers, adopted strangers, developed patron–client relationships, and, most commonly, they married and had children. In these patrilineal communities, rich men had many children and several wives with complementary talents and filiations, while women most often staked social claims through husbands and children.[41] But properly conceived children were much more than valued resources in meeting subsistence needs and, potentially, creating wealth. They were a source of affective and spiritual ties across generations and between the living and the dead. Central Kenyans named children after their grandparents to pay respect and to forge linkages between generations. In Meru, for example, the most troublesome ancestors were those who had died without children.[42] Children were the objects of attention and social energy because they enabled well-being in this life and the next.

Female initiation prepared girls for the important task of childbearing. Through its teachings and the physical rites of ear piercing, tattooing, and excision, female initiation transformed girls into women by instructing them how to behave as respectful wives and daughters-in-law. It also taught them fortitude in the face of pain and encouraged maturity and sexual control. By enabling proper sexual relations and granting reproductive entitlement, initiation, like British efforts to promote women's status and foster population growth, conflated women's sexuality with reproduction. As the *Muthirigu* verse quoted earlier put it, the unexcised could only conceive "dogs," not persons.

Beyond disciplining female desire and making reproduction possible, female initiation together with its counterpart male initiation, animated the most important political institutions in these acephalous ("chief-less") communities: age-grades and governing councils.[43] All those initiated within the span of a few years belonged to the same age-grade, fostering ties between people of the same age that countered kin-based loyalties. Status as an initiated person and, later, as the parent of an initiated person was a prerequisite for gaining admittance to the gender-segregated and gerontocratically organized councils that formulated and enforced decisions affecting the entire community. Admission also depended on demonstrating one's wealth through payment of entrance fees in livestock and agricultural produce that were then consumed by the council. As much of the work of these councils, particularly the more senior ones, was meant to be performed in secret, it is difficult to piece together a complete account of their activities. Based on the writings of colonial officials and missionaries, most of whom were interested in engaging these councils for administrative purposes, and on oral histories often gathered after such colonial initiatives had taken place, men's councils in Meru settled disputes involving bridewealth, land, and murder, and made decisions regarding cattle raiding, warfare, and male initiation.[44] Women's councils worked to ensure prosperity and fertility by performing rain-making and planting rituals, chastising unruly women, and presiding over female initiation.[45] Through these councils, people of maturity, wealth, and knowledge—as attested to by their long lives and material success—exercised power. Reproduction undergirded this political system by producing wealth and, in the case of women's councils, being both the source and object of their authority.

Women in early-twentieth-century central Kenya were not the political equals of men. Rather, women's power was grounded in difference: reproductive difference. Women, unlike men, possessed the capacity to cultivate life within their bellies or wombs. It was this capacity that situated women's councils as the ritual guardians of the land's fecundity and young women's fertility. Within households, senior men exerted substantial control over women and girls as well as junior men and boys by commanding deference, acting as family spokespersons and guardians within the wider community, and presiding over most transactions involving land and livestock. Men's councils similarly commanded the authority to make and enforce decisions on a wide range of issues that affected both men and women. Within this system, women held considerable influence in some realms but appear to have rarely challenged men's far-reaching powers. The precolonial politics of the womb flowed from an ideology of gender asymmetry.[46] Within this political system dominated by senior men, the potential to bear life differentiated women from men and, in some spheres of activity, subordinated women to men. Yet this potential also enabled women to claim certain powers.[47]

In addition to situating women and men as incommensurate beings, reproductive processes like female initiation and childbirth elaborated hierarchies of age and generation among girls and women. Female initiation transformed adolescent girls into women and differentiated them from younger girls. Through their daughters' initiations, mothers heightened their own standing within the community by becoming members of women's councils. Others affirmed their authority within the community by teaching initiates how to behave as proper women, wives, and daughters-in-law. Childbirth similarly contributed to the construction of relations of authority among women. Whereas initiation grounded a girl-turned-woman within the female hierarchies of her natal home, childbirth, especially with a woman's mother-in-law serving as midwife, located women in the female hierarchies of their marital homes. Reproductive rituals and processes were just as much about constituting and enforcing differences among females as creating a shared sense of womanhood.[48] Because of their varying reproductive capacities, young girls, initiates, brides, mothers, grandmothers, and older women possessed diverse powers. In early-twentieth-century central Kenya, the politics of the womb was rooted in differences of gender and generation.

HISTORICAL ENTANGLEMENT

During the 1920s these central Kenyan practices of female initiation and childbirth confronted British concerns about women's status, labor supplies, and maternal and child health. What exactly happened when these two sets of reproductive concerns intersected on the uneven political terrain of colonial Kenya is the subject of the following chapters. By approaching the politics of the womb as a process of intersection and entanglement, this book differs from many previous efforts to answer the question of how colonialism engaged issues of reproduction and sexuality. Scholarly and popular answers to this question have generally taken one of two approaches.

The first may be termed the "breakdown of tradition" approach. Advocates of this approach argue that colonialism entailed the clash of two radically different worldviews, one African and one European, resulting in the ultimate triumph of the latter. All of the colonial officers and missionaries who wrote on the history and culture of Meru viewed twentieth-century change in terms of "breakdown."[49] More recently, in the 1980s, a local Catholic priest, Daniel Nyaga, wrote a history of Meru in which he argued that colonialism and, in particular, the philanderings of the first British officer stationed to the area, caused the collapse of "traditional" methods for regulating sexuality, leading to widespread immorality.[50] Similarly, Jane Chege, an anthropologist from the area, has maintained that in Meru, "it is the very breakdown of pre-colonial sexual regulation under the impact of modernization" that has entrenched practices "oppressive to the female gender."[51] Such arguments fit with social scientific theories of "modernization" that describe social change in Africa and elsewhere as entailing a shift from a communal ethos to an individualistic one.[52] As we shall see in chapter 5 and the Conclusion, postcolonial politicians, religious leaders, and parents have also often blamed the "breakdown of tradition" as the root cause of contemporary reproductive problems.

This approach clearly carries political and analytical merit. It rightly emphasizes the pressing moral challenges raised and the profound political and economic inequalities imposed by colonialism. Under colonial rule, the influence of certain local practices and forms of knowledge was reduced, while other elements were abandoned or supplanted altogether. But by attributing change to a single colonial officer, the abstraction of "modernization," or a shift from an ill-defined communal to an individualist ethos, the "breakdown of tradition" approach misses how colonial subjects in Kenya and elsewhere shaped reproductive transformations by engaging, defying, and reworking them. Lost from view is how change under colonialism involved debate, negotiation, and the entanglement of the old in the new.

The second main approach to understanding colonialism and bodily affairs has been to emphasize the power of colonial discourses and categories. While not incompatible with the "breakdown of tradition" approach, this emphasis on discourses and categories is far more reluctant to assess the impact of colonialism on its subjects. Through close examination of the writings and rhetoric of colonial officials, missionaries, ethnographers, and reformers, scholarship in this vein has persuasively argued that colonial discourses and campaigns targeting black bodies were always about more than eradicating a "repugnant" practice or improving health; in delimiting standards of "civilized" behavior, colonial discourses defined racial and class hierarchies and drew sexual boundaries.[53] By unpacking the politics at work in colonial discourses, such analyses have highlighted the challenges of using colonial texts to elucidate subaltern perspectives.[54] Although these analyses have rightfully caused historians to think about their sources in more careful and critical ways, they have shed little light on the perspectives and experiences of colonial subjects. Close attention to colonial discourses and categories has left largely unanswered questions of how Africans understood and engaged colonial efforts to remake reproduction.

While this second approach is most readily recognized as an academic pursuit, it also has a popular variant, most apparent in criticism of the Western media's coverage of contemporary issues of reproduction and sexuality in Africa. Various cultural critics and national politicians have argued that Western attention to issues of population growth and HIV/AIDS plays on racist and sexist stereotypes that situate Africa as a place of promiscuity, excessive fertility, and ill-health. According to this perspective, such discourses further neocolonial relations by exaggerating the severity of such issues and distracting from the basic problem: the ever-increasing gap between the world's wealthy and poor nations. Attention to the power and longevity of colonial categories and discourses effectively illuminates the contemporary injustices and inequalities embedded in the West's relationship to Africa. It does not , however, address the reality of related injustices and inequalities within African nations and households.

This book builds upon yet moves beyond these two approaches by exploring the politics of the womb in twentieth-century Kenya as a process of historical entanglement. As Carolyn Hamilton has argued, categories and institutions forged under colonial rule should not be viewed as the wholesale creation of white authorities but as the result of "the complex historical entanglement of indigenous and colonial concepts."[55] By focusing on how disparate reproductive concerns were drawn together and, over time, became entangled, this approach enables us to elucidate the diverse and shifting interests that fueled the colonial politics of the womb, and to reveal that it was never simply about colonial subjugation and anticolonial resistance. Rather, the colonial politics of the womb entailed the uneven mixing and reformulation of local and imperial reproductive concerns. This mixing and reformulation continued in the postcolonial period as the new Kenyan nation sought to placate the reproductive concerns of domestic constituencies and international donors.

In emphasizing historical entanglement, this book joins a growing literature, mainly focused on medicine and domesticity, that analyzes the history of bodily affairs in Africa as a history of wide-ranging struggles over wealth, health, and power.[56] This study elucidates how such struggles connected and combined the material and the moral, the indigenous and the imperial, and the intimate and the global. Moreover, it insists that contests over reproductive processes and through reproductive idioms have been crucial—even universal—to the elaboration of gender differences and political hierarchies. The following chapters explore how and why the politics of the womb was such a fraught realm of intervention and debate in twentieth-century Kenya.

1 Imperial Populations and "Women's Affairs"

In his annual report for 1939, H. E. Lambert, the district commissioner of Meru, included an account of how the local population had reacted to the outbreak of World War II. According to Lambert, people generally had expressed a "calm interest" in the war, with many seeking out the latest news; headmen and elders had declared their loyalty to the British empire and readiness to assist in any way possible. Not all young men, however, were eager to join the cause. Lambert told the story of a group of young men who sought to avoid military service. He wrote that some of the "girls" had teased the group about the "indignity of head-porterage," prompting them to flee and hide in the forest for "fear of compulsory recruitment as carriers." It was the possibility of men carrying heavy loads on their heads—a form of labor usually reserved for women—that animated the girls' "jibes" and the young men's flight to the forest.[1] Lambert described with bemused approval how the local headmen and tribal police brought the situation under control: "The native authorities soon stopped the nonsense by initiating the young ladies, and the young gallants crept cautiously back."[2]

By presenting local authorities' punitive initiation of a group of girls with such candor and amusement, Lambert's anecdote reveals something of the peculiarities of colonial policy towards female initiation and excision in Meru. Rather than working toward the gradual elimination of excision, as was the colonial government's stated policy at the time, officials in Meru sought to enforce female initiation at an earlier age. As we shall see, the roots of this enforcement policy lay in a colonial desire, dating back to the 1920s, to combat abortion and encourage population growth. Lambert's story suggests how, by the late 1930s, the enforcement of female initiation also served to demonstrate the power of the colonial state at the local level. A pro-natalist initiative had become a tool for quelling young women's taunts, restoring masculine self-esteem, and convincing cowering young men that it was best to serve the British empire.

This chapter examines how and why the enforcement of female initiation became such a crucial component of colonial governance in 1920s and 1930s Meru. During this period, blacks in central Kenya instilled female initiation with the power to create adult women, ensure fertility, discipline female sexuality, and reproduce labor. By intervening in this process, colonial officers in Meru sought to fulfill the material and moral obligations of imperial rule and to secure political control. Condemnation of excision by Protestant missionaries and British feminists brought female initiation to the attention of the Colonial Office in London, but concerns over population decline convinced officers in Meru that abortion, rather than excision, was a greater threat to Kenya's colonial future. Through formulating and enforcing measures to regulate excision and prevent abortion, British colonial officers crafted a relationship between themselves and a group of local men that enabled them to intervene in women's affairs. As Charles Ambler has written of nearby Embu District, administrative involvement in female initiation "represented an unprecedented extension of male authority into the female domain."[3] These interventions also challenged hierarchies among women. They disrupted the processes through which girls became women and older women exerted authority within their communities. For all those involved, moral and political order depended upon managing the politics of the womb.

COLONIAL OPPOSITION TO FEMALE INITIATION

From their first years of activity in central Kenya, Protestant missionaries confronted the practice of female initiation. As early as 1906, Church of Scotland (Presbyterian) missionaries at Kikuyu preached against excision together with its attendant celebrations, dances, and teachings as "barbaric" and "indecent." Missionaries soon realized that female initiation posed a direct challenge to their education efforts, as girl students routinely left mission schools when their time for initiation approached. In an effort to stem these losses, missionaries experimented with holding female initiations on mission grounds. These initiations followed the model of "purified" male initiations, which had been taking place at mission stations since 1909. They were organized by local Christians and excluded ceremonies that, according to the missionaries, placed "undue emphasis on sexual life." Unlike the male procedures, which were performed by hospital staff, however, the female ones were carried out by the "usual Kikuyu woman circumciser." These procedures quickly proved too much for the missionaries to handle. Following the performance of a female initiation at the Tumutumu mission station in 1915, the senior doctor decided that because "the cruelty shown by the old woman was so great . . . he would *never* allow anything of the kind again."[4] Missionaries were particularly disturbed by the severity of the procedure and the apparent pain endured by the initiate.

As Protestant medical work expanded during the 1920s, missionaries began to ground their opposition to female initiation in health concerns. While they obliquely referred to the potential sexual consequences of excision by describing it as "sexual mutilation" and occasionally suggesting that the practice aimed to decrease "sexual passion," Protestant missionaries emphasized the health consequences. They insisted that, in the short term, excision often led to hemorrhaging and infection. Differentiating between a "minor" form, which entailed the removal of the clitoris alone, and a "major" form, which involved the removal of the clitoris, labia minora, and part of the labia majora, Presbyterian doctors argued that the "major" form produced scar tissue that led to impaired urination, menstruation, and intercourse, and, most importantly, complications during childbirth. According to this perspective, excision scar tissue, by prolonging or impeding childbirth, resulted in stillbirths, infections, vesicovaginal fistulas, and maternal deaths.[5] Female genital cutting, however, was not unknown in nineteenth- and early-twentieth-century Britain and America. Medical doctors, on occasion, performed clitoridectomies to cure epilepsy and hysteria and to curb masturbation in female patients.[6] But Protestant missionaries saw nothing therapeutic about excision as practiced in central Kenya. Instead, they charged it with confounding reproduction.

Opposition to female initiation grounded in arguments about infant and maternal mortality resonated with colonial officials' concern with low population growth rates in East Africa. Officials in Nairobi and London viewed population decreases caused by disease, famine, and war as threatening labor-intensive economic schemes and Britain's imperial reputation. Nationalist and eugenicist ideologies of the period situated population growth as a sign of a nation's or empire's vitality. With the increased scrutiny of colonial rule by international organizations, including the League of Nations, following World War I, failure to foster growth among colonized populations became a potential source of political embarrassment for European powers.[7]

Officials in interwar Kenya were especially sensitive to accusations that they were neglecting the health and welfare of Africans. In late 1919 the Kenyan government became the subject of public criticism and Colonial

Office scrutiny. Protests by missionaries and black political organizations revealed that the Kenyan government blatantly placed settler and state interests ahead of African ones through policies that encouraged forced labor. The Colonial Office sought to curb the worst abuses by compelling the Kenyan government to ensure that colonial officers' involvement in labor recruitment did not extend beyond informing men about work opportunities and by limiting the circumstances under which officers commanded compulsory labor for state projects. While these Colonial Office interventions mitigated some indignities, Kenya's system of mandatory work passes and onerous taxes continued to make it one of the most coercive labor systems in British colonial Africa.

Within Kenya, black political groups, including the East African Association and the Kikuyu Central Association, denounced oppressive labor policies and demanded that the government recognize black land rights. Together with missionaries and more conciliatory political organizations like the Kikuyu Association and Kavirondo Taxpayers' Welfare Association, they complained that too much of the tax revenue collected from black Kenyans was spent on developing infrastructure in white areas. In London, Dr. Norman Leys and W. McGregor Ross, two men who had served as colonial officers in Kenya, led similar, often coordinated, campaigns against the Kenyan government. They stirred church and humanitarian groups to action with moving accounts of abuses committed by state officials and settlers, ensuring that the plight of black Kenyans received press and parliamentary attention.[8]

Within this political context, the Kenyan colonial government felt compelled to address the issue of excision. Protestant arguments that excision contributed to infant and maternal mortality appealed to officials' concern about low population growth in the colony and their desire to demonstrate their commitment to improving the health and welfare of African populations. In the 1920s Protestant missionaries began to call for a government ban on the "major" form. In 1925 officials in Nairobi heeded missionary pressure by urging Local Native Councils (LNCs) in all districts where excision was practiced to consider restricting it. LNCs were colonial institutions comprised of African men and the British district commissioner. Colonial officials designed LNCs to be a part of the indirect-rule system, which aimed to govern colonial populations, whenever possible, through indigenous authorities. Like the indirect-rule position of headman, however, LNCs did more to create new local authorities than to engage preexisting ones. As the British district commissioners who presided over them held full veto powers, LNCs operated as tightly controlled venues for political expression.

They possessed limited authority to enact local statutes and raise local taxes. After much coaxing from the district commissioner, the Meru LNC passed resolutions in 1925 and 1927 forbidding excision without a girl's consent, prohibiting procedures that exceeded the removal of the clitoris (the "minor" form), and requiring all "circumcision operators" to register with the council.[9] While similar resolutions were passed elsewhere in central Kenya, Protestant missionaries were not satisfied with the results. To garner central government attention and resources for the cause, Protestant missionaries urged officials in Nairobi and London to introduce a colonywide ban on the "major" form as part of a new penal code then being drafted.

Colonial officials were wary of introducing such a ban. First, they were uncertain as to the relative prevalence of the "minor" and "major" forms. Second, they were beginning to appreciation the depth of local commitment to the practice. In 1929 this commitment became clear when thousands of young men and women responded to Protestant missionaries' anti-excision campaign by performing the *Muthirigu*, a dance-song that derided opponents of excision for corrupting custom, seducing girls, and stealing land. Other *Muthirigu* verses hailed the Kikuyu Central Association (KCA) and it leaders. Denouncing this dance-song as seditious, the colonial government quickly banned it.[10]

Initially, KCA leaders, the most vocal critics of colonial policies in central Kenya, did not take a strong stance on the Protestant anti-excision campaign. As late as January 1930, Jomo Kenyatta, the organization's representative in London, told Colonial Office officials that he supported the idea of hospital personnel educating central Kenyans about the ill-health consequences of excision. Kenyatta's perspective soon changed, once it became clear that the KCA's growing constituency adamantly opposed colonial interference in the practice.[11] In his 1938 anthropological account of the Kikuyu, *Facing Mount Kenya*, Kenyatta defended excision as "the very essence of an institution [initiation] which has enormous educational, social, moral, and religious implications."[12] Through the "female circumcision controversy" of 1928–31, defense of female initiation became a tenet of central Kenyan cultural nationalism.

Kenyatta was not the only London-based activist involved in the controversy. Female parliamentarians in the House of Commons proved to be particularly vocal allies for Protestant missionaries. In December 1929, during discussion of a motion condemning colonial policies that failed to foster the "social well-being" of colonized populations, the Duchess of Atholl directed attention to the ongoing controversy in Kenya. Criticizing the Kenyan government's reticent approach to the issue, she and her female colleagues argued that the "major" form of excision should be banned because of the dangers it posed to infants and mothers during childbirth.[13]

Historian Susan Pedersen has demonstrated how such maternalist rhetoric simultaneously enabled and limited the anti-excision campaign. On the one hand, it allowed for a wide range of women, from the conservative Duchess of Atholl to women's rights advocate Eleanor Rathbone, to support a prohibition. On the other, it limited their condemnation to the "major" form, as the "minor" form was not found to produce scar tissue that could lead to complications during childbirth. Like Protestant missionaries, women activists only obliquely addressed the potential sexual consequences of the procedure. According to Pedersen, these women lacked a "forthright (and anatomically explicit) public rhetoric" through which to define the clitoris as a sexual organ; the reproductive framing of excision prevailed because it was easier to defend women as mothers than as sexual beings. Pedersen's analysis effectively illuminates the discursive constraints which precluded women activists from arguing for a complete ban.[14] It does not, however, explain official refusal to institute a colonywide ban on the "major" form. That answer lies with consideration of the politics of colonial control.

The final blow to the Protestant missionaries' campaign for a colonywide ban came in September 1930 when the director of medical services in Kenya reported the findings of a health investigation into excision. The investigation revealed that officials' suspicion that the "minor" form of excision was more pervasive than the "major" form was mistaken. Of the 374 "Kikuyu women" examined by medical doctors, only three had undergone the removal of the clitoris alone and only four were unexcised.[15] In light of this revelation, the Acting Governor concluded that it would be politically impossible, given the strength of the previous *Muthirigu* protests and the related rise of the KCA, to enforce a law which would make illegal nearly all excisions in central Kenya. A well-publicized but unenforceable law could only damage colonial prestige. The Kenyan government and Colonial Office responded by stating that excision should be combated through "education and propaganda and such administrative action as can be undertaken with the assistance of the native authorities themselves."[16] In Meru, official concerns about abortion would mean that instead of gently discouraging the practice, "administrative action" would enforce it.

THE PROBLEM OF ABORTION

The earliest colonial reports filed from Meru included discussion of abortion. In 1910, Edward Horne, the first colonial officer stationed to the area, provided a description of sexual relations between young men and girls. He wrote that circumcised, unmarried men (s. *muthaka*, pl. *nthaka*), who ranged in age from sixteen to thirty years, were "free to go with any unmarried girl," although they usually married the girl with whom they had been "sleeping." He described unexcised, unwed girls (s. *mukenye*, pl. *nkenye*) as similarly free-willed, choosing their own partners without consulting their parents. Horne's description suggests that young people engaged in sexual relations that were not meant to result in procreation. According to Horne, when the time came for the warrior age-grade to marry, all "their girls" were initiated and then "b[ought]." Horne wrote that if a girl happened to become pregnant before her initiation, a "miscarriage" would be brought about.[17] As we shall see, such pregnancies were considered dangerous and undesirable. Horne's description of premarital sex, female initiation, and abortion did not condemn any of the practices involved. Early colonial officers, preoccupied with establishing military control and collecting taxes, rarely sought to reform the social order.

Horne's successors, by contrast, linked pre-initiation sexual relations and abortion to the social and political problems plaguing the district. In 1923 one officer wrote that headmen's unwillingness to cooperate with officials in "putting down abominable practices such as abortion" signaled the superficiality of colonial control within the district.[18] The following year, M. R. R. Vidal, suggested that delayed initiation contributed to abortion and other local problems. He wrote that in much of Meru, initiation had been postponed in recent years, leaving people of twenty years and older uncircumcised and unmarried. Noting that male and female initiations had resumed with the bountiful millet and bean harvests of 1924, Vidal expressed the hope that abortion would decrease and the number of labor migrants would increase with the addition of recently circumcised men. Late initiation, according to Vidal, obstructed reproduction and confounded one of his chief responsibilities as a district officer, that of ensuring a steady supply of labor for settler farms and public-works projects.[19]

While officers stationed in Meru posited the prevalence of late initiation and abortion as a sign of the district's "backward" and unproductive state, their superiors in Nairobi and London focused on the demographic consequences. Reports of abortion in Meru heightened their fear that African populations throughout East Africa were declining. In 1925 two colonywide reports singled out Meru for its low birthrate. The Acting Governor wrote in one that the district suffered from low population growth and high "infantile mortality . . . owing largely to the late date at which circumcision takes place."[20] Whereas in other areas of central Kenya female initiation took place prior to puberty, in Meru it was a prenuptial rite. Initiation and marriage in Meru usually followed the onset of puberty by five or more years, creating a period when girls were sexually mature but unexcised. Colonial officials observed that as "custom" shunned conception prior to initiation, unexcised girls who became pregnant obtained abortions. It was these abortions, officials argued, that were holding back population growth in the area.

Abortion, unlike excision, never became the subject of broad colonial debate. The colonywide reports which referred to the low birthrate in Meru did not mention abortion by name, and Protestant missionaries in Meru never made abortion the focus of a public campaign as they did with excision. In 1936 the Colonial Office rebuffed a request by the Joint Council of Midwifery for information about abortion in the colonial territories, noting that such information "might be difficult and awkward" to obtain.[21] Abortion was a familiar, if less than respectable, practice in interwar England. By the 1930s, abortion had become relatively safe and widespread, particularly among working-class women. Metropolitan debates over abortion intensified in the mid-1930s, as some eugenicists and the Abortion Law Reform Association called for the legalization of medically performed abortions while opponents argued for the protection of "infant life for its intrinsic value and for the good of the nation."[22]

In condemning the practice of abortion in Meru, colonial officials never mentioned the "intrinsic value" of human life. Instead, they argued that abortion posed a demographic threat to "the nation" as embodied in the Meru "tribe" and Kenya colony. For these officials, abortion in Meru was a moral issue because it confounded population growth, a key indicator of the health and prosperity of nations and empires. In order to stop abortion, colonial officers needed to convince people in Meru that abortion was indeed a problem.

LOCAL PRACTICES OF FEMALE INITIATION AND ABORTION

Official reports contain only brief descriptions of female initiation and abortion. To gain a fuller understanding of these practices in early-twentieth-century Meru, we must turn to two other sources: oral recollections and ethnographies. The oral recollections presented here were gathered in the 1990s by the author and a group of research assistants from older women and men living in Meru. These men and women were born between the turn of the century and the 1920s and initiated during the 1920s through 1940s. In many cases, they were either the subjects or agents of colonial campaigns to lessen the severity of excision and prevent abortion. The ethnographies were produced by a small of group of colonial officers and Methodist and Presbyterian missionaries interested in documenting and understanding the Meru "tribe." The Methodists founded their mission station at Kaaga, near Meru town and the district headquarters, in 1912, while the Presbyterians established their station in the southwestern part of the district at Chogoria in 1916. Much of their ethnographic interest in female initiation stemmed from the "female circumcision controversy" of 1928–31. After Methodist church membership plummeted from seventy members to six, church leaders took an accommodationist approach to female initiation, seeking to understand excision without either condemning or condoning it. These oral and ethnographic sources, produced by those who either staged and were subjected to colonial interventions, embody the entangled history of female initiation in twentieth-century Meru.

During the early decades of colonial rule, female initiation in Meru was an elaborate process extending from several months to a couple of years. It entailed three separate physical procedures—ear piercing *(gutura matu)*, abdominal tattooing *(gukuura ncuuro)*, and excision *(itana)*—each of which was surrounded by dances and feasts. Excision was followed by a seclusion period of three months or more, during which women cared for initiates, feeding them large amounts of food and instructing them on how to behave in their future roles as wives and daughters-in-law. The initiation process only began after a girl had passed puberty and, ideally, had become betrothed. In Mwimbe and Chuka, the southern areas of Meru, girls were initiated around the age of sixteen years, while in the remainder of the district, including in Imenti, Tigania, and Igembe, age at initiation ranged from eighteen to twenty years. Once a girl was engaged or her parents deemed her ready to marry, plans for her initiation began. As Sara Mwari, a woman from Tigania born around 1920, recalled, "Parents would say that they would circumcise that season." Expressing pride in her parents' generation, she added, "Parents organized their affairs well and those of their children."[23]

Parents alone, however, rarely commanded all the resources necessary to stage an initiation. In preparation for the various feasts, parents needed to amass enough foodstuffs to provide their guests, who included relatives, friends, neighbors, and members of their age-grade, with generous servings of meat, porridge, and beer.[24] Such feasts were especially elaborate during the initiation of firstborn children and children from wealthy families.[25] The largest feasts usually took place during the post-harvest season of September, when food was most plentiful. Not all harvests produced sufficient food to both supply initiation feasts and sustain people throughout the year. When grain and cattle were scarce, initiations were delayed. As Joseph M'Ruiga, a former colonial headman who was born at the turn of the century, explained, "You know, before a girl was circumcised, the parents had to make things, beer from millet and sorghum for the clan and then give the clan a bull. And at times, it was difficult to find these things, so one had to be given enough time."[26] Children from poor families were often initiated together with a child from a wealthy family. In these cases, the wealthy family would provide the bull and other items needed for the feasts.[27] Women from the surrounding area assisted with initiation celebrations by preparing porridge, black beans, and cowpeas.[28] In the last weeks preceding excision, initiates visited relatives and neighbors, dancing and collecting gifts of chickens, goats, beads, bangles, and money.[29] Female initiation required friends and relatives to pool resources and enabled some families to demonstrate their wealth.

In cases where the initiate was engaged to be married, female initiation also inaugurated exchanges between the initiate's family and her fiancé and his family. Fiancés provided medicinal oils to help heal initiates' pierced ears, built their seclusion houses, and supplied much of the honey beer consumed during the feasts.[30] Together with their families, they also began paying bridewealth *(ruracio)* to the initiate's family, a process that usually extended over several years and was rarely completed before the birth of the first child. In much of Meru, bridewealth consisted of five key items: a heifer, bull, ram, ewe, and one drum of honey. Bridewealth established respectful relations between two families and clans. It also declared the value of women's fertility and labor. According to E. Mary Holding, a Methodist missionary who worked with women in Meru from the mid-1930s through the 1950s, the groom's family paid bridewealth in order to demonstrate their "good intentions" and to compensate the bride's family for the services that the bride would "render both as a potential mother and as an additional worker in her husband's family."[31] Bridewealth, like female initiation, entailed material and moral exchanges that affirmed the worth and power of women's reproductive capacities. Together, these linked processes enabled the circulation and composition of wealth in things, knowledge, and people between families and across generations.

The day of the excision itself—what Holding described as "the greatest day in a girl's life"—was filled with continuous dancing and singing by women, girls, and young, unmarried men.[32] One colonial officer described this dancing as especially "excited and overwrought."[33] In the late afternoon, the crowd escorted the initiates to a nearby stream or river. There, they bathed and were then taken to a field for the excision. Veronica Ciothirangi, initiated in Tigania during the 1920s, remembered that the girls' fiancés brought the woman (s. *mutani*, pl. *atani*) who performed the excision to the field.[34] As the *mutani* approached, women encircled the initiates, singing, dancing, and ululating. The *mutani* then entered the circle and with the initiates being supported and held by other women, she performed the excisions.[35] Although the extent of the cutting varied from one area of the district to another and, depending on the *mutani*'s precision, from one initiate to the next, this first procedure usually entailed the removal of the clitoris and part of the labia minora.

In some areas, a *mutani* would perform a second cutting either immediately following on the first or a few hours or days later. This second procedure was only witnessed by a select group of very old women and entailed the further removal of the labia minora and part of the labia majora.[36] In an article published in the anthropological journal *Man* in 1913, G. St. J. Orde Browne, a colonial officer, wrote that in Mwimbe some "younger people" objected to the second cutting and tried to modify its "rigours" by bringing it in line with a less severe form of excision that they claimed was currently practiced in Kikuyu areas. These remarks suggest that female initiation was the subject of local debate even before colonial interventions commenced.[37]

While the young men, including fiancés, and children stood peering at the edge of the field, the initiates' parents remained at home, waiting for news of whether their daughters had cried or remained silent and brave. A successful initiate was one who did not flinch or show any signs of fear or pain during excision.[38] Perhaps perpetuating this ideal of stoicism, the women whom my research assistants and I interviewed never dwelt on the pain of excision. As a Kikuyu-speaking woman initiated in the 1920s explained to another researcher in 1984, initiation was a process of "buying maturity with pain."[39] The pain of excision was intended to prepare girls for future challenges and ordeals. A woman who had faced excision with determination and courage would be able to handle any subsequent hardships, particularly those of childbirth.[40] In an essay on the anthropology of pain, Veena Das has offered a further interpretation of the centrality of pain to initiation rituals. She has insightfully argued that initiations not only test the "personal courage of initiates," they are "the means by which society integrates its members into a single moral community."[41] In Meru, excision and its accompanying pain transformed children into resilient adults and grounded initiates in the moral community of women.

Women's councils *(kiama gia aka)* played a crucial role in constructing and enforcing this moral community. The primary task of women's councils was to ensure the fertility of both the land and women. Women and men whom we interviewed recounted that when the rains were late women's councils would slaughter a sheep and perform rituals beseeching the ancestors to allow the rains to begin and the crops to grow.[42] Women's councils disciplined women who misbehaved and punished all those who obstructed their efforts to ensure fertility. For instance, a man who beat his wife for attending a women's council meeting, or a woman who chose to cultivate rather than participate in the council's activities, would be cursed until he or she paid a bull to the council.[43] Women's councils further enforced morality and facilitated disciplined fertility by presiding over excision. They took initiates to the river or stream, surrounded them during the cutting, and cared for them afterwards.[44] Julia M'Mugambi, initiated in the early 1930s, recounted a song that the women's council performed as they carried initiates to their seclusion houses.

> Circumcised girl, come, we go home.
> You have come from uncircumcised girls and now return to women.
> Circumcised girl, come, we go home to be eating a goat with *nkobe* and no one will bother you.
> You will not enter that home [of your parents].
> Let the parents be told, "It [the clitoris] has been removed."
> Let her enter and get married.[45]

Through such songs, women's councils situated excision as a second birth through which initiates were "return[ed]" to women and readied for marriage.

During the 1930s and 1940s, Holding, encouraged by her Methodist colleagues and by H. E. Lambert—the chief architect of colonial campaigns targeting female initiation in Meru—investigated women's councils. Holding sought to determine whether women's councils might be engaged in administrative work or church activities. Her investigations revealed that women's councils used female initiation to establish hierarchies among girls and women. According to Holding, women's councils selected the older (post-menopausal) women who became *atani*. Holding explained that in addition to transforming girls into women through initiation, women's councils raised the social standing of initiates' mothers by granting them admit-

tance to the council upon the initiation of their first daughter. *Nthoni*, defined by Holding as "respect, deference, good manners," was the glue that
held together these hierarchical relations among women, as well as those
between husbands and wives, in-laws, and age-grades. Through excision and
the seclusion teachings that followed, older women instructed initiates how
to act respectfully; they taught them about sexual relations, their duties to
husbands and in-laws (particularly mothers-in-law), and how to interact
with people of different age-grades.[46]

One of the greatest breaches of respectful behavior was for an uninitiated
girl to become pregnant. As women in Meru explained, a being conceived
under such circumstances was not a proper person. If born and allowed to
live, he or she would endanger the lives of kin and neighbors, bringing misfortune and even death, especially to other children.[47] Pre-excision pregnancies violated *nthoni* because they occurred within bodies that had not
been prepared for procreation. Pregnancy and birth did not belong to children but to those who had become women through initiation. In discussing
this belief, Holding described how people in Meru viewed children as a link
between themselves and their ancestors; ancestors cursed children conceived by uninitiated girls in order to express their anger at those girls for
becoming pregnant before they had been consecrated to do so.[48]

Merus were not alone in this belief. Nandi, Maasai, and Kipsigis living in
the Rift Valley area of Kenya also believed that pregnancies conceived by
unexcised girls posed grave dangers.[49] According to Lambert, it was fear of
such pregnancies that motivated others in Kenya, including Kikuyus, to initiate girls prior to puberty.[50] Further afield, in the Ovambo kingdoms of
colonial Namibia and in the Bemba chiefdoms of colonial Zambia, both
places where female initiation did not usually include genital cutting, people
also believed that pre-initiation pregnancies threatened the living. As
Audrey Richards wrote in her classic 1956 study of Bemba female initiation,
Chisungu, children born to uninitiated girls were "creature[s] of ill-omen"
who brought misfortune to their home villages by stopping rain fall, making granaries empty quickly, and compelling their parents and themselves
to be driven into the bush.[51]

Both oral and ethnographic documentary sources agree that in Meru
some girls became pregnant before they were initiated. These pregnancies
occurred despite the fact that virginity at initiation was valued and ceremonies were often held as part of the initiation to ascertain whether or not
initiates were virgins.[52] Women and men recalled that the sexual relations
which resulted in pre-initiation pregnancies usually occurred at dances that

circumcised men and uninitiated girls attended in the years prior to marriage. Moses Kithinji, born in Meru during the 1920s, contrasted the sexual relations which occurred at dances in Meru with the Kikuyu practice of *ngweko*. As described by Kenyatta and others, *ngweko* was a form of sexual play practiced by young, unmarried people that stopped short of intercourse.[53] According to Kithinji, at dances in Meru, sexual play did not always remain "on the surface."[54] Philip M'Inoti, the first Methodist minister from Meru, similarly told W. H. Laughton, a mission teacher and anthropologist who worked in Meru for thirty years, that premarital sexual relations were common in 1920s and 1930s Meru. M'Inoti explained that young lovers sought to avoid pre-initiation pregnancies by practicing coitus interruptus, the entire act being performed in a standing position.[55] These accounts suggest how young people sought to engage in sexual relations that would bring pleasure without procreation.

When these methods failed and sex resulted in pregnancy, young people sought abortions. While girls tried to keep such pregnancies secret to avoid ostracism, they often became public knowledge, as abortions were usually performed at three to six months, after the pregnancy had become visible. Boyfriends, particularly those who intended to marry the pregnant girls, helped to arrange abortions.[56] Margaret Karoki, initiated during the 1920s, explained that once the pregnancy was public knowledge the girl would live in the bush in a simple shelter until her boyfriend gave a bull to her father.[57] Abortions were performed by men *(muriti wa mauu*, literally "remover of the womb")* who, according to M'Inoti and Laughton, charged one goat skin and offered no other therapeutic services. These men induced abortion in a number of ways: by administering a potion of roots and seeds which, once ingested, produced a heavy menstrual period; by placing extreme manual pressure on the girl's abdomen; or by inserting a sharp object into the vagina.[58] According to Margaret Karoki, these methods were used in combination: "The abortionist . . . would go uproot wild plants, pound them, and then, the person would drink. The abortionist would then [the following day] squeeze and kill the child and it would come out dead."[59]

Some women recalled that these procedures, especially when repeated, resulted in infertility, while others stated that some women died while obtaining abortions. If these methods failed to produce an abortion, girls committed infanticide, either by breaking the newborn's neck or abandoning it in the bush.[60] The stigma of such pregnancies clung to girls even after the fetus was aborted or infant killed. When they were eventually initiated, their procedures took place in the bush, without celebrations, and with no woman sitting behind and supporting them during excision. Those whose boyfriends refused to marry them often married older men as second or third wives.[61]

While a wide range of sources concur that pre-initiation pregnancies and abortions existed in early colonial Meru, they diverge as to the scale of these practices. In an essay on Meru customs submitted for an African-language essay contest around 1930, M'Inoti argued that pre-initiation pregnancies were so common that before they were initiated some girls had had five to ten abortions.[62] During the 1920s and 1930s, M'Inoti was the Methodist missionaries' and colonial officers' prime informant on local language and culture. His views on abortion appear to have greatly influenced Lambert. In a health and hygiene booklet addressed to "The Meru Yet to Come," Lambert claimed that girls who never committed abortions were scorned by friends as "unfashionable" and that "many girls aborted fifteen or twenty times."[63] But Laughton, the Methodist mission teacher who otherwise worked quite closely with M'Inoti and Lambert, dismissed the statements of some girls of having had upwards of five to ten abortions as "exaggeration[s] which could not be supported by statistics."[64] Lending support to Laughton's account of the scale of the practice, several women and men whom we interviewed emphasized that although abortions occurred, they were rare.[65]

Confronted with the impossibility of reconstructing reliable figures on the practice, it is difficult to assess the veracity of these competing claims. Present-day Christian sensibilities and cultural pride may have encouraged interviewees to downplay the prevalence of abortion before a foreign, white researcher and her local research assistants—all considered young adults. On the other hand, M'Inoti's and Lambert's extraordinarily high estimates of some girls having had ten to twenty abortions probably attest more to the strength of their own disapproval of the practice and their desire to justify wide-ranging interventions than to actual incidence.

It is equally difficult to determine whether the number of abortions increased from precolonial to colonial times. Lambert insisted that they had. He argued that Pax Britannica had exacerbated pre-initiation pregnancies by putting an end to cattle raiding and "inter-tribal" warfare, thus leaving the warrior age-grade with "little to do but drink and dance and dally." According to Lambert, colonial rule also fueled the problem by eliminating the harsh penalties for pre-initiation pregnancies that had existed in precolonial times. Lambert noted that in some areas of the district the couple would be banished, whereas in others they would be "spreadeagled in a public place, pinned to the ground with pegs at hand and feet," and left to die. Such punishments, Lambert argued, served as an effective and "frightful warning to all illicit lovers."[66]

In singling out the cessation of cattle raiding and the softening of punishments as having caused the increase in abortion, Lambert ignored other, often more insidious, changes engendered by early colonial rule. The colonial conditions that may have had the greatest impact on pre-initiation pregnancies and abortions were those that made it difficult for families to acquire the resources necessary for holding initiations and commencing bridewealth payments.[67] Early colonial policies that forced people to sell livestock in order to pay taxes diverted goats, sheep, and cows away from initiation ceremonies and bridewealth payments and into state coffers. Other new circumstances also made it difficult for families to accumulate the foodstuffs necessary to stage initiation and marriage celebrations. Colonial policies that forced people to build roads directed labor away from agricultural production. In central Kenya, the drought of 1917–18 drew farming to a halt, resulting in famine. These conditions were compounded by the deadly influenza epidemic spread by carrier corps returning from service in World War I.[68]

By making resources scarce and delaying the processes through which young people became adults and married, these colonial conditions frustrated young people, possibly leaving them more willing to defy parental authority and flaunt sexual prohibitions. While Lambert sought to pin the abortion problem on changes in cattle raiding and local punishments, initiation and marriage in Meru were part of a much wider web of material and moral relations.

CONSTITUTING LOCAL AUTHORITIES AND REGULATING EXCISION

As mentioned earlier, the first colonial restrictions on female initiation were passed by LNCs (Local Native Councils) in the mid-1920s. In its first few years of existence, the Meru LNC, comprised of local men and the district commissioner, passed two resolutions forbidding excision without a girl's consent, prohibiting procedures beyond the "minor" form, and requiring all "circumcision operators" to register with the LNC. These resolutions proved largely ineffectual. As one officer wryly remarked about an area near the Embu–Meru district boundary, "public opinion does not seem to be in sympathy with the cause."[69] While a few dozen individuals were prosecuted under resolutions passed elsewhere in central Kenya, it appears that in Meru, no prosecutions were made nor any "operators" registered.[70]

The enactment without enforcement of these resolutions was symptomatic of the early work of the Meru LNC. According to one colonial officer, council members "never criticize any measure submitted to them and with but few exceptions do they bring forward any suggestions of their own."[71] Rather than reflecting a lack of intelligence, as presumed by the officer, Council members' silence was most likely a product of communication problems and divergent concerns. LNC meetings were conducted in Swahili, a language which was not the mother-tongue of any of the men in attendance and whose usage within the district was limited to some trading and administrative activities. As late as 1937, a council member proposed that a Meru-speaking clerk be hired to explain the proceedings to those members who could not follow them.[72] Moreover, many observers argued that LNC agendas throughout colonial Kenya more often reflected the concerns of district commissioners than those of the local community. As one person put it, LNCs were "the 'toys' of the District Commissioners."[73]

For early participants, much of the significance of LNCs lay in their public and performative aspects rather than in who determined the agenda. As district commissioners held veto power, LNCs only ever offered the appearance of local self-government. Through LNCs, colonial officers sought to eliminate authorities beyond their purview and to constitute a group of publicly recognized local leaders under their control. In Meru, the establishment of the LNC coincided with a colonial clampdown on "secret societies."[74] Some Africans also embraced LNCs as public institutions. Older men in Meru observed LNC proceedings. In the 1930s, one officer wrote that interest was so great that all those attending could not fit inside the council building.[75] Council members themselves requested government expenditure on items such as lorry transport and distinctive badges which would make visible their status as important men.[76] Through participation in LNCs, British and central Kenyan men aimed to garner legitimacy and publicize their authority.

Throughout Kenya, LNCs were important sites of colonial collaboration and pivotal players in the expansion of African trade and business. Many LNC members were men already involved in colonial administration as headmen or elders on native tribunals, colonially appointed local courts.[77] They often began their administrative careers in the tribal police force, where British officers believed that they gained "discipline" and "a close view of the working of Government."[78] While in the 1920s, very few, if any, Meru LNC members had attended school, over time, school-educated teachers and ministers joined their ranks.[79] LNCs included the wealthiest men in the district. Some joined LNCs after they were already established as successful traders and businessmen, whereas many others used their administrative salaries and connections to develop lucrative businesses. During the interwar years, LNC members amassed wealth that established them and their families as influential figures in Kenyan politics.[80] In Meru and across Kenya, these families would dominate local and national politics after Independence in 1963.

LNCs also facilitated processes of political and class formation by elaborating colonial governance as men's work. By bringing British and central Kenyan men together to develop policies and manage revenues, LNCs defined local government as the preserve of men. British officers believed that through working closely with LNC members they could craft interventions into any area of African social life, including female initiation. Of all the issues addressed by the LNCs during the 1920s and 1930s, the regulation of excision proved to be the greatest test of these all-male bodies.

Following the "female circumcision controversy" of 1928–31, British officials agreed that further intervention against female initiation in the "Kikuyu districts proper" was politically impossible. Politically marginal Meru District, however, fell beyond these boundaries of administrative propriety.[81] In January 1932, after much encouragement from the district commissioner, the Meru LNC passed a resolution restricting excision to the removal of no "more than the tip of the clitoris and the small dark ridges of skin along the free edges of the *labia minora.*" Council member M'Ngaine, considered by colonial officers throughout the 1930s and 1940s to be among the most "intelligent and loyal" headmen and the "practically paramount Chief of the Meru," qualified his support for the resolution. He pointed out that people in the district did not see "eye to eye" on this issue and that he himself would not support further interference with the practice. The district commissioner reassured M'Ngaine by explaining that he would not "force further modification before the tribe and their Council were prepared to agree to them."[82]

The impact of these resolutions varied. In an interview, Esther M'Ithinji and Julia Simion recalled how during the late 1930s and early 1940s, *atani* carried permits on their walking sticks, certifying that they had undergone training in the new procedure.[83] In 1936 Clive Irvine, a Presbyterian (Church of Scotland) doctor and staunch opponent of excision, reported that based on "his experience with women patients," he believed that the less severe form was almost universal in the southern areas of the district. The government medical officer similarly noted a decrease in the severity of excision in the northern areas.[84] Yet, Methodist women missionaries recorded witnessing the more severe and illegal form at two initiations in 1938 and 1939, near Meru town.[85]

Some people in Meru clearly preferred a less severe form of female genital cutting. In 1931 Dr. H. W. Brassington, a Methodist missionary, wrote to the Director of Medical Services asking whether it would be a breach of medical ethics for him to lend a scalpel to a Meru female hospital assistant in order for her to perform a modified procedure (the removal of just part of the clitoris) on an assistant trainee. Brassington explained that the trainee's father had requested the hospital assistant to perform the procedure so that his daughter would maintain "her tribal rites" while being assured of receiving a more modest procedure.[86] This case suggests how some central Kenyan families negotiated the gap between defending and renouncing female initiation, and demonstrates that less severe forms of the procedure were part of the negotiations.

Lambert described other instances of girls and men insisting on milder forms of cutting. He wrote that in some cases "girls have successfully resisted attempts on the part of older women to perform second operations," while in others "men have warned operators that any excess cutting of their fiancées or daughters would result in prosecution."[87] These instances of resistance sound quite similar to Orde Brown's description in 1913 of "younger people" in Mwimbe who insisted on a less severe form. In making more severe forms of excision punishable by law, the LNC resolutions lent the force of the colonial state to those interested in ameliorating the practice.

In discussing efforts to monitor compliance with the LNC resolutions, Lambert never mentioned the involvement of women. Colonial administration, in Lambert's presentation and those of his colleagues, was always a men's affair. In an interview conducted by Jeffrey Fadiman in 1969, however, Lambert's wife, Grace, remembered that she had examined recent initiates to determine whether or not they had been cut in accordance with the resolutions. Grace Lambert, a former nurse, described how a headman requested her to undertake the examinations. As she examined each initiate, a ring of older women, including registered "circumcisors," would surround her. The men—an interpreter, headman, police, and usually Mr. Lambert— would stand nearby with "their backs discreetly turned." When Mrs. Lambert determined that an initiate's excision had exceeded the legal amount, the initiate's mother would be seized and either fined or imprisoned. She recalled that initiates vehemently protested their mothers' arrests, shouting that they had wanted the procedure and should go to prison instead of or along with their mothers.[88]

Grace Lambert's recollection is eloquent testimony to officers' ability to erase the presence of women, including their wives, from the administrative record. It also suggests how central Kenyans viewed female initiation as a woman's concern. From the headman who requested Grace Lambert to examine the initiates to the older women who surrounded her during the examinations, central Kenyans strove to keep excision within the purview of women. In 1934 H. E. Lambert wrote, "As natives frequently point out," excision is "a woman's affair, not men's." He added, "It is extremely difficult for a man (of any race) to influence the conservative opinion of the African female."[89] Yet, in spite (or, perhaps, because) of this observation, he insisted that he and his all-male LNC would succeed in regulating the practice.

STOPPING ABORTION

While colonial officers in Meru counted the resolutions regulating excision as achievements, they were more concerned about the problem of abortion. In Meru, as elsewhere, the years 1929–32 were ones of hardship. Depressed agricultural prices, unemployment, drought, and locust infestations produced scarcity. Amid these conditions no issue was discussed with more frequency by the LNC than abortion.

A. J. Hopkins, Lambert's predecessor as district commissioner, understood that abortion could only be combated by lowering the age of initiation, thereby eliminating the period when girls were sexually mature but unexcised. In 1929 Hopkins suggested to the Meru LNC that the eldest ranks of girls be initiated. Council members rejected Hopkins' suggestion. In explaining their opposition, M'Turuchio stated that initiation ceremonies could not be held because existing famine conditions precluded the requisite feasting. The timing of initiation, M'Turuchio stated, depended upon the availability of food and other resources. Council members pledged that instead of enforcing initiation, they would hold *barazas* (public meetings) to tell people to stop performing abortions.[90]

Despite council members' promises to discourage the practice, Hopkins claimed that a year later abortion was still widespread. At the November 1930 meeting of the LNC, Hopkins explicated the problem by drawing a parallel between a hen and a young woman. According to Hopkins, both beings only had a finite number of "embryo eggs." He explained that "if the Meru continued to perform abortions they would find [that] their wives would continue to have only a few children, since with every abortion performed on a girl meant possibly that she was capable of having one less child when married eventually." Hopkins' attempt to impart demographic anxiety did not sway the council. M'Ngaine voiced his opposition to early initiation by reiterating the council members' conviction that initiation could not be divorced from considerations of resources and wealth. He stated that fathers opposed early initiations because they did not want to lose their daughters' agricultural labor or the tribute that they received from men courting their uninitiated daughters. The meeting concluded with members promising to convince their constituencies to remove the "taboo" surrounding pre-initiation pregnancies, thus eliminating the need for abortion.[91] By the end of 1931, Hopkins was confident that abortion was on the wane; "an unmarried girl who becomes pregnant now is almost invariably circumcised and married instead of being sent to an aborter."[92]

Replacing Hopkins in 1933, H. E. Lambert declared his predecessor's efforts to stop abortion largely ineffectual. In voluminous reports, Lambert claimed that abortion was "the principal social problem of the Meru people" and rampant throughout the District. He noted that the seventy-seven abortion convictions within the district during 1933 equaled the total number of abortion convictions in England and Wales during that same year. At first Lambert attempted to stop abortion by prosecuting abortionists more vigorously. But he soon discovered that the prosecution of known abortionists only worsened the situation: male lovers took to performing the abortions themselves, abortifacients began to be imported, and "non-Meru natives" established themselves as abortionists. Lambert wrote that when abortion failed the newborn was simply strangled or abandoned, and that prosecuting infanticide cases was difficult since it was "impossible to obtain evidence to rebut the plea that the child was still-born."[93]

Lambert soon concluded, as had Hopkins, that the solution lay in lowering the age of initiation. For Lambert, early initiation became a panacea for Meru's social, economic, and gender ills. He argued that apart from saving the Meru from "tribal death," it would reduce the age of marriage, compel men to shoulder the responsibilities of wife and family at a younger age, encourage them to farm, and, by shifting agricultural control from women to men, facilitate the development of cash crops.[94] Working from the assumption that functioning societies were coherent systems of interdependent practices, Lambert argued that prepubescent initiation could bring colonial Meru back into balance. He wrote that according to the principles of applied social anthropology, "native law and custom" should not be viewed as "an immutable code . . . [but rather one] susceptible to change consciously or unconsciously directed to the preservation of the well-being and equilibrium of the tribe."[95] According to Lambert, early initiation was the key to restoring the "equilibrium" of the Meru.

In August 1934 Lambert guided the Meru LNC in passing the following resolution: "It shall be the duty of the parent or guardian of every girl" to have her "initiated into the tribe before she reaches sexual maturity." The resolution further stipulated that headmen should report any delayed initiations to the district commissioner, who, in conjunction with a native tribunal, would hold an inquiry into the matter. Barring discovery of a "reason" for delay, the parents or guardian would be required to undertake the girl's initiation. Those who failed to comply would be found guilty of a criminal offense. The resolution specifically exempted girls, parents, or guardians who had "repudiated initiation as a necessary tribal rite."[96]

When forwarded to Nairobi, this resolution was rejected by the Attorney General on the grounds that it implied official sanction for a custom "abhorrent to every civilized nation." Suggesting that some "civilized" individuals—namely, British women—found it more "abhorrent" than others, he wrote: "I hardly like to contemplate the position of the unfortunate Secretary of State for the Colonies when faced in the House of Commons by Lady Astor with this Resolution in her hand."[97] After consultation with other central government officials, the Attorney General approved a new phrasing: "No girl shall be initiated into the tribe *except before* she reaches the age of sexual maturity."[98] When Lambert left Meru in 1935, he informed his successor that "propaganda" encouraging early initiation had "been entirely successful." He did not specify what "propaganda" entailed.[99]

In February 1938, after nearly three years of LNC meetings with no mention of excision or abortion in official documentation, Philip M'Inoti, the Methodist minister and now headman and LNC member, announced that headmen should "force circumcision," since once again "some girls are becoming too big before being circumcised." While the other council members supported M'Inoti's suggestion, the new district commissioner, V. M. McKeag, reminded them of the government's unwillingness to support "forcible excision." The discussion concluded with all agreeing that headmen and elders should use "their influence and wake up the parents" to initiate their daughters in a timely fashion.[100]

Nine months later, council member M'Ngaine returned to the topic of abortion, blaming the 1934 resolution for a "decline in the birth rate and increase in infant mortality throughout the District." M'Ngaine explained that the threat of imprisonment for late excision discouraged pregnant girls from undergoing excision but did not subvert the "taboo" against pregnancies conceived prior to excision, making abortion and infanticide ever more common. McKeag and the council agreed that imprisonment for late excision should be replaced by a fine paid by the girl's father and the elders of his clan. Council member M'Inoti further suggested that when touring, administrators should be presented with girls to determine whether or not they should be excised.[101] M'Inoti's and M'Ngaine's determined reintroduction of the issue of early initiation signaled some LNC members' greater willingness to intervene in the women's affair of female initiation and their acceptance of demographic arguments against abortion.

These discussions also revealed that colonial efforts to stop abortion had made matters worse. McKeag, in a report to his successor, explained that the penalties instituted under the 1934 resolution had fostered a "system of blackmail." As parents continued to have their daughters initiated at marriage rather than prior to sexual maturity, McKeag wrote, they were vulnerable to being reported by a headman or "false friend"; hence, parents made "it their business to bribe, intimidate or otherwise square anyone likely to give them away." McKeag explained that in response to this problem, the LNC had reduced the penalty for late initiation so that "the people who had disregarded the Resolution [would have] a chance to get on the right side of the law."[102]

On his return to the district in 1939, Lambert claimed that the early-initiation campaigns had borne "good results," though "propaganda" needed to be maintained at "full pressure." During his second term in Meru, Lambert focused much energy on engaging indigenous institutions, particularly men's councils known as *kiama* or *njuri*, in colonial administration. Lambert believed that, as was not the case in other areas of central Kenya, where such councils had been destroyed during the installation of colonialism, in Meru, these councils remained largely intact, commanding popular allegiance and, at times, confounding colonial rule. Combining the indirect-rule principle of working through local authorities with his commitment to applied social anthropology, Lambert argued that the supreme council, the *Njuri Ncheke*, should be adapted for colonial purposes, not destroyed. He insisted that it should become the final arbiter on all matters of colonial policy involving "native law and custom."

Lambert worked to incorporate the *Njuri Ncheke* in local administration by requiring that all headmen and tribal police become *Njuri Ncheke* members and that all elected members of the LNC be chosen by the *Njuri Ncheke*. In collaboration with Methodists Laughton and M'Inoti, Lambert devised a Christian oath so that mission adherents could join the *Njuri Ncheke*. The Presbyterian and Catholic (established by Consolata Fathers in 1911) mission stations, however, remained skeptical of the ability of a "hea-

then" institution to accommodate Christians and largely refused to participate.[103] Lambert's efforts to engage the *Njuri Ncheke* and other indigenous
institutions to prevent the "disintegration" of the Meru represented one of
the most ambitious indirect-rule initiatives ever undertaken in colonial
Kenya.[104]

Following on his work with the *Njuri Ncheke*, Lambert encouraged
Methodist missionary E. Mary Holding in 1939 to investigate "indigenous
women's institutions" and to determine whether they too could be incorpo-
rated into colonial administration.[105] Although Holding's investigations became the most detailed anthropological accounts of women's councils for
colonial central Kenya, they did not lead to the councils' incorporation. Soon
after expressing his interest in "women's institutions," Lambert learned that
in some areas "women's cults" were defying LNC resolutions by performing a second excision on young women who had undergone the legal procedure. Lambert quickly encouraged the *Njuri Ncheke* to ban these "cults."
Lambert's suspicions about women's institutions were further heightened
by reports that young women in other parts of the district were either suc-
cumbing, under "the gibes and threats of older women," to second excisions,
or were being forcibly excised a second time by mothers-in-law and "midwives" immediately following childbirth.[106] These transgressions of LNC
resolutions caused Lambert to doubt the possibility of engaging women's
institutions in colonial administration. He eventually concluded that "to
more than half the tribe—the females—it [the LNC] means nothing."[107]

Early initiation was returned to the Meru LNC agenda in September
1947, when another district commissioner stated that the 1934 resolution
was once again being ignored and girls were being excised after reaching
maturity. This time, the council set a date by which "all girls of suitable age"
who had not renounced the rite would be initiated.[108] The 1934 resolution
continued to be invoked as late as 1950 and 1951, when native tribunals
heard several cases of delayed initiation.[109] Throughout this same period,
M'Inoti continued to urge his constituents to initiation their daughters in a
timely manner.[110]

KIGWARIE: "THE ONE WHICH WAS UNEXPECTED"

Interviews with those in Meru who remembered these campaigns confirm
that efforts to enforce early initiation went well beyond the legal prosecution and fining of those who defied LNC resolutions. At various times from
the mid-1930s to the beginning of the Mau Mau rebellion in the early 1950s

headmen and tribal police enforced, on short notice, mass gatherings at which all adolescent girls were excised. These mass excisions were most often referred to as *Kigwarie,* translated as "the one which was unexpected" or "the one for which we were unprepared," or they were known by the nickname of the policeman who became notorious for their enforcement, *Kiberenge.*[111] In southern areas of the district, people, again drawing attention to the unusual timing of these mass excisions, called them *Kathenya,* since they took place during the day (*muthenya*) rather than at dusk.[112] *Kigwarie* also became the nickname of the age-grade which fell victim to these mass excisions.

Nearly all the interviewees recognized that *Kigwarie* was a government effort to stop pre-initiation pregnancies and abortion. For instance, Moses Kithinji stated, "They were told to be initiated all together to avoid pregnancy, then abortion."[113] Few, however, could explain why the government opposed abortion. The two people who offered explanations, notably both of them men, spoke of demographic concerns. M'Anampiu, a headman during the later *Kigwarie* campaigns, remembered that the government thought "it was a big loss to kill people," whereas Moses Kithinji stated that whites "said it [abortion] was reducing people."[114]

Police from district headquarters, accompanied by a *mutani* certified to perform the less severe procedure, carried out *Kigwarie* by travelling from one area to another. The arrest of a local abortionist or news of an unexcised girl giving birth often prompted their arrival. Julia M'Mugambi described such an event: "During the time of *Kigwarie,* it happened that . . . one [uninitiated] girl would have a child. When she got a child, it was said that now that she has a child, all people will have children. They [the police] would surprise us in the morning. . . . We would be taken away, taken to a field full of girls."[115] After gathering all the girls in a field, the police would place them in a line and select for excision those whose breasts had begun to develop.[116]

What happened next appears to have varied by place and over time. In some cases, the police just stood at the edge of the field, leaving local women and the *mutani* to bathe the girls in a nearby river and carry out the procedure.[117] In others, the police played a more insistent role. According to Elizabeth M'Iringo, "*Kigwarie* never used to wait for women. They used to come when women are in the garden and circumcise the girls and go. Those of *Kigwarie* were circumcised by men."[118] Maritha John similarly remembered that following the excisions *Kiberenge* checked each girl to make sure that she had not been cut in the "ordinary way," but in accordance with the LNC resolutions.[119] Such intimate involvement by men horrified many. As Paul M'Kuru explained, "You know, initiation of women was not men's; women initiated their own. . . . Even men were angered [by *Kigwarie*] and women too because before it never involved men."[120] Men's participation in the initiations of *Kigwarie* marked a significant break from the past.

Although colonial officers appear to have known of these mass excisions, they did not specifically mention them in administrative correspondence. *Kigwarie* was too blatant a contravention of Nairobi's and London's policy against condoning excision to permit official inscription. Yet, set beside the oral reminiscences of *Kigwarie*, Hopkins' and Lambert's references to "pressure" and "propaganda" take on new meaning. McKeag's 1939 remark that "forcible circumcision" was not only "illegal but *now a days* impracticable" further suggests official knowledge of mass excisions.[121] Although the word *Kigwarie* never appeared in annual reports or LNC minutes, it did appear in one of Lambert's ethnographic notebooks: "*Kigwarie:* Method, for instance, of initiating all *nkenye* [unexcised girls] in an area in a few days, by order of the *Njuri*. Used when it appeared that the girls and boys were indulging too freely and when a new age-grade took over."[122] Lambert's notes suggest that unexpected initiations existed in precolonial times. While Lambert, ever concerned to administer through local institutions, would have been comforted by *Kigwarie*'s "customary status," the unexpected initiations of the 1930s and 1940s only came after much colonial prodding. By the 1990s, people in Meru remembered *Kigwarie* solely as a colonial event.

Many interviewees explained that they and others resented *Kigwarie* because it left little or no time to prepare for initiation. Maliceral Igoki remembered that because of the short notice she was unable to select the proper person to "hold her" during the excision, and Janet Kibunja recalled that older women ridiculed her because she never obtained *ncuuro*.[123] *Kigwarie* made it nearly impossible for parents to gather the resources necessary to provide feasts for their age mates, relatives, and neighbors. As Moses Kithinji explained, a girl whose father "has not given the clan a bull," or whose mother has "not ground porridge for women," was not supposed to be initiated.[124] Janet Kibunja recalled that her parents were able to hold a small celebration only because her father was a headman and had received some advance warning of *Kigwarie*.[125]

Others remembered how *Kigwarie* disrupted the timing and sequence of initiation and courtship. Ciokaraine M'Barungu recounted a song performed by girls, denouncing *Kiberenge* for disregarding the fact that initiation was supposed to follow an engagement to marry.

Ah, ii, *Kiberenge* should be cursed
Kiberenge be cursed, ii
And even if he screams
He has forced girls without young men to be circumcised.[126]

Kigwarie also upset the sequence of initiation within households. Justus M'Ikiao remembered that people "worried because traditionally . . . when circumcising, the eldest came first. But now they were being done out of order."[127] Sara Mwari similarly stated that she and her *Kigwarie* age mates wondered how they could be initiated before boys who were older than them.[128]

Yet several interviewees explained that some people welcomed *Kigwarie*. They recalled that parents were pleased that their daughters were prevented from being "spoiled" by abortion.[129] Beatrice Tiira remembered how she and her age mates felt: "We were happy because if you got pregnant before you were circumcised, it was aborted. But, if you were circumcised, the owner [of the pregnancy] used to marry you." Tiira may have recalled *Kigwarie* in such favorable terms because in her area families were given two week's notice, leaving some time to gather money and food for the celebrations.[130] But another woman who defended *Kigwarie* explained that the lack of preparation and celebration did not bother her, as she was able to have ear piercing and *ncuuro* performed in seclusion.[131] Julia M'Mugambi stated that she was not upset about missing such practices, as they were no longer popular.[132] For these interviewees, who perhaps remembered *Kigwarie* in juxtaposition to later government campaigns which sought to stop excision altogether (see chapter 3), *Kigwarie* conferred the initiate's status that they desired.

Their grandmothers, however, may have been more skeptical of the status conferred by *Kigwarie*. Women protested government interference with female initiation in secret. Whereas on other occasions, women had expressed their opposition to government policies, including burial of the dead, soil conservation measures, and prohibitions on beer brewing, by marching on Meru town, they never staged public protests against *Kigwarie*.[133] The presence of police from district headquarters appears to have been a powerful deterrent. Jennifer Karea explained that people feared the punishments the police could inflict.[134] In responding to the question of why women did not publicly protest *Kigwarie*, Elizabeth M'Iringo pointed out the futility of such protests: "If you get annoyed, do you un-circumcise her?"[135]

Women covertly resisted the LNC resolutions and *Kigwarie* by performing second excisions. Just as Lambert wrote of such procedures being performed by "women's cults," mothers-in-law, and "midwives," Margaret Karoki spoke of women secretly "circumcising again" *Kigwarie* initiates to "remove away *ukenye* [the state of being uncircumcised]." Karoki recalled one incident when a headman suspected her of performing a second excision.

> Like there was a time when this one *Njoka* [a headman] found me in the house of an initiate. He asked me, "What are you doing here? You came to circumcise?" I told him I was just taking my tobacco. I saw him bending to look [at the initiate] and then I felt very bitter because he was a man.[136]

In reasserting their control over transforming girls into women through clandestine second excisions, older women reclaimed female initiation as a women's affair. Such procedures frustrated colonial efforts to eliminate the severe form of excision and to bring female initiation within the orbit of male administrators. By performing second excisions, older women also sabotaged the efforts of young people and fathers who preferred the milder procedure. Second excisions recouped an element of initiation valued by older women, but not by all initiates, fiancés, or fathers.

During the 1930s and 1940s, the ability to intervene in female initiation in central Kenya became a mark of colonial control. The passage and enforcement of resolutions regulating excision became both constitutive and demonstrative of efficient administration. In 1934, claiming to have "learned more about the secrets of Africa in . . . three hours than one might acquire in years," Methodist missionaries in Meru boasted of the disruptive and intrusive effects of requiring initiates, perhaps some of the first *Kigwarie* initiates, to come out of their seclusion so as to receive a smallpox vaccination[137] Similarly, Lambert's anecdote of girls having been initiated during World War II because they taunted military recruits must be understood in terms of the construction and expression of a gendered colonial authority. While the policy origins of unexpected initiations lay in colonial efforts to combat abortion and promote population growth, Lambert did not mention such concerns in recounting this incident. Rather, for Lambert and the "native authorities" who enforced them, unexpected initiations had become an effective means for disciplining unruly girls, mending masculine pride, and demonstrating colonial power.

· · ·

Latter-day historians and anthropologists have most often viewed H. E. Lambert, with his attention to indigenous institutions and his willingness to criticize aspects of colonialism, as a sympathetic and astute colonial figure. Lambert's argument that colonialism caused the "breakdown" of cultural harmony and the rise of sexual immorality in Meru has resonated with a range of postcolonial sensibilities.[138] His initiatives and writings fit well with cultural nationalist narratives that characterize colonialism as a period of social and moral collapse, and that locate the possibilities of renewal in a return to "tradition."

By analyzing the efforts of Lambert and others to regulate excision and prevent abortion, this chapter reveals that these campaigns were not simply attempts to counter colonial disruption by reinvigorating indigenous practices and institutions. Through these campaigns, British officers sought to constitute themselves and a group of central Kenyan men as recognized colonial authorities, and to bring practices formally controlled by women within the purview of men. State-formation in colonial Kenya and elsewhere in Africa required the development of a working relationship between British and African "men on the spot."[139] It also entailed intervening in "women's affairs."

During the mid-1920s, Nairobi-based administrators proposed the regulation of excision, a politically sensitive customary practice, as a project that was particularly well suited for the newly founded LNCs. In Meru, officers envisioned the LNC and, later, the Njuri Ncheke, as supplanting "secret societies" and strengthening administrative hierarchies. The campaigns targeting female initiation in all their performative aspects—from the *barazas* at which officials denounced abortion to the mass gatherings of *Kigwarie*—demonstrated the status and power of colonial headmen, police, and LNC members. Moreover, by insisting that the solutions to troubling social and political problems lay in possessing detailed knowledge of local practices, district officers like Lambert asserted their own worth to the broader project of imperial governance.

British officers initially had a difficult time convincing LNC members that female initiation was an arena in which the colonial government and its male intermediaries should intervene. At LNC meetings members argued that initiation was not a discrete practice but one linked to broader material and moral concerns. They pointed out that the timing of female initiation and the attendant process of marriage depended on the availability of livestock and foodstuffs, and on parents' willingness to relinquish their daughters' labor. With equal vehemence, they insisted that excision was a women's affair. These men, like others in Meru, viewed excision as a process through which older women transformed girls into women, cultivating sexual morality and ensuring fertility. Given this gendered perspective of reproductive power, LNC members did not readily agree with British officers that female initiation fell within the scope of men's authority.[140]

Eventually, after many meetings, British officers convinced some LNC members and headmen that severe forms of excision and late initiations threatened the demographic and moral health of the Meru. But as these intermediaries anticipated, colonial efforts to regulate excision and stop abortion were never easy or very successful. Early initiations could only be ensured through police enforcement, whereas LNC restrictions on cutting were circumvented through secret second excisions. In some cases, these campaigns may have prevented abortions or lent support to those who preferred milder forms of excision. Ultimately, they strengthened colonial hierarchies by positioning officers, headmen, and LNC members as the recognized guardians of the Meru "tribe" and by weakening older women's ability to stage initiations.

Female initiation and abortion became potent realms of state intervention in the interwar period because all involved viewed them as crucial to broad material and moral concerns. It was the intersection of these diverse concerns that created the colonial politics of the womb. Black central Kenyans understood female initiation as sustaining two pillars of political order, gendered personhood and generational authority. Through initiation, girls gained sexual discipline and reproductive entitlement. As part of marriage preparations, initiation contributed to the composition and exchange of wealth in people, things, and knowledge between households and across generations. Abortion ensured that only socially consecrated women produced children. The vital meanings and transformative powers with which central Kenyans imbued female initiation caused white missionaries and, later, colonial officers and London-based women's activists to confront it. These groups variously came to view it as a "barbaric" practice, "sexual mutilation," the embodiment of African women's subjugation, and a threat to "tribal" and imperial health.

Colonial struggles over female initiation were never simply a matter of white versus black. In Meru, Methodist missionaries grew to appreciate the importance of the practice, whereas Lambert and other colonial officers saw its enforcement—albeit in a less severe form and at an earlier age—as essential to the survival of the Meru. Simultaneously, some black central Kenyans who converted to Christianity came to view excision, or at least the more severe form, as undesirable. Some headmen and LNC members also came to embrace colonial efforts to alter the severity and timing of excision as ensuring the demographic future of their "tribe." Forging affiliations defined by Christianity, ethnicity, and empire required rethinking how best to prepare female minds and bodies for reproduction. This rethinking involved mixing old and new practices rather than simply renouncing the former in favor of the latter. *Kigwarie* represented an unexpected and police-enforced mixing of the old and new, the indigenous and the imperial. Other mixing, however, took place on a smaller scale and on less coercive terms. The case of the female hospital assistant who borrowed a doctor's scalpel to perform a trainee's "tribal rites" in a modest and hygienic manner illustrates how change was negotiated in more subtle ways. As we shall see in the next chapter, hospitals, and particularly maternities, were the site of further negotiations surrounding female initiation. While the intersection of competing reproductive concerns resulted in colonial interventions and anticolonial resistance, it also entailed historical entanglement.

2 Colonial Uplift and Girl-Midwives

In July 1934 the Methodist mission station in Meru celebrated a momentous event. Ruth Mukiira, the first convert to renounce and successfully avoid excision, gave birth to a healthy baby boy. In a letter to a colleague in London, missionary Muriel Martin explained that when Ruth married Kornelio Mukiira—a Methodist evangelist, teacher, and, later, minister—without being excised, she was "cut off and cursed by her people, the curse being, she should be childless." As we have seen, many black central Kenyans understood that a child conceived by an unexcised girl posed a mortal danger to kin and neighbors. By cursing Ruth with infertility, people expressed their anger with her renunciation of excision and probably sought to protect their own lives by preventing the birth of a dangerous being. Throughout Ruth's pregnancy, Muriel Martin worried and prayed that nothing would happen that could confirm their curse. For Martin and other missionaries, the birth of Ruth and Kornelio's baby was a victory for Christianity over superstition. Moreover, they hoped that it would challenge the local conviction that successful reproduction depended upon excision.[1]

Ruth Mukiira's pregnancy and the infertility curse cast upon her occurred against the backdrop of ongoing debates in Kenya and Britain over the provision of colonial maternity care. A critical moment in these debates came in March 1930, when at the height of the "female circumcision controversy" the Colonial Office issued a despatch seeking to verify missionaries' and British feminists' claims that "circumcision" contributed to maternal and infant mortality. Lord Passfield, the Secretary of State for the Colonies, sent this despatch to the governors of Kenya, Uganda, Tanganyika, Zanzibar, Somaliland, Nyasaland, and Northern Rhodesia. The despatch linked female genital cutting to other colonial concerns by asking governors to comment on reports that the "slow increase of population" was "in large measure" attributable to female "initiation rites" and claims that "the status of native women [was] . . . scarcely distinguishable from slavery." It also solicited recommendations on how to make African women "better mothers," so as to ensure "not only an increased birth-rate, but also, what is no less important, the creation of a healthier and better-developed stock." The despatch concluded by suggesting a possible panacea for the problems of female genital cutting, demographic decline, and women's low status. It encouraged governors to provide training for "native women in maternity work" and to promote "infant and child welfare work." The Colonial Office reasoned that through the agency of state-trained African nurses, midwives, and welfare workers, reproductive crises could be abated and degrading customs curbed.[2]

This chapter explores how struggles over the introduction of hospital maternity services once again placed African women and their reproductive capacities at the center of political struggles over colonial governance, gender roles, and generational relations. Protestant missionaries, British feminists, and some colonial officials hoped that the construction of maternity wards and the training of midwives would contribute to the elimination of female genital cutting. Moreover, they argued that such initiatives would demonstrate Britain's commitment to the moral obligations of imperialism and to improving the plight of African women. For black central Kenyans, maternity wards and government-trained midwives raised profound questions about how to ensure successful reproduction and how to define governmental responsibilities and gender relations. The story of Ruth Mukiira and the infertility curse suggests the very intimate associations that existed between excision and proper procreation. These associations made many parturients wary of attending hospitals, where they might be assisted by men or unexcised women. In encouraging some births to take place at hospitals and some girls to train as midwives, colonial maternity initiatives defied local notions of who should facilitate childbirth. Examination of the debates that ensued demonstrates the persistent challenges of managing the colonial politics of the womb.

METROPOLITAN INQUIRIES AND COLONIAL ANSWERS

A reading of the correspondence generated by the Colonial Office's despatch of March 1930 offers an unparalleled opportunity to compare how colonial officials in different African territories assessed female genital cutting as a health issue and how they linked the provision of maternity and welfare services to concerns about colonial governance and women's status. Of the seven territories that responded to the despatch, only Kenya, Uganda, Somaliland, and Tanganyika reported that female genital cutting was being practiced within their borders. Significantly, these reports did not confirm anti-excision activists' claims that the practice led to complications in childbirth. For instance, the Principal Medical Officer of Somaliland wrote that infibulation, a form of female genital cutting that entailed the removal of the clitoris, labia minora, and labia majora, and the stitching together of the cut edges so that only a small opening for the passage of urine and menstrual blood remained, had "no ill effects on the health of the patient." He added that infibulation "has a very good effect on the social health of the people by preventing promiscuity and thus preventing venereal disease."[3] This assessment probably represented a blending of colonial fears of contagion with local concerns about purity and pollution. The Director of Medical and Sanitary Services for Tanganyika similarly dismissed excision as a maternal health threat. He wrote that among the thousands of births that had taken place at state-run maternity clinics, there were no reported cases of complications resulting from excision.[4]

Caught in the middle of the raging "female circumcision controversy," the Kenyan Director of Medical and Sanitary Services, J. L. Gilks, considered the question more carefully. He first noted that medical doctors in Kenya strongly disagreed on the impact of excision on childbirth. Gilks wrote that although a Presbyterian mission doctor who was an outspoken critic of the practice believed that 10 percent of excised women suffered complications later in life, a private practitioner who worked with black Kenyan patients in Nairobi considered that "the after effects of circumcision are negligible." Gilks's own inclination was to distinguish between the "minor" and "major" forms. He reasoned that the "minor" form, which entailed the removal of the clitoris alone, could "hardly be followed by undesirable results other than might occasionally result from sepsis," whereas the "major" form, involving the cutting of the clitoris, labia minora, and parts of the labia majora, was "undoubtedly followed in a proportion of cases by undesirable results." Gilks wrote that it was impossible to base an assessment of the practice on hospital admissions, as women who suffered complications from excision were much more likely to seek care at hospitals than those who did not.[5]

Gilks, therefore, appointed a health committee to investigate the issue. This committee reviewed the cases of 374 "Kikuyu women" to discover that all but a handful had had the "major" form of excision. Medical officers' suspicions that the "minor" form was the predominant form were proven wrong. Reporting its findings in September 1930, the committee neither confirmed nor denied anti-excision activists' claims that the practice contributed to complications during childbirth. Rather, it simply concluded that there was "considerable variation in the effects" of excision.[6]

Part of the difficulty that the committee faced in assessing the impact of excision on childbirth stemmed from the fact that prior to 1930 the Kenyan medical department had taken little interest in maternity work among black Kenyan women, especially those living in rural areas. Responses to the Colonial Office's despatch reveal that the limited scale of colonial maternity services in Kenya was similar to that provided in Somaliland, Zanzibar, Nyasaland, and Northern Rhodesia, but compared much less favorably to the situation in neighboring Tanganyika and Uganda. In 1929 the Kenyan Medical Department reported 18,110 attendances at its maternity and child welfare clinics in Mombasa and Nairobi, and 4,000 home visits by nursing sisters.[7] The Director of Medical and Sanitary Services for Tanganyika, by contrast, reported 342,221 attendances and 32,285 home visits for the same period. Moreover, whereas the Kenyan clinics did not include facilities for childbirth, Tanganyikan clinics had 2,503 confinements during 1929. By 1929, eight African women in Tanganyika had already undergone a three-year, government-sponsored training course in midwifery, whereas in Kenya not a single African midwife had been certified.[8]

Colonial maternity services in Uganda similarly outdid those in Kenya. During the 1920s, dozens of African women became government-certified midwives at the Lady Croyndon Maternity Training School and at the Maternity Training School at Nsambya. While mission-run, these schools, together with thirty-seven rural maternity centers, received substantial support from the Ugandan government. The Governor of Uganda boasted that in 1929 these facilities had served 4,090 inpatients, 105,078 ante-natal outpatients, and 12,333 child welfare outpatients.[9] The scale of colonial maternity schemes in Tanganyika and Uganda put Kenya's meager efforts to shame. Raymond Buell rightly remarked in his 1928 survey of the "native problem" across Africa that maternity work in Kenya, compared to Uganda, was "under-develop[ed]."[10]

In an effort to redress this embarrassing disparity, Gilks asked medical officers stationed throughout Kenya whether or not they thought that government maternity work should be expanded by building lying-in wards and labor rooms at district hospitals.[11] Nearly all medical officers responded that such expansion was unnecessary, since very few, if any, black Kenyan women had ever sought to give birth at their hospitals. Several officers stated that although women did attend government hospitals for various ill-

nesses, and a few sought treatment for "gynecological conditions," specifically, infertility, none had ever come to give birth. The medical officer at
Kiambu wrote that "the vast majority of the Kikuyu . . . will have nothing
to do with us in the matter of childbirth," although he did handle a couple of
maternity cases each month which entailed "malpresentations" or "other
serious abnormalities" that had been "neglected for periods of one to three
days" before the patient had been brought to the hospital. The medical officer at Meru was one of the few to indicate that a small maternity ward and
labor room might be useful. He added that if such facilities were built, a
black Kenyan woman would need to be trained to staff them.[12]

Gilks agreed that the presence of female nurses and midwives would be
crucial to convincing rural women to use colonial maternity facilities. In a
memorandum to the Colonial Office, he argued that nursing and midwifery
training for African women was "an influence directly antagonistic to the
practice of female circumcision," particularly the "major" form. According
to Gilks, black Kenyan nurses, midwives, and welfare workers would make
the most effective and unobtrusive anti-excision activists. The problem,
Gilks noted, was that there were neither enough school-educated women to
undertake the necessary training, nor enough maternity patients on which
to train them. He explained that while mission hospitals and the Lady Grigg
Welfare League maternity homes in Nairobi and Mombasa, founded by and
named after the wife of the governor of Kenya, had begun to train a few
black Kenyan women as midwives, their numbers would remain insufficient
until black women's "social and educational status" improved more generally.[13]

Gilks, like other agents of imperialism, viewed Western medicine or biomedicine, together with school education, as a powerful antidote to African
"barbarity." As Jean Comaroff has argued, "British colonialism in Africa, as
a cultural enterprise, was inseparable from the rise of biomedicine as a science."[14] The development of biomedical knowledge and practices convinced
colonizers of their ability to penetrate inhospitable and disease-ridden
African environments and of their duty to heal suffering and sick African
bodies. By the 1930s, few areas of colonial medicine were more central to the
"civilizing mission" than maternity work, and no African practice was more
repugnant to British sensibilities than excision. Few Britons could have
imagined a better vindication of imperial rule than that of replacing the "old
women" with dirty clothes and hands who performed excisions with
hospital-trained African midwives, described by one official as "bright, intelligent young creatures, with excellent manners . . . dressed in their white
gowns and white caps."[15] According to this color-coded logic, young black

midwives, clad in white, best embodied the power and possibility of colonial uplift.

While most colonial officials believed that teaching African women midwifery, mothercraft, and hygiene would help to "civilize" them and erode unacceptable customs, they did not agree with the assertion, made in the 1930 Colonial Office despatch, that the status of African women was "scarcely distinguishable from that of slavery."[16] British discourses bemoaning African women's lives as slavelike emerged as part of nineteenth-century campaigns to end the slave trade within Africa. By representing women as among those who suffered most at the hands of male slave traders, abolitionists situated African women as the victims of African men. The need to free African women from this predicament had been part of the moral justification of late-nineteenth-century European imperialism.[17] Eleanor Rathbone reaffirmed this image of African women in 1930 when during the House of Commons debate over female "circumcision" she described their status as "sheer slavery."[18]

Officials from African territories, however, strongly disagreed with such characterizations. In their responses to the Colonial Office despatch, they explained that women exerted a "considerable," if "frequently baneful," influence within their communities. Just as H. E. Lambert had concluded after years of trying to alter the severity and timing of excision in Meru, these officials argued that African women possessed powers that could neither be simply dismissed or controlled. A few even insisted that colonialism had made matters worse. An official in Nyasaland noted that, in fact, "the trouble lies in too rapid emancipation rather than in any tendency to slavery."[19] For these male officials, greater freedom for African women spelt colonial chaos. The pragmatics of colonial rule meant that they had little time or sympathy for humanitarian ideals of liberation.

In light of the ongoing criticism that the Kenyan government did more to assist white settlers than to ensure the welfare of black subjects, the Governor of Kenya took a different tack in answering the Colonial Office despatch. Recognizing the need to highlight colonial achievements, he claimed that British rule had improved women's status. He pointed to the elaboration of legal safeguards that promoted women's consent to marriage and the introduction of motorized transport that eased their work burdens. The governor admitted, however, that the work of elevating African women had just begun and that further progress would depend upon "improvement in their economic and social condition" and the availability of school education.[20]

Yet, education, like all welfare initiatives, required funding, and, in

Kenya, the settler-dominated legislative council was unwilling to provide the necessary money. Since 1925 Gilks had sought to secure support for maternal and child health work by linking it to the issue closest to settlers' hearts—labor: "We must reduce the present infantile mortality even if only because it represents a waste of labor."[21] Settler politicians remained unmoved by such arguments. The Kenyan Legislative Council rejected the Colonial Office's 1930 policy recommendation that "natives should receive, directly and visibly, a fair return for the direct taxation which they are called upon to pay," as well as a more specific proposal contained within Lord Moyne's 1932 report on the Kenyan tax system. Moyne had proposed that for three years, 50 percent of the yield from hut and poll tax collection should be placed in a Native Betterment Fund, which would be devoted to the improvement of educational, medical, agricultural, and trade facilities and services in African areas.[22] The Colonial Office attributed the Kenya Legislative Council's unwillingness to support these proposals to the Depression of 1929. According to the Colonial Office, the Kenyan government recognized the necessity of midwifery training but was simply unable to afford it.[23] The Legislative Council's persistent lack of support for medical initiatives in African areas throughout the 1930s, however, suggests that settler politicians never shared a strong interest in discouraging excision, improving maternal and child health, or elevating women's status. In the wake of the Depression, the Legislative Council passed on the costs for health and welfare initiatives in African areas to local governments, specifically to the Local Native Councils.

MATERNITY WORK AS A LOCAL GOVERNMENT CONCERN

Just as colonial administrators understood interventions surrounding excision as laying within the purview of Local Native Councils (LNCs), they also defined the provision of maternity services as a local government concern. In part, this designation of responsibilities reflected the fact that in post–World War I England local government authorities provided most state-run maternal and child health services.[24] This division of government labor, however, also worked to absolve the Kenyan Legislative Council of the financial burden for such welfare initiatives. In 1925, the same year that the first LNCs were established, the Acting Governor of Kenya, E. B. Denham, wrote, "It is only fair and reasonable that the natives should tax themselves for educational and medical services. No charges are made for the provision of these services, and it is but right that the natives should therefore contribute, and contribute generously, to their support."[25] This statement ignored the substantial hut and poll tax revenues that were already collected from black Kenyans, much of which were directed toward providing services and developing infrastructure in white areas.

During the 1920s and 1930s, LNCs raised revenue by imposing local head taxes, renting township plots, and collecting the fees charged by native tribunals. They directed significant sums of this money—though less than they spent on schools, roads, and agricultural services—toward medical services. Between 1927 and 1937, LNC financial support for medical services nearly quadrupled.[26] While the central government covered the costs of building district hospitals, purchasing hospital supplies, and paying staff salaries, LNCs funded dispensaries, ambulance services, and the maternity wards attached to district hospitals.[27]

The Meru LNC first began to consider the need for hospital maternity services in the late 1920s. These discussions, like those surrounding female initiation and abortion, involved men talking about women's affairs. British medical officers requested LNC members to ask "elders," assumed to be men, to encourage pregnant women to attend the district hospital for prenatal examinations and for births, "whenever any difficulty was likely to arise." These doctors, following the approach to maternity work current in interwar Britain, never sought to shift all births from homes to hospitals. Rather, they were interested in identifying and routing potentially difficult births to hospitals.[28] In addition to speaking at LNC meetings, medical officers pronounced the necessity of prenatal examinations when holding *barazas* (public meetings) and during hospital rounds, both forums in which men outnumbered women. These announcements elicited a negligible response.

The few women who attended the government hospital at Meru usually did so as a last resort, after gynecological and obstetrical problems had become dire emergencies incapable of being remedied by local practitioners. The medical officer attributed women's reluctance to attend the hospital to the lack of female staff and a separate maternity ward. In 1935 the hospital hired its first female staff member, a Kikuyu woman named Emily who had been trained as general hospital assistant at the Presbyterian mission station at Chogoria. The arrival of the first government-certified black midwife, the first white nurse, and the opening of a separate maternity, however, did not occur until the late 1940s.[29]

This delay in providing the personnel and facilities that Gilks and others had insisted in 1930 were "essential" for attracting women and children to hospitals was the product of two forces: central government inertia and local suspicions about midwifery training programs. In 1936, following the lead of LNCs in other districts, the Meru LNC voted to fund a maternity ward.[30] Medical department regulations stipulated that all maternity wards be supervised by a white nursing sister who was employed, paid, and provided housing by the central government, and that the wards be staffed by certified black Kenyan midwives, who were usually paid by LNCs. Due to the department's inability to fund the building of accommodations suitable for a single white woman, a nurse was not posted to the government hospital at Meru until 1948, ten years after nurses had been posted to all other district hospitals. Although throughout the "female circumcision controversy," officials from London to rural Kenya had heralded nurses and maternity facilities as crucial to combating excision, fostering population growth, and raising women's status, these items did not prove to be a central government priority, even for a district in which administrators had declared a reproductive practice—abortion—to be the "principal social problem." The building of the maternity ward was further confounded by local reluctance to send school-educated girls for midwifery training in Nairobi. As we shall see, parents and missionaries feared that such training would corrupt their unmarried daughters and pupils. It was not until 1949 that the first certified black midwife would join the Meru hospital and the maternity ward would finally open.[31]

In addition to financing the long-delayed maternity ward, the Meru LNC supported maternity work by providing emergency transport to the hospital and by paying the maternity fees for all those who gave birth at the Methodist hospital at Maua, in the northern part of the district.[32] This was one of two mission hospitals in the district, the other being at the Presbyterian (Church of Scotland) station at Chogoria in the south.[33] As was the case across much of colonial Africa, mission and state medicine developed in tandem. Mission doctors sometimes doubled as district medical officers and census takers, and mission hospitals trained many of the black Kenyan men and women who staffed government facilities. In turn, the colonial state often provided small but enabling grants for mission medical work.[34] Following World War II the Meru LNC further demonstrated its commitment to maternal and child health issues by using War Memorial funds to build a recreation room for maternity patients and their children at the hospital.[35]

In supporting the development of hospital maternity services in Meru, LNC members accepted childbirth as a subject upon which male administrators could deliberate and a process in which hospital personnel could intervene. LNC discussions of maternity work support Megan Vaughan's contention that by the late 1940s some African "male élite[s]" had begun to share with British missionaries and officers a vision of colonial progress that entailed the promotion of school education, welfare policies, and hospital work.[36] The adoption of this perspective paralleled the process, discussed in chapter 1, by which some LNC members gradually came to consider abortion a threat to the size and health of the Meru "tribe." Through LNC measures aimed at stopping abortion and routing problematic births from homes to hospitals, LNC members situated themselves as the progressive guardians of an ethnically defined population. Local reproductive concerns had become entangled with imperial ones. But as with the anti-abortion campaigns, LNC members did not adopt British officers' suggestions about maternity work without insisting on the difficulties of intervening in affairs normally controlled by women.

LNC members repeatedly asked that male and female patients be housed in separate wards and that parturients be further separated from other female patients. In reporting that the LNC had financed the building of a partition in the general ward in 1934, a district officer noted that the "segregation of the sexes" was "always a matter of importance to the Meru."[37] When it came to at-risk parturients, separating the sexes was not the only matter of importance. Women in danger of dying during childbirth would have been a source of heightened concern for other patients. Dr. Stanley Bell observed, based on his work at the Methodist hospital during the 1940s, that Merus believed "the body of a woman dying during childbirth is particularly powerful in bringing disease. In a similar way the living child of a woman who has died in giving it birth seems to be potent to bring disease."[38] Birth, as a potentially dangerous process, needed to be separated from other things taking place at the hospital.

In 1942 a new medical officer arrived at the Meru government hospital to find, much to his dismay, that the isolation block consisting of two small rooms had been converted to a maternity ward. He reported to his supervisor in Nairobi that even though the situation meant that infectious diseases like whooping cough were spread in the general ward, he felt that "custom and usage" made it difficult for him to reestablish the isolation block and "revert to refusing maternity cases."[39] With the absence of a nursing sister and certified midwives stalling the building of the maternity ward, some women and their families had taken matters into their own hands by insisting that they be housed in separate facilities. As LNC members had argued, maternity work could not occur in a space that mixed men and women and the sick and the birthing.

By the mid-1940s, most hospitals in Kenya handled between a few dozen to several hundred maternity cases per year. In 1945, four years prior to the opening of the maternity ward, the government hospital at Meru handled 104 maternity cases, while the Presbyterian hospital at Chogoria handled 159, and the Methodist hospital at Maua, 49.[40] This demand for maternity services, though encompassing only a fraction of the total births within the colony, marked a significant increase from the early 1930s when medical officers reported that few, if any, black Kenyan women gave birth at government hospitals. When the maternity ward at the Meru government hospital finally opened in 1949, the district commissioner wrote that it "has proved popular," handling 313 cases in the first nine months. A good portion of these cases entailed the sort of difficult labors that medical officers had hoped to route to the hospital; 39 of the cases were recorded as abnormal, with not a single maternal death.[41]

Many other cases, however, involved parturients and families who chose the hospital maternity ward because it fit with their status as members of an emergent local elite, characterized by Christianity, school education, and salaried employment. Interviewees who had given birth at hospitals during the 1940s and 1950s, as well as women who had worked at the Methodist hospital during the same period, explained that apart from those with prolonged labor or obstetrical emergencies, the women who attended hospitals for childbirth were those who had become "informed" through school education.[42] For these women and their families, the subsidized maternity fee of 2 Kenyan shillings (Ksh) was a small price to pay to ensure a successful birth and to demonstrate their enlightened status.[43] Such people transformed the maternity ward into something that colonial officers had insisted it not become, a "comfortable Lying-in Hospital for healthy women undergoing normal deliveries."[44] By giving birth in hospitals, these women and their families declared their membership in an emergent elite and contributed to local processes of class formation.

HOME VS. HOSPITAL BIRTHS

To understand more fully why some women chose to give birth in hospitals while many others did not, we need to examine the gender and generational politics of home births. Ethnographic accounts written by officials and missionaries, and oral remembrances collected during the 1990s emphasize that home births in mid-century Meru only involved a parturient's closest kin and neighbors, as people believed that the presence of outsiders endangered the lives of infants and mothers. In 1930 Edward Standleton, a district officer stationed in Tharaka, the remote eastern region of Meru, described that when a birth took place in a "village"—more aptly described as a family compound—"the village is said to be '*murindiru*' and no person from outside other than the paternal grandparents may enter it for four days." He also described how in the case of births which took place away from the "village," people worked to reinscribe them as local births: as the mother and infant approached, the husband "sacrifice[d] a goat at the entrance of the village. . . . The mother and child follow[ed] him [the husband] and when they reach[ed] the hut the child ha[d] to be passed through a circle made of [goat's] intestines and received inside the hut" by the midwife.[45] By performing these sacred gestures, relatives sought to ground infants born out of place in their social and spiritual homes.

Childbirth was a closely guarded affair because it could readily be threatened by outsiders. Based on observations made from the 1930s through the 1950s, Methodist missionary E. Mary Holding described how passersby were alerted to recent births: fathers placed three pieces of sugarcane stalk for a girl and four for a boy on the roof of the birth house to announce the newborn's gender, as well as to warn strangers to keep away and all others not to bring fire from another compound to the birth compound.[46] Less severe restrictions continued after the first several days. Rebecca Ncoro, who gave birth to all of her children at home during the 1930s and 1940s, recalled that although acquaintances could enter the compound, only parents and close female kin were allowed to hold the newborn.[47] Maritha Kaimuri, who was about ten years younger than Ncoro, similarly remembered that those suspected of practicing witchcraft (s. *murogi*, pl. *arogi*) were never allowed to enter the compound, let alone to hold the newborn. Others explained that barren women were also often prohibited from holding newborns, as "people feared that they would kill their children because of jealousy."[48] The presence of unknown patients and personnel at hospitals clearly challenged such efforts to keep childbirth an intimate affair.

As LNC members' opposition to mixing male patients and female parturients in the same room suggests, men were not supposed to be present while women were giving birth. Childbirth was managed by women who were already mothers themselves.[49] A few months into a pregnancy, based on the advice of other women and her husband, a woman would select an older woman from the immediate area to assist in childbirth. This woman was called a *mwijukia* (pl. *ejukia*), literally meaning "the one who receives." Given virilocal residence patterns, the *mwijukia* was usually a relative of the parturient's husband, and preferably, his mother. Interviewees specified that they selected either their husband's mother, the wife of one of their hus-

band's brothers, or their own co-wife to serve as their *mwijukia*. Many recalled retaining the same *mwijukia* for all subsequent pregnancies.[50] Any
woman who had passed the age of childbearing or, at least, was of an older
age-grade than the parturient could be chosen as a *mwijukia*. Such women
had fewer work obligations in their own households and possessed the
knowledge necessary to ensure successful births.[51]

Like initiation, childbirth required the attention of women who knew
how to negotiate transformative and potentially dangerous processes. In
Meru, as in many other African contexts, people believed that newborns
came from the world of the ancestors, embodying blessings and sometimes
ill-will. Older women's knowledge and experience enabled them to discern
the former from the latter and to coax newborns, who might easily decide to
return to the world of the ancestors, to remain in the world of the living.[52]
Ejukia were charged with safeguarding the fragile lives of parturients and
infants.

The presentation of gifts and services strengthened ties of respect and
obligation between the *mwijukia* and the expecting couple. A woman
would select her *mwijukia* by presenting her with a gourd of porridge.
Gifts of agricultural produce followed, with the husband offering the
mwijukia a large bunch of bananas, a local symbol of fertility and rapid
growth. The husband and wife would also, on occasion, help the *mwijukia*
in cultivation.[53] *Ejukia* assisted in childbirth by receiving infants as they
exited the womb, cutting umbilical cords, and massaging newborns' limbs
and head with oil until they assumed their proper shape.[54] Other local
women also gathered in the parturient's house to assist. With the *mwijukia* positioned in front of the parturient during the final stage of labor,
another woman would sit or crouch behind her, lending physical support
similar to that received by initiates during excision.[55] Margaret Karoki,
who gave birth to all of her children at home during the 1930s and 1940s,
explained that the severing of the umbilical cord was a *mwijukia*'s most
important task; while another woman might receive the newborn if the
mwijukia was not present, they would wait for the *mwijukia* to come and
cut the umbilical cord.[56] *Ejukia* sought to facilitate delayed labor by performing episiotomies, and if they were "courageous," by manually repositioning the baby.[57]

For several days following a home birth, or until the stump of the umbilical cord dried up and fell off, the *mwijukia* remained with the new mother
and infant day and night, bathing both and providing food for the mother.
She also managed the household, making sure that firewood and water were
collected and meals prepared. The bathing and feeding of new mothers was

similar to the care lavished on initiates following excision.[58] Before returning to her own household, the *mwijukia* would shave the head of the new mother and receive a gift of agricultural produce. The naming of the child would also take place. While the child was not necessarily named after the *mwijukia*, the *mwijukia* and the child shared a namesake relationship throughout their lives, offering each other special respect, presents, and protection.[59] Through their work of receiving newborns, *ejukia* forged intimate and powerful ties.

Like female initiation, childbirth was a crucial process through which relations of authority among women were constructed. Whereas initiation situated a girl-turned-woman within the female hierarchy of her natal home, childbirth, particularly with a woman's mother-in-law serving as *mwijukia*, situated her within the female hierarchy of her marriage home. *Ejukia*, like the older women who presided over excision, possessed the necessary knowledge and skill to facilitate reproduction, a potent and potentially precarious process. Childbirth paralleled initiation in other ways. Just as few interviewees dwelt on the pain of excision when recounting their initiations, very few who gave birth at home mentioned having problems or complications during childbirth. The ordeal of excision was, in fact, meant to prepare women for the pain of childbirth.[60] Nancy Adams, who worked at the government maternity ward in Meru during the 1950s, recalled that the behavioral ideal for parturients, as for initiates during excision, was stoicism. Adams contrasted Meru women's silence during childbirth with the loud cries of Luo women whom she assisted in childbirth while training in Nairobi. Attributing Meru women's bravery to excision, Adams explained that unexcised Luo women were not embarrassed to express their pain.[61] Adams's observation suggests how lessons learned during initiation informed women's behavior during childbirth. Such lessons initially dissuaded many women from attending maternity wards.

When asked what were the biggest differences between giving birth at hospital and at home, some interviewees spoke of the greater ability of hospital staff to intervene in complicated cases through repositioning the fetus, performing cesarean sections, and administering medicines. As Beatrice Tiira, who gave birth at home and in hospitals during the 1950s and 1960s, explained, "There was a difference because at the hospital they had more knowledge than at home. Like my last child came with legs first and refused to come out but the [nursing] sister who was there used her skills until it came out. If it was at home, I would have died."[62] People like Tiira knew that hospital personnel could sometimes save situations that eluded the expertise of *ejukia*. As in other African contexts, women resorted to colonial hospitals when cases of obstructed labor or the aftereffects of difficult deliveries threatened their lives.[63]

The suturing of episiotomies and perineum tears, the provision of cotton blankets, and cleanliness also distinguished hospital from home births. Elizabeth Kabita, perhaps recalling the rhetoric of colonial and postcolonial campaigns to persuade women to give birth at hospital, stated, "giving birth at home is difficult because at home it is dirty."[64] But not all of those who attended hospitals welcomed their routines. Muriel Chalkley, a British nurse who worked at the Methodist hospital during the 1950s, recalled that some women, accustomed to the application of oil derived from local plants to heal cuts or tears, simply refused to be sutured following episiotomies.[65] Even women who chose hospital births over home births did not easily accept all the new practices that such births entailed.

FINDING MIDWIFERY TRAINEES AND FEARING PROSTITUTION

The element of hospital maternity work that generated the greatest controversy was the figure of the girl-midwife. While imperial and local gender ideologies converged in designating childbirth as a female affair, they did not agree on which females should be involved. According to metropolitan reformers and medical officers, single and school-educated girls or young women, between the ages of 16 and 25 years, made the best midwifery trainees. They had the language and literacy skills to undertake coursework in Swahili and were free of family ties that could distract them from their careers.[66] Young midwives, reformers argued, also offered the best hope for improving African women's status and creating better mothers. Despite these high expectations, the figure of the girl-midwife in Kenya, as elsewhere in colonial Africa, was not easily accepted.[67] Parents doubted the social standing that the Nairobi-based midwifery training course would confer on their school-educated daughters, and many others questioned the wisdom of encouraging girls in maternity work. Young women were not meant to develop careers in assisting others in childbirth but to marry and give birth themselves.

Throughout the interwar period, most of the black Kenyan women who worked in hospitals were trained informally at mission stations. Early missionary involvement in childbirth focused on incorporating those marginalized by conception and childbirth gone awry—barren women and infants born to dying mothers—into nascent Christian communities. Among the

Methodists in Meru, single female missionaries, known as women's workers, spearheaded these efforts by encouraging local women who were barren and who had been shunned by kin and neighbors to join the church and place their faith in Christ. Such local women, including one named Cionkonge who served as Holding's research assistant, ranked among the Methodists' most influential early converts. Together, these white and black childless women sought to erode the "the deepest-seated superstitions" surrounding reproduction by raising orphaned children and teaching scripture and mothercraft to other women.[68] For Protestant missionaries, the development of central Kenyan congregations entailed negotiating aberrant reproduction.

At the Presbyterian mission station at Chogoria, maternal and infant health work was also pioneered by people who, in local terms, were reproductive misfits: single British women and a local woman who "by reason of disease" was unable to have children. During the 1930s and early 1940s, the Presbyterians trained and employed a couple dozen black Kenyan women in hospital work. None of these women, however, were certified midwives, as only the Lady Grigg maternity homes in Nairobi and Mombasa offered the courses that were a prerequisite for taking the state examination.[69] Similarly, the Methodist hospital at Maua, opened in 1930, employed a few local girls and women to "help out" with "babies and young children" but did not undertake any systematic training of female medical personnel until 1950.[70]

As early as 1933 the medical officer at Meru asked Methodist missionaries if they had any female students who would be interested and able to undertake the two-year midwifery training course offered at Lady Grigg in Nairobi and then return to Meru to work at the government hospital. He explained that the establishment of a maternity ward at the hospital depended upon the availability of certified midwives to staff it. A. G. V. Cozens, the Methodist superintendent, responded that because of the local premium placed on marriage it would "be very difficult, amounting almost to an impossibility, to get Meru girls [to] train with any promise of a term of service afterwards." Suggesting his own disinclination to send steadfast mission girls to Nairobi, Cozens agreed only to make inquiries among former adherents. No candidates were forthcoming.[71] Thirteen years later, the medical officer repeated the request, writing, "I have been told that no parents would allow their children to go to the Lady Grigg Training Center, Nairobi but surely the Meru are now more enlightened." The Methodist superintendent responded that although he would like to help, it was still "impossible" to offer any candidates "owing to conservatism and the early marriage age."[72] The government's need to staff the hospital maternity with certified midwives could not easily overcome local reproductive concerns about marriage and mobility.

The medical officer encouraged the Methodist superintendent to reconsider his response by explaining that the midwifery course included religious instruction and that "adequate chaperonage is laid down."[73] This reference to "chaperonage" spoke directly to missionaries' and rural parents' vision of Nairobi as a morally dangerous place. By World War II, Nairobi had become, in their eyes, a place where women became Muslims, married without bridewealth being paid, divorced, and became prostitutes.[74] Rural peoples' associations of Nairobi and prostitution were, in part, accurate. As Luise White has demonstrated, prostitutes played prominent economic and social roles in the African areas of the city. And Pumwani, where the Lady Grigg maternity home was located, was one of the most notorious areas for prostitution.[75]

In 1929 a Presbyterian missionary reported that midwives trained in Nairobi were of "little use to women in rural districts," as they were regarded as "being of a bad character."[76] Similarly, at a meeting of LNC members from across Central Province in 1938, one representative stated "that many parents were frightened of sending their daughters to be trained at Pumwani in case they become prostitutes," and suggested that the Presbyterian hospital at Tumutumu be used as an alternative training site for certified midwives.[77] LNC members were just as reluctant as missionaries and rural parents to send girls from their district to Nairobi. By 1940, the situation was so bad that rumors began to circulate that the training program at Pumwani would close due to "lack of material."[78] While the program at Pumwani remained open, in the mid-1940s the government began to allow some mission hospitals to train midwives for the certification exam.[79]

Parents' and missionaries' reluctance to send their daughters and students to train as midwives extended beyond the time that they spent in Nairobi. They were even more fearful of what might happen once girl-midwives were posted to government hospitals. In 1938 L. Olive Owen, a missionary working in Western Kenya, wrote to the Director of Medical Services to explain why black Kenyans considered midwifery, compared to teaching, an unsuitable career for school-educated girls. She first noted that at mission boarding schools precautions were taken to protect the virtue of female students by restricting them to the school grounds, prohibiting them from walking alone on the road, and censoring all letters and visitors. Owen wrote that while similar, though more lax, safeguards existed at the Lady

Grigg training center in Nairobi, they disappeared entirely once midwives began working at government hospitals. According to Owen, black Kenyan fathers and fiancés disapproved of their daughters and future wives being stationed at government hospitals, where they were housed near male staff "in such isolated proximity as no decent European girl would tolerate." Owen urged the Director of Medical Services to establish supervised hostels at all government hospitals in order to ease these men's anxieties and to "eliminate the girl who only goes into hospital training for the sake of a gay life."[80]

According to missionaries and black Kenyan men, unmarried and un-guarded black women were sexually vulnerable and free to act out their own dangerous desires. Such circumstances promised to foil missionaries' hopes that their female pupils would become stalwart Christians, marrying lead-ing men in the church and promoting Christian domesticity and mother-hood through their own example and church outreach work with other women. Similarly, Christian parents feared that a loose reputation or pre-marital pregnancy would spoil a daughter's chances for marrying a respect-able and upwardly mobile man.

The association between hospital work and promiscuity and premarital pregnancy was not limited to Kenya. Across colonial Africa, medical officers, missionaries, and members of local communities accused young unmarried midwives and nurses of engaging in illicit sex. In colonial Sudan, accusations that the young, single women initially trained at the Midwifery Training School in Omdurman were sexual perverts or lesbians convinced the school's matron, Mabel E. Wolff, to recruit older married women.[81] Dr. Albert Cook, a key figure in the development of colonial maternity services in Uganda, recalled in his memoirs that nursing and midwifery training programs attracted "troublesome girl[s]"—some even several months preg-nant.[82] Similar incidents occurred in the Belgian Congo and South Africa, where midwifery students were expelled for premarital pregnancies and parents resisted sending their school-educated daughters to nursing pro-grams for fear that they would return pregnant.[83] Government and hospital personnel preferred to train single and school-educated girls as midwives and nurses because they could read and write and were, ideally, open to learning new things and burdened with few family obligations. This prefer-ence, however, required females of marriageable age to delay, if not dismiss, sexual intercourse, marriage, and childbearing. Such requirements defied local gender roles and standards of sexual and reproductive behavior.

The first young women from Meru to undertake midwifery training at Lady Grigg directly confronted these challenges. In 1947 the Meru LNC finally sponsored two female students, a Methodist and a Presbyterian, to go to Pumwani and then return to work at the government hospital. In an interview, Martha Muirige, the Methodist recruit, remembered that it was a family friend who worked as a medical assistant at the government hospital, not the Methodist superintendent, who informed her of the opportunity. Muirige explained why most parents would not allow their daughters to attend the course: "They said any one who was going for nursing would be a prostitute so they did not want girls to go for nursing. . . . Meru people never wanted girls to be married far. They did not want them to go to Nairobi. They wanted girls, after reaching the lower classes [of school], to be married at once."[84] Muirige herself was orphaned as a child and raised by a distant relative who worked as a carpenter at the Methodist mission station. She explained that after attending school for six years, she was forced to discontinue her studies due to lack of fees. These circumstances may have caused Muirige and her guardian, unlike other mission adherents, to pay less attention to local standards of respectability and to view midwifery training as an attractive opportunity.

Once the first Nairobi-trained midwives were posted to the Meru government hospital, worries about promiscuity turned to complaints. In 1950 the district commissioner reported that the midwives had proven a "nuisance," since they are "either pursued by or send invitations to the local youths with the result that they are always being put in the family way."[85] One Presbyterian missionary at Chogoria estimated that during the early 1950s one-third of those enrolled in hospital training programs—both female and male—were compelled to resign because they either became pregnant or their girlfriends did.[86] In 1950 the Meru African District Council (formerly, LNC) "placed responsibility on the local elders to see that the female African staff at the hospital, in their leisure hours did not resort to immoral pursuits, and that they were not worried by amorously-inclined youths."[87] With this resolution, the Council situated local elders as midwives' surrogate kin, charged with policing their indiscretions and protecting them from inappropriate advances.

Hospital midwives may have pursued sexual relations with men for pleasure or for the opportunity to supplement their hospital salaries with gifts in cash and kind. At other times, these young women may have invited or accepted men's intimacy in the hope of moving a relationship toward marriage. As the practice of abortion during the 1920s and 1930s indicates, sex was not an unknown part of courtship in Meru. Moreover, as we shall see in chapters 4 and 5, by at least the 1950s some young people had begun to view premarital pregnancies as a way of prompting marriage negotiations. The LNC's concern over midwives' pregnancies, however, suggests that not all pregnancies readily resulted in marriage. Young men probably viewed girl-midwives—figures who defied gender and reproductive norms—as making better lovers than wives.

THE GENERATIONAL POLITICS OF CHILDBIRTH

In Kenya, as elsewhere in Africa, colonial officers and missionaries recognized that hospital-trained midwives threatened the authority of the old women or "grannies" who normally assisted in childbirth. Old women's persistent influence in reproductive matters represented both the greatest obstacle and the greatest inspiration for establishing maternity wards. In his notes on native law and custom in Kenya, J. S. S. Rowlands, a colonial officer who was stationed at the coast and in central Kenya, described the centrality of childbirth to older women's societies or councils. He wrote that among the coastal Pokomo such groups actively discouraged the "training of 'career-girls' in paths of hygiene and western medicine." Rowlands recalled an incident in which a Pokomo women's society held "a form of court" to punish a "poor trainee midwife" for "practicing midwifery without the necessary qualification (which is being a mother)." The older women disciplined the trainee by dancing about her, mocking her, and pinching her until she wept.[88] These Pokomo groups viewed the involvement of young unmarried and childless women in childbirth as an affront to their power to facilitate reproduction.

In an article published in a 1941 issue of the Methodist journal, *Women's Work*, E. Mary Holding similarly described how older women in Meru understood "the practice of midwifery as their special privilege." Holding told the story of two young women in the process of joining the church who were encouraged by "old midwives" to give birth alone in the bush and abandon their newborn infants. According to Holding, the "old midwives" believed that the young women were going to have stillborns and they did not want such births to bring misfortune to their "villages." Both women, in fact, gave birth to live infants, which were discovered abandoned and dying by Christians a day or two later. In response to the deaths of these infants, the local Methodist church committee decided that in the future, all women "who had joined classes for Christian instruction must engage as midwives those who were members of the church." Church-members-in-the-making would now be required to have Christian *ejukia*. Holding explained that the "old ladies" responded to this announcement by holding "an emergency meeting," at which it was agreed that "the loss of their profession would be a serious matter" and so they all decided to become Christians. The next week, thirty to forty of them turned out for Sunday service and baptism classes.[89] Through this story, Holding illustrated the "winding ways" through which the church attracted adherents, and she urged her readers to accept that strong faith can grow from "poor motives." Holding's story demonstrates how old women in Meru, like their Pokomo counterparts, strove to retain their influence over fertility and procreation.

A closer, if somewhat speculative, reading of Holding's story suggests that such struggles over childbirth were intimately related to old women's efforts to preserve and control female initiation and excision. The emergence of "career-girls" and Christian *ejukia* coincided with the enforcement of LNC resolutions regulating excision and with the *Kigwarie* episodes. While Holding claimed that the two young women had given birth in the bush because "old midwives" had predicted stillborns, it is quite likely that these were instances of pre-initiation pregnancies. As we have seen, the usual response to pregnancies conceived prior to excision was abortion. If that failed, the woman would give birth alone in the bush and then either commit infanticide or abandon the newborn to the elements and wild animals. In the mid-1930s, District Commissioner Lambert reported to the Attorney General that when such cases were investigated, the women involved normally claimed that the infants had been stillborn.[90] Holding, no doubt, knew of these practices and cover-ups. But, for her, it would have been easier to gloss these infants as stillbirths than to raise the ever-sensitive subject of excision in a Methodist outreach and fundraising magazine. In the wake of the "female circumcision controversy," the Methodists in Meru adopted a more accommodating approach to excision, an approach that may have been difficult for readers of *Women's Work* to accept.

The fact that the two pregnant women in Holding's story were young and in the process of joining the church is also noteworthy. If their pregnancies were conceived prior to excision, the women may have joined the church in the hope of finding an alternative to killing or abandoning their newborn children. Such hopes would have largely collapsed once they went into labor and the "old midwives" compelled them to give birth in the bush. Yet, it is possible that it was the young women themselves who told the Christians, albeit belatedly, where to find their abandoned infants. Missionaries were known to take in orphans. In responding to these two cases by requiring all pregnant baptismal candidates to have Christian *ejukia*, the local church committee sought to ensure that "old midwives" would never again thwart young women's efforts to embrace Christianity and defy "heathen" customs. In their decision to become Christians themselves, the old women sought to maintain their control over childbirth. For these women, midwifery was not limited to comforting laboring mothers and receiving newborn children; it also entailed protecting communities from dangerous births and, as we shall see, ensuring that all new mothers were properly excised.

Interviewees also pointed to intersections between the politics of childbirth and those of excision. They explained that women were often reluctant to give birth in maternity wards because they believed that those who assisted in hospital births were either unexcised or opposed to the practice. For instance, Elizabeth Kabita recalled that although she eventually gave birth to some of her children at the Methodist hospital during the 1950s, she, like others, feared that hospital midwives might be "children" *(aana)* or uninitiated persons. She added, "We did not want a circumcised person to be seen by an uncircumcised person."[91] Such suspicions appear to have been largely unfounded.

While hospital staff, particularly Presbyterian missionaries, may have preferred to employ unexcised women, oral evidence suggests that this preference was rarely satisfied in Meru. Nancy Adams, who was schooled at the Presbyterian mission station at Chogoria and trained as a midwife in Nairobi, explained that girls who feared that excision might jeopardize their educational opportunities simply waited until they had completed their training to be initiated.[92] Similarly, Muriel Chalkley, a British nurse, believed that all but a few of the women whom she trained as midwives and nurses at the Methodist hospital from the 1950s through the early 1980s had undergone initiation.[93] The popular perception of midwives as unexcised, however, highlights how hospitals became associated with anti-excision politics. The hopes of metropolitan, missionary, and medical reformers to construct maternity wards as institutions that opposed excision were, in part, fulfilled. Yet midwives' inability or unwillingness to avoid the practice in their own lives indicates that being "directly antagonistic" to excision was far more difficult than reformers had imagined.

Colonial medical initiatives were more successful at mitigating the severity and effects of excision than eliminating it. From the previous chapter, we know that a Methodist mission doctor probably lent a scalpel to a black Kenyan hospital assistant to perform a hygienic and more modest procedure on an assistant trainee. In her interview, Muriel Chalkley, the Methodist nurse, did not mention similar efforts to medicalize excision, but she did recount how she sought to minimize the impact of the procedure on childbirth. Chalkley explained that she instructed nursing and midwifery trainees in how to handle cases of obstructed labor caused by scar tissue resulting from excision. She taught them that when a baby's head was stuck in the birth canal, they should make a small incision, or "knick," on the scar, thereby loosening the tissue. This procedure, according to Chalkley, proved remarkably successful in preventing the need for episiotomies in that and all subsequent deliveries.[94] Chalkley's development and teaching of this technique attests to how colonial medicine adapted to excision. Within hospitals, amelioration made more sense than obstinate condemnation.[95]

While nurses and midwives took steps to accommodate excision, hospital births entailing the assistance of young and unknown women still represented a profound challenge to generational and kinship relations. In Meru, childbirth was suppose to be an intimate affair which affirmed a woman's ties to her husband's senior female kin. According to Julia Nyoroka, who gave birth to all of her children at home during the 1940s and 1950s, it was considered socially deplorable to receive assistance during childbirth from an age mate. Nyoroka stated that when this occurred, the entire age-grade was compelled to provide older women in the area with gifts of cooked food; the husband of the woman who had been assisted similarly offered a basketful of yams.[96] Amid colonial anti-excision campaigns, older women's supervision of childbirth took on additional significance. Home births provided a woman's in-laws with the opportunity to verify her initiated status. As Elizabeth Kabita explained: "If you went to hospital, women were saying it is because you are not circumcised and you did not want them to know."[97] During the 1930s and 1940s, it would have been quite rare for older women to discover a married woman who was not excised. It would have been more common for them to find a woman who had had the less severe form of excision, in accordance with the LNC regulations. Lambert reported that older women frequently used childbirth as an opportunity to perform second excisions.[98] Through second excisions, older women completed junior women's initiation and asserted control over their reproductive capacities.

A few interviewees recalled that during the 1950s some hospital-goers began to refer to nurses and midwives as *ejukia*, providing them with presents of food and instructing the children whom they had "received" to greet them as namesakes.[99] This identification was a compliment. As retired hospital midwife Martha Muirige explained: "We would be given the big name of old people because old people used to be *ejukia*. . . . . Now, you know, a *mwijukia* is not a young person. . . . They would be praising us." This naming of hospital midwives as *ejukia*, however, did not come easily. When asked whether as a young woman she ever experienced problems assisting older women in childbirth, Muirige responded: "Only women who knew me from . . . [my home place]. They did not refuse. It's me who felt *nthoni* (respect). I saw then that this is my mother [a woman of her mother's age-grade] and this other, too. Then, I would call for other midwives to come to attend them."[100] Muirige's recollection of whom she felt uncomfortable attending suggests that hospital procedures were more successful at reconfiguring childbirth as a less intimate social process than at subverting respectful relations of authority between senior and junior women of the same area. It was easier to be a girl-midwife for strangers than for one's own kin and neighbors.

．　．　．

From the 1920s through the 1950s maternal and infant health initiatives became a crucial element of British efforts to demonstrate a commitment to the moral obligations of colonial rule. At the prompting of missionaries and their metropolitan allies, colonial officials recognized that political order depended on attending to matters of the womb. Through initiatives to lower maternal and infant mortality, foster population growth, encourage Christian domesticity, and raise colonized women from a slavelike status, pregnancy, birth, and babies were made into objects of colonial governance. Calls for the Kenyan colonial government to fund midwifery training schemes, maternity wards, and infant welfare clinics were particularly strong. Throughout the 1920s black political groups, missionaries, and their metropolitan allies criticized the Kenyan government for enforcing coercive labor recruitment policies, refusing to recognize black land rights, and failing to devote significant resources to the establishment of education and health facilities for blacks. Missionaries and metropolitan women's activists, in particular, saw the provision of maternal and infant health services as an opportunity for the Kenyan government to prove that its concerns extended beyond securing white settler profits to improving the lives of black subjects. The "female circumcision controversy" of 1928–31 only strengthened their conviction. As it became increasingly clear that excision would not be made illegal, they argued that the Kenyan government could, at least, demonstrate its disapproval of the practice and its commitment to bettering maternal and infant health by building maternity wards and training black Kenyan women as nurses and midwives.

Once reformers had defined the provision of maternity services as a colonial concern, it was up to officials and politicians on the ground in Kenya to fulfill the mandate. Although senior government officials claimed that they, too, recognized the importance of such services, the settler-controlled Legislative Council refused to provide the necessary financial support.

Instead, they passed much of the monetary burden for maternal and infant health initiatives off to the LNCs. Most LNCs responded by accepting the provision of maternity services as a task worthy of their attention and expenditure, since it fit well with their self-image as the progressive and paternalistic guardians of their districts. Within Meru, the LNC's decision to build a maternity ward in 1934 coincided with its efforts to eradicate abortion by lowering the age of initiation. Through supporting these two measures, Meru LNC members embraced a colonial and pronatalist political agenda that sought to safeguard births in the name of strengthening the "tribe" and improving the lives of mothers and infants. It was also an agenda that enabled male officials to deliberate on reproductive matters and allowed young women to intervene directly in them. But as with their efforts to regulate female initiation, officials had a more difficult time implementing the resolution to establish the maternity ward at the Meru government hospital than endorsing it. The central government's delay in posting a nursing sister to Meru and local reluctance to send schoolgirls for midwifery training in Nairobi meant that the maternity ward was not opened until 1949. Once again, lack of government resources and will combined with local gender and generational relations to confound a reproductive intervention.

Competing views of African women animated much of the debate over colonial maternity services. Metropolitan women's activists and some missionaries portrayed African women as slavelike beings and posed the figure of the hospital-trained nurse or midwife as their best hope for emancipation. They imagined school-educated and white-clad African young women combating "barbaric" practices such as excision and teaching other women how to be better mothers. Senior colonial officials largely shared the hope that African nurses and midwives could become positive role models and effective agents against excision. They did not, however, accept the claim that all African women were downtrodden and disenfranchised. Instead, they complained that some young women already enjoyed too much freedom, while some old women still exerted too much influence. For officials preoccupied with the pragmatics of rule, girls and women did not so much represent victims in need of salvation as unruly subjects capable of disrupting colonial control. While metropolitan reformers denied African women's agency, colonial officials recognized and resented it. This difference in perspective made officials better able to understand the profound challenge to local gender and generational relations posed by girl-midwives.

Black Kenyans initially viewed those who trained as midwives in Nairobi as particularly ill-suited for assisting in childbirth. As unmarried young women who had yet to give birth themselves, and who had lived in a city synonymous with prostitution, they possessed neither the knowledge nor reputation to assist in the delicate and potentially dangerous work of protecting the lives of mothers and infants. Moreover, in Meru, where female initiation and childbirth were crucial and related moments in the construction of female hierarchies, allowing young and potentially unexcised women to perform maternity work threatened respectful relations of authority among different generations of female kin. The conditions under which girl-midwives labored and lived also made it an unseemly career. Employment at government hospitals, by placing girl-midwives beyond the purview of families, fiancés, and mission station protocols, subverted local techniques for regulating unmarried women's sexual behavior. It left them unguarded and free to engage in intimate relations with men, while providing them with few immediate allies to ensure that any of those relationships resulted in marriage. Parents' and missionaries' fears of prostitution and premarital pregnancies powerfully informed schoolgirls' career options. They did not want work ambitions to interfere with their daughters' and students' ability to marry respectable men and raise dutiful children. According to both local and missionary conventions, the productive labor of girls and women could not be disentangled from their procreative capacities and responsibilities. The girl-midwife was a contentious figure because she flouted reproductive roles and hierarchies.

Despite its inauspicious beginning, colonial maternity work in Kenya expanded, so that by the mid-1940s mission and government hospitals handled up to several hundred maternity cases each year. These included the types of cases that colonial officers believed should be handled by hospitals: women suffering from obstructed labor or other delivery complications. But, increasingly, they also began to handle cases of healthy parturients who simply preferred to give birth at hospitals. While maternity wards, at least government ones, were a dubious place for old schoolgirls to work, they were the most appropriate place for them to give birth. By the 1950s, giving birth in hospital had become an important sign of belonging to the enlightened and school-educated elite. Attendance at colonial maternities demonstrated affiliation to new, largely Christian, notions of morality and new forms of material prosperity. Through maternity wards, reformers' visions of uplifting African women became entangled with local processes of class formation. Colonial maternities fulfilled reformers' desire to create an alternative birthing space, free from the direct supervision of "grannies." They did not, however, satisfy reformers' hope of ending excision. Hospital personnel tended to accommodate, rather than combat, the practice. It was not until 1956 that some colonial officials in Kenya would seriously attempt to stop excision.

3   Mau Mau and the Girls Who "Circumcised Themselves"

> Those of the iron-wedge knife, stay at the side, you.
> Do not abuse those of the razor blade, you.
> A circumcised girl without water in the stomach when
>   guarded by government officials.
> A circumcised girl without water in the stomach when
>   guarded by government officials.[1]

In the mid-1950s recently excised girls in Meru sang this song as they performed punitive hard labor for having defied a ban on excision. The *Njuri Ncheke* of Meru, the men's council that H. E. Lambert had drawn into colonial administration in the late 1930s, unanimously banned excision in April 1956. When interviewed in the 1990s, people in Meru recounted how news and defiance of the ban spread quickly and widely. Ex-Headman M'Anampiu of Mikinduri remembered returning in the evening from the *Njuri Ncheke* council meeting at Nchiru only to find that "all the girls had been circumcised."[2] In the three years following the passage of the ban, over 2,400 girls, men, and women were charged in African Courts with having defied the Njuri's order.[3] Interviews suggest that many others who defied the ban paid fines in livestock to local *Njuri Ncheke* members and headmen.

As adolescent girls defied the ban by attempting to excise each other, their initiations marked a profound departure from the past. They also differed from earlier practices by foregoing the preparations and celebrations associated with initiation and the instruments typically used. While *atani* (s. *mutani*), the older women specialists who performed excisions, had previously used special triangular iron-wedge knives called *irunya* (s. *kirunya*), these girls of the mid-1950s simply used razor blades purchased at local shops. These departures caused some from Meru, both then and now, to doubt the legitimacy of these initiations. The song was, in part, an appeal by these girls to older age-grades—"those of the iron-wedge knife"—to stop abusing them and to recognize their initiation as proper. Similarly, the Meru nickname—*Ngaitana*, "I will circumcise myself"—given to these girls by older groups of men and women mocked the girls' determination and highlighted these elders' sense of the absurdity of their undertaking.

The song and the term *Ngaitana* also suggested the political exigencies of the times. Between 1952 and 1956, central Kenya and its population of approximately two million was engulfed in the Mau Mau rebellion. Originating in black Kenyans' long-standing grievances against colonial land policies, Mau Mau grew into a web of conflicts that pitted black central Kenyans against white settlers, the colonial government, and often each other.[4] The colonial government responded to and, in turn, fueled the movement by imposing a state of emergency that lasted from 1952 until 1960. Under the state of emergency, the government repatriated to their home areas over 100,000 Kikuyu, Embu, and Meru living on settler farms and in Nairobi, placed 80,000 others in detention camps, and forced over a million to live in heavily guarded "villages" meant to prevent them from providing supplies and support for rebels living in the forest. Government security forces killed an estimated 11,000 black central Kenyans suspected of being rebels, and officials executed over 1,000 others on capital crimes and imprisoned 19,000 on lesser crimes. The government held the rebels responsible for the deaths of just over 100 whites and Asians and approximately 2,000 black loyalists.[5]

Amid these circumstances, in which officials, police, and soldiers, both black and white, routinely tortured and killed black Kenyans suspected of disobeying the government, the ability of anyone, including adolescent girls, to remain calm and brave—"without water in the stomach"—when being detained in a headman's camp or police station was a remarkable feat. The term *Ngaitana* conveyed the reluctance of many adults to defy the ban for fear that their homes would be burned or that they would be fined or imprisoned. In the face of parents and *atani* who refused to assist them, some members of *Ngaitana* apparently proclaimed, "I will circumcise myself." Others, who received assistance from mothers, grandmothers, or *atani*, refused to implicate their co-conspirators, claiming before headmen and other officials that they had "circumcised themselves."

Within African, and particularly Kenyan, historiography, it is tempting to situate a history of the 1956 ban on excision within the now familiar paradigm of resistance to colonialism. The ban occurred during the waning years of the Mau Mau rebellion and the state of emergency, events that encompassed the most virulent anti-government protests in Kenyan colonial history. Moreover, historians have interpreted the "female circumcision controversy" of 1928–31 as a crucial moment in the emergence of nationalist politics within Kenya. But while the Mau Mau rebellion and the state of emergency informed the formulation and enforcement of the ban, they do not explain why so many girls and women challenged it. As Frederick Cooper, critiquing resistance historiography, has argued, "The dyad of resister/oppressor is isolated from its context; struggle within the colonized population—over class, age, gender or other inequalities—is 'sanitized' . . . and complex strategies . . . of multi-sided engagement with forces inside and outside the community, are narrowed into a single framework."[6] In other words, the resistance paradigm reifies dualities, obscuring the tangled layers of political relations which animate social protest. Applied single-mindedly to colonial controversies over excision, the resistance paradigm misses the gender and generational relations that shaped the practice and reduces excision disputes to anticolonial struggles.

This chapter examines the history of the 1956 ban in order to situate girls and women as important participants in colonial debates over excision and to demonstrate the continued importance of the politics of the womb in the post–World War II period. As we have seen, female initiation was a key institution through which gender relations and generational hierarchies were constituted. The decision in 1956 to ban excision in Meru was the brainchild of a resolute British district commissioner and group of black Kenyan men and one woman who had been educated at Methodist and Presbyterian mission schools and worked for the colonial government. The political context of the Mau Mau rebellion and related state of emergency convinced these officials that it was possible to end excision. This context also informed how girls and women assimilated news of the ban. It does not explain, however, why many chose to defy it. Their faith in the ability of excision to transform girls into women and ensure proper reproduction was something that both preceded and exceeded anticolonial resistance.

PREVIOUS EFFORTS TO REGULATE EXCISION

In the two decades prior to 1956 female initiation in Meru had undergone significant change. Many of these changes were the product of colonial interventions discussed in previous chapters. The enforcement of Local Native Council (LNC) resolutions altering the timing and severity of excision meant that many initiations occurred at puberty rather than prior to marriage and many girls received (at least prior to second excisions) a less severe form of excision. The mass excisions of *Kigwarie,* for which girls and their families had had little time to prepare, also made it more difficult for initiates to have abdominal tattooing performed or large ear holes pierced before being excised. As the most visible signs of initiated status, these two practices were falling out of fashion; in a context in which some key colonial figures, namely Protestant missionaries, opposed excision, girls and young women did not always want everyone to know whether they were initiated or not.

Throughout this period, the Methodist and Presbyterian missionaries in Meru continued to condemn excision. But while the Methodists concluded in the wake of the "female circumcision controversy" of 1928–31 that it was best to tolerate the practice even as they quietly preached against it, the Presbyterians maintained a more vocal opposition.[7] In 1947 Dr. Clive Irvine of the Presbyterian station at Chogoria stated that his church could claim one hundred unexcised women among its ranks, whereas the Methodists could claim only a handful. Although the Presbyterians appear to have stopped short of expelling excised schoolgirls, Irvine stated that all of the "leading" schoolgirls at Chogoria were unexcised.[8] According to Charity Waciuma's semi-autobiographical account of attending another Presbyterian boarding school in central Kenya during the 1950s, all schoolgirls, upon returning from holidays, were subjected to physical exams by a white doctor to determine if they had been excised over the break; if so, they were moved to a separate dormitory where "their lives were made a misery and they became very withdrawn." Waciuma described such mission actions as "revers[ing]" the situation in her rural home area, where the excised were privileged and the unexcised, chided.[9]

In addition to discouraging excision among girls in mission schools and churches, the Presbyterians continued to push for state action against the practice. They appear to have played a crucial role in the passage of an African District Council (ADC; formerly, Local Native Council) resolution in 1951 that required the consent of both parents or a guardian before a girl could be legally excised.[10] In 1953 District Commissioner F. D. Homan complained that the Presbyterians had undertaken an anti-excision initiative that provoked "a violent re-action in the Reserves."[11] During the early years of the Mau Mau rebellion, administrators kept their own interference with female initiation to a minimum. They restricted the scale of some ceremonies and in some cases required that "fees" of five shillings or fifty rat tails—in contribution to public health campaigns—be paid before initiation could be undertaken.[12] Apart from several dozen schoolgirls from strong Christian (especially Presbyterian) families, nearly all girls in post–World War II Meru still anticipated excision as the transformative moment in their passage to womanhood.

PASSING THE BAN

The decision to ban excision in 1956 was, in part, a culmination of the inter-war campaign, led by missionaries and British feminists, to stop the practice. But it was also the product of politics that were quite particular to the post-war period. In the wake of World War II, officials throughout British colonial Africa drew on Colonial Office funding for development and welfare initiatives to expand government activities. Within Kenya, this "second colonial occupation" entailed increased state support for white settler agriculture and an expansion of the government bureaucracy. For blacks, it meant coercive soil conservation campaigns, continued restrictions on cash crop production, and halfhearted attempts to improve social welfare. The cumulative effect of these measures was to compound black Kenyans' economic hardships while increasing the state's everyday presence in their lives. The state of emergency declared in response to the Mau Mau rebellion only exacerbated this situation in central Kenya by devastating countless households and granting state officials unprecedented authority and resources to intervene in local communities.[13] It was these conditions that caused some in Meru to believe that they could, at long last, end excision.

Mission-educated ADC and *Njuri Ncheke* members, and the recently appointed district commissioner, J. A. Cumber, were the key figures behind the ban. Cumber first introduced the topic at an ADC meeting in March 1956. He opened the meeting by stating that the governor's recent decision to create a Meru Land Unit, apart from the Kikuyu Land Unit, meant that the "Meru people had now gained independence from the Kikuyu." He proceeded to suggest two measures by which the Meru ADC could express its appreciation and affirm its cooperation with the government: the introduction of a tax on coffee production and a prohibition on female "circumcision." Concerning the latter suggestion, Cumber argued that in passing such a ban, "the Meru would be setting a good example to other Tribes in Kenya who persist in the enforcement of this iniquitous Tribal Tradition." Later in the meeting, the medical officer explained how he could not, in good conscience, continue to give permits to "circumcisors," as none of them practiced the "operation" in a clean and hygienic manner. The medical officer stated that boys should be circumcised between the ages of six months to one year, instead of at adolescence, and that "female circumcision" should be abandoned entirely since it resulted in complications during childbirth. Council members reportedly made no comments on the medical officer's recommendations on male circumcision, but they "wholeheartedly welcomed the suggestion" regarding excision and referred the matter to the *Njuri Ncheke* for a final decision.[14] The following month, the *Njuri Ncheke* issued an edict forbidding excision within Meru and the ADC passed a bylaw endorsing it.[15]

Cumber introduced the ban on excision as a means for the ADC and *Njuri Ncheke* to distance the Meru from the Kikuyu and to demonstrate their gratitude for being declared a separate land unit. By early 1956 officials felt that they had the Mau Mau rebellion in Meru largely under control. Cumber reported that of the 1,827 Meru estimated to have entered the forests as rebels, only 210 remained at large, while "passive" support for Mau Mau had been reduced to relatives and close friends of the rebels. In visiting Meru in February 1956 and pronouncing it a separate land unit, the acting governor fulfilled a desire among mission-educated local leaders that the Meru area should be recognized as distinct from the Kikuyu districts. Within the context of the government's post–Mau Mau reconstruction plans, this separation meant that land policies developed for Kikuyu areas could not be simply transferred to Meru and that officials and leaders within Meru would have greater say in the development and implementation of land policies. It also meant that the government could not easily use land within Meru to solve the problem of Kikuyu landlessness.[16] According to Methodist missionary W. H. Laughton, the acting governor's declaration gave "the Meru tribe a status equal to that of any of the major tribes in the Colony."[17] By situating a ban on excision as the appropriate gesture for thanking the government for increasing Meru's autonomy on land issues, Cumber continued the central Kenyan tradition of linking female initiation to land concerns. But Cumber's proposal did not share the logic, found in *Muthirigu* verses and elsewhere, that tied women's fertility to the fertility of the land. Rather, it built on the colonial recognition that excision and land were similarly charged, possibly commensurate, political issues in central Kenya; if the government was willing to give on one, local leaders should be willing to deliver on the other.

From Cumber's perspective, a successful ban on excision would also demonstrate that under his administrative leadership Meru had become a reformed and loyal district, free from Kikuyu and Mau Mau political influences. Cumber undertook a number of initiatives to bolster Meru's profile. In preparation for the March 1957 elections for the Legislative Council, Cumber orchestrated the registration of the largest number of voters in Central Province. As predicted, voters cast their ballots on a "tribal basis," and the Meru candidate, Bernard Mate, nicknamed "Cumber's Mate" in administrative circles, became the black member for Central Province.[18]

Cumber also sought to reform local administrations by recruiting young men with school education to replace retiring headmen and by "cross-posting" headmen away from their home areas.[19] The latter reform was a significant departure from previous policies of indirect rule, which stressed the importance of headmen governing in areas in which their own clans predominated.[20] In his reform program, Cumber did envision a role for the lynchpin of H. E. Lambert's indirect-rule policy, the *Njuri Ncheke.* Cumber believed that this male council, with guidance from British officers, could maintain control "over the young and undisciplined elements in the District."[21]

The history of the *Njuri Ncheke* in the twentieth century is a complex one. Although during the 1920s colonial officers in the Meru persecuted the *Njuri Ncheke* as a "secret society," arresting members and burning their meeting places, later officers embraced it.[22] As we saw in chapter 1, Lambert, working closely with Methodists W. H. Laughton and Rev. Philip M'Inoti, recognized the *Njuri Ncheke* as the supreme indigenous council of Meru District. In 1939 he granted the *Njuri Ncheke* the authority to decide on all matters of "native law and custom," and he instituted a requirement that all local government personnel, including LNC and, later, ADC members, join it. According to Lambert, the *Njuri Ncheke* was the most authentic political institution in Meru because its roots dated back to the precolonial period. Not all in Meru viewed the *Njuri Ncheke* so favorably. The Presbyterians argued that Christian headmen, police, and ADC members should not be compelled to join an institution that operated as a "secret society" and condoned excision.[23] Others in Meru questioned the authenticity of an *Njuri Ncheke* that collaborated so closely with colonial officials. They derided it as the "white man's gramophone" and doubted the qualifications of the young, mission-educated men, mainly Methodists, who joined it. Other young men with school education who were not members resented the administrative authority accorded to the "old illiterate men" of the council.[24] In spite of these criticisms, the collaboration between the *Njuri Ncheke* and colonial officers proved mutually beneficial throughout the 1940s: officers heeded the *Njuri Ncheke*'s counsel on "customary" and land matters, most notably rejecting Kikuyu claims to land in Meru, and the *Njuri Ncheke* proved effective at mustering support for government policies.[25]

Early during the Mau Mau rebellion, the *Njuri Ncheke* pledged its loyalty to the colonial government and participated in the official "rehabilitation" process by performing "cleansing ceremonies" on those who had taken Mau Mau oaths. Through oaths, men and women expressed their support for the movement and progressed upward through its ranks.[26] The

Njuri Ncheke, according to Joseph Kinyua, opposed Mau Mau as a Kikuyu movement that threatened Meru land interests, promoted violence among Africans, and wrongly involved women in "political group activities."[27] In singling out women's participation in Mau Mau as problematic, *Njuri Ncheke* members defined politics as men's domain and revealed how women's involvement in Mau Mau, more so than that of young or disenfranchised men, challenged political hierarchies within Meru.

Women did play crucial roles in Mau Mau, by providing supplies for and at times joining rebels in the forest.[28] Moreover, as Luise White has demonstrated, many of the struggles within the movement centered on gender issues, including whether rebels should be involved in monogamous or polygamous marriages, whether women should be given warrior status, and whether sexual relations should be banned in the forest.[29] Women's efforts to supply rebels with food and other necessities built upon their long-standing role as the key producers of food and, more broadly, as the guardians of the land's fertility and health. But their presence fighting and living alongside men in the forest was much more difficult to subsume within local standards of gender propriety.

By 1953, British officials, especially young district officers recruited during the state of emergency, began to question the efficacy of the *Njuri Ncheke* in eradicating Mau Mau and governing the district. While they never appear to have doubted the *Njuri Ncheke*'s loyalty to the government, they accused the members of "whole-sale corruption" in the collection of "cleansing fees" and criticized them for forcibly initiating Christians "under pagan rites" and charging exorbitant induction fees.[30] Following on these criticisms, the ban on excision became a test of the *Njuri Ncheke*'s ability to function as an effective administrative institution and to prove its political distance from the Kikuyu. The *Njuri Ncheke* responded to the test by unanimously endorsing the ban.

Oral sources cast doubt as to whether the *Njuri Ncheke* supported the ban on excision as uniformly as their edict at Nchiru suggests. On the one hand, ex-Senior Headman Naaman M'Mwirichia, a former Methodist teacher and member of the *Njuri Ncheke* and ADC who worked very closely with colonial officers and missionaries, contended that the *Njuri Ncheke* strongly supported the ban. Similarly, ex-Headman Daniel M'Iringo recalled favoring the ban after hearing a presentation by a British medical doctor on the dangers of excision.[31] But ex-Headman M'Anampiu and ex-Subarea Headman David M'Naikiuru remembered that many at Nchiru disagreed with the ban. M'Naikiuru explained, "You know, it was during the bad times of the Emergency. No one could argue with the authority then.

Because the rule came through the District Commissioner to Njuri, they [*Njuri Ncheke*] could not oppose it. . . . In my opinion, they decided to ban it during Emergency because they thought, then, no one would go against it."[32] According to M'Naikiuru, the strength of the government's presence and the dire consequences of appearing disloyal during the Mau Mau rebellion made it impossible for any *Njuri Ncheke* members to publicly dissent from the ban.

A letter written by Gerald Casey, a white settler living in an area bordering Meru, to British parliamentarian Barbara Castle corroborates the *Njuri Ncheke*'s ambivalent position. Casey undertook an investigation of the ban, interviewing officers, headmen, and African Court staff, after one of his employees was fined 400 Kenyan shillings(Ksh) when his daughter defied the ban. Complaining of the ban, Casey wrote, "The ordinary tribesmen I talk to say: 'It is not our will. If we ask the Njuri they say it comes from the Government. If we ask the District Commissioner he says it comes from the Njuri.' " Casey also claimed that mission adherents working for the government, if not missionaries themselves, played a role in organizing the ban: "I would agree that it [the ban] may represent the will of the Government servants and mission-influenced Africans: who are a minority and separated by a psychological gulf from the more primitive and illiterate tribesmen. . . . The great majority of Africans holding any position of authority in the Reserve are mission-trained and under strong missionary influence."[33]

Corroborating Casey's assertion, interviewees with the closest ties to the Methodist mission station, Stanley Kathurima and Naaman M'Mwirichia, expressed the strongest support for the ban. As Methodist, mission-educated young men in the 1950s, Kathurima and M'Mwirichia served, respectively, as secretary of the *Njuri Ncheke* and as a headman, and both played crucial roles in the formulation of the ban.[34] Although no documentary evidence reveals the direct involvement of Protestant missionaries in the ban's passage, their years of preaching against the practice was manifest in figures like Kathurima and M'Mwirichia.[35] After hearing news of the ban, both Protestant mission stations promptly sent congratulations to the ADC and the *Njuri Ncheke*, with Irvine welcoming it as "a mighty emancipation . . . [for] the girlhood of Meru."[36]

Officials outside of Meru were far less pleased with the ban. As recently as 1951 the Colonial Office and the Governor of Kenya had restated their belief that excision was best combated not by law but through "persuasion and the general spread of education and knowledge of hygiene."[37] In a secret memorandum to the Colonial Office, the governor evoked letters to the editor to explain that even school-educated black Kenyans who condemned excision insisted that the impetus to abolish it should "come from the Africans themselves." Like most district officers, the governor and the Colonial Office were reluctant to support a law that was likely to be disobeyed.[38] Provincial Commissioner Lloyd, Cumber's immediate superior, with whom he was on acrimonious terms, pressured the Meru ADC and the *Njuri Ncheke* to exempt the more "backward" locations of the district from the ban.[39]

The central government also prohibited the ban from being publicized in either the vernacular press or in Meru-language radio broadcasts, for fear that it would incite further unrest in areas of Mau Mau activity. Cumber expressed his disappointment with this prohibition on publicity: "For years, Government and Missions had pointed out the evils of this practice, so that when the decision was made congratulatory messages and some publicity were expected. . . . That there were sound reasons for such a decision [to prohibit publicity], there can be no doubt, but from the parochial point of view the ban on even moderate publicity was psychologically unsound."[40] By 1957, with widespread transgressions of the ban apparent, the provincial commissioner firmly distanced the central government from "this purely local . . . measure" by stating, "The solution to this problem [excision] lies in the progressive education of public opinion over a considerable time rather than in attempting to overcome any prejudice by sudden action."[41] Cumber and his mission-educated local officials were left with few allies.

Women's voices were notably, if not surprisingly, absent from the passage of the 1956 ban. Once again, British and black Kenyan men sought to intervene in women's affairs. Yet, the Meru ADC was no longer an all-male institution. In line with post–World War II policies to broaden and professionalize the group of black Kenyans engaged in administrative rule, Martha Musa Kanini, a former student and teacher at Chogoria, was appointed the first woman councilor in 1951, and in September 1956, five months after the ban was passed, four more women were appointed.[42] Kanini joined the ADC at the age of twenty-six after completing a year of study at Makerere University in Uganda. She was among the first women from Chogoria not to be initiated. When interviewed in 1995, Kanini remembered that the district commissioner asked her to remain quiet during discussion of the ban: "He wanted men to discuss it. Because I am concerned, I should keep quiet. . . . So long as I felt it was for their [women's] benefit, I had to keep quiet, to hear what men say."[43] In contrast to her own recollection, in which she was present but silent at the two ADC meetings at which the ban was discussed, the minutes from those meetings record Kanini as absent with apologies.[44]

After reading an earlier version of this chapter in 1999, Kanini sought to correct this discrepancy by stating that she now recalled that she had, in fact, not been in attendance at those meetings. She explained that Headman Wallace M'Mwoga, the other ADC member from the Chogoria area, had instructed the driver of the guarded land rover which transported all councilors to ADC meetings during the state of emergency not to pick her up. According to Kanini, M'Mwoga did not want her present at the meetings because the ban was an *Njuri Ncheke* matter and thus should only be deliberated by councilors who were members of the all-male *Njuri Ncheke*. Kanini further stated that M'Mwoga and other ADC members did not want to speak about excision in front of an unexcised woman.[45] While Kanini's two recollections differ in their details, they overlap in emphasizing that a male official, either District Commissioner Cumber or Headman M'Mwoga, did not want her—because she was a woman and perhaps because she was unexcised—involved in the promulgation of the ban. Even at a time when women were being drawn into administrative work, either or both of these men felt it was crucial that ADC and *Njuri Ncheke* members believed that they, as men, had had the final say on excision.

DEFYING THE BAN

Large numbers of girls and women joined the debate over the ban by defying it. Following the *Njuri Ncheke* meeting at Nchiru, headmen held *barazas* (public meetings) to inform people of the ban. Ex-Headman M'Anampiu's recollection that "all girls had been circumcised" even before he returned from Nchiru suggests that news of the ban, in some places, preceded such meetings. Caroline Kirote remembers that, in Mitunguu, girls purchased razor blades and went to the bush to "circumcise each other" while their parents sat listening to the headman announce the ban. Between 1956 and 1959 *Ngaitana* spread from one area of the district to another. Most areas of Meru experienced two or three separate episodes or "waves" of girls, of increasingly younger ages, being excised. Charity Tirindi, of the second "wave," remembers how *Ngaitana* came to her home area of Mwichiune, "It began from Igoji [to the south] and then went to Mwiriga Mieru [to the north], so we were left in the middle alone. They used to call us cowards, abusing us, and calling us *nkenye* (uncircumcised girls), so we sat down and we decided how we will circumcise ourselves."[46] Similarly, Monica Kanana recalled how she and her age mates were "beaten thoroughly" by the first group of *Ngaitana* until they too decided to join them.[47] These statements suggest how groups of recently excised girls exerted peer pressure on unexcised girls to join *Ngaitana*. Through taunts and beatings, they made *Ngaitana* into a movement, gathering even unsuspecting girls to its cause.

The ban encouraged, rather than deterred, excision. While the first members of *Ngaitana* were probably around thirteen to fourteen years old, the proper age for female initiation in the 1950s, as the practice spread the age of initiates decreased. E. Mary Holding claimed that "within a matter of days almost every uncircumcised girl under the age of eight was given the operation."[48] *Ngaitana* made it very difficult for girls and their families who opposed excision to quietly avoid it. Ex-Sub-area Headman David M'Naikiuru recalled, "Were it not for the ban, they would not have circumcised such a large number because Christianity was spreading rapidly."[49] Elizabeth Muthuuri, Rev. Philip M'Inoti's daughter-in-law and the first girl in the Methodist schools to attain a standard VII (grade seven) education in 1945, stated that schoolgirls did not participate in *Ngaitana*.[50] But other interviewees suggest that not all schoolgirls were interested or able to withstand the waves of defiance.[51]

Ngaitana initiations were a marked departure from most previous female initiations in Meru. First of all, they took place secretly, in the bush, forest, or maize fields. Previously, girls were initiated in large open fields, surrounded by crowds of women and peering children. Initiation in the bush was reserved for those who became pregnant before they were excised. *Ngaitana* initiations also lacked the necessary ceremonies. By the 1950s, female initiation in Meru had largely become a prepubescent rather than prenuptial rite and practices such as abdominal tattooing and ear piercing had faded; nevertheless, people in Meru remember *Ngaitana* as a time of profound change, when female initiation was driven "underground," stripped of its attendant celebrations and teachings, and reduced to the clandestine performance of excision.[52] Moreover, unlike with previous female initiations, the *atani* who normally performed excisions undertook few of the initial *Ngaitana* procedures. The name of *Ngaitana*—"I will circumcise myself"—reflects the fact that some girls claimed that they would cut themselves. This claim was meant to convey their determination and courage. But few, if any, girls appear to have cut themselves.[53] Rather, they banded together in groups of three to twenty and cut each other.[54]

The procedures that the girls of *Ngaitana* performed on each other fell far short of excision. In a report to the Secretary of State for the Colonies in 1957, the Acting Governor of Kenya conveyed the findings of a medical officer in Meru.

He [the medical officer] has examined girls who have been circumcised by friends, from which it is obvious that they have no idea what female circumcision entails. Most are content to make simple incisions on either side of the vulva or through the skin only on the *labia major.* Very occasionally more radical attempts are made by wider incisions which sometimes circle the vulva. He has never seen a clitoris removed, which is the object of female circumcision when performed by a professional. The only damage done in cases he has examined has been some bleeding and occasionally secondary infection, but this is surprisingly rare, and of course pain and discomfort vary with the size of the incision. In his opinion such damage would not compare with the actual removal of the clitoris as performed by professional circumcisers.[55]

The medical officer attributed the less severe procedures he viewed to girls' ignorance of the practice. In explaining why her *Ngaitana* cohort did not perform proper excisions on each other, Agnes Kirimi pointed to a lack of fortitude as well as a lack of knowledge: "We could not complete, we just tried a little by cutting just the clitoris. . . . There was this other part, the remaining part to be circumcised and we did not know. None of us knew to that extent."[56] The less severe procedures performed by *Ngaitana* members were not simply the product of ignorance. Some girls would have been familiar with the procedure from viewing it, at a distance, as young girls, hearing initiation songs that mentioned removal of the clitoris, or eavesdropping on conversations between older girls.

Four different, though not mutually exclusive, explanations could account for why they did not perform the full procedure on each other. The first centers on the instruments that they used. Whereas *atani* possessed iron-wedge knives, members of *Ngaitana* only had access to razor blades. Monica Kanana recounted that the *Ngaitana* operations were less severe because of the fragility of razor blades.[57] The second possible reason involves the pain of the procedure. While some girls may have intended to carry out excisions, once they began, the palpable distress of a friend may have prevented them from following through. It is also possible that some girls did not want the full procedure performed on them. Like the young people that Orde Browne encountered in Mwimbe during the early 1910s, some girls may have preferred a less severe procedure from the outset. For such girls, *Ngaitana,* in its ability (at least, initially) to wrench excision from the direct control of older women, may have offered the hope of a radically reduced procedure. The fourth explanation is that girls never intended to perform the full procedure but simply hoped that their "simple incisions" would compel older women to complete the task. In an ethnography of male initiation in eastern Uganda, Suzette Heald describes two cases in which young boys prompted circumcision by first cutting their own foreskins. Once they had cut themselves, their fathers were forced to find circumcisors to finish the procedure. According to Heald, their actions were "regarded as courage of a quite exceptional order, the stuff of legend."[58] A similar logic of compulsion and courage may have motivated the girls of *Ngaitana*.

Whether girls desired it or not, older women soon become involved in *Ngaitana*. Agnes Kirimi explained that when the mothers of her cohort "saw that we had already tried, they decided to finish" by calling a *mutani* to come and excise them.[59] Other interviewees recalled that while *Ngaitana* members were at home healing from the initial procedures that they had performed on each other, they would be visited and examined by *atani* and cut again.[60] These procedures were similar to the secret second excisions that older women performed during the 1930s and 1940s to circumvent the LNC resolution that restricted the amount of cutting. Like those second excisions, these procedures reasserted older women's control over the process of transforming girls into women.

In other ways, older women were involved from the start. Agnes Kirimi attributed her decision to join *Ngaitana* to her grandmother: "I remember why I got motivated. It's because my grandmother used to tell me, 'You're left here alone with your dirt.' . . . You see the grandmothers were the motivators."[61] Grandmothers' strong support for excision stemmed from the important roles that older women usually played as the organizers of initiation, as well as from the special relationship which existed between grandparents and grandchildren, enabling them to discuss intimate topics considered inappropriate for discussions between parents and children.[62] In some cases, older women followed up such encouragement by participating in the initial procedures. Evangeline M'Iringo remembered that she and her age mates had wondered how they would be able to "circumcise themselves," but when they arrived in the forest, they found a *mutani* waiting for them.[63] In still other cases, *Ngaitana* caused women who had never before performed an excision to do so. Isabel Kaimuri recounted that she excised her own daughter, whereas Isabella Kajuju recalled that she began her career as a *mutani* during *Ngaitana*, when the experienced *mutani*, fearing prosecution, failed to come to excise Kajuju's niece and other girls.[64] In households where fathers favored the ban, mothers were often blamed when their daughters joined *Ngaitana*. Monica Kanana remembered her father beating her mother after he learned of her initiation, while Lucy

Kajuju recalled how her mother fled following her initiation to escape her father's anger.[65]

Drawing on their interpretations of the Mau Mau rebellion in Meru, officials explained defiance of the ban as a conflict between young and old men. In 1957 District Commissioner Cumber wrote, "It is considered that this recurrence of female circumcision is attributable to the activities of the young men, many of whom resent the varying degree of control exercised by the *Njuri* elders."[66] Similarly, before a meeting of the *Njuri Ncheke,* Cumber claimed that young men "encouraged young girls to be circumcised with a view to undermine the authority of the *Njuri Ncheke.*"[67] Young men were a potent source of colonial anxiety during the mid-1950s. Together with "witch-doctors" and "old women," "young tribesmen" were commonly viewed as the rank-in-file of Mau Mau.[68] Colonial officers and Methodist missionaries in Meru established a Youth Training Centre to turn young men into "responsible citizens," "develop their characters," and "instill a respect for discipline and agricultural work."[69] Many young men in Meru probably did oppose the ban. According to Charity Tirindi, even most school-educated men in the 1950s still refused to marry unexcised women.[70] No evidence, however, suggests that they instigated or organized defiance of the ban. In situating young men as the real force behind *Ngaitana,* Cumber upheld a long tradition of colonial officers interpreting female protests as male-instigated.[71]

At a special meeting held in November 1957 *Njuri Ncheke* members offered their own interpretations of the defiance, some of which was linked to the Mau Mau rebellion. Yet, unlike Cumber, the members did not blame local young men. Rather, they pointed to outside agitators: "There were a number of people, most of them non-Meru in origin, who seemed to encourage female circumcision, while they would never allow their women folk to be circumcised." This statement points to Kikuyus, often perceived by the *Njuri Ncheke* as the greatest threat to the Meru. More specifically, it singled out well-educated and cosmopolitan Kikuyus, like Jomo Kenyatta, who were widely believed to be the masterminds of the Mau Mau rebellion and were suspected of embracing female initiation only to muster political support. *Njuri Ncheke* members further complained that the "tendency had sprung up recently among the women and among the government officials to disregard the *Njuri*'s authority and its existence."[72] With this statement, *Njuri Ncheke* members criticized the insolence of Cumber's junior officers, many of whom had been posted to the district during the state of emergency. These officers tended to be more skeptical than the district commissioner of the *Njuri Ncheke*'s political worth. *Njuri Ncheke* members also reproached women, a group that Cumber failed to grant political agency. As mentioned earlier, *Njuri Ncheke* members viewed women's participation in Mau Mau as one of the most disturbing elements of the movement. While they claimed that women's insubordination was a recent development, the difficulties that British officers and LNC members faced in trying to regulate female initiation during the 1920s and 1930s suggest that women's opposition to men's interference in reproductive matters was nothing new.

The Mau Mau rebellion and the state of emergency provided the political context in which girls and women decided how to defy the ban on excision. Within Meru, the two groups identified most closely with Mau Mau— young people and women—were most open in their opposition to the ban. Official documents suggest that in Meru "the unmarried girl class" was particularly active in supporting Mau Mau.[73] In an interview, Charity Tirindi illustrated how Mau Mau fighters themselves opposed the ban by recounting a gruesome tale of forced excisions: "If you were not circumcised, they [Mau Mau fighters] came for you at night, you [we]re taken to the forest [and] circumcised, and you [we]re roasted for what you have been circumcised [the clitoris] and you are told to eat it."[74] Those who supported the ban—strong mission adherents and men serving as ADC and *Njuri Ncheke* members, headmen, and home guards—ranked as government loyalists during the Mau Mau rebellion.[75] Furthermore, defiance of the ban occurred while government officials were still enforcing the state of emergency by detaining, torturing, and executing those suspected of being Mau Mau supporters or rebels. The presence of such harsh punishments caused some *atani* and older women to steer clear of *Ngaitana*. Those who defied the ban feared the worst. Caroline Kirote recalled the attitude of her *Ngaitana* group as they walked to the headman's camp to turn themselves in: "If it happened that we would be wiped out, girls would be wiped out together. . . you know, because of the way the government carried out executions at that time."[76] Veronica Kinaito also suggested how members of *Ngaitana* recognized similarities between their defiance and that of Mau Mau rebels. She recounted a song performed by her *Ngaitana* group in which they compared their one-month detention in a headman's camp to young men's imprisonment at Manyani, a camp for Mau Mau detainees.[77]

While interviewees drew parallels between *Ngaitana* and Mau Mau and described how the latter created the political context for the former, they insisted that they were two distinct movements. When asked directly, those who had been excised during *Ngaitana* stated that their actions were not a part of the Mau Mau rebellion. As Charity Tirindi explained, "We did not know things about war; we just knew about circumcision."[78] The girls of

Ngaitana defied the ban in order to gain respect and become young women. The older women who encouraged and assisted them probably had a better of sense of how *Ngaitana* related to past and present struggles against colonial law and order. Richard Cashmore, a Briton who served as a district officer in Meru during the mid-1950s, recalled how older women stood outside of his office protesting the ban through a song that was quite similar to the *Muthirigu* verses that had been performed during the "female circumcision controversy" of 1928–31. According to Cashmore, the women's song denounced the ban as a government plot to make young women infertile, eliminate the Meru, and steal their land.[79] These complaints certainly echoed those made by people who participated in the earlier controversy and the Mau Mau rebellion. But rather than viewing *Ngaitana* as something that merely mimicked these other two episodes of anticolonial resistance, it is important to recognize how all three episodes emerged from a faith that linked women's fertility to the future of the land and situated excision as enabling proper procreation. It was this faith that girls and women defended when they defied the ban. The politics of the womb infused yet surpassed anticolonial resistance.

ENFORCING THE BAN

Enforcement of the ban on excision varied tremendously over its three-year duration from 1956 to 1959, and from one area of Meru to another. In "backward" areas of the district, such as Tharaka, the ban was not enforced. In other areas, such as Igembe, Tigania, and North and South Imenti, *Ngaitana* cases consumed the attention of district officers, headmen, home guards (armed loyalists charged with eliminating local support for the Mau Mau rebellion), *Njuri Ncheke* members, and African Court staff for months on end. All suspected transgressors were supposed to be charged before African Courts—colonial courts staffed by three or more local elders—with having contravened the *Njuri Ncheke*'s order, authorized under section 17(a) of the African Courts Ordinance No. 65 of 1951.[80] Of the more than 2,400 individuals charged before African Courts, fathers of initiates accounted for approximately 43 percent; initiates, 33 percent; mothers of initiates, 20 percent; and "circumcisors," 3 percent of those accused.[81]

Fines ranged from 50 to 400 Ksh and sentences from one month in detention camp to six months without hard labor, depending on the accused's wealth and status. Gerald Casey, the white settler who complained about the ban, explained the scale of these fines, "My shepherd earns Shs 50/– a month cash wage. He will have to work eight months to realize Shs 400/–. He is one of the lucky ones. Very few old men earn half as much as he does. Some would have to work eighteen months to two years to find the money." One district officer reportedly remarked that the African Courts were "making more [money] out of it [Ngaitana fines] than out of all the rates put together."[82] In addition to those fined by African Courts, oral evidence suggests that in many cases headmen and home guards imposed and collected their own fines. Of those interviewed who were charged with defying the ban, all remembered paying their fines in livestock at headmen's camps, not in cash at African Courts.

The swiftness of girls' response to the ban appears to have caught administrators unprepared. The first group of Ngaitana in North Imenti paid no fine: "Nothing was done, even the daughters of Chiefs [headmen], askaris [home guards] . . . had circumcised themselves."[83] Ex-Headman M'Anampiu recalled sending home all the girls whom he met on his return from Nchiru and, later, fining their fathers. Ex-Home Guard Moses M'Mukindia remembered arresting initiates as they came from the forest and taking them to the Meru Civil Hospital to be examined by a British Medical Officer. At Ntakira, Monica Kanana recounted how home guards burned the homes of an early Ngaitana group that was found healing in seclusion.[84]

Later cohorts, fearing that such punishment would be inflicted on their homes, turned themselves in at headmen's camps. Charity Tirindi recounted why her group presented themselves for arrest: "We had heard that those who were caught from Igoji were beaten, so we might make ourselves to be beaten for no good reason [unnecessarily] so we decided to take ourselves." The walk to the headman's camp, according to Monica Kanana, was not easy, as each girl tried to keep her legs apart and her head shrouded in a cloth. Upon their arrival, Ngaitana members responded to headmen's and home guards' queries by claiming that they had "circumcised themselves." They remained in the headmen's camps from a few days to a few weeks until their parents paid their fines. During their stay, they ate food brought by their mothers and slept in simple shelters or on dried banana leaves. Caroline Kirote and Evangeline M'Iringo remembered that at times the camps were filled with one hundred or more girls. Many Ngaitana members, after healing at the headmen's camps or in their own homes, performed several weeks of punitive manual labor that ranged from digging roads and drainage trenches, to planting trees and clearing weeds, to plastering floors in home-guard houses.[85]

When fines were paid in bulls or goats, headmen and home guards along with local *Njuri Ncheke* members slaughtered and ate them. Historically, the *Njuri Ncheke* imposed fines in livestock on those who transgressed its rulings. By slaughtering and consuming these fines, the *Njuri Ncheke*, like other men's councils in central Kenya, asserted its authority to punish social transgressions and to cleanse moral impurities.[86] As the ban on excision was passed by the *Njuri Ncheke*, members appear to have felt entitled to collect fines in livestock. These fines, like those paid in cash, varied across time and from one individual to the next. Lucy Kajuju recounted that as a headman, her father was forced to pay a double fine of two bulls and two he-goats. Evangeline M'Iringo recalled that she and her sister decided to be excised together, even though they were five years apart in age, so their parents would only have to pay a single goat. Ex-Sub-area Headman David M'Naikiuru remembered a gradual decrease in the fines charged: "They started with imprisoning and destroying the houses, they went down to fining bulls. . . . As the number of circumcised girls increased, they saw the bulls that were suppose to be eaten were too many so they started fining goats."[87]

Based on available evidence, it is not entirely clear why some people paid fines in livestock at headmen's camps while others paid fines in cash at African Courts. From the perspective of headmen, home guards, and *Njuri Ncheke*, it was probably preferable to collect fines of livestock beyond the purview of British officers rather than forwarding cases to African Courts. Such procedures allowed them to feast on other people's wealth while masking their own inability or unwillingness to prevent defiance. Samuel Nkure, who worked at an African Court during the 1950s, suggested that the *Ngaitana* cases that ended up at African Courts involved people who disputed the charge of having defied the ban or who did not want to provide headmen, home guards, and *Njuri Ncheke* members with more livestock to eat. According to Nkure, those who insisted that their cases be heard in African Courts represented a direct challenge to the political arrangement preferred by headmen, home guards, and *Njuri Ncheke* members.[88]

Fines in livestock and labor were not the only forms of punishment meted out in headmen's camps. In some areas of the district, punishment involved attendance at the women's group meetings of *Maendeleo ya Wanawake* (Progress of Women), which had been founded by white Kenyan women who sought to teach black Kenyan women mothercraft and domesticity. During the Mau Mau rebellion, central government officials viewed *Maendeleo* as "an effective instrument against subversive elements."[89] A Methodist missionary recorded how one Christian headman in Meru similarly viewed *Maendeleo* as rehabilitation. He ordered all girls who had defied the ban to "attend [*Maendeleo*] classes instead of doing manual work for the location." Other headmen, however, regarded participation in *Maendeleo* as a privilege, and therefore, as punishment, forbade *Ngaitana* members from attending meetings for seven to ten weeks.[90] Defiance and enforcement of the ban also became entangled with sexual and marital access to initiates. Caroline Kirote recalled the following song, which chastised a headman named M'Mbuju for enforcing the ban and proclaimed that he would never "cover"—that is, have sex with—a member of *Ngaitana:*

> Yes, yes, M'Mbuju, you will die before you cover a circumcised girl.
> Yes, yes, M'Mbuju, circumcised girls have been made to dig up a road.
> Yes, M'Mbuju, circumcised girls have dug up a road, yes.

James Laiboni of Igembe recounted stories of two *Ngaitana* members who were betrothed to a headman and home guard because their parents could not afford the fines imposed.[91]

While largely ignorant of such happenings within headmen's camps, outside observers voiced concern over the work of African Courts. Following his investigation of a *Ngaitana* case involving his shepherd, Ngarui Kabuthia, settler Gerald Casey criticized African Court personnel for not allowing witnesses and for arrogantly refusing appeals. He submitted the following description of African Court procedures to MP Barbara Castle:

> In the case of my shepherd I asked to see the court record. I found that no witnesses had been called. The man was simply asked whether it was true his daughter was illegally circumcised. He replied that it was so: but it had happened without his consent or knowledge. No other evidence was proffered. The verdict "Guilty on plea: fine Shs 400/–." It was generally assumed by all those in the Administration I questioned that it was a waste of time to prove guilt. It was simply assumed and that was that. I advised my shepherd to appeal against the decision. The court clerk was astonished at this and declared that such a thing wasn't possible. He implied that the Court was infallible and no good would come of challenging it. Such a thing, he said, had never happened before. I nevertheless insisted in the face of all-round reluctance.[92]

Casey was not alone in his criticism of the handling of *Ngaitana* cases by the African Courts. In reviewing the court registers, British district officers often reduced the size of fines imposed. Central government officials, as discussed earlier, were wary of the ban from its inception. Monthly court returns from Meru reporting that hundreds of people had been charged with defying the ban only added to their unease. In response to the April 1957 returns, which listed over two hundred *Ngaitana* cases, the Nairobi-based African Courts officer wrote to the district commissioner of Meru: "Are

[you] satisfied with the number of such cases so suddenly taken as a result of the Njuri's order and the severity of the fines imposed? The P[rovincial] C[ommissioner] has stressed the matter is basically one for education of public opinion. This seems a slashing attack."[93] Following this memorandum, the number of cases and the size of fines only increased. In July 1957 another officer informed the provincial commissioner that "the avalanche does not slow up." Describing how African Courts in Meru were hearing up to 180 *Ngaitana* cases per month and charging fines as large as 400 Ksh or four months in detention camp, he complained that "if this is not 'mass action through the courts' I don't know what is."[94] Central government officials, however, did not halt "the avalanche." That took settler Casey's letter of complaint and two questions in the British House of Commons.

In his letter to Barbara Castle drawing her attention to the inappropriateness of the ban and the injustices perpetuated in enforcing it, Gerald Casey requested that Castle secure from the Colonial Office statistics on prosecutions relating to the ban. On 1 August 1957, Castle raised the issue of the Meru ban in the House of Commons before the Secretary of State for the Colonies. Unsatisfied with his response, Castle requested a further inquiry into the matter. Castle, like Eleanor Rathbone and the Duchess of Atholl, the women who had raised the subject of excision within the House of Commons in 1929–30, opposed excision: "I abhor the practice of female circumcision and certainly want to see it stamped out." But Castle, after receiving Casey's letter, was convinced that a ban was not "the right way to do it."[95]

In late December the acting governor of Kenya wrote to the secretary of state, distancing central administration as well as officers in Meru from the formulation and enforcement of the ban. Pinning the blame on school-educated local leaders, the acting governor reported: "The state of affairs brought to your attention by Mrs. Castle is the result of an excessive outburst of zeal on the part of the tribal authorities and African Courts of Meru to stamp out female circumcision, which the more enlightened leaders of the tribe have come to abhor." He further explained that officials had "already taken steps to curb this enthusiasm and to reduce not only the number of cases being brought to court, but also to temper the sentences imposed."[96] This statement represented a major retrenchment in enforcement of the ban. The secretary of state forwarded the acting governor's letter to Castle along with notification that, on appeal, Ngarui Kabuthia's sentence had been reduced from 400 to 50 Ksh.[97]

By November 1957 *Njuri Ncheke* members had already begun to feel the effects of the new policy reported by the acting governor. At a special meeting, members agreed that while the incidence of excision had only increased of late, "courts had tended to disregard hearing of circumcision cases." They proceeded to blame the failure of the ban on the erosion of the *Njuri Ncheke*'s power under colonial rule. Members explained that in the past, the *Njuri Ncheke* had effectively enforced its pronouncements by inflicting severe punishments—"most of which were cruel," but that the advent of British rule had resulted in such practices being "modif[ied]." They noted that "in the old days no one dared disobey *Njuri* but these days the British Government has tended to replace the indigenous authority, and maintenance of law and order is a responsibility of Government."[98] In this statement, *Njuri Ncheke* members both emphasized how colonial rule had weakened the position of indigenous men's councils and exonerated themselves from the ban's failure.

Although *Njuri Ncheke* members were willing to admit that the colonial state had subverted the authority of indigenous men's councils, they never acknowledged that limits had previously existed on that authority. They insisted that they were capable of intervening in all aspects of local life. Yet the failure of the 1956 ban proved, once more, that the processes of transforming girls into women and ensuring proper reproduction were not things that men could easily control.

After October 1957 the number of *Ngaitana* cases decreased dramatically in nearly all of the African Courts. By March 1959, they had ceased entirely.[99] As even young girls defied the ban, it is unlikely that by 1959 there were many girls left in Meru who had not already been excised.

．　．　．

In 1990s Meru mention of *Ngaitana* drew chuckles of laughter or, on occasion, head-shakes of knowing disapproval from those who could recall the time of the ban. For those too young to have direct knowledge of the mid-1950s, however, the term most often elicited perplexed faces and queries. Those who remembered or learned of *Ngaitana* often spoke of it as a preposterous undertaking, simultaneously absurd and amusing. When I presented a first draft of this chapter in a seminar at the University of Nairobi, the participants from Meru sought to impress upon me how ludicrous it was for girls to believe that they could initiate one another without the intervention of a *mutani* and her iron-wedge knife.[100] Others spoke of *Ngaitana* as a travesty that had ruined female initiation in Meru. For instance, Celina Kiruki, who was initiated in the late 1940s, argued that *Ngaitana* had "spoiled" female initiation by omitting the meaningful teachings and celebrations and reducing it to the practice of excision.[101] *Ngaitana* did permanently alter female initiation in much of Meru. In appearing as a travesty, *Ngaitana* lent support, in some areas and households, to a growing sentiment that female initiation was no longer necessary. In other places, *Ngaitana* helped to reduce female initiation to excision. The ban of 1956 did more to drive excision underground than to end it. As one interviewee explained, "They are still circumcised secretly, the ones who want."[102]

Analysis of the 1956 ban reveals how entangled the politics of the womb had become by the post–World War II period. Passage of the ban depended upon the existence of a cadre of *Njuri Ncheke* and ADC members, including Stanley Kathurima, Naaman M'Mwirichia, and Martha Kanini, all of whom had been educated at Protestant mission schools and had renounced excision. This group's opposition to excision demonstrates how the reproductive perspective of some in Meru had been altered by colonial rule. Their views on excision had become intertwined with those of the white missionaries and colonial officers who taught and ruled them. It was this group that gave District Commissioner Cumber the confidence that he could accomplish something that his predecessors during the "female circumcision controversy" of 1928–31 and many of his administrative superiors believed impossible. In formulating the ban, Cumber and mission-educated ADC and *Njuri Ncheke* members sought to distance the Meru from the Kikuyu in the wake of the Mau Mau rebellion, and to express gratitude for the government's having declaring Meru a separate land unit. They also sought to eliminate a practice that white missionaries had long found "repugnant" and that a small but growing number of local Christians found unnecessary. Cumber, at least, believed that the "women of Meru" as well as "future generations of the Tribe as a whole" would appreciate the ban's passage.[103]

In attempting to end excision, Cumber and his local allies displayed a tremendous confidence in the ability of the post–World War II colonial state to remake social relations. In targeting excision and linking it to land issues, their efforts demonstrate how women's bodies and their reproductive capacities continued to be important sites for the elaboration of political and moral order in colonial central Kenya. As in previous decades, the ability to intervene in female initiation remained an unparalleled mark of colonial control. But mass defiance of the ban revealed that the colonial state's intermediaries, including ADC and *Njuri Ncheke* members, headmen, and home guards, lacked the authority and, in some cases, political will to remake gender and generational relations.

For many in Meru, excision, as part of female initiation, was still a women's affair and a reproductive practice of the gravest significance. Through excision, girls were remade into young women and learned to behave as future wives and daughters-in-law. Cumber and ADC and *Njuri Ncheke* leaders interpreted girls' and women's defiance of the ban as the lingering effect of the Mau Mau rebellion. They claimed that either young men or Kikuyu sophisticates had played crucial roles in promoting defiance. While the Mau Mau rebellion and the accompanying state of emergency created the context within which girls and women decided how to defy the ban, these political circumstances do not explain why so many were willing to risk severe punishment. Girls—some fearing they would be denied adulthood, others feeling peer pressure—claimed that they would excise themselves. By performing procedures on each other that fell far short of excision, however, they demonstrated that they were either unwilling or unable to follow previous practices. In stepping in to complete the procedure, older women reclaimed responsibility for making immature girls into fertile women.

The 1956 ban was the last time that officials in colonial Kenya tried to intervene in female initiation. Their immediate postcolonial successors, all too familiar with the colonial controversies over excision, would do their best to keep excision from becoming a matter of national debate, let alone the target of state intervention. Other reproductive practices, however, did garner official attention during the late colonial and early postcolonial periods. The following two chapters explore how premarital pregnancy became the subject of new laws during the 1950s and 1960s. These laws furthered debates generated by colonial interventions surrounding female initiation, abortion, and childbirth by once again raising concerns over how to regulate girls' and women's sexuality and how to ensure proper procreation.

4 Late Colonial Customs and Wayward Schoolgirls

In late January 1967 the Kinoru African Court in Meru, comprised of three local men appointed by colonial officers, heard the "illegal pregnancy" case brought by Ayub M'Muthuri against Francis M'Muthamia. Under Meru customary law, M'Muthuri sought 700 Kenyan shillings (Ksh) in compensation from Francis for impregnating his daughter, Jennifer Kinanu, and then refusing to marry her. M'Muthuri testified that after his daughter had informed him that she was pregnant by Francis, he had sent a group of male elders to discuss the matter with Francis and his father. According to M'Muthuri, Francis initially accepted responsibility for the pregnancy by giving M'Muthuri 200 Ksh toward bridewealth. Once the child was born, however, Francis denied responsibility. Testifying on behalf of her father, Jennifer stated that she became pregnant after she and Francis had sex in January 1966. As translated from Meru and paraphrased in the English case record, Jennifer explained: "When the child was born in maternity, he came there to see me. Then he went and said to my parent that the child was not his."

In his own defense, Francis stated that he had had sexual intercourse with Jennifer in March and May 1966, and that in June 1966, Jennifer wrote him a letter informing him that she was pregnant as a result of their May encounter. Francis claimed that he then drafted, and both he and Jennifer signed, an agreement stating that he would accept responsibility if the child was born nine months from May. Francis stated that when the child was born in October 1966, just five months later, he knew the child was not his. Francis submitted this agreement, along with three love letters allegedly written by Jennifer, as evidence. Before the Court, however, Jennifer denied that she had ever signed such an agreement or written such letters. She pointed out that the letters and agreement were signed Joyce, rather than Jennifer, Kinanu.

In its ruling the Court dismissed the letters, including one with the opening epithet of "Dearest innermost super guy," and the agreement as forgeries perpetrated by Francis and two friends. Officials stated that the "standardized and fluent English" in which the letters were written could never have been produced by someone like Jennifer, who had only achieved a Standard VII (grade seven) education. The Court also noted that nowhere on Jennifer's school certificates did her name appear as Joyce. Agreeing with M'Muthuri that Francis's earlier payment of 200 Ksh toward bridewealth amounted to an admission of responsibility, the Court ruled in favor of M'Muthuri. They ordered Francis to pay Jennifer's father compensation of 500 Ksh and a bull valued at 200 Ksh, plus court costs of 76 Ksh.[1]

In 1950s and 1960s Meru "illegal pregnancy" cases like the case of *Ayub M'Muthuri v. Francis M'Muthamia* became crucial forums through which young people and their kin negotiated the politics of the womb. In Anglophone Africa, such cases were also referred to as "pregnancy compensation" or "seduction damages" cases. In Meru, people referred to them as *kuthukia mwari* ("spoiling the daughter"). Together with "illegal pregnancy," these terms situated premarital pregnancies as deviant events that harmed generational relations and required recompense. By the mid-1960s, such cases accounted for about 5 percent of the civil caseload at Meru's African Courts (known as Native Tribunals prior to 1951 and converted to Third Class District Magistrate's Courts in 1967).[2] Although premarital pregnancy cases never dominated court dockets, they did command significant official attention and were a source of considerable concern for school-educated young people like Jennifer and Francis, and their parents. For members of the local elite and those striving to join it, premarital pregnancies signified sexuality, courtship, and schooling gone awry. Fathers and guardians filed pregnancy compensation suits in order to ameliorate the moral and material damages caused by such pregnancies.

This chapter and the next ask how and why premarital pregnancy and laws relating to it became the subject of debate in late colonial and, after 1963, early postcolonial Kenya. These debates took place in family compounds, courtrooms, the Swahili press, and the national Parliament. Like the controversies examined in previous chapters, the clamor over premarital pregnancy grew from competing reproductive concerns. In Meru, the customary law of pregnancy compensation emerged in the wake of colonial efforts to lower the age of female initiation. As a result of these campaigns, official concern over adolescent reproduction shifted from pre-initiation pregnancies and abortions to premarital pregnancies. Pregnancy compensation suits aimed to prove paternity and prompt either marriage negotiations or compensation payments. During the 1950s and 1960s, cementing such social relations had become more difficult, as some school-educated young men developed attitudes and aspirations that made them reluctant to accept responsibility for out-of-wedlock pregnancies. By reconstructing the history of pregnancy compensation law and litigation, this chapter explores how premarital pregnancy disputes entailed the entanglement of old social relations with new institutions and expectations.

CONSTRUCTING THE CUSTOMARY LAW OF PREGNANCY COMPENSATION

The customary law of "illegal pregnancy," as applied in African Courts in Meru during the 1950s and 1960s, represented the colonial reconfiguring of local practices. Within British colonial Africa, the term *customary* was used to refer to laws purportedly derived from "native law and custom." Officials assumed that each "tribe" possessed its own set of customary laws, which could be applied in legal disputes not covered by colonial statutes. Various historians have argued that customary law as identified and implemented during the colonial period was more a reflection of the interests of colonial officers and African male elders than an accurate embodiment of long-standing or precolonial customs. According to this perspective, African male elders crafted a version of custom that bolstered their authority over women and younger men; colonial officers accepted this version because they recognized that colonial order depended on male elders maintaining local control.[3] Recently, a few historians have questioned this perspective, arguing that customary law more often operated as a terrain of contestation than as a set of codified rules. Emphasizing the fluidity of customary law during much of the colonial period, this scholarship has examined how, at times, women and young men engaged colonial courts and law to their own benefit.[4]

The history of the customary law of pregnancy compensation in Meru reveals how officials' interest in bolstering senior men's authority could co-exist with women's active involvement in legal proceedings. In a context in which generational and kinship relations mattered as much as gender, men and women could just as easily be courtroom allies as adversaries. Pregnancy compensation law cast premarital pregnancy cases as disputes between junior and senior men. This does not mean, however, that women were marginal to pregnancy compensation proceedings. Rather, as later sections of this chapter will demonstrate, they played crucial—if uncomfortable—roles in bringing such cases to court and determining their outcomes.

As we have seen, in interwar Meru, pre-initiation (not premarital) pregnancies, were the subject of intense debate and intervention. E. B. Horne, the
first colonial officer stationed to Meru, noted in his earliest reports that
when uninitiated girls (pl. *nkenye*, s. *mukenye*) became pregnant, they obtained abortions. Subsequent officials in Meru denounced pre-initiation
pregnancies and abortions as immoral and "backward" practices. Amid colonial fears that African populations were declining, officials in Nairobi and
London viewed abortion as threatening the demographic future of "the
Meru." Many in Meru, on the other hand, saw such abortions as remedying
the grave moral dangers posed by pre-initiation pregnancies. They believed
that beings conceived to *nkenye*, if born and allowed to live, endangered the
lives of kin and neighbors, bringing misfortune and even death.

The campaigns undertaken by colonial officials, beginning in the late
1920s, to stop pre-initiation abortions altered local categories of acceptable
and problematic reproduction. Officials ultimately focused their efforts on
transforming female initiation from a prenuptial to a prepubescent rite,
thereby eliminating the period in which girls were sexually mature but
deemed incapable of conceiving socially viable persons. By lowering the age
of initiation, the *Kigwarie* campaigns shortened the period of time when females existed as *nkenye* (uninitiated) and lengthened the period of time
when they existed as *ngutu* (initiated but unwed). Previously, the period of
being an *ngutu* was short, since initiates ideally moved directly from post-
excision seclusion to their new marital homes.

Officials were initially not concerned about this lengthening of the
ngutu period. They believed that as initiated females, *ngutu* were capable of
conceiving persons, so that even if they became pregnant they would not resort to abortion or infanticide but instead would simply marry the men
deemed responsible. Marriage was, in fact, the usual response to pregnancies
among *ngutu*. Based on his work in and around the Methodist hospital at
Maua during the 1940s, Dr. Stanley Bell observed that among initiates it
was fairly common to become pregnant and then to quickly marry. He
added, "Indeed, it seems as though her value as a wife and potential mother
is verified should she be pregnant." Rather than being a problem, a *ngutu*'s
pregnancy provided a positive impetus toward marriage.[5] While Bell described such arrangements without condemning them, Dr. Clive Irvine of
the Presbyterian mission station at Chogoria repeatedly railed against them
as "trial marriage." Irvine claimed that young people used premarital sexual
relations to test whether their union would be fertile and, hence, avoid
childlessness—"the supreme tragedy to an African." Irvine denounced

these arrangements which placed reproduction before marriage as "immoral."[6]

Within a decade of the first colonial efforts to lower the age of initiation, officials began to complain that not all pregnancies among *ngutu* were leading to marriage. In 1942 District Commissioner V. M. McKeag presented his understanding of the problem to the Meru Local Native Council (LNC).

> Formerly, a man who put a *mukenye* (unmarried [and unexcised] girl) in the family way had to pay a heifer or its equivalent in goats, but this did not apply in the case of *ngutu* (circumcised girl). Nowadays, *ngutu* live in their fathers' villages as *mukenye* used to do. Young men are taking advantage of this and, with impunity, putting them in the family way without any intention of marrying them.

To remedy the situation, McKeag proposed, and the LNC approved, extending the practice of fining to cases involving *ngutu*. A man found responsible for helping to cause any girl's pregnancy and who refused to marry her would be required to pay her father's age-grade a bull.[7] Once again, a colonial officer and his black Kenyan intermediaries sought to fix aberrant reproduction by tinkering with local practices.

While noting that young men's attitudes toward *ngutu* pregnancies had changed, McKeag did not specify how this change related to colonial campaigns and processes. Efforts to lower the age of initiation challenged local notions of who was fit to conceive and marry. People, including young men, may not have accorded the young initiates of *Kigwarie* the same respect as they had previous groups of *ngutu*. Moreover, experiences as labor migrants and students at mission schools made some young men much less willing to comply with elders' exhortations, including those to marry. In an interview conducted in 1995, Naaman M'Mwirichia, a teacher and school supervisor during the 1930s and 1940s and later a headman, explained the problem of premarital pregnancy as the product of young men's experiences working for wages and attending schools, often far from Meru. According to M'Mwirichia, "Young men started parting with old men. If you're from Makerere [the university in Uganda] or if you're from Nairobi Hospital or you're from Great Britain or you're from America, when you come it's difficult to see a person who is older than you and to stay with him and ask him about customary ways."[8] M'Mwirichia's words are eloquent testimony to the changing generational relations that challenged elders' ability to compel young men to marry those whom they had helped to make pregnant.

In the eyes of subsequent British officers, McKeag's efforts to deter premarital pregnancies proved ineffective. In 1949 another district commissioner drew the Meru LNC's attention to what he considered a moral outrage: "Parents have no control over their daughters who go with young men for weeks at a time and then return pregnant. No attempt appears to be made to see those young men nor does the public condemn this state of affairs." To encourage parents to exert more control over their sons and daughters, the LNC passed a resolution stating that in cases of premarital pregnancy, the boy or man responsible would pay a fine to the LNC rather than to the father's age-grade.[9] This reform proved short-lived. Perhaps viewing it as too great a challenge to male elders' authority, the *Njuri Ncheke* reversed the LNC's resolution in 1954 and ordered that premarital pregnancy fines should once again "be paid to the father of the girl as compensation."[10]

Over the next decade, officials further elaborated pregnancy compensation as part of broader efforts to codify customary law. From the mid-1950s until 1960, the standard amount of compensation awarded in pregnancy compensation cases in Meru was 300 Ksh plus a bull to be consumed by the woman's father (if he was deceased, her brother) and his age mates.[11] As we saw with the *Ngaitana* fines, this was a sizeable sum in an area where agricultural laborers on nearby settler farms earned upward of only 50 Ksh per month, a semiskilled migrant laborer in Nairobi earned roughly twice that amount, and a bull could cost anywhere between 100 and 200 Ksh.[12] In June 1960 the Meru Law Panel, a group of male elders charged with standardizing local customary law, set a standard rate of compensation of 500 Ksh plus one bull valued at 200 Ksh.[13]

Such efforts to systemize customary law were part of the Kenyan government's efforts to create, in the words of contemporary legal scholars, a "modern unified legal system."[14] During the 1960s, the Restatement of African Law Project was the lynchpin of state efforts to codify customary law. Financed by Colonial Development and Welfare funds and supervised by Eugene Cotran of the School of Oriental and African Studies in London, the Restatement Project sought to "ascertain and restate the customary law" on criminal offenses and on marriage, divorce, and succession for the "various tribes." These efforts were an integral element of late colonial and early postcolonial reforms aimed at dismantling the racially bifurcated judicial system created under colonial rule, by standardizing procedures in African Courts and by shifting control of them from district administrators to the judiciary. Through codification, Kenyan officials hoped to make customary principles accessible to advocates and magistrates with little firsthand knowledge of such matters, and to harmonize these principles with those of British law.[15]

The Meru Law Panel discussed the issue of pregnancy compensation a few more times in the early 1960s, and in 1968 a summary of these discussions was published as part of the Restatement of African Law Project's volume on marriage and divorce. Of the fifteen main "ethnic groups" covered in the volume, the customary law listings for ten of them included compensation for "causing pregnancy of an unmarried girl." For Meru, the work confirmed a compensation rate of 500 Ksh and one bull valued at 200 Ksh. Noting local variation, the volume stated that in all areas of the district except Tharaka division, compensation would only be payable for a girl's first pregnancy. The volume further specified that if the defendant and the girl later married, the money and livestock already paid as part of pregnancy compensation should be counted as part of the bridewealth payment *(ruracio)*. In local terms, pregnancy compensation and bridewealth payments were related forms of exchange. Suggesting how such exchanges were also tied to reproduction and its dangers, the volume indicated that if a single girl or woman died during childbirth, the boy or man responsible for the pregnancy would have to pay death compensation ranging upward of the equivalent of a standard bridewealth payment.[16]

The development of the customary law of pregnancy compensation significantly challenged the local categories of personhood through which people understood out-of-wedlock pregnancies. Up until the 1940s, initiation status had determined how such pregnancies were handled. A *mukenye*'s pregnancy, conceived by a female not yet socially consecrated to reproduce, usually ended in abortion or infanticide. On the other hand, a pregnancy to an *ngutu*—an initiated but yet unmarried female—posed few problems, particularly if it led directly to marriage. In collapsing *mukenye* and *ngutu* into "girl," the LNC's 1942 resolution and all subsequent renderings of this customary law ignored the powerful distinctions in moral personhood produced through female initiation. The 1956 ban on excision drove such categories of personhood further underground. While court records from the 1940s and early 1950s sometimes make mention of the initiation status of the girls and women involved, after 1956 such distinctions disappear from the summaries of pregnancy compensation court proceedings.

Through refusing to recognize previous categories of moral personhood, colonial officials sought to make marriage rather than initiation the decisive process in defining acceptable and problematic reproduction. Officials also challenged the categories of personhood through which people viewed the unborn and the newborn. By criminalizing abortion and infanticide, they insisted that all pregnancies could produce socially viable persons, not just those conceived by the initiated. They rejected the notion that some newborns could endanger the lives of kin and neighbors. According to this logic, no pregnancy was so deviant that it could not be remedied through compensation or marriage.

The customary law of pregnancy compensation, as developed in Meru during the 1940s and 1950s, elaborated the local principle that premarital pregnancy was an offense against a girl's or woman's guardian and other senior men. Such pregnancies injured a guardian's and family's reputation, as well as their ability to receive a large or complete bridewealth when their daughter eventually did marry. Officials intended pregnancy compensation to assuage both the moral and material disruptions caused by premarital pregnancies.

CHANGING REPRODUCTIVE CONCERNS

During the 1940s through 1960s, the period when the customary law of pregnancy compensation was developed in Meru, official concerns about reproduction underwent important changes. Whereas in previous decades, colonial officials had worried about the possibilities of African populations dying out, in the post–World War II period some began to voice concern about rapid population increase.[17] This shift in perspective drew official demographic concerns closer in line with those of white settlers, who since the early 1930s had complained of rapid population increase in African areas adjoining their farms and homesteads. This shift also occurred alongside the rise of an international discourse focused on the specter of overpopulation in parts of Asia and eastern and southern Europe.[18] Postwar demographic studies confirmed that across much of colonial Africa populations were no longer decreasing. The East African census of 1948, the first complete enumeration ever undertaken in Kenya, revealed that officials had previously underestimated the black Kenyan population by approximately 20 percent. The census results placed the number of black Kenyans at 5.37 million and estimated that the average annual rate of "natural increase" ranged between 1.5 and 2.0 percent. While some officials, including those who directed the census, did not believe that these figures represented worrisome rates of growth, others argued that they foretold an unmanageable population increase. This latter group advocated the promotion of birth control.[19]

The Colonial Office held the view that the newly determined rates of population growth did not warrant concern and that aggressive birth control programs should not be pursued. In a 1956 memorandum prepared for an advisory committee on scientific policy, Colonial Office staff argued that apart from a few locales African territories were "at the moment . . . not . . . fa[cing] rapid population growth." They further noted that the promotion of birth control was difficult due to political and racial considerations: "Even a recommendation that the matter should be discussed in the colonial legislatures would invite the imputation of a racial motive: a desire by a white government to restrict the growth of the non-white population."[20] The available demographic data combined with fears of fueling racialized anti-colonial sentiment to convince the Colonial Office that a population control policy was unnecessary and unwise. Although Colonial Office personnel no longer worried about African populations dying out, they were not prepared to focus material and political resources on managing or limiting growth. It was not until after independence that the Kenyan government, with strong encouragement from the U.S.-based Ford Foundation and the Population Council, adopted a national population policy and opened state-sponsored family planning centers.[21]

In contrast to their predecessors who understood pre-initiation pregnancy and abortion in Meru as a demographic threat, colonial officials of the 1940s and 1950s did not frame premarital pregnancies as a population issue. Rather, officials, such as those who worked to develop the customary law of pregnancy compensation in Meru, cast premarital pregnancies as a symptom of the "breakdown" of previous constraints on sexuality and courtship. This perspective was most clearly articulated in the 1953 report of a government committee charged with identifying the problems affecting young persons and children and with proposing policy solutions. Influenced by then current theories of modernization, the report situated premarital pregnancy as one of the problems that young people faced "when two or more civilizations clash" and "too rapid economic development takes place."[22] As we shall see in the next chapter, the committee would propose and the settler-dominated Legislative Council would eventually accept that the problem of premarital pregnancies in urban areas should be addressed through an affiliation law. That statutory law, adapted from British common law, would grant all single mothers the right to sue the biological fathers of their children for paternity support. Affiliation law would depart from customary laws of pregnancy compensation by situating single mothers, rather than their male guardians, as the wronged parties.

The introduction of the statutory law of affiliation and the elaboration of the Meru customary law of pregnancy compensation stemmed from the same colonial conviction that contemporary circumstances had overwhelmed previous methods for handling out-of-wedlock pregnancies. While the central government committee singled out "too rapid economic development" and saw that the solution in urban areas lay in strengthening single mothers' legal position, officials in rural Meru focused on bolstering fathers' authority over their nearly grown children. Both responses were animated by a recognition—if not admission—that colonial rule had altered generational and reproductive relations.

Black central Kenyans pointed more directly to the role of colonial circumstances in encouraging promiscuity and premarital pregnancies. Some of the earliest central Kenyan complaints against colonial labor policies and mission schools centered on fears that they rendered unmarried girls sexually vulnerable. Harry Thuku, the Kikuyu politician and secretary of the East African Association whose jailing in 1922 was the subject of large and violent protests, often singled out forced female labor in his criticism of colonial policies. According to Thuku, work on settler farms took girls and women far from their homes and left them susceptible to rape at the hands of other employees, as well as "immoral practice[s]" and premarital pregnancies.[23] When Protestant missionaries first opened schools for girls in the early 1900s, central Kenyan parents similarly worried that by sending their daughters to school they might turn them into prostitutes. As John Lonsdale has argued, parents were nervous about "their daughters' adolescent transition to full sexuality occurr[ing] in the ritual seclusion of school, subject to foreigners."[24]

This association between promiscuity and schooling lingered, even as school attendance increased. As we saw in chapter 2, one of the greatest obstacles, up through the 1940s, to recruiting Meru schoolgirls for midwifery work was parents' fear that a training stint in Nairobi would render their daughters loose women. To demonstrate that they did not condone such behavior, schools expelled pregnant students. Yet, schoolboys found responsible for such pregnancies were often immune from expulsion. By the 1970s and probably earlier, some schools subjected girls to mandatory medical examinations to determine if they were pregnant. When tests proved positive, girls were sent home.[25] Pregnancy tests, like the examinations conducted at Presbyterian schools to determine students' initiation status, sought to discipline those who transgressed the reproductive standards that schools sought to cultivate.

Central Kenyan concerns about premarital pregnancy were, of course, closely tied to colonial debates and interventions surrounding female initiation. For Meru, we have already seen how colonial efforts to lower the age of female initiation in order to prevent abortions contributed to the problem of premarital pregnancy by lengthening the period of time spent as *ngutu*. During the interwar period, Protestant missionaries' efforts to stop excision, particularly among schoolgirls, exacerbated anxieties over promiscuity and premarital pregnancy. By attacking excision, a practice that many central Kenyans believed curbed excessive female desire, Protestant missionaries strengthened local suspicions that their schools contributed to undisciplined sexuality.[26]

Reproductive predicaments faced by some of the first schoolgirls to renounce excision only confirmed these suspicions. In 1939 Dr. Clive Irvine of the Presbyterian mission station at Chogoria wrote a letter to District Commissioner H. E. Lambert, drawing attention to the "increase in immorality between men and unmarried girls." Irvine described the cases of two Chogoria schoolgirls (one being the "head girl") who had become pregnant. The man held responsible for the pregnancy—in the first case, an ex-elder of the church, and in the second, a young man training to become a medical assistant—refused to follow "native custom" and marry the girl. Irvine blamed such "immorality" on education which "quickens all the sensibilities and gives rise to increased sex desire" and causes girls to "get themselves up attractively," and stated that only heavier fines could deter married men from committing adultery and unmarried ones from "repudiat[ing] their responsibilities." Irvine, unwilling to cast his fervent opposition to excision in a negative light, only admitted in passing that these cases were "complicated by the fact that [the girls] . . . were uncircumcised."[27]

Lambert, however, responded to Irvine's letter by recognizing the girls' uninitiated status as the crux of the problem. He stated that the men were not following "native custom" and marrying the girls because they were not excised.[28] The men or, perhaps, their wives and female kin could not accept incorporating an unexcised woman into their households. Schooling, either by drawing girls outside of their parents' immediate purview or by encouraging them to renounce female initiation, complicated the transition from pregnancy to marriage. During the late 1950s and 1960s many of the daughters involved in pregnancy compensation cases were, in fact, schoolgirls.

Many of them were probably also members of *Ngaitana*. This overlap raises questions about the relationship between defiance of anti-excision policies and the problem of premarital pregnancy. Some girls may have been motivated to "circumcise themselves" by stories of girls (like the two from Chogoria) who repudiated excision only to be shunned by lovers once they became pregnant. Yet, the reproductive status conferred by *Ngaitana* was not clear-cut. *Ngaitana* continued the pattern—begun during the *Kigwarie* episodes of the 1930s and 1940s—of reducing the age of female initiation and, thereby, disrupting the previously close association between initiation, reproductive entitlement, and marriage.[29] This muddling of procreative order together with girls' own claims that they had "circumcised themselves" may have caused some boys and young men to doubt the status that *Ngaitana* conferred and to treat its members with less respect. Any such inclinations would have been enhanced by the more general tendency for juniors to disregard the authority of senior men and women. Generational strife informed many of the local struggles that made up the Mau Mau rebellion. Such tensions continued unabated in the late 1950s and 1960s, as young men, particularly those with school education and salaried employment, became ever more willing to defy elders' control, even when it came to such morally laden matters as reproduction.

By the mid-1960s, premarital pregnancy had become a much-discussed social problem and legal issue. For example, in 1966 Mrs. Julia Mburugu, a social worker, wrote a letter to the district commissioner of Meru in which she singled out "young girls in town" as the "biggest problem" in the area. Mburugu complained that girls with a few years of schooling hung out around "bars and other places dangerous to their behavior" in the hope of earning money to buy "tight dress[es], high shoes, hair oil and other cosmetics." Like Irvine, Mburugu linked schooling to changed appearances and desires. But for Mburugu, these new appearances and desires had as much to do with cash and commodities as with sex. Mburugu explained that when these ex-schoolgirls "g[o]t babies," they returned "home where they continued with such business." Suggesting ways to remedy this problem, Mburugu urged the district commissioner to enforce laws regarding legitimacy and guardianship, and to establish commercial and agricultural schools where girls who failed out of primary school could learn a trade.[30]

In contrast to Mrs. Mburugu, the Swahili press's attention to premarital pregnancy cases was motivated less by a sense of professional duty or social conscience than by an appreciation for its entertainment value. The Swahili press had become an important part of colonial popular culture in the post–World War II period, when newspapers that had initially been started by the government to stem anticolonial sentiment became profitable commercial ventures.[31] By the mid-1960s, premarital pregnancy had become a favorite topic in these papers. *Baraza*, the *Taifa Weekly*, and the *Taifa Leo* regularly featured pieces on pregnancy compensation and affiliation litigation on the letters-to-the-editor page and in sections devoted to court reporting. With a combined weekly circulation in 1964 of 180,000 copies, and with some copies being passed among people to be read aloud, the stories that were printed in these three Swahili newspapers spread news about premarital pregnancies to a significant portion of Kenya's nine million citizens.[32] A single issue containing four or more pieces on premarital pregnancy was not uncommon. The pieces often carried sensationalist headlines, such as "He who bought love to pay a big sum" and "Beautiful woman receives a big sum," and they provided titillating descriptions of the intimate relations that preceded the pregnancies.[33] The intensity and tenor of this coverage suggests how, by the 1960s, premarital pregnancies had become the subject of everyday conversations and jokes.

RESPONDING TO PREMARITAL PREGNANCIES

Court records reveal that pregnancy compensation litigation represented one phase in a protracted set of social negotiations usually aimed at transforming intimate relations into marriage. Since court procedures required litigants and witnesses to narrate the relevant events which proceeded their arrival in court, the records provide clues to earlier efforts to resolve the predicament. These clues suggest that many premarital pregnancy cases never made it to African Courts, and that girls and women played decisive, though difficult, roles in determining the course that their cases took.

Once a young unmarried woman realized that she was pregnant, she had to decide whether to carry the pregnancy to term or end it in abortion. In Meru in the 1950s and 1960s, abortion remained a practical, if illegal and often dangerous, response to an unwanted pregnancy. Since a woman's decision to abort precluded the possibility of her guardian suing for pregnancy compensation, court records only provide fragmentary evidence of abortion. In two cases from 1965 witnesses mention that they considered abortion. One woman testified that when she first realized that she was pregnant she wrote a letter to her lover asking "him whether it was good to have miscarriage and he told me that he will report me." Another stated that the defendant had requested her "to take medicine to commit abortion."[34] Other young women probably made the decision to terminate their premarital pregnancies without consulting the men involved.[35] As during the 1920s and 1930s, girls and women in late colonial and early postcolonial Kenya turned to a variety of methods to procure abortions. In a largely rural area like Meru, common methods ranged from applying external pressure to the uterine area, to the insertion of sticks, hangers, and knitting needles, to the ingestion of various supposed abortifacants, including herbal preparations, quantities of choloroquine pills, writing ink, or strong detergents. In Nairobi and large towns, some medical personnel performed clandestine dilatation and curettage procedures.[36] By whatever method, abortion was the ever present if risky alternative to maintaining a premarital pregnancy and seeking resolution through marriage negotiations or compensation payments.

After deciding to carry a pregnancy to term or while she was still deciding (as in the above cases), the young woman would contact the man deemed responsible. By informing him, she usually sought to determine whether he was interested in marriage. As Job Kinoti, who had two pregnancy compensation cases filed against him in the 1960s, explained in 1995: "Initially, the question was not to pay [compensation], it was acceptance in the hope that they will get married."[37] If the young man ignored the woman's repeated requests to discuss the pregnancy or if he categorically refused paternity, the woman would inform her guardian. Mothers and other older women probably often served as intermediaries, relaying the news to the young woman's father or brother.[38] Direct discussions between daughters and fathers would have been exceptional, given local notions of respectful behavior that discouraged discussion of sexual matters between members of adjacent age-grades.

Once a father or brother knew of the pregnancy, he usually sent a *kiama*—a group of two or three respected older men from his clan who represented both generational sets of *kiruka* and *ntiba*—to the home of the young man. The sending of a *kiama* was crucial for subsequent pregnancy compensation proceedings. African Courts interpreted *kiama* as evidence of the guardian's good-faith efforts to resolve the pregnancy through customary channels. They automatically dismissed cases in which *kiama* had never been sent.[39] *Kiamas* were charged with informing the young man's family of the pregnancy and ascertaining whether marriage would follow or compensation would be paid. The pregnant woman often accompanied the *kiama* to the man's home. If the man accepted responsibility for the pregnancy and he and his family agreed to the marriage, the woman would remain at the man's home, beginning her married life while bridewealth discussions continued. The woman would return with the *kiama* to her natal home if the man and his family agreed only to pay compensation or denied paternity altogether. In some cases, the man and his family stated that they would wait until the birth of the child before accepting or denying responsibility. If *kiama* failed to secure a firm commitment to marriage negotiations or the payment of compensation, the woman's guardian could file a pregnancy compensation suit.

SCHOOLING, MOBILITY, AND MARRIAGE

Many of those involved in premarital pregnancy disputes which ended up in African Courts came from or aspired to join the local elite. Almost all of the pregnancy compensation cases deposited at the Meru Law Courts originated in the administrative divisions of North and South Imenti. These areas participated more fully in the cash economy, particularly through the cultivation of coffee and later tea, and had a longer history of engagement with Christianity than other parts of the district. By the 1950s, part of being upwardly mobile in these areas and elsewhere in central Kenya meant attending school. Parents used hard-earned cash to pay their children's school fees. They viewed schooling as the crucial process for providing their children with the knowledge and skills necessary to succeed in a colonial and, later, postcolonial world. In Meru, those who had gained influence and wealth through serving the colonial government as headmen, LNC (later ADC) members, and Native Tribunal (later African Court) elders sent their children to school, as did those who had profited from business and trade ventures. Often, these were the same people. Others, who had fewer resources but who hoped to gain similar influence and wealth, also sent their children to school.

School education, the logic went, enabled young people, particularly men, to obtain employment as clerks, teachers, hospital personnel, and government officials. From these comfortable salaried positions, they could accumulate wealth by developing family farms, purchasing land, and owning businesses. With black Kenyans embracing schooling as the key to acquiring and maintaining prosperity during the 1960s, primary school enrollments increased by more than 50 percent, to 1.4 million students, while secondary school enrollments increased sixfold, reaching over 126,000.[40] It was within this context of parents and young people investing considerable resources in school education and expecting high returns that pregnancy compensation became such a compelling issue.

Many of the young men and women involved in pregnancy compensation cases had attended school. In the 1962 census, only 33 percent of men and 14 percent of women over the age of 15 years in Meru reported having attended school for one year or more.[41] Of the pregnancy compensation cases examined, one-third of the young men and women specifically stated that they had attended school.[42] References to the reading and writing of letters, and to jobs requiring literacy skills, however, suggest that a much larger portion of those who appeared in court, particularly of the young men, had attended school. Court records also reveal that many of those who attended school had reached relatively advanced levels. Jennifer Kinanu's eight years of schooling placed her in the elite 5 percent of women in Meru who had attended school for five years or more, and the secondary school education of Francis and his two friends placed them in the less than 1 percent of the male population that had had nine or more years of schooling. Such impressive educational achievements were not unusual for pregnancy compensation witnesses and litigants.

By the 1960s, these suits had become a perennial worry for secondary schoolboys. Interviewee James Laiboni explained how he and his classmates would peer from the classrooms, particularly during the second month after each school holiday, to see if an old man who worked at the local African Court was at the school office. If they saw the old man, they knew that one of them would soon be delivered a court summons notifying him that a holiday tryst had resulted in a pregnancy compensation suit.[43] In this way, such cases became part of secondary school routines.

Beyond the simple proportions of litigants and witnesses who had attended school, issues of education suffused pregnancy compensation litigation. Since school officials normally expelled students who became pregnant, parents viewed schoolgirl pregnancies as having spoiled their investment in school fees, dimming their hopes that schooling would bring their daughters lucrative employment or marriage to a wealthy man.[44] Given these disappointments, some interpreted pregnancy compensation as a partial repayment of school fees. In two cases, fathers specifically stated that their suits were an effort to recoup money spent on their daughters' schooling.[45]

The most common connection drawn between girls' schooling and premarital pregnancy was that by moving outside the immediate purview of their family, schoolgirls had become vulnerable to the predations of powerful men, particularly teachers. In a range of twentieth-century African contexts, in fact, missionaries, parents, and young people have complained of male teachers taking advantage of female students.[46] Several of the pregnancy compensation cases filed in Meru during the 1950s and 1960s involved fathers suing their daughters' teachers.[47] In one ruling, African Court officials indicated the power relations that animated such sexual encounters: "The Prosecutrix's evidence is taken as credible because she was a school girl whereas Defendant is a teacher who couldn't miss to trap her."[48] In another case, a schoolgirl testified that her Swahili teacher, while keeping her and a friend after school one day as punishment, "caught" and "fucked" her.[49] These statements suggest how teachers and headmasters might put

their far-reaching authority to inappropriate ends. Stories of teachers compelling students to have sex only perpetuated central Kenyan concerns, dating back to the earliest colonial controversies over excision, that schools
could render girls sexually vulnerable and prone to premarital pregnancy.

Others located the causes of pregnancy compensation litigation in boys'
schooling. As we have seen, interviewee Naaman M'Mwirichia attributed
the rise of such cases to young men's decreasing willingness to listen to
their seniors on a range of issues, including sex and marriage. According to
M'Mwirichia, young men who had attended school and worked outside of
Meru viewed themselves as sophisticates, no longer bound by the knowledge and advice of local elders. Similarly, interviewee Job Kinoti stated that
young men's brazen refusal to accept responsibility for pregnancies
stemmed directly from schooling. He explained: "It's because of the education. . . . We started seeing things differently. And we started moving freely
with the girls."[50] Although generational struggle had long been part of social relations in Meru, schooling altered the balance between young and old
men by providing the former with the knowledge and skills to negotiate
colonial and postcolonial institutions in often more effective ways than
their non-literate elders.

One colonial development that had a direct bearing on premarital pregnancy cases was schoolboys' skepticism of local oaths. In her semi-
autobiographical account of growing up in central Kenya during the 1940s
and 1950s, Charity Waciuma described how local tribunals required young
men who denied responsibility for a premarital pregnancy to take an oath to
prove their innocence. The oath involved the young man presenting a goat
to the elders, slaughtering and roasting it, and eating a portion of its heart
while declaring, "If I be responsible in this matter may the judgement of God
strike me down." According to the logic of the oath, if nothing unfortunate
occurred in the next week, the man was vindicated. Waciuma explained that
as "younger educated men did not believe in the oaths and did not fear their
power," they would take them irregardless of whether they were responsible or not.[51] Such skepticism probably also enabled some young men to disregard the Christian, Muslim, or "pagan" oaths (depending on their declared
faith) administered in African Courts. In causing young men to dismiss
oaths and elders' advice, schooling weakened previous methods for holding
young men responsible for the consequences of their sexual relations.

A letter that appeared in the "Dear Dolly" advice column of the popular
magazine *Drum* in 1972 suggests how schoolboys sometimes worked together to evade pregnancy compensation suits. It also reveals the social burdens of such evasions. "K.M." of Meru wrote to "Dolly" requesting advice

on whether he should testify in a pregnancy compensation case on behalf of his friend or on behalf of the girl whose father had brought the suit.

> I considered myself a happy and fortunate adolescent until suddenly trouble found me in a big way. It started when a friend and myself were in the home of a village girl and we asked her for sex. She preached some nasty stories which disturbed me and I quickly lost my desire. But my friend persisted and succeeded in persuading the girl. The aftermath of this immoral affair was that the girl became pregnant. When accused by the girl's father, my friend denied responsibility, so the father is taking him to court. My dilemma is that both the girl and my friend have asked me to appear as a witness, each to support their own case. Should I speak for the girl, who is of my village, or my good friend?

Predictably, Dolly replied that K.M. should tell the truth.[52] Beyond suggesting the verbal, if not, physical struggles entailed in some premarital sexual encounters, K.M.'s account reveals how young men's efforts to evade responsibility in premarital pregnancy cases could place other social relations in jeopardy. In this instance, a young man's efforts to assist an age mate and friend in outwitting a "village girl" and her father entailed betraying his own kin. Such betrayals and trickery would have been easiest for young men who did not fear the power of local oaths and who saw their futures unfolding in a world that was broader than their home areas.

In their own defense, teachers and schoolboys often claimed that the reason why they were the targets of so many pregnancy compensation suits was not because they, compared with their age mates, were more irresponsible but because they were the "best catches." According to this perspective, when it came time for a young woman to identify who was responsible for her pregnancy, she paid more attention to which of her lovers had the brightest future than to who was actually responsible. For instance, prior to appearing in court, one defendant wrote a letter stating that the plaintiff's daughter "wanted to be married by a teacher, that's what made her say that the pregnancy she has is mine."[53] Moreover, interviewees who had been the "victims" of pregnancy compensation litigation also claimed that women specifically enticed them or singled them out from a number of lovers because they were secondary school students with promising futures and, in one case, from a wealthy family.[54]

By promoting the Christian ideal of monogamy, schooling also changed how young men approached marriage. In their study of premarital pregnancy in Botswana in the 1970s, John L. Comaroff and Simon Roberts argued that the rise of such litigation was due to "the spread of monogamy within a society organised in terms of the assumption of polygyny." According to Comaroff and Roberts, premarital pregnancy cases were part of a new pattern of serial monogamy that had emerged to replace polygyny.[55] In central Kenya, too, schoolboys who planned on monogamous marriages were probably more discriminating about who and when they married than were age mates who viewed polygyny as a possibility. In a 1942 memo circulated to other missionaries in East Africa, E. Carey Francis, the principal of Alliance High School—the earliest and most prestigious Protestant secondary school in Kenya—explained such decisions as one of the dilemmas posed by Christian monogamy. He wrote that whereas with polygyny, "it is fairly easy to choose a cook cum labourer cum producer of children who can be sacked if inefficient," under monogamy "it is far harder to choose a helpmeet 'till death do us part.' "[56] Although Francis overdrew the distinction between marital decisions under polygyny and monogamy, caricaturing the former as a loveless relationship, he was right to suggest that an expectation of monogamy cast courtship and marriage in a new light.

Many school-educated young men expected their only wife also to be school-educated. In one pregnancy compensation case, a young woman testified that the defendant refused to marry her because she "was not educated."[57] Other considerations related to the prosperity that schooling was supposed to bring. A letter written by Stephen Anampiu in 1957 or 1958 to his former teacher W. H. Laughton suggests how for an upwardly mobile man the decision to marry entailed careful financial planning. Anampiu wrote, "I am no longer the Stephen who used to be suspicious of getting married. For next year my love and my coffee will support a family. My pay [salary] will support my professional standard and I hope I will then be a man!"[58] In order for Anampiu to be the sort of "professional" man, father, and husband who could provide smart clothing, decent housing, and small luxuries for himself and his family, he needed to have a coffee farm as well as a salaried position. An early marriage could have delayed or even spoiled Anampiu's attainment of financial well-being.

Intertwined issues of schooling and class mobility animated pregnancy compensation litigation. By refusing responsibility for premarital pregnancies or by paying compensation instead, school-educated young men sought to preserve their marriage options and avoid assuming the financial burden of a family too soon. Compared with their female counterparts, school-educated men were far less eager to marry in early adulthood. Whereas young pregnant women viewed marriage as a means to turn a disgraceful situation into a respectable and, perhaps, promising one, school-educated men viewed such marriages as only creating problems that just might be evaded altogether.

REPRESENTING INTIMACY BEFORE AFRICAN COURTS

For the young men being sued, pregnancy compensation cases were difficult to win. Of the fifty-seven cases examined, plaintiffs won nearly three-quarters of them.[59] Court officials generally approached these proceedings with the presumption that the defendant was responsible for the pregnancy unless proven otherwise. They started from the position that someone needed to be held accountable and that the woman had little reason to identify the wrong person. For instance, in one case, the officials baldly stated that "the burden of proof lies on the Defendant to prove he never met or had carnal knowledge with the girl on alleged date, which he has failed to prove."[60] While this ruling was eventually overturned by a Resident Magistrate, who noted that "there never is such a burden on the defendant," it nonetheless reveals how some officials approached these cases by favoring plaintiffs and their witnesses.[61]

In my sample of pregnancy compensation cases brought before an African Court, one of four basic scenarios ensued: the defendant failed to appear and the court granted an ex parte decision in favor of the plaintiff (five of the fifty-seven cases)[62]; the defendant admitted responsibility and agreed to pay compensation (fifteen cases)[63]; the defendant admitted responsibility and tried to persuade the court that he intended to marry the woman in question (ten cases)[64]; or, most commonly, the defendant sought to prove that he was not responsible for the pregnancy (twenty-seven cases).[65] When defendants failed to appear in court or immediately agreed to pay compensation, hearings ended quickly. The other two scenarios, however, entailed extended discussion and produced revealing court records.

When defendants admitted responsibility and insisted on their desire to marry, they sought to prove that they had begun to develop *uthoni*—relations of respect between in-laws—with the plaintiff. The best evidence of *uthoni* was the payment and acceptance of bridewealth items. Some defendants claimed that they had already paid bridewealth items, including cattle, sheep, goats, alcohol (both home-brewed and bottled), sugar, tea leaves, porridge, honey, blankets, clothing, and cash.[66] As one defendant explained: "I prepared food and drinks for them. One day that girl asked me to go and see her house. I went there twice. Afterwards I sent seven lbs. sugar and one lb. tea leaves to the Plaintiff to cover small brideprice for his daughter. The next time a gourd of gruel [porridge] was sent again. I then called the Plaintiff as my father-in-law."[67] Such accounts were often followed by statements of how plaintiffs had rejected their efforts toward marriage.

Plaintiffs, for their part, contested the meaning of these gifts. One plaintiff claimed that the defendant's gift of liquor did not signal the formation of *uthoni*, but rather marked the defendant's acceptance of the pregnancy.[68] When court officials were convinced that *uthoni* had already been formed between the defendant and plaintiff, they usually ruled that defendants should complete bridewealth payments and the couple should marry.[69] Even in cases in which they rejected a defendant's claim that *uthoni* existed, court officials would remind the litigants of the customary law stipulation that if they later married, the compensation already paid would count toward bridewealth.[70] Like many of the litigants and witnesses involved in these cases, court officials often recognized pregnancy compensation suits as marriage negotiations gone amiss. In ordering the completion of bridewealth payments, court officials declared such negotiations back on track.

But when defendants insisted from the outset that they were not responsible for the pregnancy in question, there was little hope of pregnancy compensation suits ending in marriage. In these cases, defendants sought to refute plaintiffs' accusations of paternity. The most crucial figure then became the young woman. She was the one who shouldered the burden of providing a persuasive account of where, when, and with whom the decisive sexual encounter took place. Plaintiffs themselves had little firsthand knowledge of these events. For instance, in response to the court's question of whether he knew that his daughter had had more than one lover, one plaintiff stated, "I never knew my daughter used to go out with others. . . . [She] was fully grown. I can only say what my daughter told me."[71] Court officials too viewed the young woman as the person best positioned to provide the necessary information. In one ruling, they explained, "In pregnancy case[s], the best evidence is that of the prosecutrix which is supported by *kiama* plus defendant's evidence."[72]

To be an effective witness for the plaintiff, a woman needed to present a confident and coherent account of the relevant events. Job Kinoti described the pressures that young women faced in discussing such intimate affairs in the public forum of the court: "The girl was asked to give graphic details about what happened and if the girl shied away, she'd lose. . . . These things . . . are supposed to be secret but those who braved the jury, court attendance, and gave details, they won."[73] Officials interpreted courage and composure as signs of truthful testimony. Given black central Kenyans' reservations about discussing sexual matters before parents and members of their parents' age-grade, it must have taken an enormous amount of strength for young women to muster such a demeanor.

A common defense strategy employed by men who denied responsibility was either to specify another man with whom the woman was involved or to argue that the woman was generally known to be promiscuous. One defendant unsuccessfully tried to pin the pregnancy on a recently deceased man, and court officials denounced as a "pack of lies" another defendant's claim that his friend had intercepted a letter written by the woman stating that another man had made her pregnant.[74] Court officials appear to have been more easily persuaded by defendants' accounts of women's generally "loose" conduct. Statements that a woman was "popular in Igoji market," "having sexual intercourse with various people," or "play[ing] sexual intercourse as a prostitute" all served as the basis for judgments in favor of defendants.[75] Assessments of women's sexual histories also appear to have shaped court officials' willingness to believe a woman's testimony. In one case, court officials explained that they accepted the testimony of the woman and her friend because they "are not lo[o]se girls."[76]

In none of the cases examined did a plaintiff ever introduce evidence about a defendant's sexual relations with other women, either to call into question the credibility of the defendant's testimony or to suggest that the defendant had a habit of refusing to marry women whom he had helped to make pregnant. All those involved deemed men's sexual reputations as irrelevant or, perhaps, beyond censure. In often commencing from the presumption that the accusations were true, officials enabled young women's testimony to powerfully shape court proceedings. But by making women's sexual histories the subject of public scrutiny, pregnancy compensation suits placed the women in an awkward and humiliating position.

These circumstances make any latter-day interpretation of young women's testimony a daunting challenge. On the one hand, pregnancy compensation records contain specific accounts of courtship and intimate relations found in few other sources from 1950s and 1960s Kenya. These records represent a largely unparalleled depository of contemporary descriptions of sexual relations. Yet, like all historical sources, they are shaped by the circumstances of their production. Pregnancy compensation litigation transgressed local notions of public decorum by requiring people to air private affairs before a mixed age and gender audience that could potentially extend to include all the readers of Swahili newspapers. The challenge of how to retain some propriety while at the same time provide a detailed and convincing account of the relevant events weighed heavily on litigants and witnesses, particularly young women. An effective witness needed to be calm and courageous. But a young woman who recounted her sexual relations with too much ease could be branded "loose." In interpreting such court records, we need to consider how the dilemma of appearing both respectful and persuasive informed the representations of intimacy provided by witnesses and defendants.

The testimony of young women brave enough to describe sexual relations before men and elders indicates that premarital pregnancies emerged from relations of varying duration and intensity. Two young women described their sexual relations with defendants as having taken place as part of long-term, quasi-marital relationships. One of these women recounted how she "was feeling as spouses" on the four separate occasions when she and the defendant had sex, and the other woman spoke of how she and the defendant had been "cohabiting" in her "small house" in the last two months of their four-month courtship.[77] Other women described how they and the defendants were already "friends" when they had consented to sex: "In 1964, we started friendship. In 1964 May 25th, Defendant asked me to play sexual intercourse with me and I agreed."[78] In describing their relationships as entailing cohabitation and friendship, these women indicated that they had good reason to believe that the defendant would marry rather than abandon them if they became pregnant. Through such descriptions, women also implied that they had willingly agreed to the intercourse that had resulted in pregnancy.

Other women claimed that their pregnancies were the result of casual or even first-time, although apparently consensual, sexual encounters. Women described meeting defendants at dance halls and then having sex with them later the same night. One woman provided the following account of what happened after she and the defendant left the hall and he proceeded to walk her home: "When we reached near our house he caught me willingly and tempered a fence. We then enjoyed ourselves playing sexual intercourse."[79] Another woman explained how she had met the defendant "on the way during the day and [he] invited me to his home and had sexual intercourse."[80] Such accounts often contributed to rulings in favor of defendants. By presenting their pregnancies as the consequence of a single meeting rather than of an enduring relationship, young women became vulnerable to accusations of promiscuity.

Other relations described in court situated men as intimidating or forcing women to have sex with them. As the accounts discussed earlier of
teachers "trap[ping]" and "ca[tching]" schoolgirls suggest, some premarital
pregnancies were the result of rape. The following account specifically mentioned the use of force: "The Defendant caught me by force at the home of
M'Rinkanya and had sexual intercourse with me".[81] Yet, based on court
records alone, it is not always easy to differentiate consensual relations from
non-consensual ones. Officials never directly addressed the issue of rape.
Such matters would have been handled as separate criminal cases, either by
Magistrate's Courts or by African Courts, under the customary offenses of
"removing an unmarried woman from the custody of her parent/guardian"
or of "indecent assault."[82] In recording pregnancy compensation proceedings, registrars at times mixed—in quite jarring ways—descriptions of consent with those of coercion. For instance, the following judgment waffled on
whether the woman had agreed to have sex or not:

> Plaintiff witness I [the woman] says that on 7/30/63 she had sexual
> intercourse with the Defendant in his father's coffee *shamba* [farm]
> when she was going to fetch firewood. It is not funny when [she] says
> the Defendant held her and had carnal knowledge with him. There is no
> question she screamed. They knew each other well and are relatives.
> Although he held [her], of course, there was willing[ness] on both
> parties.[83]

While insisting that the man's holding of the woman was a serious matter
and that the woman had screamed, the judgment concluded that it was a
consensual encounter. In this case, at least, court officials were reluctant to
interpret a woman's resistance as evidence of coercion.

Part of this reluctance probably stemmed from the prevailing cultural
and legal logic that defined female respectability in terms of sexual restraint.
A virtuous woman was one who resisted men's advances, particularly those
that offered little hope of leading toward marriage.[84] Court officials may
have interpreted women's descriptions of non-consensual sex as one way to
explain the origins of their pregnancy while at the same time defending
their reputations. In an interview, Job Kinoti made precisely this point. He
argued that women's courtroom portrayals of themselves as unwilling sexual partners lent credibility to their claims that they were either virgins or,
at least, not promiscuous.[85] In his analysis of cases of runaway women and
abductions in colonial Gusiiland, Kenya, Brett Shadle insightfully demonstrates how litigants and witnesses articulated different notions of consent;

some women defined consent in terms of whether they loved the man or not, yet some men assumed that a "good woman" would never agree to sex when first propositioned.[86] Given the less extensive discussion of consent in pregnancy compensation cases, it is more difficult to discern what litigants, witnesses, and court officials sought to convey by using words such as "caught," "held," "force," or "willing[ness]," not to mention the Meru language terms from which they were usually translated. It is safer to assume, however, that the sexual relations that led to "illegal pregnancy" ran the gamut from long-term courtships, to single but non-coercive encounters, to rapes.

By eliciting descriptions of intimate relations, court officials sought to confirm whether the defendant was responsible for the pregnancy. The weight of providing these descriptions fell more heavily on young women than on young men. Before parents, elders, and court officials, young women were compelled to walk the fine line between being convincing and confident witnesses and maintaining their sexual modesty. Although "illegal pregnancy" cases frequently commenced from the presumption that young women were telling the truth and most often resulted in defendants being found liable, they placed young women's—not young men's—reputations on trial.

PROVING PATERNITY BEFORE AFRICAN COURTS

In addition to the young woman providing a convincing account of her involvement with the defendant, successful pregnancy compensation suits hinged on the plaintiff producing evidence that specifically linked the defendant to the pregnancy in question. The most common methods for substantiating this link included pinpointing conception and birth dates, establishing previous admissions of responsibility, and demonstrating that the newborn child resembled the defendant. In assessing these claims, court officials relied on oral testimony as well as letters, visits to maternity wards, and consultations with older women. Examination of how litigants and officials evoked and refuted these various forms of evidence reveals that reproductive contests in central Kenya in the 1950s and 1960s were animated by a mix of old and new forms of social and bodily knowledge.

Proving conception and birth dates was especially salient in cases in which the defendant admitted having had sex with the young woman but disagreed over the date of the encounter(s). As explicitly stated in one pregnancy compensation judgment, court officials recognized the normal gestation period for human beings to be around 280 days.[87] Convincing testimony entailed presenting conception and birth dates that were roughly nine months apart. Yet, court officials and litigants recognized that such information was not easily within everyone's grasp. For instance, in one case, the plaintiff sought to explain his daughter's confused testimony by stating, "She does not know how to read or write and could hardly count months correctly."[88] In assessing young women's accounts of conception and birth dates, officials considered their level of school education. In two cases, officials interpreted literate women's incongruous testimony on conception and birth dates as trickery since they were familiar with "dates, months, and years."[89] Literacy meant that witnesses were expected to have fluent knowledge of calendar dates. When they did not, or if they provided inconsistent chronologies, such women became vulnerable to accusations of deception. While school education ostensibly provided witnesses with a powerful form of evidence, it also made their testimony subject to higher levels of scrutiny.

Evidence on conception dates also provides clues to how people understood fertility and the menstrual cycle. In two cases, women specified the date of conception in relation to their menstrual cycle; both women claimed that they had conceived just one or two days prior to the date on which they usually began menstruating, rather than at mid-cycle, the point at which ovulation normally occurs. Court officials apparently did not question either of these statements. One of these women was, in fact, in nurse's training at the Methodist hospital at Maua.[90] This fragmentary evidence suggests that although officials, litigants, and witnesses spoke of conception dates and 280-day gestation periods, they did not fully understand or embrace a biomedical model of conception.

Like testimony on conception and birth dates, letters and documents written in English and Meru were crucial but contested forms of evidence within African Courts. Litigants and witnesses with school education used such written evidence to corroborate claims about conception and birth dates and to demonstrate previous bridewealth agreements and admissions of paternity. For instance, in one case, court officials interpreted a letter written by the defendant, in which he requested that the young woman come and discuss the pregnancy, as proof that he was responsible.[91] As an interviewee who had been involved in such cases explained, love letters, in particular, were powerful tools for proving that the defendant and the young woman "were not just friends."[92]

The case of Francis and Jennifer, with which this chapter began, however, reveals that court officials could be quite skeptical of written evidence. In that case, officials dismissed a set of letters, submitted by Francis and allegedly written by Jennifer, as forgeries. Officials accepted Jennifer's claim that she had never written the documents and noted that someone like Jennifer, with only a Standard VII education, could never have written letters in such "standardized and fluent English."[93] Other cases, too, contained accusations of forgery.[94] As other scholars have argued, in contexts of limited literacy the written word often appears more impermanent than durable and trustworthy.[95] Compared to oral testimony, written documents were just as, likely to be products of deceit and trickery, if not more so.

In a further example of how premarital pregnancy disputes entailed the entanglement of new practices and institutions in old social relations, visits to maternity clinics and the payment of maternity fees became key points of contention within pregnancy compensation cases. Prior to World War II, few women in Meru attended hospitals. Rather, as we have seen, they gave birth at their marriage homes with the assistance of older female kin, particularly their mothers-in-law. By the 1950s and 1960s, however, for the largely school-educated women involved in pregnancy compensation cases, hospital births and visits had become markers of their enlightened and elite status, while hospital visits had become defining moments of courtship. Plaintiffs argued that by visiting the mother and child in hospital and/or paying their fees, defendants had accepted paternity and could not subsequently change their minds.

Jennifer, for instance, cited Francis's visit to the maternity clinic to "see" her as evidence that he had accepted responsibility for her newborn child. In response, Francis argued that while he had tentatively accepted responsibility for the pregnancy and visited Jennifer at the maternity clinic, he soon realized that the child's October (rather than March) birth date did not follow their May sexual encounter by nine months. In cases in which defendants claimed that they still planned on marrying the young woman, plaintiffs would cite the fact that the defendant had not escorted the young woman to the maternity clinic, visited her there, or paid her fees as evidence that he had no intention of accepting responsibility.[96]

Defendants also cited maternity visits and the payment of fees to support their own positions. Those who claimed to be committed to marrying the young woman cited their payment of maternity fees as proof. In one such case, the defendant, seeking to demonstrate that the larger community recognized him and the plaintiff's daughter as married, stated that he was told that his "wife was in maternity," so he went and paid the fees.[97] Court officials occasionally requested staff at maternity clinics and hospitals to consult clinic cards and birth registers to confirm whether a particular pregnancy was premature, full-term, or overdue.[98] These cases demonstrate how maternity clinics became sites for assessing courtroom testimony and ascertaining marriage plans.

By the 1960s, hospital births, visits, and records, like the home births which they had, in part, supplanted, were forums through which intimate relations were elaborated. While maternity clinics displaced female in-laws from directly supervising and facilitating childbirth, they did not shed the process of its potent social significance. Childbirth and the days immediately following were still a crucial time for kin and potential kin to affirm their affinity to the new mother and child. Within premarital pregnancy disputes, maternity clinics proved particularly salient. They provided a place where a young woman could demonstrate her enlightened status and either secure or lose a commitment to marriage.

Pregnancy compensation proceedings maintained a special role for older female kin when it came to discerning whether or not the newborn child resembled the defendant. Physical resemblance was one of the most common issues raised by litigants. Once the child was born, the defendant's parents, female kin, or *kiama* examined the child for resemblance.[99] In the first few days following birth, they would visit the infant to see if he or she shared facial features or "colour" with the defendant or any of his kin. As interviewee Job Kinoti explained, "There are specific areas they looked at. Maybe, the shape of the nose, lips, ears, and so forth. A child does not have necessarily [to] resemble the father but anybody from that family."[100] Such assessments could spark further disagreement between litigants. In one case in which the defendant's mother testified that the newborn child did not resemble anyone in her family, the plaintiff asked her if she had not heard "bystanders saying that [the] child resembles" her.[101]

Court officials were not consistent in their evaluation of this type of testimony. In several rulings, officials evoked resemblance as compelling proof of paternity, writing, for example, that "the head of the child is just the same as his grand-mother's with a pointed fore head," and that the child "resembles the Defendant exactly particularly face, lips, ears, colour, etc."[102] On occasion, officials either ordered the child to be brought to court or traveled to a maternity clinic themselves to judge whether the child resembled the defendant or any of his kin.[103] Yet, one ruling from the Appeal Magistrate's Court specifically rejected physical resemblance, stating it "should not be the decisive factor in pregnancy cases."[104] In other rulings, Magistrates and African Court officials simply ignored evidence of physical resemblance, instead concentrating on birth and conception dates.[105] Court officials also rejected more scientific methods for establishing affinities between defendants and children. In one case, the plaintiff unsuccessfully requested that the court order blood tests to establish that the defendant could possibly be responsible.[106] Perhaps due to expense or skepticism about the social consequences of such scientific determinations, officials did not order the test.

Physical resemblance was a reoccurring, if disputed, form of evidence within "illegal pregnancy" cases because it built on the commonsense notion that children resemble their relatives, while granting potential relatives, particularly the defendant's senior female kin, one more opportunity to declare the child their own. Evidence provided by witnesses who had examined the child's appearance nearly always coincided with the position of the litigant on whose behalf they testified. In one case, however, a defendant denied that his parents had viewed the child and had accepted it as his. The court rejected the defendant's claim, and ruled that his parents had accepted responsibility on his behalf.[107] This case suggests how examination of resemblance could become an occasion for a young man's relatives to circumvent his decision and make their own claim. Such circumstances made the acceptance or refusal of paternity a family matter rather than a personal decision.

Older women played crucial roles in these matters. As interviewee Job Kinoti explained, they were considered experts at recognizing resemblance because "they stay with children longer."[108] Within premarital pregnancy disputes, an older woman's acceptance of the child was especially crucial because quite often she became the child's main caregiver. Under Meru customary law, children born outside of wedlock were suppose to be raised by their fathers. Children were to stay with their mothers until they had finished breast-feeding (usually a couple years), after which they would then be taken to their fathers' homes. But when fathers—or mothers, in cases in which no man accepted responsibility—eventually married and established their own homes, children from previous unions often remained with their grandparents. Within new marital homes, such children were viewed as potential sources of conflict. By remaining with their grandparents, these children lived under the immediate care of grandmothers and other female kin.[109]

By the 1960s, older women had lost much of their previous authority to ensure proper reproduction. The colonial state had largely driven female initiation underground and women's councils were no longer a palpable presence. Moreover, the establishment of maternity wards meant that an increasing number of births occurred in hospitals rather than at home. Yet, as pregnancy compensation cases and their aftermath suggest, these transformations did not absolve older women from the responsibilities and, at times, burdens of mitigating the damaging effects of problematic reproduction.

. . .

Across much of late colonial and early postcolonial Africa, premarital pregnancy and laws relating to it became the subject of public debate. From Kenya to Botswana to the Ivory Coast, officials, politicians, and parents identified premarital pregnancy as a problem of increasing proportions.[110] They usually attributed the apparent rise in premarital pregnancies to the "breakdown of tradition," which decreased elders' ability to exert effective control over young people's moral and sexual behavior. To address the problem, officials and politicians often developed new laws.

In this chapter, we have seen how the problem of premarital pregnancies emerged as much from attempts to create something new as from the collapse of something old. As James Ferguson has argued in regard to anthropological analyses of marriage on the Zambian Copperbelt, interpretations that emphasize the "breakdown of functional traditional institutions" fail to appreciate "familial relations as constituting a site of struggle," in which men and women "seek to respond to the formidable difficulties and problems they face."[111] In Meru, premarital pregnancies increased at mid-century as a result of colonial campaigns targeting female initiation and more wide-ranging social transformations. Colonial efforts to lower the age of initiation undermined the local categories of personhood through which people had previously defined who was ready to conceive and bear children. By extending the period of time that females spent as unmarried initiates, and by insisting that all pregnancies be considered socially viable, these efforts made premarital (as opposed to pre-initiation) pregnancies a more common dilemma. Broader changes in gender and generational relations made it difficult for parents and elders to hold young men responsible for these reproductive dilemmas. Central government officials and politicians, influenced by post–World War II theories of development and modernization, glossed these broader changes as the "clash" of "civilizations" and as "rapid economic development."[112] Court records, however, reveal the concrete forms that these abstract processes took in rural areas like Meru. Schooling, salaried employment, and monogamous aspirations all contributed to the reworking of the politics of the womb.

The customary law of "illegal pregnancy," as crafted by colonial officials and local elders, sought to safeguard the moral and material value that fathers and families held in unmarried daughters. Like similar laws instituted elsewhere in Kenya and colonial Africa, the law situated premarital pregnancy as an offense against a girl's or woman's guardian. According to this logic, premarital pregnancy was a problem because it jeopardized a man and his family's reputation and their ability to receive full bridewealth. Through codifying such customary laws, late colonial and early postcolonial legal reforms sought to shore up senior men's authority in rural areas.

Not everyone, however, held the authority of male elders in equally high regard. Some school-educated young men did all they could to avoid paying compensation, even when they knew that they were responsible. These young men undermined the power of the elders by rejecting the efficacy of oaths, by requiring disputes to be taken to African Courts, and, once there, by providing false testimony and evidence. The ambitions of these young men did not easily accommodate the authority of elders. Rather, they embodied a faith that school education and salaried employment could catapult them into a world in which elders carried less influence and young men had more say in deciding which reproductive and familial responsibilities to accept.

Young women played decisive but often difficult roles in premarital pregnancy disputes. They determined the development of premarital pregnancy cases by deciding whether to carry the pregnancy to term and by identifying the man responsible. Moreover, African Court proceedings favored young women and their guardians, since officials often approached these cases assuming that the plaintiffs' claims were true unless proven otherwise. But when defendants refused to accept paternity, young women were placed in a very uncomfortable position. They then faced the formidable task of describing intimate sexual relations in a forthright and confident manner before fathers, court officials, and others. They also became vulnerable to having their sexual histories made the subject of courtroom scrutiny. Evidence that a woman was "loose" or promiscuous was among the most damaging testimony that a defendant could provide. Some of the young women involved in pregnancy compensation litigation probably did resort to trickery in the hope of securing marriage to a desirable man. But in both the short and long term, pregnancy compensation cases put young women and their reputations in a much more compromising position than that of men. In a context in which sexual modesty defined female virtue, girls and young women never escaped premarital pregnancy disputes unscathed.

Efforts to conduct interviews on this subject heightened my appreciation for the distress and discomfort that such courtroom dramas must have caused women. My research assistants and I located and interviewed men who had stood as plaintiffs and defendants in pregnancy compensation cases. They recounted their experiences with apparent candor and, at times, amusement. Yet we never managed to interview a woman who had been at the center of such a case. Those who we approached either declined to be interviewed or missed scheduled appointments. For these women, pregnancy compensation cases probably remained embarrassing and shameful episodes that they would rather not discuss.

During the 1950s and 1960s pregnancy compensation cases were important forums through which elders and young people sought to ameliorate reproduction gone awry. The reliance of litigants and witnesses on the intervention of *kiama* elders and on the examination of newborns by older women, when considered alongside references to schooling, maternity wards, and letter writing, suggest how these negotiations entailed the mixing of old and new forms of knowledge and social relations. These cases embodied disagreements over who could assign reproductive responsibility and who would make a suitable spouse. They entailed struggles between young men who sought to delay marriage and older men who sought to minimize the damage of spoiled daughters. In the next chapter, we will see how the affiliation law pushed premarital pregnancy cases in even more contentious directions by situating women as plaintiffs and requiring men to make ongoing child-support payments. It was this legal arrangement that generated a heated national debate over gender, generational, and reproductive relations in early postcolonial Kenya.

5   Postcolonial Nationalism and "Modern" Single Mothers

In the early 1960s Lilian Tirindi wrote to the district commissioner (DC) of Meru, asking for his assistance with providing for her six-month-old baby boy, born outside of marriage. She began by apologizing for "this shocking letter" and explaining that she was only turning to him after having consulted "so many people about this matter" without receiving assistance. She stated that while in nurse's training at Meru District Hospital, a "certain man," who was not her "boy friend," "conceived [her] by force." Lilian explained that the man had instructed her not to report the incident to "the Doctor" and had promised to marry her "if things went wrong." But when she notified him that she was pregnant, he denied responsibility. Lilian stated that both her father and her brother refused to support her and her baby. Lilian concluded her letter with the following plea: "Shall [I] put myself into death together with my son so that I may not see him suffering in future or what shall I do?"

A district officer (DO), acting on behalf of the DC, responded to Lilian's letter by instructing her to come see him and to bring along papers for filing a civil suit under the Affiliation Act. This statutory law, adapted from British common law and adopted by the colonial Kenya Legislative Council in 1959, granted all single mothers the right to sue the biological fathers of their children for paternity support. As mentioned in the previous chapter, the Affiliation Act differed from customary laws of pregnancy compensation in a number of different ways. First, it situated women rather than their male guardians as the plaintiffs in premarital pregnancy cases. Second, it provided for ongoing child-support payments of up to 200 Kenyan shillings (Ksh) per month for up to sixteen years to the woman, instead of a lump sum of compensation to her guardian. It also granted mothers, rather than fathers, custody of children born outside of wedlock.[1] Affiliation suits were a much less common occurrence in African and Magistrate's Courts in Meru than pregnancy compensation cases.[2] Given that neither Lilian's father nor her brother had filed a pregnancy compensation claim prior to the birth of her son, an affiliation suit was the only form of legal recourse left for ameliorating Lilian's premarital pregnancy. By instructing Lilian to file an affiliation suit, the DO encouraged her to exercise her rights under statutory law.

Just four days after writing her letter to the DC, the Kinoru African Court, located near Meru town, heard Lilian's affiliation suit against Joshua M'Burugu. In presenting her affiliation case, Lilian stated that after initially "refus[ing]" Joshua's advances, she had "slept" with him. She explained that when she informed him "a month and ten days" later that she was pregnant, he replied that "he did not believe it was his." In his defense, Joshua testified that Lilian had "c[o]me" to his house one night and then had claimed, a week later, that he "had made her conceive." Joshua explained that he refused to accept responsibility because he believed "it was a short period for conceiving." After hearing both sides, court officials dismissed Lilian's suit on the grounds that "Meru Law and Custom" had not been followed. They argued that for her affiliation claim to be valid, her father would have had to have sent a *kiama*, a group of clan elders, to "guard" Lilian during her pregnancy and to examine the child once it was born. Court officials dismissed Lilian's statutory law case on a point of customary law.[3]

The case of Lilian and Joshua reflects much of the strife that surrounded the Affiliation Act during its ten-year duration. Between 1959, when the act was passed by the colonial Legislative Council, and 1969, when it was repealed by an all-male National Assembly, people in Kenya argued over the relationship between the Affiliation Act and the customary laws of pregnancy compensation. Some also questioned whether single mothers should be granted the right to sue for paternity support and receive custody. Although the number of affiliation cases heard across Kenya appears not to have exceeded a few hundred per year, the act became a lightning rod for a national debate over changing gender relations and "women's status" before the law.

As was the case in immediate postcolonial contexts across sub-Saharan Africa, the birth of the Kenyan nation in 1963 generated wide-ranging consideration of the state's role in defining and ensuring women's legal rights.[4] Kenyan civic leaders, politicians, and members of the public argued over whether national independence should entail greater autonomy and guaranteed rights for women. Women's and welfare organizations held seminars at which participants discussed the "confusion" faced by single women living in the new social milieu of East Africa's towns and cities, as well as the challenges posed to the institution of marriage by women who had school education and salaried employment.[5] As an assistant minister, B. C. Maisari-Itumbo declared in 1967, "No social institution in Kenya has come under greater strain in recent years than the institution of marriage."[6] It was within this context of a perceived gender crisis that the Affiliation Act, a law ostensibly designed to ensure the welfare of children born outside of marriage, became the subject of debate over the relative powers of men and women and the value of the "modern" and "traditional" in postcolonial Kenya. While welfare and women's organizations hailed the Affiliation Act as a crucial step toward providing for children born outside of marriage and protecting women from irresponsible men, many male politicians and members of the public complained that it was a "foreign imposition" that made "men [the] slaves of . . . women" and encouraged female promiscuity and prostitution.[7]

This chapter examines how, in engaging and arguing over the Affiliation Act, Kenyans contested who should control women's sexuality, and who should bear the responsibility for and reap the rewards of their fertility. At stake were competing ideas about women's proper reproductive role and the value of children as a form of wealth. The affiliation debates also entailed arguments over the political future of the new Kenyan nation. While the most vocal supporters of the act embraced a view of Kenya's future that involved the promotion of "modern" laws aimed at elevating "women's status," opponents of the act articulated a vision of national politics in which "African tradition" would be recouped and male prerogatives upheld. Amid the tumultuous political and social changes of the late colonial and early postcolonial periods, the politics of the womb continued to shape intimate relations and inform visions of governance.

PASSING THE AFFILIATION ACT

The metropolitan origins of affiliation legislation extend back to acts promulgated by the British Parliament during the late eighteenth and early nineteenth centuries. These acts enabled single mothers to "affiliate" their children to their biological fathers and then sue fathers for weekly maintenance payments. Men found to be liable but unable to make maintenance payments faced imprisonment. The commissioners who drafted the New Poor Law of 1834 disapproved of these acts, believing that they left poor men at the mercy of unscrupulous women and encouraged women to engage in immoral behavior for financial gain. Influenced by Malthusian thought, the

Poor Law Commission argued that "Providence" had ordained that a "bastard" child "should be, a burthen on its mother," and that in seeking to ease that burden, affiliation laws had only promoted births outside of wedlock. To reverse this apparent trend, the commissioners included in the New Poor Law provisions that held paternity accusations to a higher standards of evidence, eliminated imprisonment for men who defaulted on payments, and, most significantly, situated Poor Law authorities rather than mothers as claimants. These changes proved enormously unpopular.

In 1844 the Poor Law commissioners were compelled to remove "bastardy" proceedings from the control of Poor Law authorities and to reinstate them as a civil matter between a child's parents. Thereafter, single mothers could once again affiliate their children to fathers and obtain paternity support. Apart from minor modifications, affiliation law in Britain remained largely unchanged into the post–World War II period. As we shall see, many of the issues raised during these mid–nineteenth-century British debates over affiliation law—issues concerning whether the law victimized men, unjustifiably empowered women, promoted promiscuity, or prevented abortion and infanticide—reappeared in strikingly similar form during the debates over the Kenyan Affiliation Act.[8]

Discussions over the need for affiliation legislation commenced in Kenya during the early 1930s. During the previous decade, metropolitan child welfare advocates had successfully made the problem of "illegitimate" children a target of legislative reform. In 1926 the British Parliament passed the Legitimacy Ordinance, which enabled "illegitimate" individuals to become "legitimate" upon the marriage of their parents. The Kenyan Legislative Council soon adopted this ordinance with slight amendments.[9] These efforts to improve the position of children born outside of wedlock were animated by the same maternalist activism that stirred contemporaneous campaigns to ban female genital cutting and improve maternal and child health in the colonies. In 1929 the Colonial Office forwarded to all colonial governments a League of Nations resolution urging that "illegitimate" children be treated the same as "legitimate" children "in all questions of protection and assistance."[10] Years later, white settler politician Humphrey Slade recalled that it was in 1932 that he and other members of the Law Society of Kenya first discussed the need for legislation to provide maintenance support for "illegitimate" children.[11] It was not until the post–World War II period, however, that the Kenyan colonial government drafted such a law.

In 1946 the Kenyan government appointed a multiracial committee of men and women with expertise in education, social welfare, and the law to consider legislation "relating to young persons and children" and to recommend the adoption of "more modern and comprehensive legislation" where desirable. As the Committee on Young Persons and Children explained in its final report in 1953, their mandate originated "from widespread anxiety and interest" among both government officials and "members of the public" concerning the problems caused "when two or more civilizations clash" and "too rapid economic development takes place." Further suggesting the broad post–World War II political and intellectual currents informing their mandate, the committee noted that the perception of such problems in Kenya had been "affected by the conception of the 'Welfare State.' "[12]

In 1948 the attorney general's department presented the Committee on Young Persons and Children with a draft Affiliation Bill, modeled after existing affiliation law in the United Kingdom. This draft Affiliation Bill, unlike the one that was actually passed eleven years later, excluded maintenance cases between black Kenyans. The final clause of the draft bill specified that the ordinance "shall not apply to cases where both the father and mother of the child are natives."[13] In 1950 the Committee on Young Persons and Children was reconstituted under the chairmanship of liberal white settler Humphrey Slade. In 1952, against the backdrop of the emerging Mau Mau rebellion, the committee suggested that the Affiliation Bill be broadened to apply to all the people of Kenya, regardless of race. In a political context in which it was becoming increasingly difficult to justify the introduction of new racially differentiated laws, the committee drafted its legislative recommendations relating to bastardy, adoption, maintenance, and age of majority "without racial distinction."[14]

The Affiliation Bill was finally introduced into the Kenyan colonial Legislative Council on 21 April 1959.[15] Although the version of the bill presented to the multiracial parliamentary body contained no mention of racial groups, much of the debate focused on whether or not the bill's provisions were, in fact, suitable for black women. Specifically, some members who supported the bill in principle noted that the term "single woman" needed to clarified. Pointing to possible ambiguities in African marriages, Dorothy Hughes asked whether a woman who "was married before witnesses" but for whom "bride-price had not been paid" would be considered a single woman under the bill. Voicing a similar need for clarification, John Muchara argued that the bill should distinguish between the deserving single woman who had temporarily been "led astray" and that recurrent figure of reproduction gone awry, the prostitute. Maintaining that "most of these illegitimate children" are born to prostitutes who do not care for them properly, Muchara held that such women should not be eligible to receive affiliation payments.[16]

Government ministers successfully defended the Affiliation Bill against these misgivings. Walter Havelock, the minister for local government, health, and town planning, explained the government's support for a non-racial Affiliation Bill by stating that after "considerable investigation," the government realized that "illegitimacy" was a "growing problem in the African community," particularly apparent in cities and towns, and it believed that African Courts would be capable of determining which black women were "single women." He responded to Muchara's suggestion that prostitutes be excluded from the law's provisions by arguing that a woman proven to be a prostitute would already be excluded under the clause stipulating that the mother first be deemed "a fit and proper person to have custody of the child." Similarly, the minister for housing, Musa Amalemba, justified extending the bill's provisions to black women by noting that customary laws of pregnancy compensation "benefited the parents but not the girls or the mothers and their children." Referring to the increasing number of black girls and women working in towns, Amalemba stated that they needed some protection "against the single or the married man who likes to take a little bit more than what he is entitled." Finally, Amalemba applauded the bill's non-racial character as "a step forward towards recognizing the right of everybody, not on racial grounds but as human beings."[17]

The political exigencies of decolonization propelled the Kenyan colonial government to expand the Affiliation Bill to include all racial groups. During the debate on passage of the Affiliation Bill, the "constituency elected" African members of the Legislative Council boycotted the proceedings to protest the government's refusal to hold constitutional talks prior to the 1960 general election. Unlike the "specially elected" African members—including Muchara and Amalemba—who were elected by the Legislative Council itself, the "constituency elected" members were chosen through "qualified franchise" elections and were considered to be much more vocal critics of colonial policy. "Constituency elected" African members denounced "specially elected" African members as "stooges, quislings, and black Europeans."[18] In introducing a racially inclusive Affiliation Bill, the government appears to have sought to convince boycotting African politicians of its commitment to a democratic future. As Amalemba's comment about recognizing everybody "not on racial grounds but as human beings" suggests, the Affiliation Bill pointed to a future in which universalist principles rather than ideologies of racial difference would inform all state policies, including those relating to reproduction.

In addition to extending its provisions to women of all races, the Legislative Council granted African Courts as well as Magistrate's Courts jurisdiction under the act. For some legal practitioners in Kenya, the act's expansive jurisdiction was its most striking feature.[19] Previously, the jurisdictions of African and Magistrate's Courts had remained distinct, with the purview of African Courts being largely confined to the adjudication of matters arising from customary laws, and from rules and orders promulgated under the Native Authority Ordinance.[20] For most Africans, African Courts were far more accessible legal forums than Magistrate's Courts. They were often located in closer proximity to people's homes, conducted their proceedings in local languages, charged lower court fees, and prohibited the appearance of professional lawyers. In empowering African Courts to hear affiliation cases, the government both placed the act within the reach of a greater number of black Kenyans and contributed to broader efforts to create a unified judicial system. By allowing affiliation suits to be heard in both African and Magistrate's Courts, government officials further used the act to demonstrate their commitment to the erosion of racially based legal distinctions.

While embodying universalist political principles, the Affiliation Act also demonstrated the limits of the "second colonial occupation." Throughout the post–World War II period in Africa, white officials and politicians, often responding to African demands, took a heightened interest in social welfare issues. They founded new departments of community development and welfare, undertook expansive social surveys, and enacted new social welfare legislation. Yet lack of sufficient state funds usually prevented this heightened interest from translating into substantial new programs. In their report of 1953 the Committee on Young Persons and Children stated that although their mandate was "affected by the conception of the 'Welfare State,' " they did not advocate the establishment of a welfare state in Kenya. According to the committee, the burden of solving social issues like "illegitimacy" did not belong to the state:

> If these problems are to be solved, then each community through its voluntary agencies, through the homes of its people, and through its schools, must make its maximum effort. Government will no doubt to a large extent co-operate and co-ordinate; but the real burden will fall on the people themselves. The rate of growth of the population creates absorption problems, Government alone cannot solve.[21]

Engaging the emergent discourse of rapid population growth in Africa, the committee claimed that the state alone was both ill-suited and unable to solve social problems concerning young people. The Colonial Office had disseminated a similar message in a 1944 circular sent out to dispel widespread colonial rumors that the Beveridge social security plan designed for Britain would apply throughout the empire. In that circular, the Colonial Office emphasized the difference between "traditional agricultural societies with their own basis of social security provision" and "more sophisticated and industrialized societies" like Britain, in which national systems of income redistribution and social security measures have "developed gradually."[22] The Affiliation Act, in holding fathers and mothers legally responsible for children born outside of marriage, fit well with the post–World War II colonial vision of regulating African social and reproductive relations without shifting the financial burden from family resources to state coffers.

IMMEDIATE CHALLENGES TO THE AFFILIATION ACT

Questions immediately greeted the passage of the Affiliation Act. The editor of *Baraza*, a major Swahili-language newspaper, approached government officials "with a view to obtaining advice for the information of his African readers, as a result of very considerable pressure from the public." *Baraza* readers wanted to know whether it was possible for a man to be sued twice for the same pregnancy, once by a woman's father under the customary law of pregnancy compensation, and then again by the woman herself for affiliation payments. Readers also asked whether prostitutes could bring suits under the act.[23] The British officer in charge of African Courts similarly sought the Solicitor General's advice. Asking for clarification on who was eligible to file an affiliation suit, the African Courts officer wrote: "It appears to favour the single career girl, as against one who marries."[24]

Within eight months of the act's passage, such queries had turned into outright hostility. In December 1959 and January 1960, some black members of the Legislative Council—many of whom had been boycotting its proceedings when the act was passed—called for the act's repeal. Taita arap Towett introduced the repeal motion by arguing that there was "general discontent" among black Kenyans over the act, much of it expressed in the vernacular newspapers. According to Towett, the Affiliation Act ignored the Christian principle of forgiving sinners and contradicted customary law by reducing the parent/child relationship to "financial arrangements." Francis Joseph Khamisi, a representative from the Coast and an editor of *Baraza*, argued that the limits of the act's much-touted "non-racialism" had already been demonstrated in his constituency, where a young black woman had been unable to bring a successful affiliation case against the white father of her child.[25]

Criticisms raised by other members of the Legislative Council anticipated arguments that would be used against the act in the succeeding decade. They also reiterated aspersions previously cast against young women who refused initiation or pursued careers in midwifery or nursing. Members argued that the act encouraged women to become promiscuous and morally corrupt. For example, Masinde Muliro of North Nyanza claimed that the act discouraged marriage by providing mothers with a comfortable "income" outside of marriage. He further questioned whether this "income" was being used for its rightful purposes by stating, "Women who are loose, who normally get children like this . . . seize the first chance to get out of the home and leave that child there to the poor grandmother and not even care about looking after it." Oginga Odinga similarly questioned black women's moral fortitude. He described the act as "releasing so many African women to be loose and move about in towns." Another member complained that the act fundamentally contradicted "African tribal customs" by granting custody to mothers rather than fathers.[26]

In response, others argued that the Affiliation Act was necessary because customary laws alone were no longer capable of providing for children's welfare. Dorothy Hughes explained that prior to the act's passage black women had lobbied for its universal application, on the grounds that "tribal traditions" had "broken down" and were unable to accommodate "illegitimate" children. Jemimah Gecaga, the single black woman to speak during the legislative debate, likewise defended the act by declaring that "good" customs should be preserved while "bad" ones should be abandoned. Gecaga also challenged some members' depiction of black women as irresponsible and uncaring by dismissing their suggestions that women would use affiliation payments for their "own purpose[s]" as "mere supposition." In place of her male colleagues' portrayal of women as selfish and rapacious, Gecaga offered an idealized view of the bond between mothers and children: "Mothers know that there is no love greater than that of a mother for her child."[27]

Speaking on behalf of the government, the minister of African affairs, C. M. Johnston, dismissed much of the criticism of the Affiliation Act as unfounded and then proposed an alternative to the repeal motion. He pointed out that in contrast to the "very general discontent" to which members had referred, only forty-three affiliation cases had been filed during the first eight months of the act's existence. Acknowledging the potential conflict between the act and customary laws, as well as the varying needs of rural and urban Africans, Johnston convinced the Legislative Council to table the repeal bill and, instead, allow the government to review the Affiliation Act and, if necessary, introduce amendments guaranteeing that courts would administer it with "due regard to native law and custom."[28]

While most African members expected that such a review would entail a refashioning of the act, no radical revision was ever introduced.[29] Instead, late colonial and early postcolonial officials employed the timeworn colonial strategy of recasting a contentious political issue as an administrative concern. Through pronouncements and circulars, they sought to discourage use of the act in rural areas, "where an adequate customary procedure for the upbringing of a fatherless child" still existed.[30] In Meru, African Court officials supported this position. At a meeting in June 1960, they concluded that "consideration should be given to Native Law and Custom when hearing an affiliation case." They also stated that the Affiliation Act was "more particularly suitable for application to the detribalized people in the big towns."[31] These efforts to restrict and temper application of the act in rural areas stemmed from some administrators' recognition that the act was a radical departure from customary procedures. In providing single mothers with the opportunity to raise children with the financial assistance of men, but without being subject to male authority as daughters, sisters, or wives, the act appeared to challenge the patriarchal relations that had long underwritten colonial control in rural areas.

Yet keeping the Affiliation Act out of rural areas proved more difficult than was initially imagined. As we saw in the case of Lilian that opened this chapter, not all colonial officials agreed that its application should be limited to cities. The DO in Meru believed that Lilian, as a single mother receiving no support from her father or brother, was entitled to sue for paternity support. During the 1959–60 legislative debate over whether to repeal or revise the act, some politicians pointed to the impossibility of building a legal policy on distinctions as fragile as those between the urban and rural. Justus Kandit Ole Tipis explained that urban areas had "always a very big influence on the rural areas." Similarly, Ronald Ngala noted that premarital pregnancies had already wreaked "a lot of havoc" among schoolgirls in rural areas, where the majority of schools were, in fact, located.[32]

Tipis's and Ngala's doubts about the administrative strategy of limiting the Affiliation Act to urban areas proved to be well founded. By the mid-1960s, a significant portion of the few hundred affiliation cases filed each year were heard in rural courts. For example, of the 244 affiliation cases reportedly filed in 1963, 183 originated with Kikuyus living in Central Province, 27 with the Abaluhya in Western Province, and 20 with the Kamba in the Machakos area. The remaining 14 were filed by white and black Kenyans in the Nairobi Resident Magistrate's Court.[33] Between 1964 and 1968, the Mathira African Court, located in Karatina, a Kikuyu-speaking area of Central Province, heard between 35 and 75 affiliation cases per year.[34] In Meru, a total of 35 affiliation cases were filed at the Kinoru African Court, the District Court Civil Panel, and the District Magistrate's Court between 1965 and 1969.[35] These numbers suggest that the gender and sexual relations that fueled affiliation cases were not confined to urban areas. Within the context of the affiliation debates, the distinction between the urban and the rural did not accurately reflect discrete social realms. Rather, it operated as a discursive strategy for placing the act beyond the reach of the majority of black women.

Within rural areas, the Affiliation Act intersected with the customary law of pregnancy compensation. In some instances, affiliation suits followed on successful or unsuccessful pregnancy compensation suits. Thus, as some *Baraza* readers had feared, men were sued twice for the same premarital pregnancy, once by the woman's guardian under customary law, and then by the woman herself under the Affiliation Act. In the eyes of some defendants, such an arrangement amounted to "double jeopardy." In January 1966 a man from Kiambu District wrote to the attorney general expressing his shock at receiving an affiliation summons two months after having paid "the girl and her father" 770 Ksh for pregnancy compensation.[36] Women, for their part, emphasized the distinction between their guardians' pregnancy compensation cases and their own affiliation cases by stating in court that they did not even know the amount of the sum awarded in customary cases since it was paid to their guardians and not to them.[37]

USING THE AFFILIATION ACT

As was the case with pregnancy compensation litigation examined in the previous chapter, a tangled set of social struggles informed affiliation litigation. Most obviously, affiliation cases entailed disputes between women and men. They also embodied conflicts over generational relations and class mobility. Most of the men who stood as defendants in affiliation cases were school-educated and had salaried employment. As elites or members of an emergent middle class, they worked as teachers, postal clerks, policemen, taxi drivers, shop clerks, government officials, and even national politicians. Others described themselves as students or unemployed graduates in search of such salaried positions. The women who filed affiliation cases often had also attended school. Education and employment enabled affiliation litigation by providing women with the wherewithal to engage the official legal system, and by placing men in an economic position where they could make monthly payments or have them automatically deducted from their salaries.

An affiliation case began with a woman filing an application for a summons. Once the application was complete, the court would hold a summons hearing at which the woman would explain to the judges the circumstances and dates of the child's conception and birth. At these hearings, judges sought to establish whether or not the woman's claim fell within the act's purview. For an affiliation claim to be valid, it had to be filed by a single woman, defined to include "a married woman who is living apart from her husband," and to fit one of two criteria: (1) the case needed to be filed prior to or within twelve months of the child's birth;[38] or (2) if the child had been born in the three years prior to the commencement of the act, it had to be filed by 16 June 1960, which was the one-year anniversary of the act's commencement.

If the judges were satisfied that a woman's claim fell within the above parameters and if she appeared credible, they would set a date for the affiliation hearing and issue a summons for the accused man to appear in court on that date. In vetting women's claims in this way, judges ensured that most cases that made it to full hearing were on relatively firm footing. Plaintiffs were, in fact, more than twice as likely as defendants to win affiliation hearings.[39] As in pregnancy compensation cases, court officials appear to have assumed that a woman was in the best position to identify the man responsible for her pregnancy and that, unless proven otherwise, the man was liable. Yet, according to legal experts, one of the most important procedural features that distinguished affiliation law from the customary law of pregnancy compensation was that the burden of proof for plaintiffs under the former was more stringent. Under the act, an affiliation order could only be granted if the mother's evidence could be "corroborated in some material particular by other evidence to the satisfaction of the court."[40] Much to the dismay of the African Courts officer in Nairobi, African Court officials sometimes used their decision in a pregnancy compensation case brought by a woman' guardian as the basis for granting or dismissing her affiliation suit without hearing any witnesses.[41] In practice, the distinction between evidentiary standards in affiliation and pregnancy compensation cases was not always clear.

In 1962 Samuel Waruhiu, a law lecturer at the Royal College of Nairobi, published a lay guide to the Affiliation Act. This booklet sought to explain the "general principles of the law" to those considering or involved in affiliation litigation. As mentioned previously, professional lawyers were allowed to appear in Magistrate's Courts but not in African Courts. Thus, a large number of affiliation cases involved self-representation. While the guide stemmed from Waruhiu's own initiative, two Supreme Court magistrates vetted the manuscript and the acting solicitor general approved it.[42] In the guide, Waruhiu outlined what counted as corroborative evidence in affiliation cases. He wrote that a plaintiff's claim could be corroborated by evidence ranging from the defendant's express admission of "close affection" between the plaintiff and the defendant during the relevant period of time, to the defendant's failure to deny paternity on an earlier occasion. Waruhi further stated that "contrary to common belief, facial resemblance between the defendant and the child is no corroboration," except when "the mother is not of the same racial stock as the defendant." Giving the example of an "African mother" and a "European defendant," Waruhiu wrote that the child's "European features" would be of relevance if the plaintiff could show that "she has had no association with any man other than the defendant."[43] From this perspective, the identification of shared, racially defined physical features would be corroborative evidence, whereas observed similarities between family members would not be. As we saw in the previous chapter, resemblance was a contested form of evidence in customary law cases. Yet, according to Waruhiu, the Supreme Court magistrates, and the solicitor general, racially defined similarities were above dispute. Although the Affiliation Act was, in part, meant to demonstrate the government's commitment to a "non-racial" future, its application could not escape racial logics.

Some affiliation defendants avoided having to worry about what counted as corroborative evidence by successfully evading summons and thereby ensuring that the suits against them never made it to full hearing. For instance, of the forty affiliation cases set to be heard by the Mathira African Court in 1968, roughly one-sixth were dismissed because court officials were unable to issue the summons.[44] Other forms of evasion proved only temporary. In 1965, as Joseph, Margaret, and their relatives were beginning to discuss how to resolve a premarital pregnancy that had emerged through the young pair's relationship, Joseph left Kenya to do a training course abroad. After learning of Joseph's departure "over the radio," Margaret wrote to him expressing her annoyance at his secret exit and asking how to proceed. Without admitting any responsibility for the pregnancy in writing, Joseph encouraged Margaret to handle the situation herself and not bring a suit.

> About the question you asked me, there is no point in your worry about it. What do you think could be done. We must under no circumstances

attempt to create problems where they do not or never existed before. You think of what could be done and let me hear your suggestions, please. . . . So what you can do should this happen is to use your imagination and tact and see whether a way out could be found. At any rate, keep me informed of the steps you take. I shall see whether with all the distance I could be of any help.[45]

When Joseph returned to Kenya in 1966, Margaret successfully brought an affiliation case against him. The Mathira African Court handed down the decision ex parte, as Joseph failed to appear in court despite receiving a summons. Ex parte decisions were not uncommon and almost always resulted in very high monthly sums being awarded to the plaintiff. Joseph was ordered to pay Margaret the maximum of 200 KSh per month.[46]

Those men who appeared before the courts responded to the paternity accusations against them in a variety of ways. Some denied the accusations, stating that they had never had sexual relations with the plaintiff or that the dates of their sexual relations did not coincide with the child's birth date. For instance, Gibson, a teacher, dismissed his student's accusations against him by arguing that he was away on holiday on the alleged date of conception. Gibson successfully argued before the Karatina District Magistrate that the plaintiff had forged the three love letters which she had submitted as evidence of their relationship and had stolen the photograph of Gibson which she claimed he had given her as a token of his affection.[47]

Denials like Gibson's, however, were less common in affiliation hearings than tempered admissions. Some defendants accepted responsibility, professing their desire to marry the plaintiff. Eustus, for example, explained to the Mathira African Court that just prior to the hearing he had, once again, proposed marriage to the plaintiff, Juliana: "This morning I asked her to marry me but she refused. I love and want her as well as the baby."[48] Such defendants appear to have believed that their willingness to marry the plaintiff would cast their cases in a different light. During the 1960s the attorney general's office received several letters from men expressing their astonishment at having to make affiliation payments to women who had refused to marry them or who had been prohibited from doing so by their parents. As one frustrated letter writer explained: "I told District Magistrate that the Girl refused to marry me, so why I should affiliated, I showed the Magistrate the letter which was sent by a girl that she cannot marry me but Magistrate did not pay attention to it."[49] In dismissing a marriage proposal as a basis for mitigating an affiliation claim, a Mathira court official argued that the affiliation law required him to disentangle marriage from maintenance: "Marriage is not an issue. I consider the welfare of the child."[50] By making a man's marriage proposal only as significant as a woman's acceptance, and by providing a viable financial alternative to marriage, the Affiliation Act weakened men's ability to control courtship and made single motherhood a more attractive option than it had previously been.

. Other defendants who admitted responsibility sought to mitigate the impact of affiliation suits by arguing that they were too poor or had too many other financial obligations to meet the monthly payments requested by the plaintiff. As we saw in the previous chapter, pregnancy compensation hearings often entailed much discussion about sexual relations and reputations. But because such issues had been already addressed through either a previous pregnancy compensation case or during the summons hearing, affiliation hearings contained much less discussion of sex. Rather, they often amounted to a debate over the just and proper use of a limited resource, the defendant's monthly paycheck.

Women justified their claims to receive between 40 Ksh per month and the legislated maximum of 200 Ksh per month by providing detailed lists of the expenses of raising a child. For example, in 1968 Mary Njeri told court officials that she needed to receive 70 Ksh per month to cover the costs of milk, Nestum, cod liver oil, Orange Squash, eggs, baby powder, Omo, baby oil, soap, and clothes.[51] Court officials recognized that while such a broad spectrum of commodities was not used by the majority of Kenyan mothers, such items had become a necessity for those who wished to raise their children in the "modern way."[52] Defendants responded to these lists not by dismissing any of the items as frivolous but by enumerating the various directions in which their monthly paychecks were already being pulled. The man that Mary was suing, for instance, stated that he could only afford to offer 10 Ksh per month, not the 70 Ksh that she was requesting. He explained that on his 150 Ksh monthly salary he already supported his widowed mother, paid correspondence course fees for himself, made pregnancy compensation payments to Mary's father, and maintained his sisters' two children and paid their school fees.[53]

In presenting their individual lists of expenses and responsibilities, plaintiffs and defendants situated small children as financial liabilities and social investments. Grown children were, however, widely viewed as financial and social assets. Defendants often requested that they be granted custody of the child in question. When such requests were denied, they expressed outrage that an offer to raise the child, like an offer to marry the woman, made no difference under the Affiliation Act. In arguing that the act should, like most variants of customary law, grant fathers custody, men expressed their conviction that raising children in their own homes made more sense than providing mothers with monthly payments to do the same.[54] In raising children in their homes, men could develop affective ties which would enable their children to feel endeared and indebted to them when they were grown. Compared to making monthly cash payments, men regarded caring for the child as a less significant burden. They viewed the reproductive labor normally performed by the mother as replaceable since most men could count on female kin to do much of the same. By ignoring the contributions that mothers made to their children's maintenance through daily care, some men perceived the Affiliation Act as granting women a monopoly on wealth-in-children without asking them to pay any of the investment costs.

The inability to obtain custody of their children and the obligation to make monthly affiliation payments clearly drove some men to emotional distress and financial hardship. In several instances, men wrote letters to the attorney general expressing utter dismay with their predicament. In their desperate tone, these letters were similar to the one written by Lilian to the Meru DC in 1961. For example, in January 1969 Ibrahim Mwangi accused the woman to whom he made affiliation payments of using the money to support herself and her "illigal husband" in Nairobi, and he requested that the government grant him custody of the child. After listing his other financial obligations—a wife, two children, and a "number of dependants who are always out . . . for my help"—Mwangi explained that in such circumstances "one can either be mad, have no hesitation in driving to the idea of mudering or just decide to comit suicide and quit the agony of the world."[55] Another letter writer who angrily denounced the Affiliation Act as the "ADVOCATE OF WOMEN" similarly described how the attachment of his salary had made him "very unhappy" while such hardships had driven others to violence.[56]

In court, women expressed little sympathy for men's accounts of despair and overwhelming financial obligations. Frequently, they argued that defendants had assets that they had failed to mention, including land, cars, coffee trees, or wealthy parents.[57] In one 1964 case, the plaintiff, Helena, stated that the defendant's status as a poor schoolboy made no difference to her, as "no one was capable of bringing about a child that should not be able to support it." Court officials, on the other hand, tended to be swayed by defendants' arguments that they were financially strapped. In Helena's case, the Mathira Court ruled that the defendant could not be ordered to make affiliation payments until he "might have the means to pay."[58] In a case from 1968, officials explained that they had ordered the defendant to pay less than the amount requested by the plaintiff because he maintained "his mother and other members of the family."[59] The amount of monthly payment ordered in nearly all rulings represented, in fact, a compromise between the amount requested by the plaintiff and the amount that the defendant stated he could afford. Court officials usually ordered defendants to pay between 40 and 60 Ksh per month to support babies and small children, specifying that plaintiffs could apply for a variation of the order once the child's expenses increased when he or she entered school.

Men also had the right to sue for a variation of the order if they believed that the women to whom they made their affiliation payments were misusing the money. Newspaper commentators and politicians often argued that such abuse was commonplace. In March 1964 member of Parliament (MP) G. J. Mbogoh asked the minister for justice and constitutional affairs, Tom Mboya, whether he realized that women were spending affiliation payments on "self-adornment" rather than on their children. Mboya challenged Mbogoh to produce evidence to support his claim since no such cases had been brought to his notice.[60] Some men, however, did apply for a variation of the orders against them. In 1967, Jackson, the manager of a shop in Karatina, argued that Jane did not use his payments to maintain their child, but instead left her parents to care for the child while she "roam[ed] about in Karatina." In describing Jane as moving aimlessly about town, Jackson meant to suggest that she had become a "loose" woman or prostitute. Jane and her mother, Mary, presented her situation in a different light. They explained that although Jane was living in Karatina with another man and had left the child with Mary, Jane still provided the child with clothes and other necessities. With Jane's and her parents' agreement, the court shifted guardianship of the child from Jane to Mary, making her the recipient of Jackson's payments.[61] In public debates over the Affiliation Act opponents repeatedly represented the law as including no safeguards against negligent or abusive mothers, but men's right to sue for a variation of the order provided just such a mechanism.

As has frequently been the case with paternity and maintenance suits in other national contexts, women often encountered difficulties in obtaining the affiliation payments ordered by the court. If a man did not deliver on his monthly payments, the woman could file an application for the interrogation of a judgment debtor. In 1964 Leah Gathoni poignantly explained in a written statement her reasons for filing such an application:

1. He failed to pay me six months at rate of 45/- [Ksh] per month as the court arranged.

2. He is employed in Bata shoe and he is rich, he has got Pegeout. . . .

4. I want him to come in this court and state to me why! If he is going to refuse the court is going to deal with him accordingly. He is enjoying while
I am suffering.

If the application was granted, as was Leah's, the court would issue a summons to the man and a hearing would be held. Such hearings often ended
with the court ordering that the man's salary be attached, so that the payments could be deducted directly from his paycheck. Salary attachments
proved effective as long as the man had a salaried position and remained
employed in Kenya. The father of Leah's child, for example, effectively
skirted making affiliation payments from 1966 to 1967 by leaving his job in
Kenya and travelling with his employer to Rhodesia, the Congo, Zambia,
and Tanzania.[62] As few affiliation cases were ever filed against men not in or
searching for salaried employment, it appears that the women themselves
recognized the difficulties of collecting monthly payments from men without steady and attachable incomes.

One of the most common complaints lodged against the Affiliation Act
was that greedy parents prompted much of the litigation. While the act was
premised on the principle that single mothers should be considered independent legal actors, critics of the act insisted that such women did not act
independently. Letter writers to the newspaper *Taifa* denounced parents,
particularly fathers, for using the law "as a business." George Owinoh
Omoloh contended that some "old men" prevented their daughters from
marrying so that they could collect pregnancy compensation and, then, affiliation payments.[63] Letters written to the attorney general demonstrate
that some fathers were, in fact, deeply involved in their daughters' affiliation cases. In January 1969 Ephraim Kariuki Gatu wrote a letter expressing
outrage that a Resident Magistrate could rule in favor of his pregnancy
compensation suit and then turn around and dismiss his daughter's affiliation case against the same man. Noting that "the Government is complaining a lot of times of illegitimate children," Gatu asked, "who would bring up
the child" now that his daughter's suit had been rejected.[64] Following the repeal of the act in June 1969, the attorney general received letters from angry
fathers posing the same question.[65]

In closely following and strongly supporting their daughters' affiliation
cases, parents sought to prevent the entire financial burden of raising their
daughters' children born outside of wedlock from landing on their households. Moreover, some parents appear to have viewed affiliation litigation as
a means to assuage the material and moral damage suffered when schoolgirl
daughters became pregnant. Suits involving schoolgirls and teachers were

among the most common type of affiliation cases discussed in the press. As a legal commentator for *Taifa Weekly* put it, teachers "have been beaten a lot by this law."[66] In one such case reported in *Baraza*, the judge ruled in favor of the schoolgirl and chastised the teacher and others like him for "holding back the development of women"; it was the third time that this teacher had been found liable for causing the pregnancy of one of his students.[67] Such cases were particularly disconcerting for parents, who entrusted teachers to foster the moral and intellectual growth of their daughters, not to seduce them and then leave them pregnant, unmarried, and expelled. Parents felt schoolgirl pregnancies as an acute financial and emotional hardship because of the sizeable sums of hard-earned money that they had invested in their daughters' school fees in the hope of good returns.

In cases of schoolgirl pregnancies, affiliation payments may have been viewed as a form of reparation for the young woman's entire family rather than paternity support directed toward a particular child. Such logic blurred the distinction between the Affiliation Act and the customary law of pregnancy compensation. While the act granted women a legal status independent of any male guardian, it could not dissolve the complex familial relations in which their lives were embedded. As daughters, many recipients of affiliation payments remained subject to the authority of fathers, mothers, and other kin. Because of the tangled layers of social relations that animated premarital pregnancy disputes, affiliation cases were never simply gendered conflicts that pitted female plaintiffs against male defendants. Rather, they also embodied struggles to salvage generational investments and secure upward mobility.

The scale of affiliation litigation is difficult to determine. The only two nationwide figures for affiliation litigation that I have been able to locate suggest that while the numbers of cases was never great, they probably increased over time as more women learned of the act's existence and felt able to engage it. The minister of African affairs reported that during the first six months following the act's introduction in 1959, only 43 cases were filed, whereas in 1964, the minister for justice and constitutional affairs reported that a total of 244 affiliation cases had been file in 1963.[68] Contemporary observers sympathetic to the act noted that Kenyan women used it "sparingly," given the "large number" of children born outside of wedlock.[69] In other postcolonial African countries, such as Botswana, Ghana, and Zimbabwe, where statutes similar to the Affiliation Act were introduced and still exist, such cases ranked during the 1990s as among the most common forms of civil litigation.[70] Based on the limited availability of nationwide figures, it is impossible to determine whether affiliation cases in Kenya ever accounted for such a large portion of civil suits.

What is clear, however, is that by the late 1960s, the significance of the Affiliation Act was not simply linked to the number of cases that were filed. As one politician remarked, the act was a "very rare" piece of legislation in that it "touch[ed] almost every individual citizen of this country."[71] The Swahili-language newspapers *Baraza, Taifa Weekly,* and *Taifa Leo* played a crucial role in creating such impressions. As discussed in the previous chapter, premarital pregnancy was a favorite topic in the court-reporting sections of these papers and in letters-to-the-editor columns. Reporters and letter writers alternatively referred to the Affiliation Act in Swahilli as *sheria ya mimba* (pregnancy law) or, more politely and precisely, *sheria ya kuwalea watoto* (the law of maintaining children). The more commonly used *sheria ya mimba* linked the Affiliation Act to customary cases of pregnancy compensation, in which it was the fact of pregnancy itself, not the need to care for the child, which entitled women's guardians to compensation. The focus on pregnancy also emphasized the illicit event that had sparked the affiliation litigation rather than the law's intended purpose.

While readers expressed opinions both in favor and in opposition to the act, the editorial perspective of the newspapers was decidedly against it. Editors often attached negative-sounding headlines to letters that were, in fact, supportive of the act. For instance, in May 1968, *Baraza* headlined a letter lamenting the fact that the Affiliation Act was not used more widely with the phrase, "The Law of Maintaining Children Does Not Have a Strong Future in Kenya."[72] Similarly, *Taifa Weekly* used the subheading "It's Bad" in the middle of a full-page legal commentary that stressed the act's worth.[73]

Through their reporting of affiliation cases, these newspapers provided their readers with detailed knowledge about the mechanics of bringing affiliation cases and the best strategies for winning them. Summaries of affiliation cases provided newspapers with titillating and sometimes scandalous copy. Some readers took offense at the graphic sexual content contained within the summaries. In 1968 a letter writer from Mombasa urged the *Taifa Weekly* to stop "advertising" the "dirty things that a boy and girl exchange in secret."[74] The year before, in fact, the minister for information and broadcasting had summoned the editors of *Baraza* and *Taifa Leo* to his office to urge them to stop using "obscene" and "unpalatable" language, particularly in their reporting of affiliation cases.[75] In spreading the word about the Affiliation Act, Swahili newspapers most likely helped to encourage its use. In 1967 one MP asked if the government would discourage the Swahili newspapers from covering affiliation cases heard at Makadara—a

Nairobi court that became renowned for such litigation—"on the grounds that this publicity increased tendencies to demoralize women." Implying that this MP's efforts to halt reporting of affiliation cases stemmed more from a fear of becoming the subject of such reporting than from a desire to protect public morality, the assistant minister for information and broadcasting advised the MP simply to "be careful not to become a victim of Makadara Court."[76]

INTRODUCING THE REPEAL BILL

On 9 May 1969, six years after political independence, the Kenyatta government, introduced a bill in the all-male National Assembly to repeal the Affiliation Act and immediately end all affiliation payments. While criticism of the act had been long-standing, the government's decision to push for its repeal emerged quite unexpectedly. Between 1964 and 1968, Minister for Justice and Constitutional Affairs Tom Mboya and Attorney General Charles Njonjo, the government's key spokespeople on legal matters, had vigorously defended the act against attacks in the National Assembly.[77] Although no official at the time offered an explanation for the government's reversal, the immediate motivation behind the introduction of the repeal bill appears to have stemmed from two sources.

First, by 1969 the Affiliation Act had begun to hit too close to home. Affiliation suits were being brought against national politicians. The attorney general's office itself had provided one woman with advice on how to file an affiliation case against an MP from western Kenya.[78] Throughout the raucous parliamentary debates over the bill, MPs accused their colleagues of having "personal interests" in favoring repeal. Although some of these accusations were probably made in jest, others referred to past or pending suits. In favoring the repeal of the Affiliation Act, some politicians surely sought to eliminate from their own lives the unwelcome payments and untoward publicity generated by affiliation litigation.

By introducing the repeal bill, the Kenyatta government probably also sought to recapture political support. The year 1969 was an election year, and Kenyatta and his inner circle were concerned about their declining popularity. They viewed opposition in the upcoming election as potentially stemming from two different sources: the Kenya People's Union (KPU), a self-styled socialist party led by the Luo politician Oginga Odinga; and Kenyatta's own party, the Kenya African National Union (KANU), which was rife with internal wrangling. The KPU was comprised of radical politicians and trade unionists, including the famed Kikuyu freedom fighter Bildad Kaggia, who had accused the Kenyatta regime of advocating "tribalism and capitalism" and of refusing to share the "nation's wealth equitably."[79] KANU was riddled with factional conflicts, as "individuals and groups struggled for control over patronage, licenses, contracts, and other fruits of office."[80]

The repeal bill seemed to be part of a broader strategy (including a mass oathing campaign throughout central Kenya) in the lead-up to the December 1969 election, to deflect the KPU's populist critique and to solidify support within KANU by reasserting the Kenyatta government's commitment to African nationalism and the concerns of the common people. By 1969, critics of the Affiliation Act had popularly branded it as a colonial imposition and a corrupting influence. As a newspaper editorial in support of the repeal bill argued, the act was a "foreign law" that had made parents prod their daughters to become pregnant by wealthy men, encouraged women to have children in order to buy things to make themselves "more beautiful," and enabled prostitutes to obtain "pensions by a way that isn't from sweat or long employment."[81]

In a interview conducted in 1999, Samuel Waruhiu, the lawyer who wrote the lay guide to the Affiliation Act and was a supporter of the Kenyatta government in the late 1960s, explained the repeal bill as an effort to recoup the government's waning popularity among some segments of the Kikuyu electorate. Son of the staunchly loyal Senior Chief Waruhiu, who had been assassinated by Mau Mau supporters in October 1952, Samuel Waruhiu, perhaps not surprisingly, explained the debates over the Affiliation Act in terms of the lingering politics of the Mau Mau rebellion. Waruhiu maintained that although Kenyatta favored the act, he felt compelled to support its repeal in order to prove to the "extreme Mau Mau Kikuyus" that the government was not partial to the "moderate Kikuyus," who as loyalists had fought against the Mau Mau rebellion.[82] Waruhiu's remarks further suggest how opposition to the Affiliation Act came to be equated with a long-standing nationalist position that shunned disorderly women and viewed increased female autonomy as morally suspect.

Such a campaign strategy, however, seemingly begs the issue of support from women voters, who made up more than half of the electorate. During the National Assembly debate, in fact, one MP noted that the repeal bill had been introduced at an inopportune time, as it would "frustrate" women in the lead-up to the election. A. R. Tsalwa stated that women who had sold "their sacred bodies" to "whites" during the Mau Mau rebellion to obtain armaments would be especially annoyed by the act's repeal.[83] With this remark, Tsalwa alluded to the view that Nairobi prostitutes, especially Kikuyu ones, had played important roles during the Mau Mau rebellion by contributing money to the forest fighters and stealing military secrets and guns from British and black loyalist clients. As some of the wealthiest black property owners in Nairobi, prostitutes had long ranked among the most influential women in the city. Throughout the colonial period, they had offered sexual services, companionship, and domestic comforts to male migrants and urban residents.[84] According to Tsalwa, repealing the Affiliation Act would mean alienating this powerful and patriotic, if morally suspect, segment of the female electorate.

The Christian newspaper *Target* criticized the repeal bill as part of a broader government campaign to crack down on prostitution without addressing its underlying causes. In February 1969 the government began implementing the Vagrancy Act, which aimed to clear Kenya's cities of prostitutes and street beggars by sending them back to the rural areas from which they came. By ridding cities of prostitutes and beggars, MPs believed that they would ease urban unemployment and crime.[85] In passing this act, postcolonial politicians failed to acknowledge how rural poverty often compelled people to move to cities like Nairobi in the first place. In criticizing both the Vagrancy Act and the government's effort to repeal the Affiliation Act, *Target* stated: "It is sheer wishful thinking to hope that prostitution can be wiped out of a modern society. . . . The Government seems to be tackling the results instead of examining the causes and dealing with them first."[86] By attacking prostitution as a corrupting and criminal activity, postcolonial politicians sought to demonstrate their commitment to moral order.

Just two years before implementing the Vagrancy Act and proposing the repeal bill, the Kenyatta government had initiated a national debate over elevating "women's status" through legal reforms. In May and April 1967, Attorney General Njonjo announced the creation of two Commissions to study existing customary, Islamic, Hindu, and statutory laws on marriage, divorce, and inheritance, and to propose new, uniform laws to replace them. Njonjo noted that the Commissions were "to pay particular attention to the status of women . . . in a free democratic society." The Commission on the Law of Succession and the Commission on the Law of Marriage and Divorce were each comprised of a dozen or so politicians, legal experts, and civic leaders. Advocate Samuel Waruhiu, politician A. R. Tsalwa, and President Kenyatta's daughter, Margaret, all were members of the Commission on Marriage and Divorce. Eugene Cotran, a British advocate and supervisor of the Restatement of African Law Project served as the secretary for both Commissions.

The commissions solicited input on how to unify and reform marriage, divorce, and inheritance laws by distributing questionnaires to "religious and social organizations" and "representative bodies and individuals," by holding public meetings, and by inviting the submission of memoranda through press and radio publicity. They released their reports and draft legislation in 1968. The most important legislative recommendation of the Commission on Succession was that when a married man died without a will, the man's wife, as opposed to other relatives, should automatically assume control of his property.[87] In its report, the Commission on Marriage and Divorce explained that it had tried to balance a desire to bring about "equal rights and responsibilities for everyone" with a recognition of the variety and continued strength of "religious and customary practices." The commission's key recommendations centered on requiring all spouses to consent to polygamous unions, on maintaining bridewealth as a "social custom" but not as a "legal essential," and on criminalizing adultery.[88]

When the Kenyatta government announced the bill to repeal the Affiliation Act in May 1969, the national debate over the commissions' recommendations was well underway. Supporters viewed the recommendations as successfully reconciling the various sets of law and improving women's legal status, but critics argued that the recommendations steamrolled over "African tradition." In speaking of the Affiliation Act, some MPs made direct reference to the commissions. For example, Arthur Ochwada, a strong opponent of the act, denounced both commissions as being led by "foreigners" and for implying in their reports that "anything African is terrible, everything foreign is excellent."[89]

The Commission on Succession's proposed legislation was eventually passed in October 1972, although its particulars did not come into effect until 1981. The recommendations of the Commission on Marriage and Divorce, on the other hand, were never enacted. Several times during the 1970s and 1980s, the commission's recommendations were placed before the National Assembly. But supporters of the so-called Marriage Bill were never able to convince a majority of the MPs that it was anything but a "Western imposition."[90] In introducing the bill to repeal the Affiliation Act just months after the publication of the commissions' reports, it is quite possible that the Kenyatta regime was responding to a rising tide of opposition toward legal reforms aimed at improving "women's status." In retrospect, the repeal bill appears to have been the first major setback for women's legal-reform efforts in postcolonial Kenya and a harbinger of future failures.[91]

By proposing that the Affiliation Act be repealed, the Kenyatta government sought to demonstrate its commitment to a political perspective that emphasized the moral dangers of granting women greater autonomy. As Audrey Wipper, a Canadian sociologist and contemporary observer of the Affiliation and Marriage Bill debates, argued, the public denouncement of women who worked as prostitutes and wore provocative "Western" fashions by Kenyatta and other postcolonial politicians was part of a broader effort to construct the nation as "a large, extended family" with the politicians playing the role of puritanical and authoritarian fathers.[92] Within central Kenya, at least, the association between women's autonomy, prostitution, and civic corruption was long-standing. In previous chapters, we have seen how people feared that the ending of initiation and the training of hospital midwives would lead to sexual and moral chaos. While the Kenyatta government surely anticipated that the repeal bill would anger some women, it counted on many more women and men viewing it as an affirmation of the government's desire to cleanse the nation of colonial corruption and (re)establish moral order.

DEBATING THE REPEAL BILL

Following the government's announcement of the repeal bill in early May 1969, women's welfare and church organizations immediately began to speak out against it. In newspaper interviews, leaders of *Maendeleo ya Wanawake* (Women's Progress), the National Council of Women of Kenya (NCWK), and the Child Welfare Society expressed their surprise and opposition to the repeal bill. Jael Mbogoh, the former president of *Maendeleo ya Wanawake*, described the repeal bill as "the latest move to show up how badly represented women are in Kenya." Other leaders explained that although a few women might have abused the Affiliation Act by making a "trade" out of it, the law nevertheless played a crucial role in providing for children born out of wedlock, and in protecting girls and women from men who "feel they can do as they please." They warned that the passage of the repeal bill would lead to increases in illegal abortion and "cases of destitution and unavoidable neglect of young children."[93] Women's and welfare organizations submitted letters to government officials and MPs stating their annoyance at not having been consulted before the bill was introduced, and requesting that abuses be corrected by reforming rather than repealing the law. In their letters, the National Christian Council of Kenya, the NCWK, and the Kenya Association of Social Workers suggested that the issue be deferred until a commission could be appointed to inquire into the "achievements and failures of the Act," and, if necessary, propose amendments.[94]

At least one MP summarily dismissed these letters and their bearers. Arguing that defenders of the Affiliation Act had personal interests at stake, J. W. Khaoya noted that Margaret Kenyatta—the president's daughter and chair of the NCWK—had children but no husband. For Khaoya, Margaret Kenyatta's position as a prominent member of the nation's first family and a single mother was proof of the "very dangerous situation" into which Kenya was drifting, a situation that the Affiliation Act was only encouraging.[95] The well-known Kenyan journalist Philip Ochieng similarly sought to discredit the women's organizations that defended the Affiliation Act. He claimed that they "were mainly Western-oriented and out of step with the African way of thinking on these issues."[96] The leaders of Kenya's women's and welfare organizations, like Margaret Kenyatta, represented the country's political elite. Most were married or related to men who were national politicians and prominent professionals. But in contrast to their husbands and male kin, these women were far more vulnerable to accusations of being inauthentic.[97] Whenever a woman like Margaret Kenyatta stepped beyond her prescribed roles as tea-party hostess and charity matron to lobby for women's rights, critics sought to dismiss her as a member of a "Westernized" elite, incapable of understanding or representing the common Kenyan woman.

With "far more women than usual" in the public galleries, Attorney General Njonjo opened the National Assembly debate on the repeal bill on June 10 to "thunderous applause" and cries of "pass it without debate."[98] Some MPs shouted that Njonjo had "a personal interest" in introducing the repeal bill. Njonjo had a reputation as a long-standing bachelor and an avid Anglophile.[99] The London-educated Njonjo never appeared in public without a three-piece, pin-striped suit replete with braces and a pocket watch. Within Kenyatta's cabinet, Njonjo ranked among the least likely candidates to embrace "African custom" over British law. For those who opposed the Affiliation Act as an affront to "tradition," it must have been particularly satisfying to see Njonjo introduce the repeal bill. Njonjo acknowledged his deep ambivalence. Explaining how, as a student recently returned from the UK, he had agitated for the act in the late 1950s and how he had later defended it against criticism, Njonjo stated that the repeal bill left him with a "very heavy heart." He went on to advise that if it passed, "our girls . . . should not have any association with men, unless the man takes her first of all to the altar and she becomes a wife to him."[100]

Njonjo's lukewarm endorsement of the repeal bill was followed by strident speeches that enumerated the evils that had been fostered by the Affiliation Act. J. W. Khaoya argued that the objections raised against the

Affiliation Bill in 1959 had proven true; prostitutes had taken advantage of the law to enrich themselves and to create "a lot of havoc amongst the population of Kenya." Other MPs similarly protested that the act had encouraged promiscuity for profit. MP Munyi optimistically claimed that the repeal bill would bring the "prostitution industry" to an end, while MP Ochwada stated that it would force women "to be closing doors to their houses and not leaving them [open] as if they were toilets." MPs accused affiliation claimants of selecting their defendants with money in mind. Wasonga Sijeyo said women had gone "hunting for the men with big salaries and with wealth." Martin Shikuku and Minister for Co-operatives and Social Services Ronald Ngala further accused women of having brought affiliation cases against different "boyfriends" in different courts for the same pregnancy.[101] Such accounts of Affiliation Act abuses cast women as amoral and calculating predators who used sex to lure and ensnare men and their money.

Opponents of the act also accused women of having misused affiliation payments once they received them. They argued that women used the cash not to provide for their children but instead to buy wigs, miniskirts, and the skin-lightener *Ambi* that enabled them to "attract" new "boyfriends."[102] The wearing of Western fashions by African women and their use of cosmetics to "whiten" their appearance were the subjects of heated debates in Kenya and in other postcolonial African countries in the late 1960s. Critics of Western fashions and cosmetics argued that they were an affront to African nationalism because they demonstrated that women who used them were not "proud of being Africans" and were "ashamed of the colour of their skins."[103] In accusing women of misusing affiliation payments to purchase clothing and cosmetics that would enable them to appear "Western" and white, the MPs portrayed women as vain and selfish betrayers of "African culture" and the Affiliation Act as a corrupting influence.

Dismissing affiliation law and litigation as "foreign ideas" became one of the most common rhetorical strategies adopted by those who supported the repeal bill. MP Mwangi Karungaru, for example, described the abolition of the act as an important step in transforming Kenya from a colony into a nation: "We do not . . . want to become cowards or copiers of the British Empire or imperialists by imitating them as if they were the only champions to tell us what to do in our nation." Mark Mwithaga similarly branded the Affiliation Act as "absolutely un-African." For Mwithaga, as well as for Martin Shikuku, the act's greatest affront to "African tradition" was its definition of children as belonging to mothers rather than fathers. Shikuku explained:

We, as Africans, in this country—and even on the Continent of Africa—
believe that a man is in charge of the family. . . . So this idea of
affiliation is encouraging the idea that the son or the daughter belongs
to the woman. This is wrong. Where did we get this idea from? . . . Are
we going out of our minds? Mr. Speaker, I believe we are not. We are
still clear in our thinking. Western civilization has not quite demoralized
us. We can overcome this threat from the women to try and own
children instead of letting us own them.[104]

Through such statements, Shikuku and other MPs argued that the
Affiliation Act had enabled the corrupting drive of "Western civilization" to
combine with women's predatory instincts to challenge fathers' "traditional" rights to "own" their progeny.

Shikuku also suggested that women in some areas of Kenya had been
more susceptible to the insidious forces of "Western civilization" and the
Affiliation Act than those in others. Shikuku, who represented a western
Kenyan constituency, stated that once the repeal bill was passed, all the babies that had been taken to Kiambu—the Kikuyu home area of both
President Kenyatta and Attorney General Njonjo—should be returned to
their fathers: "We want all those babies back; we will take care of them."[105]
With these remarks, Shikuku highlighted the fact that a large proportion of
affiliation cases had been filed in central Kenya. In 1963, for instance, three-
quarters of all cases had been filed there.[106] Shikuku's remarks also suggest
that the affiliation debates were inflected by ethnic tensions. By situating
Kikuyu women as the prime users of the Affiliation Act, Shikuku insinuated
that prior to the repeal bill, senior Kikuyu politicians like Kenyatta and
Njonjo had been content to allow such women to prey on men from elsewhere and hoard their booty in central Kenya.

But not all MPs believed the Affiliation Act to have been such an abominable affront to "African tradition." A small group of men staged a vocal
defense of the act, twice introducing motions aimed at postponing a vote on
the repeal bill for several months until more careful consideration could be
given to the issues involved. Though both motions failed, defenders of the
Affiliation Act like Dr. Munyua Waiyaki of Eastleigh responded vigorously
to their colleagues' criticisms of the act. Waiyaki argued that although some
women had "commercialized the law," the act was used not by prostitutes,
who rarely knew who was responsible for their pregnancies, but by young
working women—like "the girls in our offices"—who were involved in
steady relationships and had been promised marriage. With these words,
Waiyaki challenged the previous speakers' descriptions of affiliation
claimants as distant and undeserving women. Waiyaki further declared that

support for the repeal bill was motivated more by some men's desire for "a free feasting" (sexual relations without social and financial repercussions) than for a concern for the act's intended objective of providing for children. In concluding his speech, Waiyaki informed his colleagues that he planned to encourage the women of his constituency to "kick" MPs when they encountered them: "They will kick you because you are busy trying to destroy them."[107]

Through his speech, Waiyaki demonstrated that one's sex did not determine one's views on the Affiliation Act. At the same time, like so many other participants in the debate, he framed the debate as a battle between the sexes. Another MP who also opposed the repeal bill described it as "one of the most discriminatory pieces of legislation that we have ever made against other people while we favour ourselves as men."[108] Yet the repeal bill did not "favour" all men. Some fathers, particularly those with schoolgirl daughters, strongly opposed the act's repeal, while some women voiced support for it. On a few occasions, the press captured these alternative perspectives. In a letter to the *Daily Nation*, two women who identified themselves as married mothers with daughters voiced their strong support for the repeal bill. J. Anyoso and J. Akeyo of Endebess argued that with the act gone, young women like their daughters would learn to "never agree to be 'wastepaper baskets' of men till they get married" and "to live decent lives, like our grandmothers and mothers used to live."[109] In an interview with the *Daily Nation*, Patricia Oloo, the executive officer of *Maendeleo ya Wanawake*, voiced similar criticisms of the act. Responding to news of the repeal bill's introduction, Oloo criticized the act for making "many young girls get more loose than they should be." Two days later, the newspaper printed a correction in which Oloo stated that the *Daily Nation* had "highly accentuated" her comments and that her remarks on the act's loopholes reflected only her personal view and not that of *Maendeleo ya Wanawake*.[110]

Although Oloo's original remarks reveal that some women doubted the act's worth, her retraction indicates that women's and welfare organizations felt that they could not afford for women to appear divided on the issue. Just as some male politicians depicted the act as an attack on the "traditional" authority of *all* men, women's and welfare organizations defended the act as protecting *all* women's interests. By casting the affiliation debate as a gender conflict, participants ignored how men's and women's political convictions, moral beliefs, and social positions informed their various and shifting views of affiliation law and litigation. In casting the affiliation debates as a battle of the sexes or a conflict between the "traditional" and the "modern," participants obscured the complex gender, generational, and class relations that fueled premarital pregnancy litigation.

PROPOSING A REPLACEMENT BILL

Participants in the affiliation debates took greatest notice of these complexities when discussing the possibilities of replacing the Affiliation Law with a new one. On the first day of debate, one MP insisted—over shouts of disapproval from colleagues—that a new bill be introduced to provide for children born of out wedlock. Minister Tom Mboya opened the second day of debate by announcing that the government was in the process of drafting just such a bill. Strong criticism of the repeal bill by civic organizations appears to have prompted the government's decision to draft a replacement bill. Mboya's wife, Pamela Mboya, was, in fact, the executive officer of the Child Welfare Society. Challenging the notion put forth in the affiliation debates that the problem with the act was one of simple gender conflict, Tom Mboya stated: "The question is not whether we are for or against the women, nor is it a question of whether we defend the men. The real issue here, and essential point of concern, is the children." But apart from stating the need to incorporate "traditional approaches" into the new law, Mboya provided few details of the planned replacement bill.[111]

Several MPs doubted the government's sincerity in promising such a bill. Some interrupted Mboya's speech with disparaging shouts of "Show us the new Bill!" They noted that it was a highly unusual parliamentary procedure to introduce a replacement bill only after the original one had been repealed. Under normal procedures, any new bill introduced would containing a final clause that repealed the previous legislation.[112] Some MPs, however, took the government's word seriously enough to offer suggestions on what a replacement bill should look like.

One of the most common suggestions centered on maintaining affiliation provisions for schoolgirls. MPs argued that there should be protection for schoolgirls who committed their "first mistake" or who were lured by presents and false promises offered by teachers, government officials, and others with "fat salaries" and "big positions and cars."[113] Even J. W. Khaoya, an ardent critic of the act, supported the introduction of a new bill to protect schoolgirls. He stated:

> We are all fathers and we have daughters. In the rural areas, Mr.
> Speaker, we have case after case where a school master has made a

school girl pregnant, we have heard of these cases. We have heard of cases where a county council clerk, or a district commissioner himself, have made school girls pregnant. I think we have a big danger there because without some form of protection we might regret this later on.[114]

Relationships between schoolgirls and wealthy "Big Men" or "sugar daddies" have been a staple moral concern across postcolonial sub-Saharan Africa.[115] The press and popular fiction have portrayed such relationships as a common means by which schoolgirls acquire cash for school-related expenses, clothes, and cosmetics.

During the National Assembly debate, another MP explained why schoolgirl pregnancies annoyed fathers. He argued that in forcing young women to drop out of school, such pregnancies "disrupted" fathers' "investment[s]."[116] This remark points to the financial rewards that fathers hoped to gain in shared wages, bridewealth payments, and long-term support when their school-educated daughters obtained good-paying jobs and married upwardly mobile men. MPs' calls for the protection of schoolgirls challenged depictions of the affiliation litigation as a struggle between predatory women and victimized men by identifying some women as deserving of affiliation payments. These calls also cast some men, namely fathers, as beneficiaries of the Affiliation Act and others—Big Men and sugar daddies—as its rightful targets. Such remarks offered a more complex, if contradictory account (many parliamentarians were themselves both fathers and Big Men) of the social relations animating the affiliation litigation than the notion of a battle between the sexes. Nonetheless, the MPs' focus on schoolgirls privileged patriarchal interests. Schoolgirls' position as a deserving group derived from their status as daughters, whereas Big Men's position as the rightful targets of any new legislation stemmed from their disruption of fathers' strategies for investing and accumulating wealth.

A second common suggestion for the replacement bill centered on granting fathers rather than mothers custody of children born out of wedlock. Like the focus on schoolgirls, discussion of changing custody provisions amounted to a defense of what MPs viewed as fathers' "traditional" rights. This time, though, it was the rights of the child's father, not the woman's father, that were in question. Tom Mboya elucidated the material reasons why so many men found the Affiliation Act's custody provisions objectionable. He explained that men viewed the act as holding fathers financially responsible for children while placing mothers in the position to "reap the benefit when the child is a grown up person."[117] According to this perspective, a grown child was more likely to feel close to and care for a parent who had raised him or her rather than one who had simply provided financial support. Like the description of schoolgirls as an "investment," Mboya's remarks suggested that receiving material support from grown children was a crucial part of the "traditional" authority of fathers.

Other MPs lobbied for the replacement bill to shift the role of raising "illegitimate" children from mothers to the state. Such suggestions entailed a tacit recognition that not all men wanted custody of children that they fathered outside of marriage. Early in the debate, Wasonga Sijeyo argued that instead of compelling men to make payments "to these women or to these prostitutes," the new law should require men to make payments directly to the government, which would then care for the children. John Gatuguta agreed with Sijeyo's suggestions, explaining that with the state as guardian women would no longer be able to misuse affiliation payments and they would be more inclined to marry.[118] These politicians preferred to transfer patriarchal authority from fathers to the state than allow mothers to care for children with the financial support of men while remaining beyond their immediate control. Commentators and editors at the English-language newspapers the *Daily Nation* and the *East African Standard* also supported this suggested reform. In an editorial, Philip Ochieng argued that the state's care of such children would be "the modern equivalent of the fact that in tradition all children . . . were the responsibility of the whole family or extended-family or clan."[119] This confidence in the government's ability to care for such children reflected a broader early postcolonial optimism in the state's capacity to tackle and solve social problems.

Not all citizens and politicians, however, shared this faith. Two social workers employed by the National Christian Council of Kenya vehemently opposed the *Daily Nation*'s advocacy of institutional care as a replacement for family care. Throwing the epithet of "un-African" back at opponents of the Affiliation Act, Audrey Parker and Rosemary Kairu wrote, "Institutional care is an unfortunate characteristic of a Western-type developed society, completely un-African in nature, and we are surprised to see it being advocated by a newspaper such as yours."[120] Others opposed placing children under the state's care on logistical and financial grounds. Echoing the sentiments expressed by the Committee on Young Persons and Children in 1953, Minister Ronald Ngala argued that Kenya could not afford to become a welfare state that would raise all children born outside of marriage.[121]

The Kenyatta government ultimately reneged on its promise to replace the Affiliation Act with new legislation. On 17 June 1969 the repeal bill was passed by an "overwhelming majority." All affiliation payments were stopped and all pending case files were closed.[122] In spite of extended discussion of how to reform the act, no replacement bill was ever introduced. Opponents of the repeal bill had all along doubted the government's sincerity in promising such legislation. Any remaining hope for a replacement bill quickly faded in early July when Tom Mboya, the government's most vocal advocate of reform legislation, was assassinated. The only legal recourse that remained in premarital pregnancy cases was for fathers of single mothers to sue for pregnancy compensation under customary law. The repeal of the Affiliation Act and the persistence of customary laws of pregnancy compensation represented a compromise between the rights of two groups of fathers and a significant diminution of single mothers' legal rights. Fathers of single mothers continued to receive some financial compensation, and fathers of children born outside of marriage still faced some financial repercussions. Single mothers, on the other hand, lost all legal recourse to obtain paternity support.

The repeal of the Affiliation Act also sparked debate over abortion and birth control. In defending the Affiliation Act, women's and church leaders warned that passage of the repeal bill would result in a marked increase in illegal abortions "for girls whose consciences urge them not to bring children into the world with no one to look after them."[123] Following the act's repeal, one MP, M. Jahazi, argued that abortion laws should be liberalized.[124] Jahazi's colleagues greeted his suggestion with shouts of "shame," while one MP summarily denounced abortion—like the Affiliation Act itself—as "un-African."[125] With such comments, male politicians denied the long history of abortion within Kenya and claimed that local reproductive traditions had always been single-mindedly pronatalist. A few years later, another MP, E. C. K. Mulwa, returned to the topic. Stating that since the repeal of the Affiliation Act, "parents of school girls" have been "shouldering the burdens of . . . illegitimate children," Mulwa asked the government to liberalize abortion laws and make birth control "more easily available to school girls." Attorney General Charles Njonjo responded to Mulwa's suggestion by stating that it was not necessary to make contraceptives more widely available, and that, as a Christian, he could not support a change in abortion law.[126] These issues of access and morality stood at the heart of reproductive debates in Kenya during subsequent decades.

Calls for the greater distribution of birth control, the teaching of sex education in schools, and the liberalization of abortion law faced debilitating opposition from many religious leaders, politicians, and parents. These groups argued that all three policies would corrupt single girls, particularly schoolgirls, and women, by encouraging them to have sex without fearing the possible consequences.[127] Studies done in the late 1980s and 1990s and publicized in local newspapers estimated that over 250,000 illegal abortions were performed each year in Kenya and that the majority of these involved women who were 25 years of age or younger. Other research indicated that 60 percent of all gynecological admissions at public hospitals stemmed from induced abortions, and that between 1,000 and 5,000 Kenyan women died each year from botched abortions.[128] Newspapers frequently carried reports of women who had died in the attempt to terminate their pregnancies, either by taking an overdose of the anti-malarial medication chloroquine or by procuring the services of an underground practitioner.

By repealing the Affiliation Act in 1969, the National Assembly eliminated an important option available to women who became pregnant outside of marriage. The Kenyan government's reluctance to make birth control available to unmarried women, to require sex education in schools, and to liberalize abortion law further narrowed the reproductive options available to young women. The cumulative effect of these reproductive policies was to place the burdens of preventing and handling premarital pregnancies squarely upon the shoulders of young women and their families. By repealing and refusing to replace the Affiliation Act, Kenyan politicians left many pregnant young women either hoping for compassion and support from their families or seeking resolution in a bottle of chloroquine tablets.

. . .

Over the next three decades, debates over the Affiliation Act continued. Although few scholars of postcolonial Kenyan politics took notice of these debates, the act remained the focus of vivid recollections among those who both supported and opposed it at the time. Moreover, female MPs, as well as women's, welfare, and church organizations, repeatedly called for the introduction of reformed affiliation legislation.[129] Through the wide-ranging Children Act of 2001, the Kenyan National Assembly reintroduced, in a very limited way, elements of the Affiliation Act. Under sections 25 and 94 of the new act, a single mother could once again sue the biological father of her child for paternity support if the father had already accepted parental responsibility, either by legal agreement or by cohabiting with the mother for twelve or more months after the birth of the child. The Children Act aimed to bring Kenyan law in line with the Convention on the Rights of the Child adopted by the United Nations in 1989.[130] While government officials heralded the sections on parental responsibility and maintenance, advocates for women's rights and child welfare argued that the sections did not make it any easier for single mothers to compel the fathers of their children to accept responsibility. They also doubted whether the Kenyan government had the resources or political will to enforce even these limited provisions.[131]

The Kenyan Legislative Council passed the Affiliation Act in 1959 in an effort to allay the social problem of "illegitimacy" and to demonstrate its commitment to a "non-racial" future. Like the failed administrative ban on female excision in 1956, the passage of the Affiliation Act illustrates both the ambitions and limitations of post–World War II efforts to remake African social and reproductive relations. The Affiliation Act and the Committee on Young Persons and Children that drafted it were among the final influences of interwar feminist politics to be felt in colonial Kenya. The committee sought to address in a colonial context many of the social issues such as "illegitimacy," delinquency, and maintenance that had been placed on metropolitan political agendas through campaigns to improve maternal and child health and welfare. Yet the policies that the Kenyan committee advocated to address these issues differed markedly from those offered by contemporary commissions in Britain. Rather than arguing that these social problems should be solved through the elaboration of a welfare state, the Kenyan committee prescribed the state's role in fixing reproductive relations gone awry as the coordination of voluntary efforts and the enforcement of parental obligations.

Black Kenyan politicians, many of whom were boycotting Legislative Council proceedings when the Affiliation Act was passed, quickly made known their disapproval. Like others throughout the twentieth century, these late-colonial politicians linked reproduction to political and moral order. They opposed the Affiliation Act because they believed that it unfairly distributed the costs and benefits of children born outside of wedlock. They branded it an anathema to "African tradition" because it granted mothers custody and compelled fathers to pay children paternity support for up to sixteen years. Insisting that such children had always belonged to their fathers, many MPs argued that single mothers could not be trusted to use paternity payments appropriately. Informing these doubts were deep-seated notions of the propensity of women, located beyond the control of men, to become promiscuous, greedy, and irresponsible.[132] Opponents of the act defined this corrupt behavior as antithetical to "African tradition" and a product of "Western modernity."

These oppositions of "traditional" and "modern," "African" and "Western," powerfully structured the affiliation debates. In a political context in which it was no longer possible to justify the differential application of laws in racial terms, late colonial and early postcolonial administrators used these oppositions to define the act as a "modern" piece of legislation, to demarcate rural areas as "traditional," and to place the majority of African women beyond the act's purview. During the National Assembly debates in 1969, many effectively evoked these oppositions to denounce the act as an inappropriate law for their new nation. By dismissing the Affiliation Act as a "foreign" imposition that turned African women into skin-lightening and wig-wearing prostitutes, parliamentarians defined "African tradition" as morally superior to the "West's modernity." The "African tradition" that they envisioned, however, was one that would do little to curb men who desired "a free feasting."

The jocular and defiant tone of the National Assembly debates over the Affiliation Act resonates strongly with Achille Mbembe's description of the politics of the "obscene" and "grotesque" in postcolonial Africa. According to Mbembe, "the unconditional subordination of women to the principle of male pleasure" is one of the underlying principles of the "phallocratic system" of postcolonial politics.[133] Through jesting about their own philandering, these male politicians fashioned a postcolonial political culture that flaunted the moralistic tenets of "modernity." By the 1960s, the oppositions of "traditional" and "modern," "African" and "Western" operated less as accurate descriptions of discrete political realms than as popular idioms through which to contest the nation's future. During the affiliation debates and those that followed over the marriage law, these oppositions became powerful rhetorical tools for safeguarding men's privileged legal position and sabotaging efforts to legislate greater equality.

Another opposition that structured the affiliation debates was that of women versus men. MPs, civic leaders, and the press frequently framed the affiliation debates as a battle between the sexes. Yet men and women never lined up so neatly. Women's organizations did vigorously defend the act, but the press captured at least one member of a woman's organization and a pair of mothers who attacked the act as a corrupting influence. Not all men opposed the act. In addition to a small but vocal group of MPs who vigorously defended the act, fathers of single mothers voiced their strong disapproval of the act's repeal in letters to the attorney general. Affiliation debates, like disputes over female initiation and pregnancy compensation, were generational as well as gender struggles.

These generational contests were most clearly elaborated through the figure of the schoolgirl. Even MPs who vehemently opposed the Affiliation Act supported provisions that would protect schoolgirls, objects of their parents' investments and aspirations, from Big Men and "sugar daddies" who lured and then left them pregnant and unmarried. Affiliation cases, like pregnancy compensation cases, often entailed a contest between fathers, the father of the single mother and the father of her child. In casting the affiliation debates as a simple gender conflict, contemporary observers and participants obscured the complex generational as well as class issues that informed affiliation litigation and people's passionate perspectives on it.

Debates over the Affiliation Act that took place in the press, Parliament, and courtrooms were fundamentally struggles over the changing relations between different kinds of men and women and the changing strategies for accumulating and consuming wealth. Litigants, letter writers, and politicians argued over who should care for and incur the expenses of raising a child born outside of marriage, and over who should reap the benefits once the child was grown. In early postcolonial Kenya, men sought to come to terms with women's increasing social and economic options, and both men and women began to reassess the expenses and benefits of raising children. School fees, salaried employment for women, and the commodities needed to rear a child in the "modern way" cast ill-timed pregnancies in a new light. By the 1960s in much of Kenya, career options and cash considerations rather than initiation status determined whether a child was socially viable or not.

Yet, as in earlier periods, these out-of-sync reproductive episodes prompted moral and material quandaries over the relationship between education, fertility, and marriage. Through the figures of the pregnant schoolgirl and the predatory prostitute, postcolonial Kenyans distinguished between "modern" women who were deserving and those who were not. They also considered whether women could and should live respectable and comfortable lives as single mothers. Ultimately, these debates furthered the construction of a national political culture that was reluctant to hold men responsible for the social consequences of their sexual encounters. As the more recent debates over the Children Act attest, it is an outcome that continues to be contested.

Conclusion

Throughout the twentieth century, struggles over reproduction were crucial to the construction of political and moral order in Kenya. Of particular concern was how to ensure that daughters became well disciplined—not wayward—mothers and wives. Late precolonial and early colonial central Kenyan communities situated the regulation of female initiation, pregnancy, and childbirth as underlying successful social relations. In communities in which properly conceived children embodied wealth and ties to the spiritual world, procreation was a matter of material as well as moral importance. It also enabled the elaboration of gender differences and generational hierarchies. Women's power was rooted in their ability to cultivate life within their wombs. This reproductive capacity differentiated them from and, in certain realms, subordinated them, to men. It also distinguished women from girls. Through their involvement with female initiation and childbirth, older women sought to promote and safeguard the maturity and fertility of their juniors.

Beginning in the 1920s these reproductive politics intersected with those brought to Kenya by white colonial officers, settlers, and missionaries. Like those whom they sought to govern, hire, and convert, colonizers invested procreation with tremendous significance. During the early decades of colonial rule, officers and settlers understood population increase to be a sign of imperial peace and prosperity. Protestant missionaries together with their metropolitan allies, concerned with eliminating "barbaric" customs and elevating women's status, drew attention to local reproductive practices. They denounced female initiation as a degrading "custom" that contributed to complications during childbirth, and they argued for the expansion of colonial maternity services. Although officials in Nairobi and London were initially reluctant to attempt such reforms, the need to demonstrate Britain's commitment to improving "native" welfare and the desire to encourage population growth prompted them to condemn female genital cutting and to support the movement of some births from homes to hospitals. By the 1930s, colonial governance in Kenya depended upon skillfully navigating the politics of the womb.

As indigenous and imperial reproductive concerns intersected, they became entangled. It was the depth of local commitment to female initiation that caused Protestant missionaries to devote so much attention to it and convinced colonial officials in Meru that the problem of low population growth could be solved by altering its timing. Just as black central Kenyans understood female initiation as ensuring proper gender and generational relations, white missionaries and officials understood the ability to either alter or end female initiation as promoting health and demonstrating colonial control. Over time, some black Kenyans—particularly mission converts, headmen, and Local Native Council members—embraced white missionaries' and colonial officers' reproductive concerns, reworking them in the process. They accepted low population growth as a threat to ethnically defined populations, questioned the necessity of female initiation, and identified giving birth in colonial maternities with membership in an emergent elite. During the 1950s and 1960s, officials, politicians, parents, and young people further blended indigenous and imperial reproductive concerns by developing and engaging both a customary law of pregnancy compensation that sought to shore up senior men's authority, and a statutory law that asserted women's right to live as single mothers. As the failure of the 1956 ban on excision and the repeal of the Affiliation Act attest, the most radical innovations were not easily accepted. Nonetheless, the fact that black Kenyans stood on all sides of these debates by the late colonial period suggests just how entangled reproductive politics had become.

COLONIAL POWER

By analyzing the politics of the womb in twentieth-century Kenya as a process of historical entanglement, this book departs from many previous interpretations of the history of colonialism, reproduction, and sexuality in Africa. Scholarly and popular approaches to these issues have tended either to attribute change to the "breakdown of tradition" or to emphasize the power of colonial discourses and categories to frame reproductive and sexual concerns. Both of these approaches carry analytical and political merit: under colonialism, the authority of certain local practices and forms of

knowledge was reduced or supplanted altogether, while the power of colonial discourses to define Africa as a place of promiscuity and ill-health continues into the present day. These approaches miss, however, how reproductive change under colonialism entailed debate, negotiation, and the uneven
mixing of the indigenous and the imperial. Moreover, while elucidating the
injustices that have informed the West's relationship with Africa, these approaches fail to examine how related inequalities within African households, communities, and nations have also structured reproductive and sexual relations.

Approaching reproductive change as a process of historical entanglement
means attending to a wide range of power relations. Entanglement never
entailed an exchange between equals. Which reproductive visions held sway
in colonial Kenya depended upon both the political strength of the figures
involved and the political significance of the issues at stake. In addition to
the racialized divide between colonizers and colonized, intersecting distinctions of gender, generation, and wealth influenced whose visions were enacted, with what force, and in which realms. Yet British officers, the men
who in many respects sat atop colonial hierarchies, were often unsuccessful
in implementing policies targeting female initiation, pregnancy, and childbirth. Colonial officers could only be certain that unpopular measures were
enforced by dispatching and, in some cases, accompanying police to each
community. At times, reproductive practices, particularly female initiation,
garnered such interventions. On other occasions, colonial rhetoric on reproductive issues far outstripped the resources devoted to them. Colonial power
in Kenya alternated between extreme brutality and minimalist control. It
was precisely this unevenness of colonial power together with the depth of
reproductive concerns on all sides that made matters of the womb such contentious sites of intervention.

The challenges that British officers and other agents of colonialism faced
in affecting reproductive change raise important questions about the character of colonial power. Since the 1980s a number of scholars have sought to
assess the usefulness of Michel Foucault's notions of power to understanding European colonialism. In particular, they have considered the relevance
of bio-power, defined by Foucault as a "political technology" that emerged
in eighteenth-century Europe and "brought life [as opposed to death] and
its mechanisms into the realm of explicit calculations" by defining political
subjects as members of populations and making their sexual and reproductive conduct matters of national importance. For Foucault, European preoccupations with cultivating populations, defining racial hierarchies, and regulating sexuality were all a part of bio-power.[1] Developing Foucault's ideas,

Ann Stoler has argued that bio-power with its intertwined focus on race and sex emerged through the history of European imperialism.[2] Other scholars of colonialism have asked whether colonial power was bio-power.[3] Did colonialism discipline individual bodies as sexual and reproductive beings, and situate them as members of aggregate populations? Did colonial power, like Foucault's bio-power, have an expansive reach, transforming everyday bodily practices into sites of self-regulation and resistance?

In considering these questions, historians of Africa have tended to conclude that bio-power is of limited usefulness in making sense of colonialism. Megan Vaughan has argued that colonial institutions in Africa, especially in the pre–World War II period, were largely unable and uninterested in fostering individual and self-regulating subjectivities.[4] Frederick Cooper has further questioned the applicability of Foucault's diffuse notion of power to colonialism in Africa. Cooper has described colonial power in Africa as "more arterial than capillary—concentrated spatially and socially, not very nourishing beyond such domains, and in need of a pump to push it from moment to moment and place to place."[5] Vaughan's and Cooper's critiques suggest the potential pitfalls of applying bio-power wholesale to an analysis of bodily debates and interventions in colonial Africa.

Yet much of the reproductive change that occurred in twentieth-century Kenya involved the elaboration and reworking of reproductive concerns that coincide with Foucault's concept of bio-power. Campaigns to increase the size of African populations and to improve their health through abolishing "repugnant" practices, teaching mothercraft, and establishing maternity wards reveal that colonialism sometimes did operate through a political technology that promised life rather than threatened death. These campaigns drew Africans into the ambit of discourses of race, demography, women's status, and biomedicine. They connected black Kenyans to imperial and, later, international reform movements that simultaneously promoted reproductive health and welfare and challenged local methods for safeguarding pregnancy, childbirth, and childrearing. Over the twentieth century, as more black Kenyans attended schools and hospitals, and the number of organizations—in and outside of Kenya—interested in African reproduction multiplied, these reform efforts gained influenced. It would be a mistake, however, to view bio-power as simply replacing local reproductive visions. As the critical events examined in the previous chapters have demonstrated, reproductive concerns introduced by white missionaries and colonial officers vied and eventually became entangled with a politics of the womb rooted in the precolonial past. Historians of twentieth-century Africa must attend to the complex intersection of reproductive concerns stemming from previous centuries of both African and European history.

Like Foucault's bio-power, the colonial politics of the womb produced sites of regulation and resistance. In some cases, these sites further elaborated the racialized divide between colonizer and colonized. Through the "female circumcision controversy" of 1928–31, for example, white missionaries elaborated standards of "civilized" behavior while black politicians framed defense of female initiation as a nationalist cause. Colonial campaigns targeting female initiation, childbirth, and premarital pregnancy also contributed to the reworking of other hierarchies. They challenged generational relations by insisting that girls should come of age through schooling, not initiation, and that some women were better off giving birth in maternity wards, beyond the purview of female kin and under the care of girl-midwives. These reforms provided girls and young women with alternative routes to move from their natal to marital homes and to accrue material prosperity and moral authority. These routes also enabled girls and young women to revise their relations with fathers, brothers, lovers, and husbands. Colonial reforms generated new reproductive options. These options, however, depended upon racialized distinctions between the "barbaric" and the "civilized," and, later, between the "traditional" and the "modern." Moreover, they rarely escaped intergenerational and patriarchal controls. By the end of the colonial period, girls' and young women's bodies and reputations remained crucial sites for constructing and contesting political and moral order.

POSTCOLONIAL AMBIVALENCE

By examining premarital pregnancy laws in 1950s and 1960s Kenya, the final two chapters of this book reveal some of the continuities and disjunctures between the colonial and postcolonial politics of the womb. Postcolonial reproductive debates continued to be animated by material and moral concerns. The customary law of pregnancy compensation and the Affiliation Act sought to ameliorate the damage done to household finances and to personal reputations by premarital pregnancies. The history of the Affiliation Act, in particular, reveals how the reproductive concerns of rural households became entangled with the efforts of London- and Nairobi-based social reformers to improve the status of "illegitimate" children. In the postcolonial period, such entanglement became untenable for some male politicians and members of the public. Over the protests of welfare and women's organizations, led largely by black Kenyans, opponents argued that the act was a colonial imposition and "absolutely un-African." While such nationalist arguments had existed prior to political independence, they had never before carried the force of the state. During the early postcolonial period, male politicians effectively cast such reproductive reforms as antithetical to the task of building a truly African nation.

The Kenyatta government's position on the Affiliation Act also embodied an ambivalence that was to mark much reproductive policy in the early postcolonial period. This ambivalence, evidenced in Attorney General Njonjo's lukewarm endorsement of the repeal bill and Minister Tom Mboya's unfulfilled promise that a replacement bill would be introduced, reveals how the Kenyatta government sought to juggle competing reproductive concerns.[6] On the one hand, such ambivalence was nothing new. The colonial state often lacked the political will and resources to undertake the reproductive reforms that it promised. Colonial rulers bequeathed to their postcolonial successors an appreciation for the difficulties of displacing reproductive visions grounded in local moralities of gender, generation, and wealth. Leaders like Kenyatta, Njonjo, and Mboya, however, also faced dilemmas particular to their postcolonial condition. They needed to weigh any desire to undertake reproductive reforms against the need to define and defend a commitment to "African values." The strains of this balancing act resulted in ambivalent approaches in which different constituencies received different messages and in which public pronouncements did not match policy implementation. To highlight such inconsistencies and contradictions is not to suggest that reproductive matters were unimportant in the early postcolonial period. Rather, it is precisely because these matters meant so much to such diverse constituencies that ambivalence most frequently prevailed.

This ambivalence is well illustrated in the Kenyatta government's position on female genital cutting. In December 1964, just a year after political independence, a schoolteacher from central Kenya named Josuah Muchiri Benjamin wrote to the minister of health urging that excision be banned. Benjamin argued that the practiced needed to be stopped for the good of "our dear beautiful girls" and the building of a "healthy, educated and well cultured *Jamhuri* [republic]."[7] A ministry of health official, A. S. Mbuthia, responded to Benjamin by writing that while he agreed that excision "serves no useful purpose," it was impossible to abolish. Reminding Benjamin that previous anti-excision efforts had resulted in a "near revolution," Mbuthia insisted that "education" was the "only solution."[8] Mbuthia's response typifies the Kenyan government's position on female genital cutting throughout the 1960s and 1970s. While some officials and politicians disapproved of the practice, none proposed a ban.

Even women's and welfare organizations avoided the issue. Although such groups frequently spoke out against "tribal customs" and laws that discriminated against girls and women in schooling, marriage, and inheritance, they rarely broached the subject of female genital cutting.[9] When asked by international women's activists for their position on the practice, Kenyan women's organizations explained that it was a "very sensitive subject" that was best combated through school education.[10] For organizations that sought to work with the government to improve women's status and to foster national unity, female genital cutting was too divisive an issue to raise. After all, President Kenyatta had furthered his political career just a few decades earlier by defending the practice.

Postcolonial population policies illustrate how such ambivalence was fueled by financial considerations as well as nationalist concerns. As we saw in chapter 4, by the 1950s, some colonial officials had begun to voice concern about rapid population growth in Kenya. Their concerns were part of an emerging international movement that feared that population growth in poor countries and colonies would soon outstrip global resources. The Colonial Office, however, refrained from promoting family planning for fear that it could be misinterpreted as a racist scheme to limit the "non-white" population. After independence, the Kenyatta government faced great pressure from expatriate advisors and international donors, particularly the United States–based Ford Foundation and the Population Council, to recognize rapid population growth as an obstacle to economic development. The new Kenyan government soon succumbed to this pressure; in 1967 it became the first country in sub-Saharan Africa to adopt a national population program. The key plank of the program was to make modern contraceptives, mainly birth control pills and intrauterine devices, available on a free and voluntary basis, as part of a nationwide system of maternal and child health services. By incorporating family planning within the provision of basic healthcare, the Kenyatta government hoped to appease donor demands while fulfilling its national promise to tackle "ignorance and sickness" through the establishment of more schools, hospitals, and health centers.[11]

During the late 1960s and through the 1970s the Kenyan government demonstrated its ambivalence toward population control policies by accepting millions of donor dollars to expand family planning services but doing little to promote their use. Prominent politicians openly expressed suspicions that family planning was a "colonial hang-over" and a genocidal plot.

In 1967 Oginga Odinga, an influential Luo politician and former vice-president, stated that population control was unnecessary, as Africa remained a sparsely populated continent. Kenyatta himself never publicly voiced support for family planning and forbid his name or photograph from being used in any family planning campaigns. Although dismayed by such attitudes, foreign donors continued to fund family planning programs in Kenya in the hope that politicians and the public would eventually be won over to the cause and provide a model for the rest of Africa. During the Kenyatta administration (1963–78), the average number of children born alive to a Kenyan woman actually rose from 7.0 to 7.9, leading Kenya to have the highest rate of natural population increase in the world.[12]

The Kenyatta government's decisions not to promote family planning, condemn female excision, or replace the Affiliation Act stemmed from a nationalist desire to develop policies that were neither simply derivative of colonial campaigns nor fully determined by the demands of international donors. They also stemmed from a deep-rooted concern that such "modern" reproductive reforms would promote immorality and promiscuity, and skew gender and generational relations. Just as opponents of the Affiliation Act claimed that monthly paternity payments encouraged female prostitution, some politicians and members of the public defended female excision as a practice that fostered morality and maturity in young women. Family planning programs faced similar condemnation, with critics arguing that birth control enabled promiscuity by reducing the social consequences of premarital and extramarital sexual relations. One government official expressed this sentiment in a 1970 survey of attitudes toward birth control: "Yes, now women can move loosely, some leaving their husbands shrunk cold in their houses. They do all the nonsense because they are sure the contraceptives will hide them. Unmarried girls are in fact worse. They feel that sexual intercourse is a normal and common link with men. This is morally damaging."[13] Reforms that appeared to increase women's reproductive options could easily be construed as promoting female depravity, undermining masculine authority, and challenging generational hierarchies. Such sentiments contributed to government policies that paid more attention to defending the status quo than to altering reproductive relations.

ONGOING POLITICS OF THE WOMB

Over the course of the 1990s, the decade during which this book was mostly researched and written, the national and international contexts within which reproductive debates took place changed significantly. The decade opened with demographic data revealing that the Kenyan national fertility rate had decreased to 6.7 births per woman. Another survey conducted in 1998 found that the rate had dropped further, to 4.7. Demographers attributed this dramatic decrease to changing attitudes about ideal family size and the increased use of modern contraceptives. After having invested billions of dollars and weathered substantial criticism, the international population movement and the national government proclaimed Kenya a family planning success story.[14]

The immediate roots of this demographic trend lay in the 1980s, when Kenyatta's successor, Daniel arap Moi, adopted a more aggressive stance toward population increase. Compelled by slow economic growth and the persistent need to secure donor support, Moi proclaimed that smaller families made economic sense for couples and the nation and endorsed the expansion of family planning services: the number of health workers trained in family planning doubled to more than two thousand, while the facilities distributing contraceptives rose from fewer than a hundred to more than four hundred.[15] While this expansion of services improved access to birth control, Kenya's worsening economy probably convinced many to use it. In the late 1970s, as world prices for Kenyan exports like tea and coffee fell, oil prices rose, and the Kenyan government went further into debt, per capita income began to drop; between 1980 and 1984 alone, the official minimum wage declined by 36 percent in real terms.[16] In the face of lower wages and the rising costs of raising children, a growing number of Kenyans began to use birth control. What population experts and politicians deemed a family planning success story was, for many Kenyans, part of a broader tale of increasing hardship.

The HIV/AIDS epidemic was another part of this tragic tale. When press reports of AIDS cases in Kenya first began to appear in the mid-1980s, some government officials and politicians denounced them as alarmist and racist. Voicing criticisms quite similar to those raised against family planning programs during the 1960s and 1970s, they argued that journalists were exaggerating the prevalence of AIDS and playing to deep-rooted Western stereotypes of Africa as a place of disease and promiscuity. Theories that located the origins of HIV in Africa only heightened official defensiveness. Pressing financial constraints also shaped the government's response. Some officials worried that too much attention to HIV/AIDS would hurt tourism. As the single largest earner of foreign currency in the Kenyan economy, tourism was crucial to the government's repayment of international loans and the purchasing of expensive imports, particularly oil.[17] Any thoughts of staging aggressive HIV/AIDS awareness and prevention campaigns also quickly confronted the reality that Kenya's healthcare system was already overburdened. Across much of sub-Saharan Africa, the onset of the AIDS epidemic coincided with the implementation of structural adjustment policies aimed at liberalizing economies by, among other things, reducing government spending on social services, including healthcare.[18] Faced with shrinking health budgets and mounting foreign debts, countries like Kenya had few internal resources to devote to combating HIV/AIDS. Moreover, few international and African leaders possessed the political will to raise the resources necessary to combat the epidemic in Africa.[19]

While global economic inequalities and inadequate leadership shaped international and national responses to HIV/AIDS, widespread poverty and imbalanced gender relations influenced its spread on the ground. By the end of the 1990s, the HIV infection rate among Kenyan adults (15–49 years) was estimated at 14 percent. Across Kenya, infection rates were disproportionately high for girls and young women; females between the ages of 15 and 24 are more than twice as likely as their male counterparts to be infected.[20] This disparity probably reflects the facts that the sexual organs of girls and young women are more vulnerable to the virus and that girls and young women are more inclined to have older sexual partners. Girls and young women with few material resources often use such relationships to acquire food, clothes, and cash to pay school fees and support their families. East and Central Africans frequently have attributed the spread of HIV/AIDS to women's and young people's insatiable desire for material things and unrestrained movement outside their homes.[21] Such popular perceptions cast HIV/AIDS as a moral problem while obscuring the disparities in wealth and power that facilitate its transmission.

In addition to growing poverty, decreasing fertility rates, and the spreading AIDS epidemic, the 1990s saw the proliferation of non-governmental organizations focused on reproductive matters. This proliferation stemmed from the intensification of second-wave feminism's global reach and donors' desires to steer resources into "grassroots" organizations and away from government ministries, which are often viewed as bloated, inefficient, and corrupt. Such shifts are well illustrated in debates over female genital cutting. While the decade of the 1990s began with few, if any, organizations in Kenya undertaking public education campaigns to discourage the practice, it ended with more than a dozen non-governmental organizations, supported by international funders like the Population Council and the United States Agency for International Development (USAID), engaged in such work.[22] International funding for these efforts was a direct result of activism undertaken by feminists from the United States and Europe and, later, the Middle East and Africa during the 1970s and 1980s. Deploying the term "female genital mutilation" (FGM), these activists cast female genital cutting as a human rights violation that promotes patriarchy, threatens women's health, and deprives women of experiencing sexual pleasure.[23] The influence of the anti-FGM movement was manifest in the 1994 Cairo Conference on Population and Development and in the 1995 Beijing Conference on Women, two United Nations' meetings that condemned FGM and urged governments to work toward its elimination. The movement's influence was also felt in Kenya, as women's and health organizations received encouragement and funding to campaign against FGM.

As with the international movement for population control, the anti-FGM movement both paralleled and fostered developments within Kenya. A few years after assuming office in 1978, President Moi publicly denounced female "circumcision" as a harmful practice that should end. Although this pronouncement did not criminalize the practice, it did signal to international donors that Moi, unlike Kenyatta, was willing to speak out against the practice.[24] Moi's condemnation also resonated with a growing number of Kenyans who were deciding not to have their daughters "circumcised." A 1998 survey found that whereas 54.2 percent of Meru/Embu women between the ages of 15 and 49 reported that they had been "circumcised," only 36.6 percent reported that their eldest daughters had been "circumcised."[25] Since the "female circumcision controversy" of 1928–31, the decision of whether or not to "circumcise" in central Kenya had been tied to issues of Christianity, schooling, and economic prosperity. In 1990s Meru, people who had repudiated the practice claimed that excision was most common in remote or "traditional" areas of the district, where Christian churches and school education had a shorter history of influence. Over the twentieth century, many Kenyan parents gradually accepted school as a more appropriate forum than initiation for preparing their daughters for their future roles as wives, mothers, and salaried employees.[26] Yet opposition to excision cannot be seen as an easy or enduring byproduct of school education. In Meru and elsewhere in East Africa, schoolgirls have often been excised.[27] Moreover, worsening economic conditions in Kenya may cause others to reconsider excision and female initiation. Fragmentary evidence suggests that as families find it increasingly difficult to pay rising school fees and job opportunities for school-educated young men and women become ever more scarce, schooling appears as a less attractive alternative to female initiation.[28]

During the 1990s a recognition that school education alone would not result in the "natural death" of excision combined with a growing international anti-FGM movement to encourage some non-governmental organizations to propose more interventionist approaches. One of the most publicized anti-FGM interventions undertaken by a non-governmental organization was the "ritual without cutting," or *ntanira na mugambo* (circumcision by words) held in the Tharaka area of Meru. Through this initiative, the national women's organization *Maendeleo ya Wanawake* and the Seattle-based Program for Appropriate Technology in Health (PATH) worked with local community groups to organize a week-long "seclusion" during which girls and young women were taught "traditional wisdom" and "family life skills" on topics ranging from personal hygiene to reproductive health to respectful behavior. The week culminated with a "coming-of-age ceremony" that included initiates' performance of songs and dramas with anti-FGM messages, feasting, gift giving, and the presentation of graduation certificates. The "ritual without cutting" was hailed by many opponents of excision within and outside Kenya as a culturally sensitive alternative. Yet it was also the subject of local rumors claiming that it was engineered by foreigners to promote the use of birth control among unmarried girls, including the injection of contraceptives into their clitorises.[29] Such rumors suggest how some still associated reproductive interventions—even interventions that work through "traditional wisdom" and local organizations—with imperialism, immorality, and anti-natalism.

Throughout the 1990s some anti-FGM activists urged the Kenyan government to introduce a law banning the practice. In addition to repeating long-standing arguments, these activists condemned the continuation of FGM for violating the "Platform for Action" adopted at the 1995 Beijing Conference and for facilitating the spread of HIV/AIDS through the use of unsterile instruments. Their opponents defended excision as a practice with "dignity" and took offense at arguments that linked it to AIDS, claiming that areas where the practice was prevalent had lower rates of HIV infection.[30] In 2001 the Kenyan government introduced a legal provision prohibiting "female circumcision" on those under the age of eighteen years. This provision was Section 14 of the expansive Children Act that, as mentioned in Chapter 5, also reintroduced limited elements of the Affiliation Act.[31] The Children Act aimed to bring Kenyan law in accordance with the 1989 United Nations Convention on the Rights of the Child prior to President Moi's attendance at a U.N. Special Session on Children, held in September 2001.[32] By introducing a ban on female genital cutting, the Kenyan government followed the lead of other African countries, including Senegal, Ghana, Burkino Faso, and Guinea, which during the 1990s responded to pressure from international funders and, in some instances, local constituencies by outlawing the practice.[33] While most Kenyan anti-FGM activists welcomed the ban as part of a multipronged strategy to end the practice, some voiced skepticism over whether the government would be willing or able to commit the resources necessary to enforce it.[34] In the months following the passage of the Act, Kenyan newspapers featured stories documenting the continuance of the practice, even at government hospitals.[35]

The intensity of FGM debates during the 1990s and the passage of the Children Act in 2001 underscore the persistent relevance of female genital cutting and other reproductive practices to struggles over political and moral order. Like colonial opponents of the practice, more contemporary anti-FGM activists have viewed excision as a brutal practice and intolerable manifestation of women's oppression. By denouncing it for endangering "tribal" populations, threatening maternal and infant health, violating human rights, or denying women sexual pleasure, colonial and postcolonial activists have tied the elimination of excision to broader visions of political and moral reform. Postcolonial FGM debates, however, also highlight important shifts in the politics of the womb over the twentieth century. By the 1990s, a wider range of people had declared themselves to be opponents of the practice. They included African-American novelist Alice Walker, countless journalists, and the leaders of many women's and community organizations in Kenya and other African countries.

The material resources at stake in such campaigns had also changed dramatically. Colonial campaigns ultimately foundered on the threat that they posed to political stability and imperial prosperity. The Kenyan colonial government's decision in 1930 not to prohibit excision, and its eventual dismissal of the 1956 ban, arose from the realization that these measures were unenforceable without time-consuming and costly administrative action. Such action risked undermining Kenya's position as a viable and, for some, profitable colony. By contrast, postcolonial anti-FGM initiatives have been tied to the influx rather than the outflow of material resources. The dramatic increase in anti-FGM work by Kenyan non-governmental organizations during the 1990s and the passage of the Children Act was fueled by ubiquitous donor interest in ending the practice. The opposition of Kenyan activists and politicians to FGM cannot be disentangled from the preoccupations of their funders; female genital cutting and other local reproductive practices have become enmeshed in a global web of political hierarchies and economic inequalities. Within this context, it remains to be seen whether those who defy the Children Act's provision on excision will be prosecuted, and whether the "ritual without cutting" or similar interventions can provide enduring strategies for ensuring material prosperity and constructing moral persons.

. . .

Across the twentieth century, reproduction was such a fraught realm of state intervention in Kenya because it stood at the heart of people's efforts to cultivate successful families, communities, empires, and nations. Through managing female initiation, pregnancy, and childbirth, parents and elders sought to create respectful and prosperous descendants and juniors. The colonial and, later, postcolonial state similarly saw such processes as crucial to cultivating loyal and productive subjects and citizens. Competing reproductive concerns prompted some of the most intrusive episodes of colonial intervention and the most virulent moments of anti-colonial protest. But the colonial politics of the womb was never simply a matter of black versus white. Rather, it entailed entanglement: the uneven mixing of the old and the new, the indigenous and the imperial. Over time, the colonial politics of the womb changed the way many central Kenyan women came of age and gave birth. Through reworking reproductive processes, politicians, reformers, parents, and young people elaborated new distinctions based in schooling, Christianity, and class. By the early postcolonial period, one's approach to matters of female initiation, pregnancy, and childbirth had become a sign of belonging to either the "modern" or the "traditional." Yet even the lives of the "modern" could never be fully detached from older hierarchies rooted in local notions of gender, generation, and wealth.

Contemporary politics of the womb need to be understood as part of a long history of struggles over who should control women's sexuality and who should bear the responsibility for and reap the rewards of women's fertility. Over the course of the twentieth century, reproductive concerns within central Kenya became increasingly entangled with those emanating from outside—first, from Nairobi and London and, later, from New York, Cairo, and Beijing. This entanglement was a piece of the far-reaching political projects of colonization, modernization, and, more recently, globalization. Although these projects have been enormously influential, they have never been all encompassing. The reproductive concerns that they have introduced vied and combined with those that already existed in Kenya. In the twenty-first century, perhaps more than ever, we need to understand how reproductive and sexual politics in Africa and elsewhere encompass struggles to accumulate material resources and fulfill moral ambitions, struggles that bind the global to the local.

Notes

INTRODUCTION

1. Notes of T. H. R. Cashmore (in Cashmore's personal possession) concerning the following document: S. H. Fazan, DC, Kiambu, report on performance of Muthirigu, 12 January 1930, KNA, ADM/1. Cashmore graciously shared with me notes that he had taken of Fazan's report.

2. Throughout this book, I use *female genital cutting* as an umbrella term to refer to practices ranging from removal of part of the clitoris to the removal of all of the clitoris, labia minora, and most of the labia majora. The term *excision* more specifically denotes the removal of the clitoris and all or part of the labia minora, the most common form of female genital cutting practiced in twentieth-century central Kenya. Unlike the use of "female circumcision," *excision* does not suggest equivalency between the genital cuttings performed on women and male circumcision. I use the term *circumcision* in quoting oral sources, as it is the most widely accepted translation from both the Kikuyu and Meru languages and reflects the fact that in those languages the same term is used to refer to male and female genital cutting. I refrain from using the term *female genital mutilation* (FGM) except when referring to postcolonial campaigns against the practice because of the term's condemnatory denotation. For more on terminological issues, see Shell-Duncan and Hernlund, "Female 'Circumcision' in Africa," 3–13. To reflect the change to adult status which initiation conferred, I will refer to all unexcised females as girls even though, during the 1920s and 1930s, some initiates appear to have been 25 years of age or older.

3. Rosberg and Nottingham, *The Myth of "Mau Mau,"* ch. 4; Murray, "The Kikuyu Female Circumcision Controversy"; Murray, "The Church Missionary Society"; Tignor, *The Colonial Transformation of Kenya,* ch. 10; Spencer, *The Kenya African Union,* 72–79; Sandgren, *Christianity and the Kikuyu,* 90–95; Clough, *Fighting Two Sides,* ch. 7; Pedersen, "National Bodies"; Lonsdale, "The Moral Economy"; Hetherington, "The Politics of Female Circumcision"; Karanja, *Founding an African Faith,* 181–90.

4. Clive Irvine, "Chogoria, 1930," KNA, MSS; Church of Scotland, "Memorandum prepared by the Kikuyu Mission Council on Female Circumcision," 1 December 1931, PRO, CO/533/418; Macpherson, *The Presbyterian Church*, 104–16; Nthamburi, *A History of the Methodist Church*, 72.

5. Bayart, *The State in Africa*.

6. Madan and Johnson, *A Standard Swahili–English Dictionary*, 478. Other dictionaries list a more precise phrase for "womb": "*tumbo la uzazi*" (the belly of reproduction); see Madan and Johnson, *A Standard English–Swahili Dictionary*, 628; Snoxall, *A Concise English–Swahili Dictionary*, 314; Perrott, *The E.U.P. Concise Swahili and English Dictionary*, 183; Rechenbech, *Swahili–English Dictionary*, 539. In English, too, "womb" is an obsolete term for "belly"; see *Webster's New World College Dictionary*, 1646. Today, Swahili-speakers in Kenya commonly use the phrase "*nyumba ya mtoto*" (house of the child) to refer to the womb. In the Meru language, the words for womb *(iu)* and belly *(kiu)* are closely related terms.

7. While Bayart pays little attention to reproduction, sexuality, or gender, he does acknowledge *(The State in Africa*, xviii) that the "politics of the belly are also the politics of intimate liaisons" and that in many precolonial societies women were "the substance of wealth itself."

8. Stoler and Cooper, "Between Metropole and Colony," 18–21. For an earlier statement of the "moral and material obligations" of imperial rule, see Lugard, *The Dual Mandate*, 58.

9. Feierman and Janzen, Introduction, 12.

10. Das, *Critical Events*, 5–6.

11. I use the adjective "premarital" to describe pregnancies among unmarried girls and women, usually in their teens or early twenties. In using this term, I do not intend to suggest that all these girls and women eventually did marry.

12. Hunt, "Placing African Women's History." Hunt's *A Colonial Lexicon* goes a long way toward correcting this silence. Amadiume, *Male Daughters*, and Oyewùmí, *The Invention of Women*, have similarly pointed to Western feminists' refusal to examine the centrality of fertility and maternity in African women's lives as an example of how exogenous rather than indigenous categories and concerns continue to inform Africanist scholarship. Yet social and cultural anthropologists, through their interest in kinship, have long taken matters of the womb quite seriously. This study engages that anthropological literature by casting many of its key insights into historical perspective. Other scholarship that has been crucial to my thinking about reproduction includes Meillassoux, "From Reproduction to Production"; Harris and Young, "Engendered Structures"; Collier and Yanagisako, *Gender and Kinship*; Handwerker, *Births and Power*; Ginsburg and Rapp, "The Politics of Reproduction"; Meillassoux, *The Anthropology of Slavery*; Ginsburg and Rapp, *Conceiving the New World Order*; and Stevens, *Reproducing the State*.

13. For instance, see D'Emilio and Freedman, Introduction; and Vance, "Anthropology Rediscovers Sexuality."

14. For more on my research methodology, see the Interviews section of the Bibliography.

15. Spivak, "Can the Subaltern Speak?"; Mohanty, "Under Western Eyes"; Alcoff, "The Problem of Speaking for Others."

16. Kenya Bureau of Statistics, *The 1999 Population and Housing Census*, xxxiii.

17. Kenyatta, *Facing Mount Kenya*, xv.

18. Haugerud, *The Culture of Politics*, 60; Ambler, *Kenyan Communities*. Central Kenyan languages, including Kikuyu, Chuka, Embu/Mbeere, Sonjo, Tharaka, Meru, Kamba, and Daiso, all belong to the Thagicu subgroup of Northeast Coast Bantu (Spear, *Kenya's Past*, 38–40).

19. On the colonial construction of "tribal" identities in East Africa, see Iliffe, *A Modern History of Tanganyika*, ch. 10; Willis, *Mombasa*; and Bravman, *Making Ethnic Ways*.

20. Fadiman, *The Moment of Conquest*; Bernard, "Meru District"; Maupeu, *L'Administration indirecte*.

21. It is important to note that not all Kenyan communities practiced or continue to practice female genital cutting as part of female initiation. Female genital cutting has largely been limited to communities living in the central highlands and Rift Valley areas.

22. Robinson, "Kenya Enters the Fertility Transition"; Brass and Jolly, *Population Dynamics of Kenya*; Egero and Mburugu, "Kenya"; National Council for Population and Development, Central Bureau of Statistics (Office of the Vice President and the Ministry of Planning and National Development) [Kenya], and Macro International, Inc., *Kenya Demographic and Health Survey, 1998*.

23. Packard, *Epidemiologists*; Treichler, "AIDS and HIV Infection."

24. Jordan, *White Over Black*, ch. 4; Davis, *Women, Race and Class*, chs. 1–2; Omolade, "Heart of Darkness"; Morgan, "Women in Slavery"; Morgan, "Some Could Suckle over Their Shoulder."

25. Ferguson, *Subject to Others*; Midgley, *Women Against Slavery*; Burton, *Burdens of History*.

26. Foucault, *The History of Sexuality*; Weeks, *Sex, Politics, and Society*; Riley, *"Am I that Name?,"* ch. 3; Teitelbaum and Winter, *Population and Resources*; Soloway, *Demography and Degeneration*; Koven and Michel, *Mothers of a New World*; Horn, *Social Bodies*; Quine, *Population Politics*.

27. Davin, "Imperialism and Motherhood"; Hunt, "Le bébé en brousse"; Hunt, *A Colonial Lexicon*, chs. 1, 5–6; Summers, "Intimate Colonialism"; Vaughan, *Curing Their Ills*; Stoler, "Carnal Knowledge"; Stoler, *Race and the Education of Desire*; Beinert, "Darkly Through a Lens"; Allman, "Making Mothers"; Burns, "Reproductive Labors"; Odinga, "Criminalizing the Sick"; Ram and Jolly, *Maternities and Modernities*.

28. Hardinge, *Report on the East Africa Protectorate*, 25; Eliot, *Report on the East Africa Protectorate* (18 April 1903), 29, cited in Kuczynski, *Demographic Survey*, 3:216; Eliot, *The East Africa Protectorate*, 57.

29. Turshen, *The Political Ecology of Disease;* Turshen, "Population Growth"; Dawson, "Health, Nutrition, and Population"; Iliffe, *A Modern History,* ch. 5; van Zwanenberg with King, *An Economic History,* ch. 1.

30. Paterson, "Population in Kenya," 301.

31. Kennedy, *Islands of White,* 22–23, 138–55, 197; Berman, *Control and Crisis in Colonial Kenya,* 143–60.

32. Kennedy, *Islands of White,* 142–44. On black peril scares elsewhere, see van Onselen, "The Witches of Suburbia," 45–54; Hansen, *Distant Companions,* 98–106; Stoler, "Carnal Knowledge," 67–70; and McCulloch, *Black Peril.*

33. Kennedy, *Islands of White,* 174; Hyam, *Empire and Sexuality,* 160–70; Strobel, *European Women,* 4, 49–51; Stoler, "Carnal Knowledge," 57–62.

34. Gillan, "Notes on the Kikuyu Custom"; Church of Scotland, "Memorandum prepared by the Kikuyu Mission Council on Female Circumcision," 1 December 1931, PRO, CO/533/418; Pedersen, "National Bodies," 656–66.

35. U.K., *Report of the East Africa Commission* (1925), 54, cited in Kuczynski, *Demographic Survey,* 3:188; Kenya Colony and Protectorate, Medical Department, *Annual Report* (1925), 17.

36. Herbert, *Iron, Gender, and Power;* Schoenbrun, *A Green Place,* esp. ch. 3.

37. Rimita, *The Njuri-Ncheke,* 30–31. A similar legend is contained in M'Inoti, "Asili ya Wameru." Laughton, "An Introductory Study," describes a time when bridewealth (properly called dowry) went from the bride's to the groom's family rather than vice versa.

38. Kenyatta, *Facing Mount Kenya,* 5–10; Lambert, "History of the Tribal Occupation of the Land," 19–21; Leakey, *The Southern Kikuyu,* 1:48–50; Shaw, *Colonial Inscriptions,* 33–36; Haugerud, *The Culture of Politics,* 113.

39. Guyer and Belinga ("Wealth in People") insightfully argue that within African studies the concept of wealth in people has often been wrongly used to situate "material adaptation and social simplicity" as the keys to understanding precolonial societies. This study shares with Guyer and Belinga a desire to rid the concept of wealth in people of its evolutionary underpinnings by emphasizing knowledge composition as an important part of why people were and are valued, and by insisting on reproduction as a site of political struggle. Recent works that identify population growth as the central theme in the longue durée of African history, or low population densities as the greatest challenge facing postcolonial states, attest to the continued power of biological and demographic determinism within African studies. Such works overlook the varied interests and ideas that have informed procreative practices and underwritten population trends. See, for example, Iliffe, *Africans;* and Herbst, *States and Power in Africa.*

40. Ambler, *Kenyan Communities,* 25.

41. Lonsdale, "The Moral Economy," 327; Kenyatta, *Facing Mount Kenya,* 168–70; Ciancanelli, "Exchange, Reproduction."

42. Kenyatta, *Facing Mount Kenya,* 157–58; E. Mary Holding, "Meru Names," n.d., KNA, MSS/7; Laughton, "An Introductory Study," 22–23, 77.

On the need to understand sexuality in Africa as a religious and moral matter, see Ahlberg, "Is There a Distinct African Sexuality?"; and Heald, *Manhood and Morality*, ch. 8.

43. Kenyatta, *Facing Mount Kenya*, ch. 9; Muriuki, *A History of the Kikuyu*, ch. 5; Ambler, *Kenyan Communities*, ch. 1. Generational sets were another key political institution in precolonial central Kenya; in Meru, each age-grade belonged to one of two alternating generational sets named *kiruka* and *ntiba* (Lambert, *The Use of Indigenous Authorities*, 4; Bernardi, *The Mugwe*, ch. 1; Bernardi, *Age Class Systems*, 133–34; Peatrik, "Age, generation et temps").

44. Laughton, "An Introductory Study," 128–34; Holding, "Some Preliminary Notes"; Laughton, *The Meru*, 3–5; Lambert, *The Use of Indigenous Authorities*, 1–6; Kangoi, "A History of the Tigania"; Mwaniki, "The Chuka Struggle for Survival"; Muthamia, "A Study of Political Development"; Riungu, "Political History of Imenti"; Fadiman, "The Meru Peoples"; Fadiman, *An Oral History of Tribal Warfare*.

45. Holding, "Women's Institutions"; Holding, "Some Preliminary Notes." For accounts of women's councils in Kikuyu areas, see Kenyatta, *Facing Mount Kenya*, 108; Clark, "Land and Food"; Stamp, "Kikuyu Women's Self-Help Groups"; Wipper, "Kikuyu Women"; Ahlberg, *Women, Sexuality*, 6, 62; Presley, *Kikuyu Women*, 27–28, 181; and Robertson, "Grassroots in Kenya," 617.

46. Laughton, "An Introductory Study"; Kenyatta, *Facing Mount Kenya*, esp. ch. 1; Leakey, *The Southern Kikuyu*, 1:6–12; Clark, "Land and Food"; Ahlberg, *Women, Sexuality*, ch. 10. Based on similar evidence, others (Lonsdale, "The Moral Economy," esp. 340–41, 385; Kershaw, *Mau Mau from Below*, esp. 23–24) have argued that male and female roles in early-twentieth-century central Kenya were different but "essentially equal."

47. In reference to precapitalist societies in southern Africa, Guy ("Gender Oppression," 46–47) similarly speaks of women's fertility as the basis of both their "oppression" and their "social standing and social integrity." Some anthropologists have interpreted contemporary practices of female genital cutting in closely related terms. Janice Boddy (*Wombs and Alien Spirits*, 319) has argued that in Sudan "circumcision and its social implications are strategically used by women as bargaining tools with which to negotiate subaltern status and enforce their complementarity with men." Based on research among the Okiek of Kenya, Corinne Kratz (*Affecting Performance*, 347) describes female initiation as "the primary context in which women come together as a group, constituting a ritual community and a forum for social critique."

48. On the problematic prominence of a "female solidarity model" over a "stratification model" within studies of African women, see Bledsoe, "The Political Use."

49. Laughton, "An Introductory Study"; Laughton, *The Meru*; H. E. Lambert, "The Meru Yet to Come," 25 December 1941, KNA, PC/CP/4/4/7; Lam-

bert, *The Use of Indigenous Authorities;* Holding, "Women's Institutions"; E. M. Holding, "The Understanding of Indigenous Sex Relationships," essay submitted as part of final exam, 1940, MOM, 17; E. Mary Holding, "The Education of a Bantu Tribe," unpublished manuscript, c. 1963–64, RH, MSS/Afr/r/117.

50. Nyaga, *Mĩkarĩre na Mĩtũũrĩre ya Amĩĩrũ;* and a revised version published in English, *Customs and Traditions of the Meru.*

51. Chege, "Dynamics of the Regulation of Sexuality," 2. Also see Greeley, "Men and Fertility Regulation"; Greeley, "Planning for Population Change"; and Fadiman, *When We Began,* chs. 10–13. Jeater (*Marriage, Perversion, and Power*) presents an updated version of the "breakdown of tradition" thesis by analyzing debates over marriage and morality in Southern Rhodesia as clashes between two fundamentally incongruent epistemes, an African one that judged sexual acts "in terms of their impact upon the lineage," and an ultimately victorious European one that assessed sexual acts as "right or wrong in themselves" (260).

52. See Ferguson, *Expectations of Modernity,* ch. 5, for a discussion of the influence of the "breakdown" approach within studies of family life on the Zambian Copperbelt.

53. Important works in this vein that address African bodies and colonialism include Gilman, "Black Bodies"; Mitchell, *Colonising Egypt,* esp. ch. 4; Vaughan, *Curing Their Ills;* Comaroff, "Medicine"; McClintock, *Imperial Leather;* Shaw, *Colonial Inscriptions;* and Butchart, *The Anatomy of Power.*

54. The piece that most forcefully highlights these methodological challenges is Spivak, "Can the Subaltern Speak?," esp. 298–308. Works on colonialism in Africa that have considered these same issues include Hunt, Introduction; and White, *Speaking with Vampires.*

55. In this passage, Hamilton (*Terrific Majesty,* 3–4) is critiquing the scholarship on ethnicity and "customary" law in colonial Africa, specifically that of Mamdani in *Citizen and Subject.* For other discussions of the importance of "entanglement" to understanding colonial and postcolonial history, see Thomas, *Entangled Objects;* and Mbembe, *On the Postcolony,* esp. 14–17.

56. Cohen and Odhiambo, *Burying SM;* Hansen, *African Encounters;* Burns, "Louisa Mvemve"; Burke, *Lifebuoy Men;* Landau, *The Realm of the Word;* Comaroff and Comaroff, *Of Revelation and Revolution,* vol. 2; Feeley-Harnik, "Dying Gods"; Feldman-Savelsberg, *Plundered Kitchens;* Hunt, *A Colonial Lexicon;* Sadowsky, *Imperial Bedlam;* Setel, *A Plague of Paradoxes;* and White, *Speaking with Vampires.*

CHAPTER 1: IMPERIAL POPULATIONS AND "WOMEN'S AFFAIRS"

1. On British military recruitment in colonial East Africa, see Parsons, *The African Rank-and-File,* chs. 2–3.

2. Meru District, Annual Report [hereafter AR], 1939, KNA, DC/MRU/1/1/4.

3. Ambler, "The Renovation of Custom," 149.

4. Church of Scotland, "Memorandum prepared by the Kikuyu Mission Council," 1 December 1931, PRO, CO/533/418/2; Rosberg and Nottingham, *The Myth of "Mau Mau,"* 114; Murray-Brown, *Kenyatta*, 51–52.

5. Philp, "Native Gynecology"; Philp, "Artificial Atresia"; Philp, "Vescical Fistula"; Gillan, "Notes on the Kikuyu Custom"; Church of Scotland, "Memorandum prepared by the Kikuyu Mission Council," 1 December 1931, PRO, CO/533/418/2.

6. Sheehan, "Victorian Clitoridectomy"; Jalland and Hooper, *Women from Birth to Death*, 250–65; Masson, *A Dark Science*, 137–38.

7. Davin, "Imperialism and Motherhood"; Hunt, " 'Le bébé en brousse' "; Summers, "Intimate Colonialism"; Hunt, *A Colonial Lexicon*, chs. 1, 6; van Beusekom, "From Underpopulation to Overpopulation."

8. Wylie, "Confrontation Over Kenya"; Wipper, "Kikuyu Women"; Berman, *Control and Crisis*, ch. 4; Clough, *Fighting Two Sides*, chs. 3, 5.

9. O. F. Watkins, Ag. Chief Native Commissioner, Native Affairs Department, Circular No. 36, 21 September 1925, KNA, DC/KBU/7/3, reproduced in Murray, "The Kikuyu Female Circumcision Controversy," 122–23; Meru LNC, Minutes, 8 August 1925, 12 October 1925, and 1–3 June 1927, MCC, LNC/1; Meru District, AR, 1926, KNA, DC/MRU/1/1/2.

10. Murray, "The Kikuyu Female Circumcision Controversy," 136–44.

11. Lord Passfield, Secretary of State for the Colonies, London, to Edward Grigg, Governor, Kenya, "Despatch No. 123," 6 February 1930, PRO, CO/533/394/10; Murray-Brown, *Kenyatta*, chs. 11, 16.

12. Kenyatta, *Facing Mount Kenya*, 128.

13. *Parliamentary Debates*, Commons, 5th ser., 233 (11 December 1929), cols. 443–45, 581–616. See also *Parliamentary Debates*, Commons, 5th ser., 233 (12 December 1929), cols. 680–81; ibid. (13 December 1929), col. 844; ibid. (16 December 1929) cols. 1001–1004; ibid. (23 December 1929), col. 1948.

14. Pedersen, "National Bodies," 666–74.

15. J. L. Gilks, Director of Medical and Sanitary Services, Nairobi, to Chief Native Commissioner, Nairobi, "Female Circumcision," 6 September 1930, KNA, Health 2/164.

16. H. M. Moore, Ag. Governor, Kenya, to Lord Passfield, Secretary of State for the Colonies, London, 6 November 1930, PRO, CO/533/394/11; Drummond Shiels, Under-Secretary of State for the Colonies, London, to Duchess of Atholl, member of the House of Commons, London, 1 January 1931, PRO, CO/533/394/11.

17. Meru District, AR, 1910, KNA, PC/CP/1/9/1.

18. Meru District, AR, 1923, KNA, DC/MRU/1/1/1.

19. Meru District, AR, 1924, KNA, DC/MRU/1/1/1.

20. E. B. Denham, Ag. Governor, Kenya, "Reports by the Acting Governor on His Visits to the Nyanza and Kikuyu Provinces and the District of Kitui,"

15 September 1925, PRO, CO/533/333. See also Great Britain, *Report of the East African Commission* (1925), 54, cited in Kuczynski, *Demographic Survey*, 3:188.

21. A. B. Cohen to T. Stanton, Colonial Office, London, file notes, 21 December 1936, PRO, CO/323/1463/5.

22. Brookes, *Abortion in England*, 41–42.

23. S. Mwari, interview, 22 April 1995.

24. S. Imathiu and M. Zachary, interview, 15 September 1990; M. Roben, R. M'Mwendwa, T. M'Angaine, and I. M'Arimba, interview, 15 September 1990; C. M'Barungu, interview, 8 May 1995; M. Kaimuri, interview, 12 May 1995; G. M'Itiri and W. M'Rarama, interview, 18 May 1995; V. Ciothirangi, interview, 6 June 1995.

25. Orde Brown, "Circumcision Ceremonies," 137.

26. J. M'Ruiga, interview, 19 May 1995.

27. G. Kirimi, interview, 1 August 1995; J. M'Itwaruchiu, interview, 5 August 1999; Meru District, AR, 1934, KNA, DC/MRU/1/1/2.

28. Z. Karegi, interview, 7 August 1995; C. M'Barungu, interview, 8 May 1995; M. Kaimuri, interview, 12 May 1995.

29. B. Tiira, interview, 30 March 1995; E. Mary Holding, "The Understanding of Indigenous Sex Relationships," 1940, MOM, 17.

30. M. Ncence, interview, 12 September 1990; B. Tiira, interview, 30 March 1995; V. Ciothirangi, interview, 6 June 1995; E. Mary Holding, "The Understanding of Indigenous Sex Relationships," 1940, MOM, 17.

31. E. Mary Holding, "The Understanding of Indigenous Sex Relationships," 1940, MOM, 17. See also Laughton, "An Introductory Study"; Laughton, *The Meru*, 13–16.

32. E. Mary Holding, "The Understanding of Indigenous Sex Relationships," 1940, MOM, 17.

33. Orde Browne, "Circumcision Ceremonies among the Amwimbe," 138.

34. V. Ciothirangi, interview, 6 June 1995.

35. M. Ntuti, interview, 24 January 1995; B. Tiira, interview, 30 March 1995; S. Mwari, interview, 22 April 1995; M. Karoki, interview, 5 April 1995; E. M'Iringo, interview, 4 August 1995; Z. Karegi, interview, 7 August 1995.

36. Orde Brown, "Circumcision Ceremonies among the Amwimbe," 139–40; Orde Brown, "Circumcision Ceremony in Chuka," 66–67; Clive Irvine, "Yaws in East Kenya," unpublished manuscript, 1925, Chogoria Mission Archive, Clive Irvine papers; E. Mary Holding, "Notes on Girls' Circumcision" and "The Functions of Women's Institutions in Meru Society," typescripts, n.d., KNA, MSS/7; M. Karoki, interview, 5 April 1995.

37. Orde Brown, "Circumcision Ceremonies among the Amwimbe," 140.

38. S. Mwari, interview, 22 April 1995; B. Tiira, interview, 30 March 1995; M. Karoki, interview, 5 April 1995.

39. Davison, *Voices from Mutira*, 60.

40. Nyaga, *Customs and Traditions of the Meru*, ch. 8.

41. Das, *Critical Events*, 178.

42. M. Karoki, interview, 5 April 1995; P. M'Kuru, interview, 22 April 1995; M. Kaimuri, interview, 12 May 1995; J. M'Mugambi, interview, 10 June 1995; P. Mwirichia, interview, 15 June 1995; E. M'Iringo, interview, 4 August 1995.

43. C. M'Lithara, interview, 30 January 1995; G. Mwitiabi, interview, 31 March 1995; J. Karea, interview, 24 March 1995; C. M'Barungu, interview, 8 May 1995; J. M'Ruiga, interview, 19 May 1995; V. Ciothirangi, interview, 6 June 1995; P. Mwirichia, interview, 15 June 1995.

44. M. Karoki, interview, 5 April 1995; R. Kanini, interview, 18 May 1995; E. M'Iringo, interview, 4 August 1995.

45. J. M'Mugambi, interview, 10 June 1995.

46. E. Mary Holding, "The Understanding of Indigenous Sex Relationships," 1940, MOM, 17; Holding, "Women's Institutions"; Holding, "Some Preliminary Notes"; E. Mary Holding, "The Functions of Women's Institutions in Meru Society," typescript, n.d., KNA, MSS/7; E. Mary Holding, "*Nthoni,*" typescript, n.d., KNA, MSS/7. On *nthoni,* see also Laughton, "An Introductory Study"; Chege, "Dynamics of the Regulation of Sexuality," 11–12; and Thomas, "Old Age in Meru, Kenya," ch. 6.

47. T. Maigene, interview, 17 October 1990; M. Igoki, interview, 18 October 1990. See also M'Inoti, "Asili ya Wameru na tabia zao," 4–5.

48. Holding, "Women's Institutions," 296–97.

49. C. M. Dobbs, Ag. Chief Native Commissioner, "Memorandum on Infanticide," 12 January 1930, RH, MSS/Afr/s/665/1; Lema and Njau, "Abortion in Kenya," 42–45; Kanogo, "The Medicalization of Maternity in Colonial Kenya," 89–92.

50. H. E. Lambert, "Notes on Difference between Kikuyu and Meru Tribe," 1 January 1934, JKML, Lambert/1/7/1; and H. E. Lambert, "The Meru Yet to Come," 25 December 1941, KNA, PC/CP/4/4/7.

51. Richards, *Chisungu,* 33–34; McKittrick, "Faithful Daughter," 268. See also Schapera, "Premarital Pregnancy"; and Setel, *A Plague of Paradoxes,* 45.

52. S. Ayub and E. Evangeline, interview, 12 September 1990; S. Mwari, interview, 22 April 1995; P. Mwirichia, interview, 15 June 1995. On the value of virginity in central Kenya, see Nyaga, *Customs and Traditions of the Meru,* 93–96; and Shaw, *Colonial Inscriptions,* 82–89.

53. Kenyatta, *Facing Mount Kenya,* 149–54; Leakey, *The Southern Kikuyu,* 1:418–19, 2:703–6, 813; Ahlberg, *Women, Sexuality,* 61–62; Shaw, *Colonial Inscriptions,* 72–74.

54. M. Kithinji, interview, 9 June 1995.

55. Laughton, "An Introductory Study," 60.

56. S. Ayub and E. Evangeline, interview, 6 September 1990; M. Ncence, interview, 12 September 1990; E. M'Ithinji and J. Kiruja, interview, 14 October 1990; B. Tiira, interview, 30 March 1995; J. M'Ikiao, interview, 1 May 1995.

57. M. Karoki, interview, 5 April 1995.

58. M'Inoti, "Asili ya Wameru na tabia zao," 4–5; Laughton, "An Introductory Study," 59; S. Ayub and E. Evangeline, interview, 6 September 1990; T.

Maigene, interview, 17 October 1990; M. Igoki, interview, 18 October 1990; I. M'Arimba and I. Ntui, interview, 13 October 1990; R. Ncoro, interview, 8 February 1995; J. Karea, interview, 24 March 1995; E. Kabita, interview, 3 May 1995; V. Ciothirangi, interview, 6 June 1995.

59. M. Karoki, interview, 5 April 1995.

60. M'Inoti, "Asili ya Wameru na tabia zao," 4–5; S. Ayub and E. Evangeline, interview, 6 September 1990; M. Ncence, interview, 12 September 1990; E. M'Ithinji and J. Kiruja, interview, 14 September 1990; T. Maigene, interview, 17 October 1990; M. Igoki, interview, 18 October 1990; Alice Thirindi, interviewed by Jeffrey Fadiman, c. 1969–70, BLUCB, 96/49.

61. S. Ayub and E. Evangeline, interview, 6 September 1990; M. Ncence, interview, 12 September 1990; E. M'Ithinji and J. Kiruja, interview, 14 October 1990; T. Maigene, interview, 17 October 1990; M. Igoki, interview, 18 October 1990; Z. Kagugira, interview, 28 December 1994; E. Kabita, interview, 3 May 1995.

62. M'Inoti, "Asili ya Wameru na tabia zao," 4.

63. H. E. Lambert, "The Meru Yet to Come," 25 December 1941, KNA, PC/CP/4/4/7. This booklet, which was translated into Meru and published by the East African Literature Bureau, sold with little success.

64. Laughton, "An Introductory Study," 60.

65. P. M'Kuru, interview, 22 April 1995; S. Ayub and E. Evangeline, interview, 6 September 1990; I. M'Arimba and I. Ntui, interview, 13 October 1990; E. M'Ithinji and S. Kiruja, interview, 14 October 1990; F. M'Rintari, interview, 3 November 1990.

66. Quotes from H. E. Lambert, "The Meru Yet to Come," 25 December 1941, KNA, PC/CP/4/4/7. For similar accounts, see D. M'Kaiga, interview, 6 June 1995; N. M'Imanyara, interview, 27 October 1990; Laughton, "An Introductory Study," 60–61; E. Mary Holding, "The Understanding of Indigenous Sex Relationships," 1940, MOM, 5–6.

67. For other accounts of how poverty, famine, and land scarcity led to delayed initiation and marriage, see Reining et al., *Village Women*, 16; White, *The Comforts of Home*, 35–40; Kershaw, *Mau Mau from Below*, 6; and Setel, *A Plague of Paradoxes*, 47.

68. van Zwanenberg, *An Economic History*, ch. 1; Dawson, "Health, Nutrition," 187–200; Fadiman, *When We Began*, ch. 10.

69. J. G. Hopkins, District Commissioner, Embu, to Provincial Commissioner, Kikuyu, 27 December 1928, KNA, PC/CP/8/1/1.

70. Meru LNC, Minutes, 26 September 1967, MCC, LNC/1; F. M. Lamb, District Commissioner, Meru, to Provincial Commissioner, Kikuyu, 20 December 1928, KNA, PC/CP/8/1/1.

71. Meru District, AR, 1927, KNA, DC/MRU/1/1/2.

72. Meru LNC, Minutes, 17 March 1937, MCC, LNC/3.

73. Howman, *African Local Government*, 32, cited in Berman, "Bureaucracy and Incumbent Violence," 247. See also "Draft of Dr. Sheils' Interview with Mr. Kenyatta," 23 January 1930, PRO, CO/533/384/9; Secretary of State

for the Colonies to the Governor of Kenya, 9 July 1930, PRO, CO/533/398/11; S. V. Cooke, Killincoole, Ireland, to Undersecretary of State for the Colonies, London, 18 March 1931, PRO, CO/533/409.

74. Meru District, AR, 1928, KNA, DC/MRU/1/1/2.

75. Meru District, AR, 1925, 1933, and 1934, KNA, DC/MRU/1/1/2.

76. Meru LNC, Minutes: 29 August 1928, 23 November 1928, MCC, LNC/1; 27 November 1930, MCC, LNC/2; 25 May 1938, 8–9 August 1939, 7 December 1939, MCC, LNC/3; 21 March 1941, MCC, LNC/4.

77. Meru District, AR, 1928, KNA, DC/MRU/1/1/2; Meru LNC, Minutes, 29 August 1928, MCC, LNC/1.

78. Lambert, *The Use of Indigenous Authorities,* 21.

79. Meru District, AR, 1927, 1928, KNA, DC/MRU/1/1/2.

80. Kitching, *Class and Economic Change,* ch. 7; Berman, *Control and Crisis,* 216–17; Stamp, "Local Government"; Bayart, *The State in Africa,* 73, 111.

81. S. H. La Fontaine, Ag. Provincial Commissioner, Kikuyu, to A. de V. Wade, Ag. Chief Native Commissioner, Nairobi, 24 July 1931, KNA, PC/CP/8/1/2.

82. Meru LNC, Minutes, 29 January 1932, MCC, LNC/1. In 1934 Lambert convinced the Meru LNC to amend the 1932 resolution to limit excision to the removal of the *glans clitoridis* (Meru LNC, Minutes, 8 August 1934, MCC, LNC/2). On M'Ngaine, see Meru District, AR, 1931 and 1934, KNA, DC/MRU/1/1; and Meru, Handing Over Report, 1935, KNA, DC/MRU/1/3/1.

83. E. M'Ithinji and J. Kiruja, interview, 14 October 1990.

84. Meru District, AR, 1936, KNA, DC/MRU/1/1/2; and 1939, KNA, DC/MRU/1/1/4.

85. E. Mary Holding, "The Functions of Women's Institutions in Meru Society," typescript, n.d., KNA, MSS/7; Jones, *Kenya Kaleidoscope,* 22–25.

86. Dr. H. W. Brassington, Berresford Memorial Hospital, Maua, to Dr. J. L. Gilks, Director of Medical Services, Nairobi, 16 October 1931, KNA, Health/BY/1/61. The Director of Medical Services assured Brassington that he would not be violating medical ethics by lending the nurse his scalpel (Dr. J. L. Gilks, Director of Medical Services, to Dr. H. W. Brassington, United Methodist Church Mission, Meru, 29 October 1931, KNA, Health/BY/1/61).

87. Meru District, AR, 1934, KNA, DC/MRU/1/1/2.

88. Grace Lambert, interviewed by Jeffrey Fadiman, 1969, BLUCB, 96/49. Mrs. Lambert recalled that in some areas, including Chuka, thirty out of every hundred initiates had had illegal excisions.

89. Meru District, AR, 1934, KNA, DC/MRU/1/1/2.

90. Meru LNC, Minutes, 10 June 1929, 20 August 1929, MCC, LNC/1; Meru District, Handing Over Report, 1929, KNA, DC/MRU/1/1/2; Meru District, AR, 1929, 1930, KNA, DC/MRU/1/1/2.

91. Meru LNC, Minutes, 27 November 1930, 19 March 1931, MCC, LNC/1.

92. Meru District, AR, 1931, KNA, DC/MRU/1/1/2.

93. Meru LNC, Minutes, 8 August 1934, MCC, LNC/2; Meru District, AR,

1933, 1934, KNA, DC/MRU/1/1/2; Meru District, Handing Over Report, 1935, KNA, DC/MRU/1/3/1. Abortion was an offense against the Indian Penal Code, Sections 312–16, and infanticide was an offense under Section 302 (C. M. Dobbs, Ag. Chief Native Commissioner, "Memorandum on Infanticide," 12 January 1930, RH, MSS/Afr/s/665/1; see also Dickens and Cook, "Development of Commonwealth Abortion Laws").

94. Meru, AR, 1934, KNA, DC/MRU/1/1/2; Meru, Handing Over Report, 1935, KNA, DC/MRU/1/3/1; H. E. Lambert, "The Meru Yet to Come," 25 December 1941, KNA, PC/CP/4/4/7.

95. H. E. Lambert, District Commissioner, Meru, to Provincial Commissioner, Central, 13 November 1934, KNA, AG/5/991.

96. Meru LNC, Minutes, 8 August 1934, MCC, LNC/2; H. E. Lambert, District Commissioner, Meru, to Attorney General, Nairobi, "Meru Local Native Council," n.d., KNA, AG/5/991.

97. Attorney General, Nairobi, to Chief Secretary, Nairobi, 12 October 1934, KNA, AG/5/991; Meru District, AR, 1934, KNA, DC/MRU/1/1/2. The Director of Medical and Sanitary Services also expressed concern that the Meru resolutions appeared "to make circumcision compulsory" (A. R. Paterson, Ag. Director of Medical and Sanitary Services, Nairobi, to J. C. Callahan, Medical Officer, Meru, 23 August 1933, KNA, Health/BY/1/61).

98. S. H. La Fontaine, Provincial Commissioner, Central, to H. E. Lambert, District Commissioner, Meru, 5 November 1934, KNA, AG/5/991 (my emphasis). See also S. H. La Fontaine, Provincial Commissioner, Central, to Attorney General, Nairobi, 24 November 1934, KNA, AG/5/991; Attorney General, Nairobi, to Provincial Commissioner, Central, 20 March 1935, KNA, AG/5/991.

99. Meru District, Handing Over Report, 1935, KNA, DC/MRU/1/3/1. Convictions for abortion decreased from 10 to 1 from 1934 to 1935, and transgressions of the excision resolutions decreased from 70 to 17. Ex-headman M'Anampiu stated that *Kiberenge* was from Central Imenti in Meru, had served in World War I, and even had his own daughters excised as part of *Kigwarie* (Chief M'Anampiu, interview, 10 May 1995). Convictions for "illegal" excision rose again in 1936 to 34 (Meru District, AR, 1935, 1936, KNA, DC/MRU/1/1/2).

100. Meru LNC, Minutes, 19–22 February 1938, MCC, LNC/2.

101. Meru LNC, Minutes, 22 November 1938, MCC, LNC/3.

102. Meru District, Handing Over Report, 1939, KNA, DC/MRU/1/3/3. The fine of 5 Ksh was to double every three months.

103. Lambert, *The Use of Indigenous Authorities*, passim; Kinyua, "A History of the *Njuri*." On the central role played by Methodists in elaborating "indirect rule" in Meru and fostering a "Meru" ethnic identity, see Maupeu, *L'Administration indirecte*.

104. Read, "Patterns of Indirect Rule," 272, 293–94.

105. Meru District, AR, 1939, KNA, DC/MRU/1/1/4; "Notes of a Meeting

Held at the District Commissioner's Office, Meru, on 23 April 1940," KNA, VQ/11/2.

106. Meru District, AR, 1940, KNA, DC/MRU/1/1/4.

107. Lambert, *The Use of Indigenous Authorities*, 34.

108. Meru LNC, Minutes, 23–26 September 1947, MOM, 18; Meru District, AR, 1947, KNA, DC/MRU/1/1/4. The 1947 report specified that sexually mature girls were required to pass a medical examination before being granted permission for a late excision by the district commissioner.

109. Criminal Appeal Nos. 11–13/51, Native Tribunal Appeal Book No. 12, 1951, KNA, AHD/1/11; Imenti Native Tribunal Criminal Register, 596/50–1194/50, KNA, AHD/2/7; Native Tribunal Criminal Register, 1950–51, KNA, AHD/2/8. For a delayed initiation case brought by Presbyterian missionary Dr. Clive Irvine against a headman, see Meru District, AR, 1951, KNA, DC/MRU/1/1/6; and D. Joseph, interview, 13 June 1995.

110. Philip M'Inoti, personal diaries in the possession of Stephen Mugambi, Nairobi.

111. Thomas Mpunia stated that the term *Kigwarie* was derived from the verb *kugwiirirua*, "to be unexpected," whereas former Methodist missionary Bertha Jones suggested an etymology relating to the verb *kugwa*, "to fall" (T. Mpunia, interview, 18 October 1990; B. Jones, interview, 6 December 1995). In Swahili, *kiberenge* is a "light locomotive" (Johnson, *A Standard Swahili–English Dictionary*, 186).

112. J. M'Ruiga, interview, 19 May 1995.

113. M. Kithinji, interview, 9 June 1995.

114. Chief M'Anampiu, interview, 10 May 1995; M. Kithinji, interview, 9 June 1995.

115. J. M'Mugambi, interview, 10 June 1995. See also J. Nyoroka, interview, 29 March 1995; and M. Karoki, interview, 5 April 1995.

116. T. Maigene, interview, 17 October 1990; N. M'Imanyara, interview, 27 October 1990; M. Nthang'i, interview, 28 December 1994; P. Paul, interview, 10 January 1995; M. Kagwania, interview, 16 March 1995.

117. S. Nkure, interview, 26 January 1995; M. Ngeta, interview, 8 February 1995; S. Mwari, interview, 22 April 1995; J. M'Ruiga, interview, 19 May 1995; J. M'Mugambi, interview, 10 June 1995.

118. E. M'Iringo, interview, 4 August 1995. See also E. M'Ithinji and J. Kiruja, interview, 14 October 1990.

119. J. Stanley and M. John, interview, 3 May 1995.

120. P. M'Kuru, interview, 22 April 1995. See also E. M'Tuaruchiu, interview, 3 February 1995.

121. Meru District, Handing Over Report, 1939, KNA, DC/MRU/1/3/3 (my emphasis).

122. H. E. Lambert, *"Kigwarie"* and "Note on Early Initiation," n.d., JKML, Lambert/1/7/1.

123. M. Igoki, interview, 18 October 1990; J. Kibunja, interview, 19 October

1990. For another description of how Lambert's efforts to lower the age of excision led to the abandonment of *ncuuro*, see Paulo M'Itoke, interviewed by Jeffrey Fadiman, c. 1969–70, BLUCB, 96/49.

124. M. Kithinji, interview, 9 June 1995. See also M. Karoki, interview, 5 April 1995; and G. M'Itiri and W. M'Rarama, interview, 18 May 1995.

125. J. Kibunja, interview, 19 October 1990.

126. C. M'Barungu, interview, 8 May 1995.

127. J. M'Ikiao, interview, 1 May 1995.

128. S. Mwari, interview, 22 April 1995.

129. M. Mongeru, interview, 5 January 1995; C. M'Lithara, interview, 30 January 1995.

130. B. Tiira, interview, 30 March 1995.

131. V. Ciothirangi, interview, 6 June 1995.

132. J. M'Mugambi, interview, 9 June 1995.

133. Meru District, AR, 1934, KNA, DC/MRU/1/1/2; Meru District, AR, 1949, KNA, DC/MRU/1/1/4; Meru District, AR, 1950, KNA, DC/MRU/1/1/5/1; Lambert, *Kikuyu Social and Political Institutions*, 100.

134. J. Karea, interview, 24 March 1995.

135. E. M'Iringo, interview, 4 August 1995.

136. M. Karoki, interview, 5 April 1995.

137. A. J. Hopkins, Superintendent, Methodist Missionary Society, Meru, to Ayre, Secretary, Methodist Missionary Society, London, 11 April 1934, SOAS, MMS/GC/39/1542. See also Dr. Brassington, Methodist Missionary Society, Meru, to Secretary, Methodist Missionary Society, London, 12 June 1934, SOAS, MMS/GC/39/1547. Interviewees recounted that a vaccination campaign had occurred at the same time as the early *Kigwarie* episodes (E. M'Ithinji and J. Kiruja, interview, 14 October 1990; S. Mwari, interview, 22 April 1995; J. Karea, interview, 24 March 1995).

138. See Fadiman, *When We Began*, 147–50, ch. 13; Chege, "Dynamics of the Regulation of Sexuality"; and Nyaga, *Customs and Traditions of the Meru*, 144–50.

139. Willis, " 'Men on the Spot.' " For an earlier statement of the importance of African intermediaries to the Kenyan colonial state, see Berman and Lonsdale, "Coping with the Contradictions."

140. On how debates over *sati* in India similarly contributed to men's colonial authority while silencing the women at the center of that practice, see Spivak, "Can the Subaltern Speak?," 297–307, and Mani, *Contentious Traditions*.

CHAPTER 2: COLONIAL UPLIFT AND GIRL-MIDWIVES

1. Muriel Martin, Methodist Missionary Society, Meru, to Mrs. Duncan Leith, General Secretary, Women's Work, Methodist Missionary Society, Bishopsgate, London, 26 January 1934 and 3 July 1934, SOAS, MMS/WW/5/189; Mr. and Mrs. Laughton, interviewed by Jeffrey Fadiman, c. 1969–70, BLUCB, 96/49.

2. Lord Passfield, Secretary of State for the Colonies, London, to Governors, East African Dependencies, 8 March 1930, PRO, CO/822/27/10. The despatch and edited responses were eventually published in 1931 as Colonial No. 65, *Health and Progress of Native Populations in Certain Parts of the Empire.*

3. Harold B. Kittermaster, Governor, Somaliland, to Lord Passfield, Secretary of State for the Colonies, London, 17 April 1930, PRO, CO/822/27/10.

4. J. O. Shircore, Director of Medical and Sanitary Services, Tanganyika, forwarded by Donald Cameron, Governor, Tanganyika, to Lord Passfield, Secretary of State for the Colonies, London, 5 May 1930, PRO, CO/533/407/14.

5. J. L. Gilks, Director of Medical and Sanitary Services, Nairobi, to Lord Passfield, Secretary of State for the Colonies, London, 15 March 1930, PRO, CO/533/394/11. Jomo Kenyatta *(Facing Mount Kenya,* 147) similarly noted that missionaries' perspective on excision was unduly influenced by complicated cases that turned up at hospitals.

6. J. L. Gilks, Director of Medical and Sanitary Services, Nairobi, to Chief Native Commissioner, Nairobi, "Female Circumcision," 6 September 1930, KNA, Health 2/164. For responses to the committee's findings, see Henry Moore, Ag. Governor, Kenya, to Lord Passfield, Secretary of State for the Colonies, London, 6 November 1930, PRO, CO/533/394; and Colonial Office, "Memorandum," December 1930, PRO, CO/533/407.

7. Kenya Colony and Protectorate, Medical Department, *Annual Report* (1929), 30.

8. J. O. Shircore, Director of Medical and Sanitary Services, Tanganyika, forwarded by Donald Cameron, Governor, Tanganyika, to Lord Passfield, Secretary of State for the Colonies, London, 5 May 1930, PRO, CO/533/407/14.; Donald Cameron, Governor, Tanganyika, to Lord Passfield, Secretary of State for the Colonies, London, 22 May 1930, PRO, CO/822/27/10.

9. P. W. Perryman, Ag. Governor, Uganda, to Lord Passfield, Secretary of State for the Colonies, London, 30 September 1930, PRO, CO/822/27/10. See also Foster, *The Church Missionary Society;* Summers, "Intimate Colonialism"; and Vaughan, *Curing Their Ills,* 58–59, 129–42.

10. Buell, *The Native Problem,* 390.

11. A. Williams for J. L Gilks, Director of Medical and Sanitary Services, Nairobi, "Med. Dept. Circ. No. 413: Treatment of Maternity Cases in Native Hospitals," 21 March 1930, KNA, Health/1/173. State support for maternity services in rural areas was limited to the treatment of pregnant women as part of an anti-syphilis campaign in South Nyanza and government grants-in-aid to mission societies (Kenya Colony and Protectorate, Medical Department, *Annual Report* [1925], 66). For an analysis of the South Nyanza campaign, see Odinga, "Criminalizing the Sick."

12. KNA, Health/1/173 contains over fifteen medical officers' responses, written during March and April 1930, to the "Med. Dept. Circ No. 413."

13. J. L. Gilks, Director of Medical and Sanitary Services, Nairobi, to Lord Passfield, Secretary of State for the Colonies, London, 15 March 1930, PRO,

CO/533/394/11. The Lady Grigg maternity homes catered to Asian and African women and were supported by private donations raised by the Lady Grigg Child Welfare League and government grants. In his memoirs, Edward Grigg, the governor of Kenya between 1925 and 1931, describes the league's maternity and welfare work as a direct challenge to the practice of excision (Altrincham, *Kenya's Opportunity*, 98–103). For more on the early history of colonial maternity work in Nairobi and Mombasa, see Thomas, "Regulating Reproduction," 89–97.

14. Comaroff, "Medicine, Colonialism" (quote from 215–16). See also Vaughan, *Curing Their Ills;* Burke, *Lifebouy Men*, chs. 1–2; and Butchart, *The Anatomy of Power.*

15. Donald Cameron, Governor, Tanganyika, to Lord Passfield, Secretary of State for the Colonies, London, 22 May 1930, PRO, CO/822/27/10.

16. Lord Passfield, Secretary of State for the Colonies, London, to Governors, East African Dependencies, 8 March 1930, PRO, CO/822/27/10. See also Vaughan, *Curing Their Ills*, 66; Vaughan, "Health and Hegemony," 194.

17. Burton, *Burdens of History*, ch. 3; Midgley, "Anti-Slavery," 161–79. For more on British feminists' efforts to uplift their colonized "sisters," see Pedersen, "National Bodies," 677–80; and Strobel and Chaudhuri, *Western Women and Imperialism.*

18. *Parliamentary Debates*, Commons, 5th ser., 233 (11 December 1929), cols. 606–8.

19. All of the following responses to Lord Passfield, Secretary of State for the Colonies, are contained in PRO, CO/822/27/10: Harold B. Kittermaster, Governor, Somaliland, 17 April 1930; J. Moffat Thomson, Secretary for Native Affairs, Northern Rhodesia, 29 April 1930; J. A. Taylor, Director of Medical and Sanitary Services, Zanzibar, 5 May 1930; Donald Cameron, Governor, Tanganyika Territory, 22 May 1930; R. Rankine, British Resident, Zanzibar, 10 June 1930; T. S. W. Thomas, Governor, Nyasaland, 19 July 1930; P. W. Perryman, Ag. Governor, Uganda, 30 September 1930. For similar sentiments expressed in other colonial contexts, see Hunt "Noise over Camouflaged Polygamy"; and Allman, "Rounding up Spinsters."

20. Edward Grigg, Governor, Kenya, 14 August 1930; and J. L. Gilks, Director of Medical and Sanitary Services, Kenya, 14 August 1930, PRO, CO/822/27/10.

21. Kenya Colony and Protectorate, Medical Department, *Annual Report* (1925), 17.

22. Berman, *Control and Crisis*, 194 n. 111. For further information on Moyne's report, see "Report of the Sub-Committee of Provincial Commissioners on the Native Betterment Fund," 7 July 1932, KNA, PC/CP/8/4a/10; and H. M. Moore, Colonial Secretary, Nairobi, 28 September 1932, KNA, AG/2/6.

23. Colonial Office, "Memorandum," December 1930, PRO, CO/533/407.

24. Lewis, *The Politics of Motherhood*, 21, 103–4, 129–30; Peretz, "A Maternity Service," 30–45; Marks, "Mothers, Babies," 50.

25. E. B. Denham, Ag. Governor, Kenya, "Reports by the Acting Governor on his Visits to the Nyanza and Kikuyu Provinces and the District of Kitui," 15 September 1925, PRO, CO/533/333.

26. Kenya Colony and Protectorate, African (Native) Affairs Department, *Annual Reports* (1927–37); Kenya Colony and Protectorate, Medical Department, *Annual Report* (1937); Munro, *Colonial Rule*, 172–77.

27. Kikuyu Province, AR, 1932, KNA, PC/CP/4/1/2; Meru LNC, Minutes, 24–25 July 1935, MCC, LNC/2; Ag. Provincial Commissioner, Central, Nyeri, to Member for Health and Local Government, Nairobi, 20 August 1947, KNA, Health/BY/4/219. For another account of the involvement of central Kenyan LNCs in maternity work, see Kanogo, "The Medicalization of Maternity in Colonial Kenya," 75–86.

28. Meru LNC, Minutes, 20 August 1929, MCC, LNC/1; Meru LNC, Minutes, 24–25 July 1935, MCC, LNC/2; Meru LNC, Minutes, 17 March, 25–27 November 1937, MCC, LNC/3. On the predominance of home over hospital births in interwar Britain, see Lewis, *The Politics of Motherhood*, chs. 4, 5; and Peretz, "A Maternity Service."

29. Meru District, Medical AR, 1926, 1935, and 1936, KNA, DC/MRU/1/1/1; R. C. Speirs, Senior Medical Officer, Central Province, Nyeri, to Director of Medical Services, Nairobi, 1 April 1945, KNA, Health/BY/3/165. Ndirangu, *A History of Nursing*, 42, writes that in hospitals men were trained to be "dressers" and women to be "nursing orderlies," but officials were not so precise with their terminology.

30. Central Province, AR, 1935, KNA, PC/CP/4/3/1; Meru District, Medical AR, 1936, KNA, DC/MRU/1/1/1.

31. Meru District, AR, 1939, 1948, KNA, DC/MRU/1/1/4; Meru LNC, Minutes, 25–27 November 1937, 22 November 1938, MCC, LNC/3; A. H. Bonwell, Medical Officer, Meru, to Director of Medical Services, Nairobi, 22 October 1948, KNA, Health/3/166.

32. Meru LNC, Minutes, 23 June 1930, MCC, LNC/1. The Meru LNC purchased its first ambulance vehicle in 1947 (Meru District, AR, 1947, KNA, DC/MRU/1/1/4).

33. The Meru LNC justified paying maternity fees at the Methodist hospital and not at the Presbyterian one by noting that the former was located in a more "backward" area of the district, whereas around Chogoria husbands were willing to pay for their wives to give birth in the hospital. The fact that two Methodists, Chief M'Ngaine and Rev. M'Inoti, ranked among the most influential LNC members, and that a number of interwar district commissioners, particularly McKeag and Lambert, maintained close connections to the Methodist missionaries, probably also facilitated this differential treatment (A. J. Hopkins, Superintendent, Methodist Missionary Society, Meru, "Kenya District Letter," n.d., MON, KD/B/1; Meru LNC, Minutes, 21 February 1939, CMA, AE; Meru LNC, Minutes, 26–28 March 1945, MCC, LNC/4).

34. Hunt, " 'Le bébé en brousse' "; Fabian, "Religious and Secular Colonization"; Summers, "Intimate Colonialism"; Vaughan, *Curing Their Ills*, 23,

56–57; Vaughan, "Health and Hegemony," 173–20; and Hunt, *A Colonial Lexicon*, ch. 4. For an analysis that argues for a sharper distinction between mission and state medicine, see Comaroff, "Medicine, Colonialism."

35. Meru District, AR, 1949, KNA, DC/MRU/1/1/4. In 1947 the Meru LNC also discussed financing a "home for motherless infants," as it was not "always possible for the father to find a foster-mother for an infant whose mother had died" (Meru LNC, Minutes, 10 December 1947, MCC, LNC/4).

36. Vaughan, "Health and Hegemony," 195.

37. Meru District, AR, 1934, KNA, DC/MRU/1/1/2. For more on LNC members' desire to separate and distinguish male and female patients, see Meru District, Medical AR, 1927, KNA, DC/MRU/1/1/1; Meru LNC, Minutes, 24–25 July 1935, MCC, LNC/2; Meru LNC, Minutes, 8 June 1937, 22 November 1935, MCC, LNC/3; Meru LNC, Minutes, 6–8 November 1948, MOM, 18; and Philip M'Inoti, personal diaries in the possession of Stephen Mugambi, Nairobi.

38. Dr. Stanley Bell, "Treatment of Diseases by the Ameru," n.d., MOM, 17.

39. H. O. Watkins-Pitchford, Medical Officer, Native Civil Hospital, Meru, to Director of Medical and Sanitary Services, Nairobi, 21 May 1942, KNA, Health/BY/4/28. For more on isolating patients prior to the completion of the maternity ward, see Meru LNC, Minutes, 25–27 November 1937, 19–22 February 1938, MCC, LNC/3; and Meru LNC, Minutes, 3 March 1943, MCC, LNC/4.

40. Kenya Colony and Protectorate, Medical Department, *Annual Report* (1945), 28, 35.

41. Meru District, AR, 1949, KNA, DC/MRU/1/1/4; Meru District, Handing Over Report, 1950, KNA, DC/MRU/1/3/9. The ward cost 88,000 Ksh, or 4,400 British pounds sterling, to build.

42. M. Ntuti, interview, 24 January 1995; I. Kaimuri, interview, 20 March 1995; E. Nyambura, interview, 11 April 1995; E. Kabita, interview, 3 May 1995.

43. The sum of 2 Ksh was relatively modest. In 1949 a semiskilled worker in Nairobi earned on average 46 Ksh per month, while the annual tax levied by the Meru LNC amounted to 13 Ksh (White, *The Comforts of Home*, 150; Meru District, AR, 1949, KNA, DC/MRU/1/1/4).

44. H. O. Watkins-Pitchford, Medical Officer, Native Civil Hospital, Meru, to Director of Medical and Sanitary Services, Nairobi, 21 May 1942, KNA, Health/BY/4/28. On the need to develop domiciliary midwifery services so that normal births could continue to take place at home, see Kenya Colony and Protectorate, Medical Department, *Annual Report* (1934), 22.

45. Edward R. Standleton, Assistant District Commissioner, Meru, "Tharaka," 2 May 1930, JKML, Lambert 1/5/3.

46. E. Mary Holding, "The Education of a Bantu Tribe," unpublished manuscript, c. 1963–64, RH, Afr/r/117, 8–12. Holding's account of childbirth is very similar to an account written by W. H. Laughton ("An Introductory

Study," 20–24), and another by either officer J. G. Hopkins or H. E. Lambert ("Miscellaneous Customs," unpublished manuscript, n.d., JKML, Lambert 1/5/3).

47. R. Ncoro, interview, 8 February 1995.

48. M. Kaimuri, interview, 12 May 1995; G. Kaburo, interview, 30 December 1994.

49. "Miscellaneous Customs," unpublished manuscript, n.d., JKML, Lambert 1/5/3; S. Mbuthu, interview, 11 January 1995; J. Karea, interview, 24 March 1995. Some interviewees with knowledge of childbirth in the northern areas of the district, Igembe and Tigania Divisions, recalled that men, skilled in cutting, sometimes helped to perform episiotomies and extract dead fetuses (M. Ntuti, interview, 24 January 1995; V. Ciothirangi, interview, 6 June 1995; and M. Chalkley, interview, 2 December 1995).

50. G. Kaburo, interview, 30 December 1994; R. Ncoro, interview, 8 February 1995; J. Karea, interview, 24 March 1995; J. Nyoroka, interview, 29 March 1995; B. Tiira, interview, 30 March 1995; M. Kimwe, interview, 31 March 1995; M. Kaimuri, interview, 12 May 1995; T. Likicha, interview, 29 May 1995; V. Ciothirangi, interview, 6 June 1995; D. Joseph, interview, 13 June 1995; J. M'Mugambi, interview, 10 June 1995. See also Nyaga, *Customs and Traditions*, 25–26.

51. E. Mary Holding, "The Education of a Bantu Tribe," unpublished manuscript, c. 1963–64, RH, Afr/r/117, 9; J. Stanley and M. John, interview, 3 May 1995.

52. Holding, "Women's Institutions," 296–97; Holding, "Meru Names," typescript, n.d., KNA, MSS/7. On such beliefs elsewhere in Africa, see Riesman, "The Person," 83–85; Piot, *Remotely Global*, 78–79.

53. E. Mary Holding, "The Education of a Bantu Tribe," unpublished manuscript, c. 1963–64, RH, Afr/r/117, 9; Laughton, "An Introductory Study," 21; "Miscellaneous Customs," unpublished manuscript, n.d., JKML, Lambert 1/5/3; M. Kimwe, interview, 31 March 1995; M. Karoki, interview, 5 April 1995; S. Mwari, interview, 7 May 1995.

54. On the process of massaging the newborn (*kuthithia mwana*) in order "to bring the bones together," see G. Kaburo, interview, 30 December 1994; and S. Mwari, interview, 7 May 1995.

55. G. Kaburo, interview, 30 December 1994; B. Tiira, interview, 30 March 1995; C. Mutiria, interview, 12 June 1995; and D. Joseph, interview, 13 June 1995.

56. M. Karoki, interview, 5 April 1995.

57. G. Kaburo, interview; 30 December 1994; I. Kajuju, interview, 20 March 1995; J. Nyoroka, interview, 29 March 1995; M. Muthoni, interview, 3 April 1995; E. Nyambura, interview, 11 April 1995; C. Mutiria, interview, 12 June 1995; D. Joseph, interview, 13 June 1995; and J. M'Mugambi, interview, 5 July 1995. Bianco, "The Historical Anthropology," 217, 220, and Davison, *Voices from Mutira*, 176–78, describe Pokot and Kikuyu midwives using the same

techniques to assist with delayed labor. During the "female circumcision controversy," mission doctors argued that excision made episiotomies or perineum tears unavoidable, particularly with first births. These doctors did not categorically oppose episiotomies. With the medicalization of childbirth, episiotomies had become increasingly common in interwar England. Rather, they decried the "very crude and ineffective manner" in which "old women in the village" performed them (Philp, "Vescical Fistula," 126–28; Dr. Gillan, Church of Scotland Mission, Tumutumu, to Director of Medical Services, Nairobi, 23 February 1930, KNA, Health/2/164; C. Viney Braimbridge, Surgical Specialist, Nairobi, to Director of Medical and Sanitary Services, Nairobi, 10 June 1935, KNA, Health/BY/1/61; Lewis, *The Politics of Motherhood*, 126).

58. Laughton, "An Introductory Study of the Meru People," 21; E. Mary Holding, "The Education of a Bantu Tribe," unpublished manuscript, c. 1963–64, RH, Afr/r/117, 10; "Miscellaneous Customs," unpublished manuscript, n.d., JKML, Lambert 1/5/3. See also G. Kaburo, interview, 30 December 1994; M. Ntuti, interview, 24 January 1995; M. Kaimuri, interview, 12 May 1995; T. Likicha, interview, 29 May 1995; and M. Manene and S. Karambu, interview, 7 June 1995. For a discussion of postnatal seclusion in another African context, see Hunt, *A Colonial Lexicon*, 71, 276–80.

59. R. Ncoro, interview, 8 February 1995. See also E. Mary Holding, "The Education of a Bantu Tribe," unpublished manuscript, c. 1963–64, RH, Afr/r/117, 10; Laughton, "An Introductory Study," 22; M. Karoki, interview, 5 April 1995; M. Ngeta, interview, 18 February 1995; and M. Kagwania, interview, 16 March 1995.

60. For other discussions of how female genital cutting is meant to prepare and purify women for reproduction, see Boddy, *Wombs and Alien Spirits*, ch. 2; Brett-Smith, *The Making of Bamana Sculpture*, 43–47; and Ahmadu, "Rites and Wrongs," 297–98.

61. N. Adams, interview, 26 June 1995. For a West African context in which excision is also practiced and the cultural ideal is to give birth not only stoically and silently but alone, see Sargent, *Maternity, Medicine, and Power*, 1, 166–80. For a Northeast African context in which childbirth is female initiation, see Hutchinson, *Nuer Dilemmas*, 190–96. Other hospital personnel noted that with school education, Meru parturients became less capable of bearing pain in silence and without expression (Clive Irvine, "Chogoria Days," 1954, CMA, booklets; M. Chalkley, interview, 2 December 1995).

62. B. Tiira, interview, 30 March 1995. See also J. Nyoroka, interview, 29 March 1995; and J. Stanley and M. John, interview, 3 May 1995.

63. Hunt, *A Colonial Lexicon*, 250–51, and Burns, "Reproductive Labors," 326, argue that in the Belgian Congo and South Africa, respectively, the roots of colonial maternity work lay in such obstetrical and gynecological emergencies.

64. E. Kabita, interview, 3 March 1995. See also B. Tiira, interview, 30 March 1995; and J. Stanley and M. John, interview, 3 May 1995.

65. M. Chalkley, interview, 2 December 1995.

66. Lady Grigg, Welfare League, African Maternity and Child Welfare Hospital and Training Centre, Nairobi, "Rules for Candidates for Acceptance as Probationers," forwarded by D. M. Blomfield, Medical Officer, Native Civil Hospital, Meru, to the Superintendent, Methodist Missionary Society, Meru, 2 July 1946, MOM, 16. While the rules stipulated that married women were eligible, the medical officers' emphasis was always on recruiting single women.

67. Bell, *Frontiers of Medicine*, esp. 205–6; Hunt, *A Colonial Lexicon*, ch. 5; Mager, *Gender and the Making of a South African Bantustan*, 185. My term "girl-midwives" was inspired by Hunt's "girl-nurses." For another account of the training of African women as midwives and nurses in colonial Kenya, see Kanogo, "The Medicalization of Maternity in Colonial Kenya," 101–11.

68. A. J. Hopkins, Chairman, Methodist Missionary Society, Meru, "Kenya District Letter," n.d., MON, KD/B/1; Alice Walton, Secretary, Women's Work, Methodist Missionary Society, London, to A. J. Hopkins, Chairman, Methodist Missionary Society, Meru, 2 August 1934, MON, WW/A/6; Holding, "The Woman Who Was Too Old"; Holding, "The Functions of Women's Institutions in Meru Society," typescript, n.d., KNA, MSS/7; Dr. Stanley Bell, "Treatment of Diseases by the Ameru," n.d., MOM, 17; Jones, *Kaaga Girls*, 10–13, 22–24.

69. Dr. Clive Irvine, Church of Scotland Mission, Chogoria, to Senior Medical Officer, Central Province, Nyeri, 21 February 1945, KNA, Health/BY/27/1; F. C. Smith, Convener, "Conference on Medical Missions: Record of Ad Hoc Meetings Held on 20th and 23rd February 1945," 24 February 1945, MOM, 12; and "The Presbyterian Church of East Africa—Chogoria Hospital," c. 1968, CMA, HB/1.

70. Joy Bannister, Nursing Sister, Methodist Hospital, Maua, to Alice Walton, Secretary, Women's Work, London, 7 February 1938 and 10 April 1939, SOAS, MMS/WW/5/211. Systematic training of male medical personnel— called "hospital dressers"—began at Maua in the early 1940s (Dr. Stanley Bell, "Methodist Mission in Meru, Berresford Memorial Hospital, Maua—General Report and Numerical Returns for December 1941–November 1942," MOM, 16).

71. Dr. Callahan, Medical Officer, Native Hospital, Meru, to A. G. V. Cozens, Superintendent, Methodist Missionary Society, Meru, 24 October 1933, MOM, 16; A. G. V. Cozens, Superintendent, Methodist Missionary Society, Meru, to Dr. Callahan, Medical Officer, Native Hospital, Meru, 25 October 1933, MOM, 16.

72. D. M. Blomfield, Medical Officer, Native Hospital, Meru, to Superintendent, Methodist Missionary Society, Meru, 2 July 1946, MOM, 16; Superintendent, Methodist Missionary Society, Meru, to Medical Officer, Native Hospital, Meru, 2 September 1946, MOM, 16.

73. Medical Officer, Meru, to Superintendent, Methodist Missionary Society, Meru, 15 October 1946, MOM, 16.

74. "Minutes of the Combined Meeting of Representatives of LNCs of Central Province on 23 Feb. 1943," and "Minutes of the Combined Meeting of Representatives of LNCs of Central Province on 1 April 1944," MCC,

ADC/30/3/8. See also Wipper, "Kikuyu Women"; John Lonsdale, "The Moral Economy of Mau Mau," 320–21, 386–87; and Robertson, *Trouble Showed the Way*, chs. 3–4.

75. White, *The Comforts of Home*, 147–84.

76. "Statement by Mrs. Hooper," forwarded by the Duchess of Atholl, London, to the Secretary of State for the Colonies, London, 4 December 1929, PRO, CO/323/1067/1.

77. "Minutes of the Combined Meeting of Representatives of LNCs of Central Province on 7–8 Sept. 1938," MCC, ADC/30/3/8. See also Meru LNC, Minutes, 22 November 1938, MCC, LNC/3.

78. Medical Officer, Native Hospital, Fort Hall, to Director of Medical and Sanitary Services, Nairobi, 17 October 1940, KNA, Health/BY/27/1.

79. Norman Maclennan, Director of Medical and Sanitary Services, Nairobi, to Chief Native Commissioner, Nairobi, response to "Record of a Meeting Held in the Office of the Chief Native Commissioner on Saturday, March 1946," 29 March 1946, KNA, Health/2/425.

80. L. Olive Owen, Church Missionary Society, Ng'iya, Kisumu, to Director of Medical Services, Nairobi, 24 June 1939, KNA, Health/BY/27/1. For more on the sexual politics of hostels for midwives and nurses in Kenya, see Ndirangu, *A History of Nursing*, 42–43. At Ortum hospital, secondary-school boys nicknamed the nursing school dormitory "Soweto" because of its "locked gates and formidable walls" (see Bianco, "The Historical Anthropology," 203).

81. Bell, "Midwifery Training," 205–6.

82. Cook, *Uganda Memories*, 335; thanks to Luise White for this reference. See also Holden, "Colonial Sisters," 75.

83. Hunt, *A Colonial Lexicon*, 258; Marks, *Divided Sisterhood*, 73–74, 103–4.

84. M. Muirige, interview, 28 April 1995. Concerns about the conditions under which a woman working away from home would marry were common. In 1948 Eunice Nyambura, a Kikuyu woman from Nyeri, ventured away from home to work at the Methodist hospital at Maua. Nyambura recalled that in reluctantly granting her permission to go to Maua, her parents advised her "to take care of debts because if I fail to pay, I might be forced to marry someone who I do not like" (E. Nyambura, interview, 11 April 1995).

85. Meru District, Handing Over Report, 1950, KNA, DC/MRU/1/3/9.

86. M. S. C. Burt, Church of Scotland Mission, Chogoria, to Foreign Mission Committee, Church of Scotland Mission, Edinburgh, 31 December 1954, NLS, Acc/7548/C13; M. S. C. Burt, Presbyterian Church of East Africa, Chogoria, to Home Offices, Church of Scotland, Edinburgh, "PCEA Hospital, Chogoria, Sister's Report, December 1961," NLS, Acc/7548/C27.

87. Meru LNC, Minutes, 16 March 1950, KNA, PC/CP/2/1/9.

88. J. S. S. Rowlands, notes for a volume on "anthropology, native law and custom in Kenya," n.d., RH, MSS/Afr/s/1497/2.

89. Holding, "Winding Ways."

90. H. E. Lambert, DC, Meru, to Attorney General, Nairobi, "Meru Local Native Council," n.d., KNA, AG/5/991.

91. E. Kabita, interview, 3 May 1995. See also M. Muthoni, interview, 3 April 1995; and C. Mutiria, interview, 12 June 1995.

92. N. Adams, interview, 26 June 1995.

93. M. Chalkley, interview, 2 December 1995.

94. M. Chalkley, interview, 2 December 1995.

95. For other instances in which health professionals have chosen either to accommodate or medicalize female genital cutting, see Bella, "Sudanese Village Midwives"; Bell, "Midwifery Training"; Gwako, "Continuity and Change"; and Shell-Duncan and Hernlund, *Female "Circumcision,"* chs. 1, 4–6, 10.

96. J. Nyoroka, interview, 29 March 1995.

97. E. Kabita, interview, 3 May 1995.

98. Meru District, AR, 1940, KNA, DC/MRU/1/1/4.

99. E. Nyambura, interview, 11 April 1995; B. Tiira, interview, 30 March 1995; and M. Kaimuri, interview, 20 March 1995.

100. M. Muirige, interview, 28 April 1995.

CHAPTER 3: MAU MAU AND THE GIRLS WHO "CIRCUMCISED THEMSELVES"

1. V. Kinaito, interview, 5 July 1993.

2. C. M'Anampiu, interview, 10 May 1995.

3. Meru African Courts, Monthly Returns, 1956–58, KNA, ARC(MAA) /2/9/27/II, ARC(MAA)/2/10/27/III, MAA/7/282, and MAA/7/283.

4. On Mau Mau as a fractured and multivalent, rather than unified, movement, see Ogot, "Revolt of the Elders"; White, "Separating the Men from the Boys"; Berman and Lonsdale, *Unhappy Valley,* bk. 2; Cooper, *Decolonization and African Society,* 348–51; and Kershaw, *Mau Mau from Below.* For a critique of this perspective, see Maloba, *Mau Mau and Kenya,* 12–14.

5. Corfield, *The Origins and Growth of Mau Mau,* 316; Clayton, *Counter-Insurgency in Kenya,* 53–54; Berman, *Control and Crisis,* ch. 8; White, "Separating the Men from the Boys," 17; Elkins, "Forest War No More." Anderson, "Capital Crimes, Colonial Law," argues that the number of black central Kenyans killed by government security forces is closer to 20,000.

6. Cooper, "Conflict and Connection," 1533.

7. Nthamburi, *A History of the Methodist Church,* 70–88.

8. Dr. Clive Irvine, Church of Scotland Mission, Chogoria, to Secretaries, Foreign Mission Committee, Church of Scotland, Edinburgh, "General Report for 1947," NLS, Acc/7548/C4.

9. Waciuma, *Daughter of Mumbi,* 82–83. For another account of such exams, see Gillan, "Notes on the Kikuyu Custom of Female Circumcision," 201.

10. Meru, ADC, Minutes, 7 March 1951, CMA, AE.

11. Meru District, Handing Over Report, 1953, KNA, DC/MRU/1/3/12. Although Homan did not describe what the Presbyterian initiative entailed, the minutes from the ADC meeting of 1–2 December 1953 (MCC, ADC/5) suggest that it may have been a rigorous enforcement of the ADC resolution requiring parental or guardian approval.

12. T. Nikobwe and M. Mwakinia, interview, 20 September 1990; Mwaniki, "A History of Circumcision in Mount Kenya Zone."

13. The term "second colonial occupation" was first coined by Low and Lonsdale ("Introduction," 12–16). For other accounts of this period, see Bennett and Smith, "Kenya," 109–35; Throup, *Economic and Social Origins,*140–70; Berman, *Control and Crisis,* chs. 6–8; Cashmore, "A Random Factor in British Imperialism," 125–27; Atieno-Odhiambo, "The Formative Years"; and Lewis, *Empire State-Building.*

14. Meru, ADC, Minutes, 8–9 March 1956, KNA, CS/1/14/100, and MCC, ADC/6. Later in the controversy, some people did wrongly believe that the ban also applied to male circumcision (J. A. Cumber, District Commissioner, Meru, to Secretary, *Njuri Ncheke ya Meru,* "Meeting of the *Njuri Ncheke* on 10 January 1957 in the ADC Hall," 8 January 1957, MCC, ADM/15/16/6/II).

15. Meru, ADC, Minutes, 12 April 1956, MCC, ADC/6; Meru District, AR, 1956, KNA, DC/MRU/1/1/12/1. Cumber reported that the ADC in neighboring Embu District passed the same by-law in late 1956. The only previous ban on excision in colonial Kenya was passed by the North Nyanza LNC in 1925 (see KNA, PC/NZA/3/1/100). Within North Nyanza, however, excision was limited to small populations, namely the Nyangori, who were, in fact, exempted from the ban. The unsuccessful 1946 law prohibiting infibulation in Sudan represents the only other noteworthy attempt in colonial Africa to outlaw female genital cutting (see Bella, "Sudanese Village Midwives").

16. Meru District, AR, 1955, KNA, DC/MRU/1/1/11/2, and 1956, DC/MRU/1/1/12/1; Homan, "Land Consolidation and Redistribution"; Kamunchuluh, "The Meru Participation in Mau Mau." See also the minutes of *Njuri Ncheke* meetings held from 1956–57 in MCC, ADM/15/16/6/II.

17. W. H. Laughton, Methodist Missionary Society, Meru, circular letter, 4 November 1956, KNA, MSS/124/5.

18. As voter eligibility was dependent on possession of "loyalty certificates," accorded to those of specified age and wealth who had denounced Mau Mau, Cumber was accused by some observers of enforcing less stringent criteria for the distribution of "loyalty certificates" than other areas of Central Province (Meru District, AR, 1956, KNA, DC/MRU/1/1/12/1, and 1957, DC/MRU/1/1/13; R. Cashmore, interview, 6 December 1995). On Mate's election, see Ogot, "The Decisive Years," 54–58.

19. Meru District, AR, 1957, KNA, DC/MRU/1/1/13, and 1958, DC/MRU/1/1/14. See also N. M'Mwirichia, interview, 18 September 1995.

20. Lambert, *The Use of Indigenous Authorities,* 21.

21. Meru District, AR, 1957, KNA, DC/MRU/1/1/13.

22. Meru Political Record Book, 1908–21, KNA, PC/CP/1/9/1; Meru District, ARs, 1910–1924, KNA, DC/MRU/1/1/1; Meru District, ARs, 1925–1928, KNA, DC/MRU/1/1/2.

23. Jediel Micheu, Clerk of Presbytery, Church of Scotland Mission, Chogoria, to District Commissioner, Meru, "Initiation of Men into the Njuri," 7 April 1955; and Dr. Clive Irvine, Church of Scotland Mission, Chogoria, to R. G. M. Calderwood, CSM, Nairobi, Kenya, "Njuri Ncheke," 9 April 1955, both in NLS, Acc/7548/B279. See also correspondence in *Njuri Ncheke* file, MCC, ADM/15/16/6/II.

24. E. K. Mbogori, Makerere University College, Kampala, to District Commissioner, Meru, 4 October 1952, MCC, ADM/15/16/6/II.

25. Kinyua, "A History of the *Njuri*."

26. F. D. Homan, District Commissioner, Meru, "Minutes of a Meeting of the Njuri Ncheke of Meru held at Ncheru on 2nd December 1952," and "Minutes of the Annual Meeting of Njuri Ncheke held at Nchiru on 12th October, 1954," MCC, ADM/15/16/6/II.

27. Kinyua, "A History of the *Njuri*," 46.

28. Kanogo, *Squatters,* 143–49, states that women only totaled 5 percent of rebels in the forests, but a much larger "civilian army" of women supplied them with food and other necessities. See also Santilli, "Kikuyu Women"; Gachihi, "The Role of Kikuyu Women"; Presley *Kikuyu Women,* chs. 7–8.

29. White, "Separating the Men from the Boys."

30. Meru District, Handing Over Report, 1953, KNA, DC/MRU/1/3/12; and the following correspondence in MCC, ADM/15/16/6/II: A. Buxton, District Officer, Meru, to District Officer, Tigania, "CID Investigation of Alleged Njuri Corruption at Karama," 19 March 1955; J. Grands, Medical Officer, Meru, to District Commissioner, Meru, 20 March 1955; K. P. Khow for District Commissioner, Meru, to Reconstruction Committee, Meru, 21 May 1955; J. A. Cumber, District Commissioner, Meru, 4 July 1955; District Officer, South Imenti Division, Meru, to District Commissioner, Meru, "*Peza za Njuri Ncheke,*" 7 August 1956.

31. N. M'Mwirichia, interview, 18 September 1995; D. M'Iringo, interview, 25 June 1995.

32. D. M'Naikiuru, interview, 29 April 1995; C. M'Anampiu, interview, 10 May 1995.

33. Gerald Casey, Timau, to Barbara Castle, Member of Parliament, London, 2 July 1957, PRO, CO/822/1647.

34. S. Kathurima, interview, 15 September 1995; N. M'Mwirichia, interview, 18 September 1995.

35. In correspondence to the secretary of the Presbyterian Church of East Africa, Irvine stated that the ban came "quite suddenly and unexpectedly" (Calderwood, General Secretary, Church Offices, Presbyterian Church of East

Africa (PCEA), Nairobi, "The PCEA, Annual Report for 1956," NLS, Acc/7548/C17).

36. Clive Irvine, Church of Scotland Mission, Chogoria, "Chogoria 1956," NLS, Acc/7548/C17; Berta Allan, Church of Scotland Mission, Chogoria, to Isa Brown, Secretary, Women's Foreign Mission, Church of Scotland, Edinburgh, 1 April 1956, NLS, Acc/10231/2; Meru District, AR, 1956, KNA, DC/MRU/1/1/12/1.

37. J. Griffiths, Lord Chancellor, House of Lords, London, to Vincent Jowitt, Lord, House of Lords, London, 16 March 1951, PRO, CO/537/7213.

38. Governor, Kenya, to Secretary of State for the Colonies, London, "Secret—Female Circumcision," 7 June 1951; and file note by R. W. Newsam, 10 March 1951, both in PRO, CO/537/7213. On the colonial state's imperative to avoid giving orders that would be disobeyed, see Cashmore, "A Random Factor in British Imperialism," 125.

39. Meru ADC, Minutes of a "Special Meeting," 3 July 1956, KNA, CS/1/14/100; Acting Governor, Kenya, to Secretary of State for the Colonies, London, 27 December 1957, PRO, CO/822/1647.

40. Meru District, AR, 1956, KNA, DC/MRU/1/1/12/1.

41. Central Province, AR, 1957, KNA, MAA/1/5.

42. Meru ADC, Minutes, 7 September 1956, KNA, CS/1/14/100. On the post–World War II broadening of the range of people included in colonial administration, see Low and Lonsdale, "Introduction," 15.

43. M. Kanini, interview, 16 September 1995. For an account of Kanini's more active participation in the ADC's passage of the 1951 resolution requiring the consent of both parents before a girl could be excised, see Berta Allan, Church of Scotland Mission, Chogoria, to Isa Brown, Secretary, Women's Foreign Mission Commission, Church of Scotland, 1 March 1951, NLS, Acc/10231/2.

44. Meru ADC, Minutes, 8–9 March and 12 April 1956, KNA, CS/1/14/100.

45. M. Kanini, interview, 8 August 1999.

46. C. M'Anampiu, interview, 10 May 1995; C. Kirote, interview, 9 June 1995; C. Tirindi, interview, 10 February 1995.

47. M. Kanana, interview, 23 March 1995.

48. E. Mary Holding, "Notes on Girls' Circumcision," typescript, n.d., KNA, MSS/7.

49. D. M'Naikiuru, interview, 29 April 1995.

50. E. Muthuuri, interview, 3 January 1995. Standard VII in the British school is basically the equivalent of grade seven in the U.S. system.

51. For example, see A. Kirimi, interview, 12 June 1995.

52. M. M'Mukindia, interview, 10 January 1995; J. M'Lithara, interview, 6 February 1995; C. Tirindi, interview, 10 February 1995; C. Kirote, interview, 9 June 1995; A. Kirimi, interview, 12 June 1995; C. Kiruki, interview, 30 June 1995.

53. Only one documentary source contradicts this generalization;

Methodist missionary Merle Wilde ("Meru Women's Work Report, Synod 1958," MOM, 1) wrote that *Ngaitana* went "against all previous custom, some circumcised themselves, others one another and others were circumcised by their own mothers." This may have been a misunderstanding on Wilde's part.

54. C. Tirindi, interview, 10 February 1995; C. Kirote, interview, 9 June 1995; A. Kirimi, interview, 12 June 1995.

55. Ag. Governor, Kenya, to Secretary of State for the Colonies, London, 27 December 1957, PRO, CO/822/1647. In 1957 Clive Irvine, another medical doctor and fierce opponent of excision, noted the continuing dangers of excision, reporting how one thirteen-year-old girl had recently "died of hemorrhage" from excision (Clive Irvine, Church of Scotland Mission, Chogoria, to Secretary of State for the Colonies, 21 December 1957, PRO, CO/822/1647).

56. A. Kirimi, interview, 12 June 1995.

57. M. Kanana, interview, 23 March 1995. For another account of the use of razor blades leading to less severe forms of excision, see Davison, *Voices from Mutira,* 66.

58. Heald, *Manhood and Morality,* 12.

59. A. Kirimi, interview, 9 June 1995.

60. C. Tirindi, interview, 10 February 1995; and C. Kirote, interview, 9 June 1995.

61. A. Kirimi, interview, 12 June 1995.

62. Holding, "Women's Institutions"; Holding, "*Nthoni,*" n.d., KNA, MSS/7.

63. E. M'Iringo, interview, 16 March 1995.

64. I. Kaimuri, interview, 20 March 1995; L. Kajuju, interview, 23 March 1995.

65. M. Kanana, interview, 23 March 1995; L. Kajuju, interview, 23 March 1995.

66. Meru District, AR, 1957, KNA, DC/MRU/1/1/13.

67. "Minutes of Meeting of *Njuri Ncheke* held at Nchiru on 15th April 1958," MCC, ADM/15/16/6/III.

68. Altrincham, *Kenya's Opportunity,* 103.

69. Meru District, AR, 1955, KNA, DC/MRU/1/1/11/2; Meru District, AR, 1957, KNA, DC/MRU/1/1/13. See also file on Youth Schemes Meru, 1956, KNA, AB/16/16.

70. C. Tirindi, interview, 10 February 1995.

71. For other instances of this tradition, see Ifeka-Moller, "Female Militancy"; and Wipper, "Kikuyu Women."

72. "Minutes of a Special Meeting of Njuri Committee held in the A.D.C. Office on 6th November, 1957," MCC, ADM/15/16/6/II.

73. Provincial Commissioner, Central, Nyeri, to Minister for African Affairs, Nairobi, "Female Rehabilitation Centre, Meru," 23 September 1954, KNA, AB/2/51.

74. C. Tirindi, interview, 10 February 1995.

75. Kamunchuluh, "The Meru Participation in Mau Mau."

76. C. Kirote, interview, 9 June 1995.

77. V. Kinaito, interview, 5 July 1995.

78. C. Tirindi, interview, 10 February 1995. See also I. Kaimuri, interview, 20 March 1995; and C. Kirote, interview, 9 June 1995.

79. R. Cashmore, interview, 6 December 1995. They also chided Cashmore for having "skin like a pig."

80. Like the Native Tribunals which they replaced in 1951, African Courts existed under administrative rather than judicial control. The salaries for African Court elders were paid by ADCs and, after 1958, the central government. ADCs, in turn, received African Court revenues, which routinely exceeded expenses by 200 percent (Ghai and McAuslan, *Public Law*, 156–59; Meru District, AR, 1957–58, KNA, DC/MRU/1/1/13 and DC/MRU/1/1/14).

81. Meru African Courts, Monthly Returns, 1956–58, KNA, ARC(MAA)/2/9/27/II, ARC(MAA)/2/10/27/III, MAA/7/282, and MAA/7/283; these percentages are estimates, since it was sometimes difficult to determine an individual's status from the court registers.

82. Gerald Casey, Timau, to Barbara Castle, Member of Parliament, London, 2 July 1957, PRO, CO/822/1647.

83. M. Manene and S. Karambu, interview, 7 June 1995.

84. C. M'Anampiu, interview, 10 May 1995; M. M'Mukindia, interview, 11 January 1995; M. Kanana, interview, 23 March 1995.

85. C. Tirindi, interview, 10 February 1995; M. Kanana, interview, 23 March 1995; C. Kirote, interview, 9 June 1995; E. M'Iringo, interview, 16 March 1995.

86. Leakey, *The Southern Kikuyu*, vol. 3; Smith, "Njama's Supper."

87. L. Kajuju, interview, 23 March 1995; E. M'Iringo, interview, 16 March 1995; D. M'Naikiuru, interview, 29 April 1995.

88. S. Nkure, interview, 7 May 1995.

89. Kenya Colony and Protectorate, Community Development Department, *Annual Report, 1954*, 12–13, cited in Presley, *Kikuyu Women*, 166. See also Wipper, "The Maendeleo ya Wanawake Movement"; and Wipper, "The Maendeleo ya Wanawake Movement in the Colonial Period."

90. Merle Wilde, "Meru Women's Work Report, Synod 1958," MOM, 1.

91. M. Kanana, interview, 23 March 1995; C. Kirote, interview, 9 June 1995; J. Laiboni, interview, 23 July 1995.

92. Gerald Casey, Timau, to Barbara Castle, Member of Parliament, London, 2 July 1957, PRO, CO/822/1647. District and provincial officers were responsible for overseeing African Court proceedings and record keeping. The African Court appellate system largely followed administrative hierarchies, with cases moving from district-level African Courts of Appeal, to district commissioners, to provincial commissioners, to a Court of Review composed of the Chief Native Commissioner, African Courts officers, a black Kenyan appointed by the governor, and a judicial official appointed by the Chief Justice (Ghai and McAuslan, *Public Law*, 156–59).

93. R. F. D. Rylands, African Courts Officer, Nairobi, to District Commis-

sioner, Meru, "re: Meru African Court returns, 29 May 1957," KNA, (ARC)MAA/2/9/27/III.

94. J. B. Carson, African Courts Officer, Nairobi, to Provincial Commissioner, Central, "re: Meru African Court returns, 16 July 1957," KNA, (ARC)MAA/2/9/27/III. For another mention of the failure of the ban to effect "the right spirit" against excision, see Stephen Anampiu, G.T.T. College, Meru, to W. H. Laughton, 16 September 1957, KNA, MSS/124/6.

95. Barbara Castle, MP, London, to Alan Lennox-Boyd, Secretary of State for the Colonies, London, 16 October 1957, PRO, CO/822/1647.

96. Acting Governor, Kenya, to Secretary of State for the Colonies, London, 27 December 1957, PRO, CO/822/1647.

97. Secretary of State for the Colonies, London, to Barbara Castle, MP, London, 20 January 1958, PRO, CO/822/1647.

98. "Minutes of a Special Meeting of Njuri Committee held in the A.D.C. Office on 6th November, 1957," MCC, ADM/15/16/6/II.

99. See Meru African Courts, Monthly Returns, 1956–58, KNA, ARC (MAA)/2/9/27/II, ARC(MAA)/2/10/27/III, MAA/7/282, and MAA/7/283.

100. Seminar held by the Department of History, University of Nairobi, 8 November 1995. Ntai wa Nkararu was especially emphatic on this point.

101. C. Kiruki, interview, 30 June 1995.

102. I. Kajuju, interview, 20 March 1995. See also L. Kajuju, interview, 23 March 1995; and J. M'Lithara, interview, 6 February 1995. Survey research conducted by *Maendeleo ya Wanawake* ("Harmful Traditional Practices") indicated in the early 1990s that 73.5 percent of all females fourteen years of age or older in Meru had been "circumcised."

103. Meru ADC, Minutes, 12 April 1956, MCC, ADC/6.

CHAPTER 4: LATE COLONIAL CUSTOMS AND WAYWARD SCHOOLGIRLS

1. Kinoru African Court [hereafter KAC], Civil Case [hereafter CC] No. 1376/66. This and all other cases mentioned in this chapter were found in the storage room at the Meru Law Court (MLC) at Meru town. The names of all litigants and witnesses have been changed to protect their identities. While the proceedings were largely conducted in the Meru language, court registrars recorded the testimony in English using only occasional Meru phrases. For each litigant or witness who appeared, the registrar noted his/her sex, adult status, religion (Christian, Muslim, or "pagan"), and the fact that s/he had been sworn in. The registrar then recorded their opening statements and responses to questions posed by the court elders and the opposing litigant. The resulting records represent detailed translated summaries of the proceedings, probably capturing most major issues and points of contention within a case, rather than translated transcriptions.

2. This figure is a rough estimate based on examination of the Meru court

civil registries deposited at the Kenya National Archives, Nairobi (AHD, 1/19–1/71) and on the perusal of over one thousand civil court records in the Meru Law Court storage room. In examining the latter, I found fifty-seven cases of "illegal pregnancy."

3. This argument was originally formulated by Chanock, "Making Customary Law"; and Chanock, *Law, Custom, and Social Order.* See also Ranger, "The Invention of Tradition in Colonial Africa"; Moore, *Social Facts and Fabrications;* Mann and Roberts, "Law in Colonial Africa"; Schmidt, *Peasants, Traders, and Wives;* and Jeater, *Marriage, Perversion, and Power.*

4. Berry, *No Condition is Permanent,* esp. ch. 2; McClendon, "Tradition and Domestic Struggle"; Mutongi, " 'Worries of the Heart' "; Shadle, " 'Changing Traditions' "; Shadle, " 'Girl Cases.' " Hirsch, in her study of Islamic courts in postcolonial Kenya, *Pronouncing and Persevering,* similarly examines how women use court proceedings to their own advantage.

5. Bell, "The Ameru People of Kenya: Part I," 233. See also Dr. Clive Irvine, Church of Scotland Mission, Chogoria, to H. E. Lambert, District Commissioner, Meru, 10 October 1939, quoted in Meru District, AR, 1939, KNA, DC/MRU/4/5.

6. Dr. Clive Irvine, Church of Scotland Mission, Chogoria, to Foreign Mission Committee, Church of Scotland, Edinburgh, "Let's Be Honest," 1 November 1944, NLS, Acc/7584/B275; Dr. Clive Irvine, Church of Scotland Mission, Chogoria, to Foreign Mission Committee, Church of Scotland, Edinburgh, Annual Report, 1944, NLS, Acc/7548/C1.

7. Meru LNC, Minutes, 15 July 1942, and 28–29 October 1942, MCC, LNC/4. These LNC discussions were probably prompted by complaints like that lodged by Dr. Clive Irvine in 1939 in the letter cited in note 6.

8. N. M'Mwirichia, interview, 18 September 1995.

9. Meru LNC, Minutes, 8 December 1949, KNA, PC/CP/2/19.

10. "Minutes of the Annual Meeting of the *Njuri Ncheke* held on 12th October 1954," MCC, ADM/15/16/6/III.

11. See KAC, CC Nos. 873/56, 427/60, 463/60, MLC.

12. Gerald Casey, Timau, to Barbara Castle, Member of Parliament, London, 2 July 1957, PRO, CO/822/1647; Kenya, *The Pattern of Income;* White, *The Comforts of Home,* 188.

13. Meru Law Panel, Minutes, 16 June 1960, MCC, ADM/15/16/6/III.

14. Ghai and McAuslan, *Public Law,* 359–74 (quote is from p. 359). On Kenyan officials' previous reluctance to codify "customary" law, see Shadle, " 'Changing Traditions.' "

15. Njonjo, Foreword, v. For more on these efforts to "modernize" the Kenyan judiciary, see Thomas, "Regulating Reproduction," 321–27.

16. Cotran, *Restatement of African Law,* 40–42. See also "Special Law Panel Meeting to Record Customary Criminal in Meru District—25/9/61," and "Meeting of the Meru (including Tharaka) Law Panel, 28th–30th Nov. 1962," MCC, ADM/15/16/6/IV.

17. For an example of this new perspective, see Paterson, "The Human Situation in East Africa—Part I." For West Africa, see van Beusekom, "From Underpopulation to Overpopulation."

18. Duden, "Population"; Sharpless, "Population Science."

19. Martin, "Some Estimates of the General Age Distribution"; Searle, Phillips, and Martin, "Colonial Statistics"; Goldthorpe, "Appendix 7: The African Population of East Africa." For a fuller account of the 1948 census, see Thomas, "Regulating Reproduction," ch. 3.

20. Research Department, Colonial Office, "Population Trends in British Colonial Territories and Policy in Regard to Population Growth," memorandum distributed to the Advisory Committee on Scientific Policy, 20 January 1956, PRO, CO/859/666.

21. Brass and Jolly, *Population Dynamics of Kenya*, 130–32.

22. Kenya Colony and Protectorate, *Report of the Committee on Young Persons and Children*, 28.

23. Wipper, "Kikuyu Women," 302–7, appendix A.

24. Lonsdale, "The Moral Economy of Mau Mau," 392. See also Davison, *Voices from Mutira*, 85, 105, 119.

25. "Pregnancy Testing in Our High Schools," *Viva* 3 (September 1976): 41–42; "Womansvoice" [letter to the editor], *Viva* 3 (October 1976): 69; Rogo, Bohmer, and Ombaka, "Developing Community-based Strategies," S18, S60–S61. In 1980s and 1990s Kenya expulsion was still the most common response to schoolgirl pregnancies (Karani, "Educational Policies and Women's Education"; Ferguson, Gitonga, and Kabira, *Family Planning Needs;* Bledsoe and Cohen, *Social Dynamics of Adolescent Fertility*, 109–13).

26. Lonsdale, "The Moral Economy of Mau Mau," 380–97.

27. Dr. Clive Irvine, Church of Scotland Mission, Chogoria, to H. E. Lambert, District Commissioner, Meru, 10 October 1939, quoted in Meru District, AR, 1939, KNA, DC/MRU/4/5.

28. Meru District, AR, 1939, KNA, DC/MRU/4/5.

29. Meru LNC, Minutes, 15 July 1942, 28–29 October 1942, MCC, LNC/4.

30. Mrs. Julia Mburugu, social worker, Gitoro Women's Institute, to G. K. Gicogo, District Commissioner, Meru, 15 November 1966, MM, DC/ADM/18/5. In his sociological study of young prostitutes in early 1960s Nairobi, Carlebach *(Juvenile Prostitutes in Nairobi)* noted that premarital pregnancies prompted some girls to become prostitutes.

31. Abuoga and Mutere, *The History of the Press in Kenya*, chs. 2–3.

32. *Baraza* and *Taifa Weekly* sold 33,000 and 32,000 copies per week, whereas *Taifa Leo* sold 23,000 copies each day. In comparison, the leading English weeklies, the *East African Standard* (published on Friday) and the *Sunday Nation*, had circulations of 44,000 and 31,000, respectively, whereas the leading English dailies, the *East African Standard* and the *Daily Nation*, had circulations of 28,000 and 17,000, respectively (Soja, *The Geography of Modernization in Kenya*, 40–43).

33. *Baraza,* 16 May 1968, 23 May 1968.

34. KAC, CC Nos. 147/65, 862/65, MLC.

35. Based on research conducted in 1989–90, Lema and Kabeberi-Macharia (*A Review of Abortion in Kenya,* 15) argue that in "most cases" the decision to terminate a pregnancy is a woman's own.

36. Bell, "The Ameru People of Kenya," 233, 236; Akinla, "Abortion in Africa." On similar methods used in 1980s and 1990s Kenya, see Lema and Kabeberi-Macharia, *A Review of Abortion in Kenya;* Barker and Rich, "Influences on Adolescent Sexuality"; Rogo, Bohmer, and Ombaka, "Developing Community-based Strategies," S24–S27; and Lema and Njau, "Abortion in Kenya."

37. J. Kinoti, interview, 28 June 1995.

38. While court records contain no specific references to daughters first telling mothers, in 1990s Meru mothers often served as go-betweens between daughters and fathers. I thank Agnes Odinga for encouraging me to make this point.

39. KAC, CC Nos. 1988/65, 517/66, MLC.

40. Kitching, *Class and Economic Change in Kenya,* esp. 309–11, 438–55; Leys, *Underdevelopment in Kenya,* chs. 5–6; Leonard, *African Successes,* chs. 2–4; Ogot and Ochieng', *Decolonization and Independence in Kenya,* chs. 3–5.

41. Kenya, Ministry of Finance and Economic Planning, Statistics Division, *Kenya Population Census, 1962,* 3:44–46.

42. Cases which indicated that the woman had attended school include District Court of Kenya at Meru [hereafter DCKM], CC No. 246/68, MLC; Appeal Magistrate's Court at Meru [hereafter AMCM], CC No. 155/64, MLC; KAC, CC Nos. 133/65, 147/65, 443/66, 517/66, 885/66, 1376/66, 4500/66, 555/67, 58/67, MLC; and Imenti Native Tribunal [hereafter INT], CC No. 873/56, MLC. Those which indicated that the man had attended school included DCKM, CC No. 246/68, MLC; and KAC, CC Nos. 397/64, 766/64, 123/65, 133/65, 147/65, 1233/65, 1312/65, 1909/65, 1988/65, 443/66, 517/66, 1367/66, 1376/66, 538/67, MLC.

43. J. Laiboni, interview, 23 July 1995.

44. Elsewhere in colonial Kenya and Africa, people also associated premarital pregnancy litigation with schoolgirls (see Penwill, *Kamba Customary Law,* 73–75; and Vellenga, "Arenas of Judgement"; see also Bledsoe and Cohen, *Social Dynamics of Adolescent Fertility,* 107–8; and Puja and Kassimoto, "Girls in Education—And Pregnancy At School").

45. KAC, CC Nos. 450/66, 133/65, MLC.

46. Donald M. McFarlan (former missionary in Nigeria), Glasgow, to Rev. J. W. C. Dougall, Secretary, Foreign Mission Committee, Edinburgh, 1 March 1943, NLS, Acc/7548/B404; Penwill, *Kamba Customary Law,* 74–75; Mbembe, "Provisional Notes on the Postcolony," esp. 23; Rogo, Bohmer, and Ombaka, "Developing Community-based Strategies," S61; Mager, *Gender and the Making of a South African Bantustan,* 138–39, 203; Isak Niehaus, "Towards a Dubious Liberation."

47. KAC, CC Nos. 517/66, 443/66, 397/64, 1233/65, 1909/65, MLC.

48. KAC, CC No. 1233/65, MLC. See also J. Kinoti, interview, 28 June 1995.

49. KAC, CC No. 1909/65, MLC.

50. J. Kinoti, interview, 28 June 1995.

51. Waciuma, *Daughter of Mumbi*, 40–41.

52. K.M., "Should I lie and speak up for my friend," and response, *Drum*, November 1972, n.p. This edition of *Drum* was published out of Lagos, Nigeria. Thanks to Kenda Mutongi for sharing this letter with me. For more on "Dear Dolly," see Mutongi, " 'Dear Dolly's' Advice."

53. KAC, CC No. 397/64, MLC.

54. J. Kinoti, interview, 28 June 1995; J. Laiboni, interview, 23 July 1995.

55. Comaroff and Roberts, "Marriage and Extra-Marital Sexuality," 97.

56. E. Carey Francis, Principal, Alliance High School, Kenya, "Polygamy," 3 July 1942, NLS, Acc/7548/B404.

57. KAC, CC No. 1312/65, MLC.

58. Stephen Anampiu, Government Teacher Training Centre, Meru, to W. H. Laughton, Kagumo Government Teacher Training Centre, Nyeri, c. 1957–58, KNA, MSS/124/6.

59. Cases which plaintiffs won include KAC, CC Nos. 427/60, 463/60, 146/61, 513/63, 544/63, 632/63, 691/63, 693/63, 739/63, 198/64, 345/64, 397/64, 766/64, 780/64, 791/64, 123/65, 148/65, 592/65, 862/65, 876/65, 885/65, 1233/65, 1262/65, 1312/65, 2043/65, 2046/65, 2111/65, 443/66, 450/66, 456/66, 583/66, 1255/66, 1337/66, 1367/66, 1376/66, 58/67, 518/67, 849/67, MLC; INT, CC No. 873/56, MLC; AMCM, CC No. 206/66, MLC; and DCKM, CC No. 246/68, MLC. Cases which defendants won include KAC, CC Nos. 704/63, 200/64, 359/64, 133/65, 147/65, 889/65, 1909/65, 1988/65, 2052/65, 517/66, 1257/66, 538/67, 555/67, MLC; and AMCM, CC Nos. 155/64, 213/66, 165/67, MLC.

60. KAC, CC No. 538/657, MLC. For similar presumptions that women were telling the truth, see Waciuma, *Daughter of Mumbi*, 40; B. A. Rwezaura, "Tanzania: More Protection for Children," 263–64; Rwebangira, "Maintenance and Care in Law and Practice"; Shadle, "Rape and Justice in Kenya, c. 1940–1970"; and Shadle, " 'Girl Cases' "

61. Resident Magistrate's Court at Meru (hereafter RMCM), CC No. 146/67, MLC.

62. KAC, CC Nos. 791/64, 2046/65, 2111/65, 456/66, 1257/66, MLC.

63. DCKM, CC No. 246/68, MLC; and KAC, CC Nos. 463/60, 146/61, 544/63, 691/63, 693/63, 345/64, 592/65, 885/65, 1262/65, 1312/65, 2043/65, 583/66, 1367/66, 849/67, MLC.

64. INT, CC No. 873/56, MLC; and KAC, CC Nos. 427/60, 513/63, 739/63, 200/64, 780/64, 133/65, 450/66, 1255/66, 555/67, MLC.

65. AMCM, CC Nos. 155/64, 206/66, 213/66, 165/67, MLC; and KAC, CC Nos. 632/63, 704/63, 198/64, 359/64, 397/64, 766/64, 123/65, 147/65, 148/65, 862/65, 876/65, 889/65, 1233/65, 1909/65, 1988/65, 2052/65, 443/66, 517/66, 1337/66, 1376/66, 58/67, 518/67, 538/67, MLC.

66. KAC, CC Nos. 133/65, 739/63, 200/64, 780/64, 450/66, 538/67, MLC. On *uthoni*, see E. Mary Holding, "*Nthoni*," KNA, MSS/7.

67. KAC, CC No. 427/60, MLC.

68. KAC, CC No. 450/66, MLC.

69. KAC, CC Nos. 513/63, 200/64, 133/65, 538/67, MLC. For a case in which officials denied that that they had the right to consider the "matter of marriage" within "illegal pregnancy" cases, see KAC, CC No. 1255/66, MLC.

70. KAC, CC Nos. 513/63, 739/63, 450/66, MLC.

71. AMCM, CC No. 165/67, MLC.

72. KAC, CC No. 147/65, MLC.

73. J. Kinoti, interview, 28 June 1995. For similar difficulties that young women faced in discussing intimate matters in courts and before parents in a South African context, see Mager, *Gender and the Making of a South African Bantustan*, 104, 136–38.

74. AMCM, CC No. 254/66, MLC; KAC, CC No. 443/66, MLC.

75. AMCM, CC Nos. 155/64, 213/66, MLC; KAC, CC No. 2052/65, MLC.

76. KAC, CC No. 862/65, MLC.

77. KAC, CC Nos. 198/64, 397/64, MLC.

78. KAC, CC No. 123/65, MLC.

79. AMCM, CC No. 165/67, MLC.

80. AMCM, CC No. 213/66, MLC.

81. KAC, CC No. 1337/66, MLC.

82. Shadle, "Rape and Justice in Kenya"; "Special Law Panel Meeting to Record Customary Criminal in Meru District—25/9/61," MCC, ADM/15/16/6/IV.

83. KAC, CC No. 538/67, MLC.

84. For other accounts of how "proper" girls and young women in post-colonial Kenya were expected to be "coy and reluctant" in sexual encounters, see Mutongi, " 'Dear Dolly's' Advice"; and Nelson, " 'Selling Her Kiosk,' " 223.

85. J. Kinoti, interview, 28 June 1995.

86. Shadle, " 'Girl Cases,' " ch. 6.

87. AMCM, CC No. 213/66, MLC.

88. AMCM, CC No. 213/66, MLC.

89. AMCM, CC No. 155/64, MLC; KAC, CC No. 147/65, MLC.

90. KAC, CC No. 1909/65, MLC; D.C. Civil Panel at Meru [hereafter DCCPM], Case No. 147/65, MLC.

91. KAC, CC No. 518/67, MLC.

92. J. Laiboni, interview, 23 July 1995.

93. KAC, CC No. 1376/66, MLC.

94. KAC, CC Nos. 2052/65, 147/65, 1233/65, MLC.

95. Hofmeyer, "*We Spend Our Years as a Tale that is Told*," 65–66.

96. AMCM, CC No. 155/64, MLC; INT, CC No. 873/56, MLC; KAC, CC Nos. 1312/65, 1367/66, MLC.

97. KAC, CC No. 133/65, MLC.

98. KAC, CC Nos. 147/65, 632/63, MLC; AMCM, CC No. 155/64, MLC.

99. For parents as the primary assessors of resemblance, see KAC, CC Nos. 359/64, 1312/65, 58/67, MLC; M. M'Mwigwika, interview, 15 June 1995; and J. M'Mbogori, interview, 10 July 1995. For female kin, see AMCM, CC No. 254/66, MLC; KAC, CC Nos. 632/63, 198/64, MLC; D. Joseph, interview, 13 June 1995; S. M'Muraga and E. Mucheke, interview, 13 June 1995; J. Kinoti, interview, 28 June 1995; and S. M'Mukiiri, interview, 1 August 1995. On *kiama,* see INT, CC No. 873/56, MLC; and KAC, CC Nos. 632/63, 704/63, 198/64, MLC.

100. J. Kinoti, interview, 28 June 1995.

101. KAC, CC No. 632/63, MLC.

102. AMCM, CC No. 213/66, MLC; KAC, CC No. 198/64, MLC.

103. KAC, CC Nos. 632/63, 625/64, 198/64, MLC.

104. AMCM, CC No. 155/64, MLC.

105. AMCM, CC No. 213/66, MLC; KAC, CC Nos. 359/64, 1233/65, MLC.

106. AMCM, CC No. 213/66, MLC.

107. KAC, CC No. 58/67, MLC.

108. J. Kinoti, interview, 28 June 1995.

109. This discussion of the ongoing support for such children provided by grandparents, particularly grandmothers, is based on my interview with J. Kinoti (28 June 1995), as well as many other conversations with people in 1990s Meru. For a similar analysis of another African context, see Bledsoe, "Marginal Members."

110. Vellenga, "Attempts to Change the Marriage Laws"; Levasseur, "The Modernization of Law in Africa"; Comaroff and Roberts, "Marriage and Extra-Marital Sexuality," 97–123; May, *Changing People,* 74–81; Griffiths, "Support for Women with Dependent Children"; Kazembe, "Methodological Perspectives on Research and Maintenance Law in Zimbabwe"; Molokomme, "*Children of the Fence*"; Rwebangira and Liljeström, *Haraka, Haraka;* Tumbo-Masabo and Liljeström, *Chelewa, Chelewa;* Launay, "The Power of Names"; Mikell, "Pleas for Domestic Relief."

111. Ferguson, *Expectations of Modernity,* 189–92.

112. Kenya Colony and Protectorate, *Report of the Committee on Young Persons and Children,* 28.

CHAPTER 5: POSTCOLONIAL NATIONALISM AND "MODERN" SINGLE MOTHERS

1. Kenya Colony and Protectorate, "The Affiliation Ordinance, 1959, No. 12 of 1959"; and Waruhiu, *Affiliation Law in Kenya,* 1–9. It was originally called the "Affiliation Ordinance." After independence, it was among a series of statutory laws re-adopted as Acts.

2. A set of registers from the Kinoru African Court, the District Court Civil Panel, and District Magistrate's Court, held at the Kenya National Archives (AHD/1/50–67) and covering the period between 1965 and 1969 (the

peak period for affiliation litigation), indicates that these three courts heard only 35 affiliation cases, compared with 126 "illegal pregnancy" cases.

3. Letter to District Commissioner, Meru, MM, DC/ADM/18/5; KAC, CC No. 2/Af, MLC. The district officer ordered the court elders to rehear the case, but they reached the same conclusion. Throughout this chapter, the names of all litigants and witnesses have been changed to protect their identities. In Lilian's case, I have also omitted specific references to the year.

4. Vellenga, "Attempts to Change the Marriage Laws"; Levasseur, "The Modernization of Law in Africa"; Wipper, "Equal Rights for Women in Kenya?"; Armstrong, *Women and Law in Southern Africa;* Mbeo and Ooko-Ombaka, *Women and Law in Kenya;* Pitshandenge, "Marriage Law in Sub-Saharan Africa"; Rwebangira, "What Has the Law Got To Do With It?"

5. John Dumoga, "East African Women Look Ahead—2," *Daily Nation,* 4 April 1964, 6; The Kenya Council of Women, Nairobi, October 1962, KNA, MSS/57/28; Sheila Dixon, "Shauri ya Wanawake," *Kenya Weekly News,* 12 March 1965, KNA, MSS/57/30; and Wipper, "Equal Rights for Women in Kenya?"

6. "Greatest Strain on Marriage," *Daily Nation,* 31 May 1967.

7. Quotation is from Kenya, *National Assembly Debates* (12 June 1969), 1110.

8. Henriques, "Bastardy and the New Poor Law"; Middleton, *When Family Failed;* Wilkinson, *Affiliation Law and Practice;* U.K., House of Commons, "Appendix 5: The History of the Obligation to Maintain," 115–21; Thane, "Women and the Poor Law."

9. The Kenyan Legitimacy Ordinance, unlike the British Ordinance, covered situations in which either the father or mother was married to a third person when the "illegitimate" person was born (Colony and Protectorate of Kenya, "A Bill Relating to Children Born Out of Wedlock," 1930, KNA, AG/1/625; Colony and Protectorate of Kenya, "A Bill to Amend the Legitimacy Ordinance," 1930, KNA, AG/1/626).

10. Colonial Office, "Circular Despatch: League of Nations, Illegitimate Children," 5 October 1929, KNA, AP/1609.

11. Kenya Colony and Protectorate, *Legislative Council Debates* (22 April 1959), 44.

12. Kenya Colony and Protectorate, *Official Gazette* (2 April 1946), 165; Kenya Colony and Protectorate, *Report of the Committee on Young Persons and Children,* 1, 28–29.

13. In Tanganyika an Affiliation Ordinance was introduced in 1949 that excluded cases between "natives" (Rwebangira, "Maintenance and Care in Law and Practice"; Tanganyika, "An Ordinance to Provide for the Maintenance of Illegitimate Children. 1949, No. 42 or 1949.")

14. Kenya Colony and Protectorate, *Report of the Committee on Young Persons and Children,* 21, 83–87.

15. This bill was modeled after the Affiliation Proceedings Act introduced in 1957 in the United Kingdom. That act consolidated previous legislation on

"illegitimacy" and maintenance by repealing in whole or in part earlier legislation, including the Bastardy Laws Acts of 1845 and 1923, the Poor Law Amendment Act of 1844, the Bastardy Laws Amendment Act of 1872, the Affiliation Orders Act of 1914 and 1952, the Age of Marriage Act of 1929, and the Magistrate's Courts Act of 1952 (Zambia, *Report on Affiliation and Maintenance Orders Project*, 28).

16. Kenya Colony and Protectorate, *Legislative Council Debates* (22 April 1959), 51, 53–57.

17. Ibid., 42–43, 59, 52–53.

18. Bennet and Rosberg, *The Kenyatta Election*, 10–17, 33–35; Low and Smith, *History of East Africa*, 3:135–45; Berman, *Control and Crisis in Colonial Kenya*, 399–400; Ogot, "The Decisive Years, 1956–1963," 54–61.

19. Waruhiu, *Affiliation Law in Kenya*, i. More than 165 courts were empowered to hear affiliation cases (U.K. Colonial Office, *Report on the Colony*, 73; and Kenya, *National Assembly Debates* [7 December 1966], 2445).

20. Ghai and McAuslan, *Public Law and Political Change in Kenya*, 149.

21. Kenya Colony and Protectorate, *Report of the Committee on Young Persons and Children*, 28.

22. Colonial Office, "Social Security in the Colonial Territories," 12 December 1944, PRO, CO/859/125/8.

23. B. B. F. Russell for Permanent Secretary, Ministry of Health, to Registrar to the Supreme Court, Nairobi, "The Affiliation Ordinance No. 12 of 1959," 8 August 1959, AGCK, 527/3.

24. P. D. McEntee, African Courts Officer, Ministry of African Affairs, to the Acting Solicitor General, Attorney General's Chambers, Nairobi, 9 October 1959, AGCK, 527/3.

25. Kenya, *Legislative Council Debates* (22 December 1959), 1171–79; (6 January 1960), 1434.

26. Kenya, *Legislative Council Debates* (22 December 1959), 1179; (6 January 1960), 1415–18, 1424, 1427.

27. Kenya, *Legislative Council Debates* (6 January 1960), 1422, 1425, 1443–44. During the late colonial period, the administration held one or two of the specially elected slots for women (Wipper, "The Politics of Sex," 465).

28. Kenya, *Legislative Council Debates* (6 January 1960), 1418–21, 1430.

29. In 1962 the Ordinance was revised to clarify procedures for holding summons hearings, making affiliation payments through the court, and filing variation orders (Mavisi and Kyalo, "The Affiliation Act," 104–5).

30. Advisory Committee on African Courts, Nairobi, "Minutes of a Meeting held on 20 Aug. 1962," KNA, DC/MRU/2/11/3.

31. Meru Law Panel, Minutes, 16 June 1960, MCC, ADM/15/16/6/vol. III.

32. Kenya, *Legislative Council Debates* (6 January 1960), 1430, 1435.

33. Kenya, *House of Representatives Debates* (12 March 1964), 747.

34. KNA, Mathira. Mathira African Court materials are used throughout this chapter, as it is the only court that both handled a significant number of

affiliation cases and deposited its civil case registries and case records at the Kenyan National Archives.

35. District Court Civil Panel at Kinoru, "Applications for an Affiliation Order, 1/65–5/69," KNA, AHD/1/50.

36. Letter to the Attorney General, Nairobi, 14 January 1966, AGCK, 527/3. The names of all private citizens who sent letters to the Attorney General that are contained in this file have been changed or omitted.

37. For example, see KNA, Mathira/5154, 5195.

38. Cases could be filed later if the woman could prove either that the alleged father had paid money for the child's maintenance during his or her first year or that he had recently returned to Kenya after ceasing to reside there within the child's first year (see Kenya Colony and Protectorate, "The Affiliation Ordinance, 1959, No. 12 of 1959," clause 3[1]).

39. This estimate is based on the forty affiliation cases heard at the Mathira African Court in 1968 and the thirty-five cases heard by the District Court Civil Panel and Magistrate's Court at Kinoru (Meru) between 1965 and 1969 (KNA, Mathira/7259–98 and AHD/1/50). A less systematic examination of the Mathira records between 1964 and 1967 suggests that plaintiffs' rate of success was even higher in the years preceding 1968.

40. Kenya Colony and Protectorate, "The Affiliation Ordinance, 1959, No. 12 of 1959," Section 5(2); and Waruhiu, *Affiliation Law in Kenya*, 10–14.

41. T. A. Watts, African Courts Officer, Nairobi, to Magistrate, Nyeri, 27 April 1966, KNA, Mathira/7382. See also KNA, Mathira/7281, 7286, 7299.

42. Waruhiu, *Affiliation Act in Kenya*, i–ii; Ag. Solicitor General to Director, East African Literature Bureau, "Ms. Affiliation Law in Kenya," 6 December 1961, AGCK, 527/3.

43. Waruhiu, *Affiliation Act in Kenya*, 11–13. Waruhiu also mentioned that blood tests could be used to rule out some "candidates for fatherhood."

44. KNA, Mathira/7259–98.

45. Letter of 19 April 1965, evidence submitted as part of MAC, CC No. 206/66, KNA, Mathira/6040.

46. MAC, CC No. 207/66, KNA, Mathira/6041. For other instances in which plaintiffs were awarded the full amount that they requested in ex parte decisions, see KNA, Mathira/5484, 5492, 6041, 7277.

47. District Magistrate's Court at Karatina, Affiliation Case No. 2/69, KNA, Mathira/7300.

48. MAC, CC No. 33/68, KNA, Mathira/7291. See also KNA, Mathira/5082, 5154.

49. Letter to Resident Magistrate, Nyeri, 10 June 1969, AGCK, 527/3.

50. MAC, CC No. 33/68, KNA, Mathira/7291.

51. MAC, CC No. 25/68, KNA, Mathira/7283. For other examples of such lists, see Mathira/5097, 5490, 5492, 6041, 7264, 7271, 7277, 7285, 7287, 7288, 7289, 7291, 7300, 7301, 7302.

52. KAC, CC No. 793/64, MLC.

53. MAC, CC No. 25/68, KNA, Mathira/7283.

54. Letters dated 15 September 1962, 9 November 1964, 12 July 1966, 19 July 1966, and 9 January 1969, contained in AGCK, 527/3; and "Kulipa Mimba" (Paying pregnancy), *Baraza*, 15 May 1968.

55. Letter to Attorney General, 9 January 1969, AGCK, 527/3.

56. Letter to Attorney General, 28 September 1968, AGCK, 527/3.

57. KNA, Mathira/5082, 5097, 5201, 5490, 5063.

58. MAC, CC No. 1/64, KNA, Mathira/5063.

59. MAC, CC No. 29/68, KNA, Mathira/7287.

60. Kenya, *National Assembly Debates* (12 March 1964), 746–47. For similar exchanges, see *National Assembly Debates* (7 December 1966), 2444–47, and (28 February 1967), 450–52.

61. MAC, CC No. 4/65, KNA, Mathira/5484. Similarly, see "Ngari Sasa Atalipa 45/- Badala ya 80/-" (Now Ngari will pay 45/- instead of 80/-), *Taifa Weekly*, 11 January 1969.

62. MAC, CC No. 139/1964, KNA, Mathira/5201.

63. George Owinoh Omoloh, Ruiru, "Biashara ya Mimba" (The business of pregnancy), *Taifa Weekly*, 5 April 1969, 3. See also Henry Njoroge, Lanet, "Kufuta Sheria ya Mimba" (Repeal the pregnancy law), *Taifa Weekly*, 7 June 1969, 3; and editorial, "Sheria Mpya ya Kulipa Malezi ya Watoto?" (A new law for paying children's maintenance?), *Taifa Weekly*, 19 June 1969.

64. Letter to Attorney General, Nairobi, 14 January 1969, AGCK, 527/3.

65. Letters to Attorney General, Nairobi, 4 July 1969 and 18 September 1970, AGCK, 527/3.

66. Paul Kiambu, "Sheria nchini Kenya: Malipo ya Mimba" (Law in Kenya: Pregnancy payments), *Taifa Weekly*, 7 June 1969, 3.

67. Hamisi correspondent, "Kesi za Mwalimu Huyu Zimenichokesha—Hakimu" (The cases of this teacher have tired me—Judge), *Baraza*, 22 May 1969.

68. Kenya Colony and Protectorate, *Legislative Council Debates* (6 January 1960), 1418–21, 1430; Kenya, *House of Representatives Debates* (12 March 1964), 747.

69. Wipper, "African Women, Fashion, and Scapegoating," 348. See also Paul Kiambu, "Sheria nchini Kenya: Malipo ya Mimba" (Law in Kenya: Pregnancy payments), *Taifa Weekly*, 7 June 1969, 3.

70. Maboreke, "The Love of a Mother"; Griffiths, "Support for Women with Dependent Children"; Molokomme, *"Children of the Fence"*; Mikell, "Pleas for Domestic Relief."

71. Kenya, *National Assembly Debates* (11 June 1969), 1036.

72. H. A. Kusindi, Maseno, "Sheria ya kuwalea watoto itiwe nguvu milele Kenya" (The law of caring for children doesn't have a strong future in Kenya), *Baraza*, 16 May 1968, 5.

73. Paul Kiambu, "Sheria nchini Kenya: Malipo ya Mimba" (Law in Kenya: Pregnancy payments), *Taifa Weekly*, 7 June 1969, 3.

74. P. W. W. Ommott, Mombasa, "Korti Itupe Kezi za Mimba" (Courts should throw out pregnancy cases), *Taifa Weekly*, 20 January 1968, 3.

75. Kenya, *National Assembly Debates* (5 July 1967), 1778–79.

76. Kenya, *National Assembly Debates* (29 November 1967), 2616–17.

77. Kenya, *National Assembly Debates* (12 March 1964), 746–47; (7 December 1966), 2444–47; (31 October 1968), 2564–66.

78. Letters to Attorney General, Nairobi, 11 April 1969 and 21 October 1969; file note by Attorney General, 14 April 1969; Letter by J. R. Hobbs, Deputy Public Prosecutor, Attorney General's Office, 15 April 1969, all in AGCK, 527/3.

79. Ochieng', "Structural and Political Changes," 98–100. By September 1969 the Kenyatta regime had pressured Kikuyus within the KPU leadership, including Kaggia, to return to KANU. In October 1969 the government banned the KPU and detained its remaining leadership. With the only viable opposition party banned, the December 1969 KANU primary elections became the equivalent of a general election (Goldsworthy, *Tom Mboya*, 285–86).

80. Leys, *Underdevelopment in Kenya*, 234–35.

81. Editorial, "Sheria Mpya ya Kulipa Malezi ya Watoto?" (A new law for paying children's maintenance?), *Baraza*, 19 June 1969, 3.

82. S. Waruhiu, interview, 2 September 1999. Samuel Waruhiu himself was in the United Kingdom during the Mau Mau rebellion, studying to become a lawyer.

83. Kenya, *National Assembly Debates* (12 June 1969), 1112.

84. Bujra, "Women 'Entrepreneurs' of Early Nairobi"; White, *The Comforts of Home*; Lonsdale, "The Moral Economy of Mau Mau," 320–21, 386–87; Robertson, *Trouble Showed the Way*, chs. 3–4.

85. "Sheria ya kusafisha miji ya Kenya kuanza kazi wiki Ijayo" (The law of cleaning Kenyan cities begins next week), *Taifa Leo*, 14 February 1969. For the National Assembly debate on the Vagrancy Bill, see Kenya, *National Assembly Debates* (20 November 1968), 3238–70; (21 November 1968), 3329–46; (25 November 1968), 3435–77; and (26 November 1968), 3512–27.

86. "Christian Paper Against Repeal," *East African Standard*, 16 June 1969.

87. For a more detailed lay account of the Succession Act, see FIDA–Kenya, *A Kenyan Woman's Guide to the Law*, 23–24; and Mutongi, *"Worries of the Heart,"* ch. 5.

88. Kenya, *Commission on the Law of Marriage and Divorce Report*, i, 2–3.

89. Kenya, *National Assembly Debates* (17 June 1969), 1258.

90. Asiyo, "Legislative Process and Gender Issues in Kenya"; Thomas, "Contestation, Construction, and Reconstitution."

91. Nzomo, "Kenyan Women in Politics and Public Decision Making," 241.

92. Wipper, "African Women, Fashion, and Scapegoating," 335–38, 347–48.

93. "Affiliation Act Repeal Annoys Women's Leaders," *Daily Nation*, 10 May 1969; "Affiliation Act Move Attacked," *Daily Nation*, 24 May 1969; "Sheria ya kulea watoto isifutwe—Bi. Mboya" (The law of caring for children should not be repeated—Madame Mboya), *Taifa Weekly*, 24 May 1969;

"Women Appeal on Affiliation Act," *East African Standard*, 28 May 1969; "Kenya Women to Seek Talks Over Act Plan," *Daily Nation*, 28 May 1969; and "More Opposition to Repeal of Affiliation Act," *Daily Nation*, 10 June 1969. On the political marginalization of women in postcolonial Kenya, see Nzomo and Staudt, "Man-Made Political Machinery in Kenya."

94. "Women Protest at Bill to Repeal Affiliation Act," *East African Standard*, 31 May 1969; "Protest to MPs on Affiliation Act," *Daily Nation*, 31 May 1969; "Plea to MPs: Don't Repeal Affiliation Bill," *Daily Nation*, 1 June 1969; "Women's Letter Queried," *East African Standard*, 4 June 1969; and "Delay in Acts' Repeal Urged," *Daily Nation*, 10 June 1969.

95. Kenya, *National Assembly Debates* (10 June 1969), 977–80.

96. "Affiliation Act 'War' Hots Up on Television," *Daily Nation*, 25 June 1969.

97. Wipper, "The Politics of Sex," 472–74.

98. "Heckling Greets Affiliation Bill," *East African Standard*, 11 June 1969; and "Affiliation Act Repeal Hailed," *Daily Nation*, 11 June 1969.

99. For parliamentary chiding of Njonjo as a member of "the bachelor's club," see Kenya, *National Assembly Debates* (7 December 1966), 2447.

100. Kenya, *National Assembly Debates* (10 June 1969), 977–79.

101. Kenya, *National Assembly Debates* (10 June 1969), 979–80; (17 June 1969), 1246, 1257; (11 June 1969), 1051, 1045, 1032, 1069–70.

102. Kenya, *National Assembly Debates* (10 June 1969), 985; (11 June 1969), 1032; (12 June 1969), 1115, 1125.

103. Ali Mazrui, "A Discourse on Mixed Reactions to—Miniskirts," *Sauti ya Mabibi* (Voice of Women) 1, no. 8 (1969): 2–5, 8, 17, 21; Wipper, "African Women, Fashion, and Scapegoating"; Burke, *Lifebouy Men, Lux Women*, 180–93; Ivaska, " 'Anti-Mini Militants Meet Modern Misses' "; Stambach, "Curl Up and Dye." On a couple of occasions, Kenyan MPs tried to introduce prohibitions on Western fashions and cosmetics. The Kenyatta government responded to all of these efforts by affirming that fashion was a matter of personal choice and not national legislation (Kenya, *National Assembly Debates* [4 April 1968], 1589–90; [28 November 1968], 3660–61). Efforts to ban Western fashions were more successful in Tanzania and Malawi.

104. Kenya, *National Assembly Debates* (12 June 1969), 1125; (10 June 1969), 990–92; (11 June 1969), 1070–71.

105. Kenya, *National Assembly Debates* (11 June 1969), 1071. For further discussion of central Kenya as a hotbed of affiliation litigation, see Kenya, *National Assembly Debates* (11 June 1969), 1049; and P. W. W. Ommott, Mombasa, "Korti Itupe Kezi za Mimba" (Courts should throw out pregnancy cases), *Taifa Weekly*, 20 January 1968, 3.

106. Kenya, *House of Representatives Debates* (12 March 1964), 747. The use of the Affiliation Act in Kikuyu areas was probably facilitated by the fact that Kikuyu customary law on premarital pregnancy, as practiced and codified in the 1960s, largely coincided with the custody provisions contained in the Affiliation Act. Kikuyu and Kamba customary law, unlike that of other groups,

granted the custody of children born outside of marriage to maternal grandfathers rather than to fathers (Cotran, *Restatement of Africa Law, Kenya*, 1:18, 30). Politicians and others commonly described these provisions as granting custody to mothers (Kenya, *National Assembly Debates* [11 June 1969], 1056).

107. Kenya, *National Assembly Debates* (11 June 1969), 1038–49, 1054–79; (10 June 1969), 977–92.

108. Kenya, *National Assembly Debates* (12 June 1969), 1121.

109. J. Anyoso and J. Akeyo, Endebess, "Two Mothers Support Repeal of that Act," *Daily Nation*, 28 June 1969. See also Rachel Samuel, Mombasa, "Wasichana Watuaibisha na Mimba" (Girls disgrace us with pregnancies), *Taifa Leo*, 4 January 1969, 3. In a survey conducted in the 1990s, Mavisi and Kyalo ("The Affiliation," 119) found that many married women opposed the reintroduction of affiliation legislation.

110. "Repeal of Affiliation Act Hailed," *Daily Nation*, 10 May 1969; "Headline Error," *Daily Nation*, 12 May 1969.

111. Kenya, *National Assembly Debates* (10 June 1969), 981–83; (11 June 1969), 1024–31.

112. Kenya, *National Assembly Debates* (11 June 1969), 1030, 1037–42; (12 June 1969), 1119.

113. Kenya, *National Assembly Debates* (10 June 1969), 985; (11 June 1969), 1050; (12 June 1969), 1114.

114. Kenya, *National Assembly Debates* (10 June 1969), 981.

115. For accounts in Kenyan fiction, see Owino, *Sugar Daddy's Lover;* and Mwangi, *Striving for the Wind*. For an overview of the anthropological and demographic literature on "sugar daddies," see Bledsoe and Cohen, *Social Dynamics of Adolescent Fertility*, 108–9.

116. Kenya, *National Assembly Debates* (11 June 1969), 1054.

117. Kenya, *National Assembly Debates* (11 June 1969), 1026.

118. Kenya, *National Assembly Debates* (11 June 1969), 1050; (12 June 1969), 1110.

119. Philip Ochieng, "Affiliation—The Racket: The Remedy," *Sunday Nation*, 1 June 1969. See also "Abandoned Children," *Daily Nation*, 12 June 1969, 6.

120. Audrey Parker and Rosemary Kairu, Social Workers, National Christian Council of Kenya, Nairobi, "Letter to the editor," *Daily Nation*, 16 June 1969.

121. Kenya, *National Assembly Debates* (11 June 1969), 1033.

122. "Affiliation Bill to Go," *Daily Nation*, 18 June 1969. President Kenyatta gave his assent to the repeal bill on 25 June 1969 ("Affiliation Act Done Away With," *Daily Nation*, 28 June 1969). On the closing of the pending case files, see A. A. Kneller for Chief Justice, High Court of Kenya, to All Magistrates, "Chief Justice's Circular No. 1 of 1969," 2 July 1969, AGCK, 527/3.

123. "Christian Paper Against Repeal," *East African Standard*, 16 June 1969. See also "Affiliation Act Move Attacked," *Daily Nation*, 24 May 1969; and Kenya, *National Assembly Debates* (10 June 1969), 987.

124. Kenya, *National Assembly Debates* (12 June 1969), 1116–18.

125. "Heckling as MP Calls for Law to Legalise Abortion," *East African Standard,* 13 June 1969; Kenya, *National Assembly Debates* (12 June 1969), 1112–13

126. Kenya, *National Assembly Debates* (6 April 1972), 454–55.

127. For debates over distributing birth control to single girls and women, see Silberschmidt, *"Women Forget that Men are the Masters,"* 142; Egero and Mburugu, "Kenya: Reproductive Change under Strain," 58; Rogo, Bohmer, and Ombaka, "Developing Community-based Strategies," S60–S61; and Kaler and Watkins, "Disobedient Distributors." On sex education, see Maathuis, "To Teach or Not to Teach Family Planning in Kenyan Primary Schools"; Radel, "Kenya's Population and Family Planning Policy," 114; Koronya, "Female Circumcision and Family Life Education in Kenya"; and Rogo and Njau, "Newspaper Articles on Family Life Education/Sex Education in Kenya."

128. Lema and Kabeberi-Macharia, *A Review of Abortion in Kenya,* 19–27; Kulczycki, "Abortion in Kenya"; Rogo, Bohmer, and Ombaka, "Developing Community-based Strategies."

129. See Mavisi and Kyalo, "The Affiliation Act," and the following newspaper articles: John Esibi, "Affiliation Act: Should It Return?" *Sunday Nation,* 20 June 1976, 3; "Is Affiliation Bill the Answer?" *Daily Nation,* 21 May 1978; "Affiliation Act to be Revived—Muli," *Daily Nation,* 28 April 1984; Muthui Mwai, "Population Conference Calls for Return of Affiliation Act," *Daily Nation,* 15 September 1989; "Parliament Urged to Revive Affiliation Law," *Kenya Times,* 31 August 1990; Tony Kagoh, "M.P. to Push for Affiliation Act," *Sunday Times,* 14 March 1993; "Reinstate Affiliation Act—Don," *Daily Nation,* 28 February 1995; "Re-Introduce Affiliation Act," *Daily Nation,* 21 September 1996; "Affiliation Act 'Needed Again,' " *Daily Nation,* 20 May 1997; Lucy Oriang', "Didn't the Children's Bill Ignore Something?" *Daily Nation,* 20 November 2000.

130. Kenya, "The Children Act, 2001, No. 8 of 2001"; Zachary Ochieng, "What Will Kenya Say in New York?" *Daily Nation,* 29 August 2001; Arthur Okwemba, "Long Wait May Pay Off for Children," *Daily Nation,* 20 November 2001.

131. Lucy Oriang', "Didn't the Children's Bill Ignore Something?" *Daily Nation,* 20 November 2000; "State to Protect Children," *Daily Nation,* 21 November 2000; "Judge Faults Children's Bill," *Daily Nation,* 23 November 2000, 5; Zachary Ochieng, "Young and Wretched," *Daily Nation,* 31 March 2001, 8; editorial, "What an Appalling Debate," *Daily Nation,* 4 August 2001; Kennedy Obara, "There Is a Desperate Need for a Children's Act," *Daily Nation,* 30 August 2001; Emman Omari and Claire Gatheru, "Bill to Allow Men Custody of Children," *Daily Nation,* 8 November 2001; Joachim O. Ouko, "Why the Children's Bill Won't Work," *Daily Nation,* 22 November 2001; Judy Thongori, "A Children's Act at Last," *Daily Nation,* 20 January 2002.

132. Ferguson (*Expectations of Modernity,* 188–98) found similar sentiments among working-class men in 1980s Zambia. Although Ferguson locates

such misogyny in a postcolonial political economy of "shrinking real wages" and heightened familial and social demands, the repeated vilification of women in twentieth-century Kenya suggests the relevance of deeper and broader historical roots.

133. Mbembe, "Provisional Notes on the Postcolony," 9.

CONCLUSION

1. Foucault, *The History of Sexuality* (quote is from p. 143); Foucault, "Governmentality."

2. Stoler, *Race and the Education of Desire.* The first chapter also contains a useful discussion of colonial studies' varied engagement with Foucault.

3. Mitchell, *Colonising Egypt;* Arnold, *Colonizing the Body;* Butchart, *The Anatomy of Power;* Gilroy, *Against Race.*

4. Vaughan, *Curing Their Ills,* 8–12.

5. Cooper, "Conflict and Connection," 1533.

6. Some scholars (Bhahba, "Of Mimicry and Man"; Hunt, "Domesticity and Colonialism in the Belgian Congo"; McClintock, *Imperial Leather,* esp. 62–65) have engaged the concept of ambivalence to convey how colonial discourse held the promise but denied the possibility that the colonized could become "civilized"; even the most accomplished colonial intermediaries remained "not quite white." Here, however, the concept of ambivalence is deployed to illuminate the plight of the postcolonial state rather than the condition of the colonial subject.

7. Joshuah Muchiri Benjamin, Kahurura C.E.B. School, Nanyuki, to Minister for Health, Nairobi, 9 December 1964, KNA, Health/BY/1/61.

8. A. S. Mbuthia for Permanent Secretary, Ministry of Health, Nairobi, to Mr. J. M. Benjamin, Kahurura C.E.B. School, Nanyuki, 17 December 1964, KNA, Health/BY/1/61.

9. See the early issues of *Women in Kenya: Journal of the East African Women's League* and *Voice of Women (Sauti ya Mabibi),* published by *Maendeleo ya Wanawake.* In a rare public pronouncement of the issue, the president of *Maendeleo ya Wanawake,* Jael Mbogo, called for a "commission to scrutinize female circumcision" in January 1967 (Hosken, *The Hosken Report,* 168).

10. E. W. Gachukia, "Implications of Women's Situation for Individual and Family Health," paper presented to the World Health Organization seminar on Women and Family Health, Geneva, 27–30 November 1978, KNA, MSS/57/15; Jane Kirui, Chief Executive Office, National Council of Women of Kenya, Nairobi, to Fran P. Hosken, Publisher/Editor, WIN NEWS, Lexington, Massachusetts, USA, 20 December 1978, KNA, MSS/57/15.

11. Radel, "Kenya's Population and Family Planning Policy"; Maxon, "Social and Cultural Changes," 122–24. On anticolonialism, nationalism, and birth control in other African contexts, see Brown, "Facing the 'Black Peril' "; Lindsay, "The Politics of Population Control in Namibia"; West, "Nationalism,

Race, and Gender"; Klugman, "Population Policy in South Africa"; Kaler, "Fertility, Gender, and War"; and Kaler, " 'Who Has Told You to Do This Thing?' "

12. "The Kenya National Family Planning Programme," c. 1970, KNA, Health/BY/58/6; Bondestam, "The Foreign Control of Kenyan Population"; Warwick, *Bitter Pills,* 12–15, 74–78, 94–98, 159–60; Ndeti and Ndeti, *Cultural Values and Population Policy in Kenya,* esp. ch. 4; Hartmann, *Reproductive Rights and Wrongs,* 83–88; Brass and Jolly, *Population Dynamic of Kenya;* Watkins and Hodgson, "From Mercantalists to Neo-Malthusians."

13. Warwick, *Bitter Pills,* 159–60. See also Silberschmidt, "*Women Forget that Men are the Masters,*" 142; Egero and Mburugu, "Kenya: Reproductive Change under Strain," 58; Rogo, Bohmer, and Ombaka, "Developing Community-based Strategies," S60–S61; and Kaler and Watkins, "Disobedient Distributors."

14. Robinson, "Kenya Enters the Fertility Transition"; Brass and Jolly, *Population Dynamics in Kenya,* ch. 4; Maxon, "Social and Cultural Changes," 122–24; and National Council for Population and Development, Central Bureau of Statistics (Office of the Vice President and the Ministry of Planning and National Development) [Kenya], and Macro International, Inc., *Kenya Demographic and Health Survey 1998,* ch. 3. Some of the earliest evidence for a decrease in Kenyan fertility rates came from Chogoria, the Presbyterian hospital located in southern Meru (Goldberg, McNeil, and Spitz, "Contraceptive Use and Fertility Decline in Chogoria, Kenya").

15. Miller et al., "The Situation Analysis Study of the Family Planning Program in Kenya," 131–43; Brass and Jolly, *Population Dynamics of Kenya,* 130–32; Egero and Mburugu, "Kenya: Reproductive Change under Strain," 53–54; and Kaler and Watkins, "Disobedient Distributors."

16. Working Group on Demographic Effects of Economic and Social Reversals, *Demographic Effects of Economic Reversals in Sub-Saharan Africa,* esp. 68–81.

17. Fortin, "The Politics of AIDS in Kenya"; Fleming, "African Perceptions of AIDS"; Nzioka, "Policies in Kenya"; United States Agency for International Development, AIDSCAP, and Family Health International, *AIDS in Kenya,* ch. 1.

18. Maxon and Ndege, "The Economics of Structural Adjustment," 177; Nzioka, "AIDS Policies in Kenya," 161–63; Good et al., "Clinical Realities and Moral Dilemmas"; Turshen, *Privatizing Health Services in Africa;* Baylies, "Overview: HIV/AIDS in Africa."

19. The leaders of Uganda and Senegal are notable exceptions. Combining strong political will with highly coordinated and relatively well-funded testing and prevention programs, the rate of infection was lowered in both countries (Nzioka, "AIDS Policies in Kenya," 170; Baltazar et al., *AIDS in Kenya,* 46; Stewart, "Unprecedented Millions in U.S. Aid to Fight HIV/AIDS in Africa"; Scott, "Political Will, Political Economy, and the AIDS Industry in Zambia"; van der Vliet, "AIDS: Losing 'The New Struggle'?"; Booker and Minter, "Global Apartheid."

20. United States Agency for International Development, AIDSCAP, and

Family Health International, *AIDS in Kenya*, 18; Baltzaar et al., *AIDS in Kenya*, 4–7; and World Health Organization, *Kenya Epidemiological Fact Sheet*.

21. Bledsoe, "The Politics of AIDS, Condoms, and Heterosexual Relations in Africa"; Weiss, " 'Buying Her Grave' "; Balmer et al., "The Negotiating Strategies Determining Coitus in Stable Heterosexual Relationships"; Ogden, "Producing Respect"; Kielmann, " 'Prostitution,' 'Risk,' and 'Responsibility' "; Schoepf, "AIDS, Gender, and Sexuality during Africa's Economic Crisis"; Setel, *A Plague of Paradoxes;* and Stewart, "Toward a Historical Perspective on Sexuality in Uganda."

22. For a website devoted to indexing the range of anti-FGM initiatives in Kenya, see http://www.fgmkenya.org.

23. Daly, "African Genital Mutilation"; Hosken, "The Epidemiology of Female Genital Mutilations"; McLean, *Female Circumcision, Excision, and Infibulation;* El Saadawi, *The Hidden Face of Eve;* El Dareer, *Woman, Why Do You Weep?;* Hosken, *The Hosken Report;* Dorkenoo, *Cutting the Rose;* and Walker and Parmar, *Warrior Marks.*

24. "Kenya Girls Saved from the Knife," *Viva* (October 1982); and Hosken, *The Hosken Report,* 178. As a Kalejin, Moi was raised in a community that practiced excision as part of adolescent female initiation.

25. National Council for Population and Development, Central Bureau of Statistics (Office of the Vice President and the Ministry of Planning and National Development) [Kenya], and Macro International, Inc., *Kenya Demographic and Health Survey 1998,* 167–69.

26. Murray, "The Kikuyu Female Circumcision Controversy," 334–59; Browne, "Christian Missionaries, Western Feminists, and the Kikuyu Clitoridectomy Controversy."

27. *Maendeleo ya Wanawake,* "Harmful Traditional Practices"; Shuma, "The Case of the Matrilineal Mwera of Lindi"; Walley, "Searching for 'Voices.' "

28. Imanene Imathiu, "Wives in Circumcision Ordeal," *Daily Nation,* 19 September 1990; and M. Mongeru, interview, 5 January 1995. In explaining the resurgence of female genital cutting in northeastern Tanzania in the late 1980s, Nypan ("Revival of Female Circumcision") argued that the declining economic value and social status of schooling had prompted some young women to view initiation as a means of enhancing their social standing and marriage prospects within local communities. These initiations were often organized with the support of grandmothers and behind the backs of mothers, who themselves had rejected excision during the 1960s and 1970s in order to become "modern" women and members of the new Tanzanian nation.

29. Lilian Adhiambo, "Cut No More: At Last an Alternative to F.G.M.," *East African Standard,* 19 December 1996; Maina Waruru, "Alternative 'Female Cut' Winning Acceptance," *Daily Nation,* 1 April 1999; World Health Organization, Department of Women's Health, Health Systems, and Community Health, "Female Genital Mutilation Programmes to Date," 107–11. On "rituals without cutting" elsewhere in Africa, see Hernlund, "Cutting Without Ritual and Ritual Without Cutting."

30. See, for example, press coverage of an opposition MP's 1996 introduction of a parliamentary motion urging the Attorney General to draft a bill to outlaw female genital cutting: "Bid to Outlaw Female Circumcision Defeated," *Daily Nation*, 14 November 1996; Margaretta wa Gacheru, "Should the 'Cut' Motion Have Sailed Through?" *Sunday Nation*, 17 November 1996; and "MPs Support Mutilation," *Weekly Review*, 22 November 1996.

31. Kenya, "The Children Act, 2001, No. 8 of 2001." Under Section 20 of the Act, those found responsible for subjecting a child to "female circumcision" are liable to "a term of imprisonment not exceeding twelve months, or to a fine not exceeding fifty thousand shillings, or to both such imprisonment and fine." The Children Act came into force on 1 March 2002 (Kenneth Kwama, "The Children Act Comes into Force," *East African Standard*, 28 February 2002). In addition to the sections addressing FGM and the Affiliation Act, the other much-discussed provision of the Act was Section 6, which guaranteed every child the right to free and compulsory primary education (David Aduda, "Bill Provides for Free Compulsory Learning," *Daily Nation*, 3 December 2001; editorial, "Children's Bill a Landmark," *Daily Nation*, 3 December 2001; Francis Openda, "Children Bill Outlaws FGM, Calls for Free Basic Learning," *East African Standard*, 6 December 2001; "State Seeking Funds to Boost Children's Welfare," *Daily Nation*, 15 May 2002).

32. Zachary Ochieng, "What Will Kenya Say in New York?" *Daily Nation*, 29 August 2001; Arthur Okwemba, "Long Wait May Pay Off for Children," *Daily Nation*, 20 November 2001; Judy Thongori, "FGM: President Did the Right Thing" (letter to the editor), *Daily Nation*, 18 December 2001; "Judge Faults Children's Legislation," *Daily Nation*, 20 May 2002.

33. "Female Genital Mutilation: Is it Crime or Culture?" *The Economist* (13 February 1999): 45–46.

34. Editorial, "Anti-FGM Campaign Vital," *Daily Nation*, 13 December 2001; Gitau Warigi, "Fighting the FGM Kiss of Death is a Must," *Daily Nation*, 16 December 2001; Rebecca Wanjiku, "Legislation Alone Won't End Female Circumcision," *The People*, 16 December 2001; "Enforce Moi Order on FGM," *The People*, 20 December 2001; Mcantony Agnes, "The Only Way to Eradicate FGM is to Change Strategy" (letter to the editor), *Daily Nation*, 20 December 2001; "Law of Children's Rights Comes into Force Today," *Daily Nation*, 1 March 2002; Lucas Keya, "Why Ban on FGM May Not Be Effective," *East African Standard*, 20 March 2002; Peter Oriare, "Criminalising Circumcision Won't Help," *Daily Nation*, 2 May 2002; Murithi Mutiga, "Chief Justice Flayed Over Children's Act," *The People*, 10 May 2002; editorial, "Children Still Ignored," *The People*, 18 June 2002. See the following articles for other, more critical perspectives on the Act: Joachim O. Ouko, "Why the Children's Bill Won't Work," *Daily Nation*, 22 November 2001; Mugumo Munene, "Challenges Abound over Ban on Cut," *Daily Nation*, 21 December 2001; Paul Udoto, "Keep Unkind Cut Battle Out of Courts," *Daily Nation*, 16 January 2002; and "Group Scoffs at Children's Act," *East African Standard*, 21 March 2002.

35. See, for example, "Female 'Cut' Thrives in Pokot," *The People,* 13 January 2002; David Mageria, "FGM is Now Illegal But Some Still Want It," *East African Standard,* 16 January 2002; Richard Chesos, "Girls Flee Homes in Fear of FGM," *Daily Nation,* 16 April 2002; Faiza Jama Mohammed, "Law Has Its Uses in War Against FGM" (letter to the editor), *Daily Nation,* 20 May 2002; and "How Govt. Foots the FGM Bill," *Daily Nation,* 5 July 2002.

Bibliography

ARCHIVAL SOURCES

Attorney General's Chambers of Kenya, Nairobi (AGCK)
    527/3   Affiliation Act

Bancroft Library at the University of California at Berkeley (BLUCB)
    96/49   Fadiman Collection

Chogoria Mission Archives, Chogoria (CMA)
  Church of Scotland mission documents, c. 1920–c. 1960
    Booklets
    Clive Irvine papers
    AE   Official papers
    HB   History of Hospital

Jomo Kenyatta Memorial Library Archives, University of Nairobi (JKML)
    Lambert   H. E. Lambert papers

Kenya National Archives, Nairobi (KNA)
  Official documents and private papers, c. 1900–c. 1965
    ARC(MAA)   African Affairs Department
    AB   Community Development Department
    AG   Attorney General's Office
    AHD   Meru District court records
    AHU   Meru District court records
    AP   Ministry of Legal Affairs
    CNC   Chief Native Commissioner's Office
    CS   Chief Secretary's Office
    DC/KBU   Kiambu District
    DC/MRU   Meru District
    DC/NN   Kakamega District

Health   Medical Department
Jud   Attorney General's Office
MAA   African Affairs Department
Mathira   Mathira Deposit Book
MSS   Church of Scotland papers
MSS/7   E. Mary Holding papers
MSS/9   Clive Irvine papers
MSS/37   T. C. Colchester papers
MSS/57   National Council of Women of Kenya papers
MSS/115   Statistical and Census-related papers
MSS/120   T. O. Askwith papers
MSS/124   W. H. Laughton papers
PC/Coast   Coast Province
PC/CP   Central Province
PC/NZA   Nyanza Province
VQ   Central Province

Kenya National Archives on microfilm at Syracuse University, New York
   (KNA-SU)
   Official documents, c. 1900–c. 1960
      Nyanza   Nyanza Province
      PC/CP   Central Province

Meru County Council Offices, Meru town (MCC)
   Official documents, c. 1920–c. 1960
      ADC   African District Council minute books
      ADM   District Commissioner's correspondence
      LNC   Local Native Council minute books

Meru Law Courts, Meru town (MLC)
   Native Tribunal and African Court records, c. 1945–c. 1965
      AMCM   Appeal Magistrate's Court at Meru
      DCCPM   District Commissioner's Civil Panel at Meru
      DCKM   District Court of Kenya at Meru
      INT   Imenti Native Tribunal
      KAC   Kinoru African Court
      RMCM   Resident Magistrate's Court at Meru

Meru Museum, Meru town (MM)
   Official documents, c. 1945–c. 1965
      DCM   Meru District
      DC/ADM   District Commissioner's correspondence

Methodist Church of Kenya Offices, Meru town (MOM)
   Methodist Mission Society documents, c. 1920–c. 1960

Methodist Church of Kenya Offices, Nairobi (MON)
  Methodist Mission Society documents, c. 1920–c. 1960
    KD   Kenya District
    Med   Medical Work
    WW   Women's Work

National Library of Scotland, Edinburgh (NLS)
  Church of Scotland Mission documents, c. 1929–1964
    Acc/7548   Foreign Mission Committee
    Acc/10231, 10232 Women's Association for Foreign Missions

Public Record Office, Kew Gardens, England (PRO)
  Colonial Office (CO) files
    323   Replies to Circular Despatches
    533   Kenya, original correspondence
    537   Kenya, supplementary correspondence
    822   East Africa, original correspondence
    852   Economic, original correspondence
    854   Circular Despatches
    859   Social Services, original correspondence
    927   Research Department, original correspondence
    962   Colonial Conferences, East Africa
    994   Colonial Advisory Medical Committee, minutes and
              papers
    1034   Conference of Colonial Government Statisticians and
              Colonial Statistics, original correspondence

Rhodes House, Oxford (RH)
    MSS/Afr/r/117   "The Education of a Bantu Tribe" by E. Mary Holding
    MSS/Afr/r/191   "Christian Impact on Meru Institutions" by E. Mary
                    Holding
    MSS/Afr/s/504   M. W. Dobbs
    MSS/Afr/s/633   Coryndon papers
    MSS/Afr/s/665   C. M. Dobbs papers
    MSS/Afr/s/742   T. C. Colchester papers
    MSS/Afr/s/993   Richmond F. Anderson papers
    MSS/Afr/s/1189 V. M. McKeag papers
    MSS/Afr/s/1163 R. D. Harland papers
    MSS/Afr/s/1269 G. Hale papers
    MSS/Afr/s/1380 E. Mary Holding papers
    MSS/Afr/s/1497 R. S. S. Rowlands papers

School of Oriental and African Studies, University of London (SOAS)
  Methodist Missionary Society (MMS) documents, c. 1920–c. 1960
    GC   General Correspondence

SS   Synod Minutes
WW   Women's Work

Wellcome Institute for the History of Medicine Archival Collection, London
(Well)
    FPA   Family Planning Association papers
    NBTF   National Birthday Trust Fund papers

NEWSPAPERS AND PERIODICALS

Baraza, 1966–69
Daily Nation, 1964–2002
Drum, 1972
East African Standard, 1969–2002
Kenya Times, 1990–2002
The People, 1998–2002
Sunday Nation, 1969–2002
Sunday Times, 1993
Taifa Leo, 1969
Taifa Weekly, 1969
Viva, 1976–1982

INTERVIEWS

During my first visits to Meru in 1989–90 and 1993, I stayed with a young couple, Zipporah and Kiautha Arithi. Zipporah was a secretary who later became the owner of a store in Meru town; her husband works as an attorney. The Arithi house was located two kilometers uphill from Meru town, in a suburb called Kinoru. Most of what I learned about history and everyday life in Meru during those visits was gained through interacting with them, their family, and their friends. When I returned to Meru in December 1994 for my dissertation research, I again stayed with the Arithis. After two months, I moved into a nearby rental house. Apart from a few trips to Nairobi, I lived in that house until September 1995, working in archives in Meru town and conducting interviews in the surrounding areas.

In Meru, almost all of the interviews were conducted with the assistance of paid research assistants. Since I sought to conduct interviews in a wide range of locales within the District, and since any single research assistant's network of relatives and friends was usually limited to specific areas therein, I employed seven different assistants during 1995: Carol Gatwiri, Doreen Kathure, Richard Kirimi, Rosemary Kithiira, Thomas Mutethia, Nkatha

Mworoa, and Diana Rigiri. These five women and two men were between the ages of 22 and 26 years and in the process of completing or just having completed a university degree or a postsecondary school training course. As research assistants, their responsibilities included helping me to identify potential interviewees, scheduling interviews, and providing translation assistance during interviews. All of them except for Nkatha Mworoa also transcribed and translated interview tapes. During earlier visits to Meru, Dan Imanyara, Grace Kirimi, Kinanu Mwithia, and Charity Nduru similarly provided invaluable assistance with interviews.

As most interviewees, particularly women, felt most comfortable conversing in Meru, the basic Swahili language skills I had acquired during coursework in graduate school were of little use during interviews. Through work with a language tutor, Ntai wa Nkararu, and everyday practice, my Meru language skills improved during my research. While I was able to ask and understand the replies to basic questions and follow the general content of more complicated responses, I was unable to conduct Meru language interviews by myself.

Research assistants and I arranged most interviews two to three weeks in advance, by visiting a person's home, explaining my research project, and, if the person agreed, scheduling an interview. A typical interview day consisted of leaving my house early in the morning with a notebook, tape recorder, and presents (usually, sugar, tea, tobacco, or head scarves) in my backpack, meeting a research assistant at the public transportation stage, boarding a vehicle, alighting after a fifteen minute to one hour ride, walking to the interviewee's home, conducting a couple-hour interview, going to the house of a neighbor, conducting another interview, and returning home before dusk. Successful days meant kept appointments and engaging conversations. Most interviewees also provided gracious meals and going-away presents ranging from potatoes to passion fruits. Unsuccessful days consisted of forgotten appointments or, much less frequently, suspicious interviewees.

Roughly three-quarters of those whom we interviewed agreed to be tape recorded. Interviews began with a standard set of questions regarding age-grade; years of birth, initiation, and marriage; place and clan of birth and marriage; and school attendance, marriage, childbirth, work experiences, and church membership. Responses to these questions helped us to determine on which of the following topics to focus: initiation, courtship, childbirth, maternal and child health, government affairs, or men's and women's councils. Apart from the opening questions, interviews did not follow a standard set of questions. Rather, they meandered from one topic to another.

In the list below, unless otherwise specified, interviews in Kenya were conducted in the Meru language and those in England, in English. For the interviews conducted in Meru, the first place-name indicates either the market, location, or sub-location nearest to where the interview took place, in almost all cases, the interviewee's home. The second place-name is the pre-1992 administrative division. All interview tapes and notes remain in my possession.

Meru District

'Asuman, Amina. Interviewed by Rosemary Kithiira and author. Tape recording. Meru town, North Imenti, 26 July 1995.

Adams, Nancy. Interviewed by Rosemary Kithiira and author. Notes. Meru town, North Imenti, 26 June 1995.

Aritho, Margaret. Interviewed by author (in English). Notes. Kinoru, North Imenti, 8 April 1995.

Ayub, Sara. Interviewed by Rosemary Kithiira and author. Tape recording. Makutano, North Imenti, 7 August 1995.

Ayub, Sara, and Esther Evangeline. Interviewed by Charity Nduru and author. Notes. Makutano, North Imenti, 6 September 1990.

————. Interviewed by Charity Nduru and author. Notes. Kinoru, North Imenti, 12 September 1990.

Bailey, Margaret. Interviewed by author (in English). Notes. Meru town, North Imenti, 31 July 1995.

Bashir, Haju Limti Sheik Adam . Interviewed by Rosemary Kithiira and author. Tape recording. Meru town, North Imenti, 26 July 1995.

Ciothirangi, Veronica. Interviewed by Thomas Mutethia and author. Tape recording. Mikinduri, Tigania, 6 June 1995.

Gakethi, Jennifer. Interviewed by Doreen Kathure and author. Tape recording. Mulathankari, North Imenti, 29 December 1994.

Igoki, Maliceral. Interviewed by Charity Nduru and author. Tape recording. Kionyo, South Imenti, 18 October 1990.

Ikirima, Timothy. Interviewed by Thomas Mutethia and author. Notes. Ruiri, North Imenti, 1 February 1995.

Imathiu, Sabera, and Maritha Zachary. Interviewed by Grace Kirimi and author. Notes. Kathera, South Imenti, 15 September 1990.

John, Salome. Interviewed by Rosemary Kithiira and author. Tape recording. Mpuri, North Imenti, 21 April 1995.

Joseph, Doris. Interviewed by Rosemary Kithiira and author. Tape recording. Igoji, South Imenti, 13 June 1995.

Kabita, Elizabeth. Interviewed by Nkatha Mworoa and author. Tape recording. Kangeta, Igembe, 3 May 1995.

Kaburo, Grace. Interviewed by Carol Gatwiri and author. Tape recording. Mpuri, North Imenti, 30 December 1994.

Kagugira, Zipporah. Interviewed by Doreen Kathure, Carol Gatwiri, and author. Tape recording. Mulathankari, North Imenti, 28 December 1994.

―――. Interviewed by Doreen Kathure and author. Tape recording. Mulathankari, North Imenti, 14 August 1995.

Kagwania, Martha. Interviewed by Rosemary Kithiira and author. Notes. Mpuri, North Imenti, 16 March 1995.

Kaimuri, Isabel. Interviewed by Rosemary Kithiira and author. Tape recording. Mpuri, North Imenti, 20 March 1995.

Kaimuri, Maritha. Interviewed by Thomas Mutethia and author. Tape recording. Miathene, Tigania, 12 May 1995.

Kajege, Solome Nkoroi. Interviewed by Thomas Mutethia and author. Tape recording. Ruiri, North Imenti, 11 May 1995.

Kajuju, Isabella. Interviewed by Rosemary Kithiira and author. Tape recording. Mpuri, North Imenti, 20 March 1995.

Kajuju, Lucy. Interviewed by Rosemary Kithiira and author. Notes. Ntakira, North Imenti, 23 March 1995.

Kamincura, Sara. Interviewed by Carol Gatwiri and author. Tape recording. Mpuri, North Imenti, 4 January 1995.

Kananu, Julia. Interviewed by Rosemary Kithiira and author. Notes. Mpuri, North Imenti, 21 April 1995.

Kanana, Monica. Interviewed by Rosemary Kithiira and author. Tape recording and notes. Ntakira, North Imenti, 23 March 1995.

Kanini, Martha Musa. Interviewed by Richard Kirimi and author. Tape recording. Chogoria, South Imenti, 16 September 1995.

―――. Interviewed by author. Notes. Chogoria, South Imenti, 8 August 1999.

Kanini, Rael. Interviewed by Rosemary Kithiira and author. Tape recording and notes. Mpuri, North Imenti, 29 April 1995.

―――. Interviewed by Rosemary Kithiira and author. Notes. Mpuri, North Imenti, 18 May 1995.

Karea, Jennifer. Interviewed by Rosemary Kithiira and author. Tape recording and notes. Ntakira, North Imenti, 24 March 1995.

Karegi, Zipporah. Interviewed by Rosemary Kithiira and author. Mpuri, North Imenti, 7 August 1995.

Karigu, Evelyn. Interviewed by Rosemary Kithiira and author. Notes. Igoji, South Imenti, 30 March 1995.

Karimi, Kacera. Interviewed by Rosemary Kithiira and author. Tape recording. Igoji, South Imenti, 3 April 1995.

Karoki, Margaret. Interviewed by Rosemary Kithiira and author. Tape recording. Igoji, South Imenti, 5 April 1995.

Kathurima, Stanley. Interviewed by Rosemary Kithiira and author. Tape recording. Katheri, Central Imenti, 15 September 1995.

Kibunja, Janet Nthongo . Interviewed by Charity Nduru and author. Tape recording. Kionyo, South Imenti, 19 October 1990.

Kimwe, Mama. Interviewed by Rosemary Kithiira and author. Tape recording. Ntakira, North Imenti, 31 March 1995.

Kinaito, Veronica. Interviewed by Rosemary Kithiira and author. Tape recording. Urukuu, South Imenti, 5 July 1995.

Kinene, Jennifer. Interviewed by Rosemary Kithiira and author. Tape recording. Mpuri, North Imenti, 18 March 1995.

Kinoti, Job. Interviewed by author (in English). Tape recording. Kaaga, North Imenti, 28 June 1995.

Kireru, Elizabeth. Interviewed by Rosemary Kithiira and author. Tape recording. Kithirune, Central Imenti, 25 July 1995.

Kireru, Jacob. Interviewed by Rosemary Kithiira and author. Notes. Kithirune, Central Imenti, 25 July 1995.

Kirimi, Agnes Nyoroka. Interviewed by Rosemary Kithiira and author. Tape recording. Igoji, South Imenti, 12 June 1995.

Kirimi, George. Interviewed by author (in English). Notes. Kathera, South Imenti, 1 August 1999.

Kirote, Caroline. Interviewed Rosemary Kithiira and author. Tape recording. Mitunguu, South Imenti, 9 June 1995.

Kiruki, Celina. Interviewed by author (in English). Tape recording. Makutano, North Imenti, 30 June 1995.

Kithinji, Moses. Interviewed by Rosemary Kithiira and author. Tape recording. Mitunguu, South Imenti, 9 June 1995.

Laiboni, James. Interviewed by author (in English). Tape recording. Kangeta, Igembe, 23 July 1995.

Likicha, Tabitha Gatuma. Interviewed by Nkatha Mworoa and author. Tape recording. Kangeta, Igembe, 29 May 1995.

M'Akwalo, Stanley. Interviewed by Nkatha Mworoa and author. Tape recording. Kangeta, Igembe, 16 June 1995.

M'Anampiu, Chief. Interviewed by Thomas Muthethia and author. Tape recording. Mikinduri, Tigania, 10 May 1995.

M'Arimba, Isabella, and Isabella Mathiu. Interviewed by Grace Kirimi and author. Tape recording. Kathera, South Imenti, 20 July 1993.

M'Arimba, Isabella, and Isabella Ntui. Interviewed by Grace Kirimi and author. Tape recording. Kathera, South Imenti, 13 October 1990.

M'Barungu, Ciokaraine. Interviewed by Nkatha Mworoa and author. Tape recording. Maua town, Igembe, 8 May 1995.

M'Chala, Murungi M'Ichara. Interviewed by Nkatha Mworoa and author. Tape recording. Kangeta, Igembe, 29 May 1995.

M'Chokerachokera, Joseph. Interviewed by Thomas Mutethia and author. Tape recording. Mituntu, Tigania, 1 May 1995.

M'Ikiao, Justus. Interviewed by Rosemary Kithiira and author. Tape recording. Mpuri, North Imenti, 1 May 1995.

M'Imanyara, Naftaly. Interviewed by Dan Imanyara and author. Tape recording. Mariene, Central Imenti, 27 October 1990.

M'Imiongo, M'Mwereria. Interviewed by Nkatha Mworoa and author. Tape recording. Maua town, Igembe, 8 May 1995.

M'Inoti, John, and M'Mugambi M'Kiara. Interviewed by Rosemary Kithiira and author. Tape recording. Urukuu, South Imenti, 3 July 1995.

M'Iringera, Zachia, and Gerrard M'Ithangatha. Interviewed by Nkatha Mworoa and author. Tape recording. Maua town, Igembe, 26 May 1995.

M'Iringo, Daniel. Interviewed by Nkatha Mworoa and author. Tape recording. Kangeta, Igembe, 25 June 1995.

M'Iringo, Elizabeth. Interviewed by Grace Kirimi and author. Tape recording. Kathera, South Imenti, 19 July 1993.

———. Interviewed by Rosemary Kithiira and author. Tape recording. Kathera, South Imenti, 4 August 1995.

M'Iringo, Evangeline. Interviewed by Rosemary Kithiira and author. Tape recording. Mpuri, North Imenti, 16 March 1995.

M'Iringo, Joyce. Interviewed by Nkatha Mworoa and author. Notes. Kangeta, Igembe, 9 May 1995.

M'Ithinji, Esther. Interviewed by Grace Kirimi and author. Tape recording. Kathera, South Imenti, 19 July 1993.

M'Ithinji, Esther, and Julia Simion Kiruja. Interviewed by Grace Kirimi and author. Tape recording and notes. Kathera, South Imenti, 14 October 1990.

M'Itiri, Gerrard, and William M'Rarama. Interviewed by Rosemary Kithiira and author. Tape recording. Mpuri, North Imenti, 18 May 1995.

M'Itwaruchiu, Jackson. Interviewed by Doreen Kathure and author. Tape recording. Mulanthankari, North Imenti, 9 January 1995.

———. Interviewed by Doreen Kathure and author. Notes. Mulanthankari, North Imenti, 5 August 1999.

M'Kaiga, Daniel. Interviewed by Thomas Mutethia and author. Tape recording. Mikinduri, Tigania, 6 June 1995.

M'Kirera, Moses. Interviewed by Rosemary Kithiira and author. Tape recording. Mpuri, North Imenti, 10 January 1995.

M'Kuru, Paul. Interviewed by Thomas Mutethia and author. Tape recording. Mituntu, Tigania, 22 April 1995.

M'Lithara, Ciabaikio. Interviewed by Thomas Mutethia and author. Tape recording. Mituntu, Tigania, 30 January 1995.

M'Lithara, Jacobu, and Jacobu M'Mwirigua. Interviewed by Thomas Mutethia and author. Notes. Mituntu, Tigania, 6 February 1995.

M'Mbogori, Jacobu. Interviewed by Rosemary Kithiira and author. Tape recording. Mpuri, North Imenti, 10 July 1995.

M'Mugambi, Julia. Interviewed by Rosemary Kithiira and author. Tape recording. Urukuu, South Imenti, 10 June 1995.

M'Mugambi, Julia, and Veronica Kinaito M'Iruru. Interviewed by Rosemary Kithiira and author. Tape recording. Urukuu, South Imenti, 5 July 1995.

M'Mukindia, Moses. Interviewed by Rosemary Kithiira and author. Notes. Mpuri, North Imenti, 10 January 1995.

M'Mukiiri, Stephen. Interviewed by Rosemary Kithiira and author. Tape recording. Mpuri, North Imenti, 1 August 1995.

M'Munyua, Daudi. Interviewed by Rosemary Kithiira and author. Tape recording. Kaaga, North Imenti, 28 June 1995.

M'Munyua, Lydia. Interviewed by Rosemary Kithiira and author. Tape recording. Kaaga, North Imenti, 7 July 1995.

M'Muraga, Silas, and Erastus Mucheke. Interviewed by Rosemary Kithiira and author. Igoji, South Imenti, 13 June 1995.

M'Mutiga, Secondo, and Gertrude Gaitu. Interviewed by Rosemary Kithiira and author. Mujwa, South Imenti, 29 June 1995.

M'Mutithia, Francis. Interviewed by Thomas Mutethia and author. Notes. Kianjai, North Imenti, 26 January 1995.

M'Mwigwika, Michael. Interviewed by Nkatha Mworoa and author. Tape recording. Kangeta, Igembe, 15 June 1995.

M'Mwirichia, Naaman. Interviewed Richard Kirimi and author. Tape recording. Makutano, North Imenti, 18 September 1995.

M'Naikiuru, David. Interviewed by Rosemary Kithiira and author. Tape recording. Mpuri, North Imenti, 29 April 1995.

M'Rintari, Francis. Interviewed by author (in English). Notes. Meru town, North Imenti, 3 November 1990.

M'Ruiga, Joseph. Interviewed by Rosemary Kithiira and author. Tape recording. Igoji, South Imenti, 19 May 1995.

M'Terenge, Ibrahim. Interviewed by Thomas Mutethia and author. Notes. Mituntu, Tigania, 24 January 1995.

M'Tuaruchiu, Elijah. Interviewed by Rosemary Kithiira and author. Tape recording. Mpuri, North Imenti, 3 February 1995.

Maigene, Tabitha. Interviewed by Charity Nduru and author. Tape recording. Kionyo, South Imenti, 17 October 1990.

Manene, Marieta, and Saberena Karambu. Interviewed by Rosemary Kithiira and author. Mitunguu, South Imenti, 7 June 1995.

Manyara, Gerrishon. Interviewed by Rosemary Kithiira and author. Tape recording. Mpuri, North Imenti, 3 February 1995.

Manyara, Julia. Interviewed by author (in English). Tape recording. Kinoru, North Imenti, 2 April 1995.

Marete, Harriet, and Charles Marete. Interviewed by Doreen Kathure and author. Tape recording. Naari, North Imenti, 6 January 1995.

Maria-Pia, Sister. Interviewed by author (in English). Notes. Kirua, North Imenti, 8 August 1995.

Matiri, Jacob Kiruga. Interviewed by Rosemary Kithiira and author. Notes. Katheri, Central Imenti, 21 January 1995.

Mbarabari, Stanley M'Murithi. Interviewed by Nkatha Mworoa and author. Tape recording. Kangeta, Igembe, 17 May 1995.

Mbijiwe, Margaret. Interviewed by author (in English). Tape recording. Kinoru, North Imenti, 9 August 1995.

Mbogori, Eustace. Interviewed by Richard Kirimi and author. Tape recording. Chogoria, South Imenti, 16 September 1995.

Mbuthu, Sara. Interviewed by Rosemary Kithiira and author. Tape recording. Mpuri, North Imenti, 11 January 1995.

Mongeru, Margaret. Interviewed by Gideon Ndwaru and author. Tape recording. Kianjai, Tigania, 5 January 1995.

Mpindi, Veronica. Interviewed by Charity Nduru and author. Tape recording. Kinoru, North Imenti, 25 October 1990.

Mpunia, Thomas Kinika. Interviewed by Charity Nduru and author. Tape recording. Kionyo, South Imenti, 18 October 1990.

Muthoni, Madeline. Interviewed by Rosemary Kithiira and author. Tape recording. Igoji, South Imenti, 3 April 1995.

Muthuuri, Elizabeth. Interviewed by Doreen Kathure, Carol Gatwiri, and author. Tape recording. Kirua, North Imenti, 3 January 1995.

Mutiria, Catherine. Interviewed by author (in English). Tape recording. Igoji, South Imenti, 12 June 1995.

Murangu, Mary, and Julia Muthoni. Interviewed by Rosemary Kithiira and author. Tape recording. Igoji, South Imenti, 26 April 1995.

Mwambia, Sarah Karegi. Interviewed by Thomas Muthethia and author. Tape recording. Miathene, Tigania, 12 May 1995.

Mwari, Sara. Interviewed by Thomas Mutethia and author. Tape recording. Kianjai, Tigania, 22 April 1995.

———. Interviewed by Thomas Mutethia and author. Tape recording. Kianjai, Tigania, 7 May 1995.

Mwirichia, Philipo M'Ananga. Interviewed by Nkatha Mworoa and author. Tape recording. Kangeta, Igembe, 15 June 1995.

Mwitiabi, Grace. Interviewed by Rosemary Kithiira and author. Tape recording and notes. Ntakira, North Imenti, 28 and 31 March 1995.

Mwongo, Francis. Interviewed by Doreen Kathure, Carol Gatwiri, and author. Tape recording. Mulathankari, North Imenti, 29 December 1994.

———. Interviewed by Doreen Kathure and author. Notes. Mulathankari, North Imenti, 14 August 1995.

Ncence, Margaret. Interviewed by Charity Nduru and author. Notes. Makutano, North Imenti, 12 September 1990.

Ncoro, Rebecca. Interviewed by Diana Rigiri and author. Tape recording. Mwichiune, South Imenti, 8 February 1995.

Ndwaru, Gideon. Interviewed by author (in English). Notes. Kianjai, Tigania, 23 January 1995.

Ngeta, Mariamu. Interviewed by Diana Rigiri and author. Tape recording. Mwichiune, South Imenti, 8 February 1995.

Nikobwe, Tarsila, and Margaret Mwakinia. Tape recording. Interviewed by Charity Nduru and author. Kinoru, North Imenti, 20 September 1990.

Nkatha, Zipporah. Interviewed by Rosemary Kithiira and author. Tape recording. Mpuri, North Imenti, 18 March 1995.

Nkure, Samuel. Interviewed by Thomas Mutethia and author. Tape recording. Kianjai, Tigania, 26 January 1995.

————. Interviewed by Thomas Mutethia and author. Notes. Kianjai, Tigania, 7 May 1995.

Nkure, Samuel, and Gerald Mwithia. Interviewed by Kinanu Mwithia and author. Notes. Kianjai, Tigania, 19 November 1989.

Nthang'i, Martha. Interviewed by Doreen Kathure and author. Tape recording. Mulathankari, North Imenti, 28 Dec. 1994.

Ntimbu, Jusufu. Interviewed by Doreen Kathure, Carol Gatwiri, and author. Tape recording. Naari, North Imenti, 3 January 1995.

Ntonyia, Peter Rinkanya. Interviewed by Charity Nduru and author. Tape recording. Kionyo, South Imenti, 18 October 1990.

Ntuti, Margaret. Interviewed by Thomas Mutethia and author. Tape recording. Mituntu, Tigania, 24 January 1995.

Nyambura, Eunice. Interviewed by Thomas Mutethia and author. Tape recording. Uringu, Tigania, 11 April 1995.

Nyoroka, Julia. Interviewed by Thomas Mutethia and author. Tape recording and notes. Mituntu, Tigania, 29 March 1995.

Nyoroka, Teresa. Interviewed by Rosemary Kithiira and author. Tape recording. Mujwa, South Imenti, 29 June 1995.

Paul, Priscilla. Interviewed by Rosemary Kithiira and author. Tape recording. Mpuri, North Imenti, 10 January 1995.

Roben, Martha, Rebecca M'Mwendwa, Tabitha M'Angaine, and Isabella M'Arimba. Interviewed by Grace Kirimi and author. Tape recording. Kathera, South Imenti, 15 September 1990.

Stanley, Julia, and Maritha John. Interviewed by Nkatha Mworoa and author. Tape recording. Kangeta, Igembe, 3 May 1995.

Tiira, Beatrice. Interviewed by Rosemary Kithiira and author. Tape recording. Igoji, South Imenti, 30 March 1995.

Tirindi, Charity. Interviewed by Diana Rigiri and author. Tape recording. Mwichiune, South Imenti, 10 February 1995.

Other locations in Kenya

Irvine, Geoffrey. Interviewed by author (in English). Notes. Nairobi, 29 July 1993.

Kairo, Redan. Interviewed by author (in English). Notes. Nairobi, 3 August 1993.

Muirige, Martha. Interviewed by Doreen Kathure and author. Tape recording. Isiolo town, 28 April 1995.

Mwathi, Samson. Interviewed by author (in English). Notes. Nairobi, 6 August 1993.

Nyanga, Daniel. Interviewed by author (in English). Notes. Embu District, 31 October 1990.

Waruhiu, Samuel Waruhiu. Interviewed by author (in English). Tape recording. Nairobi, 2 September 1999.

England

Cashmore, Richard. Interviewed by author. Tape recording and notes. Twickenham, England, 6 December 1995.

Chalkley, Muriel. Interviewed by author. Notes. Bournemouth, England, 2 December 1995.

Jones, Bertha. Interviewed by author. Notes. Devon, England, 5 December 1995.

Wilde, Merle. Interviewed by author. Tape recording. Derby, England, 19–20 September 1994.

OTHER WORKS

Abuoga, John Baptist, and Absalom Aggrey Mutere. *The History of the Press in Kenya.* Nairobi: African Council on Communication Education, 1988.

Ahlberg, Beth Maina. *Women, Sexuality, and the Changing Social Order: The Impact of Government Policies on Reproductive Behavior in Kenya.* Amsterdam: Gordon and Breach Science Publishers, 1991.

Ahlberg, Beth Maina, Wangui Njau, Karanja Kiiru, and Ingela Krantz. "Gender Masked or Self-Inflicted Pain: Female Circumcision, Eradication, and Persistence in Central Kenya." *African Sociological Review* 4, no. 1 (2000): 35–54.

Ahmadu, Fuambai. "Rites and Wrongs: An Insider/Outsider Reflects on Power and Excision." In *Female "Circumcision" in Africa: Culture, Controversy, and Change,* edited by Bettina Shell-Duncan and Ylva Hernlund, 283–312. Boulder, Colo.: Lynne Rienner, 2000.

Akinla, Oladele. "Abortion in Africa." In *Abortion in a Changing World,* edited by Robert E. Hall, 291–301. New York: Columbia University Press, 1970.

Alcoff, Linda. "The Problem of Speaking for Others." *Cultural Critique,* no. 20 (1991–92): 5–13.

Allen, Kenneth. "Some Kikuyu Customs of Interest to Medical Men." *Kenya Medical Journal* 1, no. 11 (1925): 332–36.

Allman, Jean. "Making Mothers: Missionaries, Medical Officers, and Women's Work in Colonial Asante, 1924–1945." *History Workshop* 38 (autumn 1994): 23–47.

———. "Rounding up Spinsters: Gender Chaos and Unmarried Women in Colonial Asante." *Journal of African History* 37, no. 2 (1996): 195–214.

Altrincham, Edward. *Kenya's Opportunity: Memories, Hopes, and Ideas.* London: Faber and Faber, 1955.

Amadiume, Ifi. *Male Daughters, Female Husbands: Gender and Sex in an African Society.* London: Zed Books, 1987.

Ambler, Charles H. *Kenyan Communities in the Age of Imperialism: The Central Region in the Late Nineteenth Century.* New Haven, Conn.: Yale University Press, 1988.

———. "The Renovation of Custom in Colonial Kenya: The 1932 Generation Succession Ceremonies in Embu." *Journal of African History* 30, no. 1 (1989): 139–56.

————. "Drunks, Brewers, and Chiefs: Alcohol Regulation in Colonial Kenya, 1900–1930." In *Drinking: Behavior and Belief in Modern History*, edited by Susanna Barrows and Robin Room, 65–83. Berkeley and Los Angeles: University of California Press, 1991.

Anderson, Benedict. *Imagined Communities: Reflections on the Origin and Spread of Nationalism*. Revised ed. New York: Verso, 1991.

Anderson, David. "Depression, Dust Bowl, Demography, and Drought: The Colonial State and Soil Conservation in East Africa during the 1930s." *African Affairs* 83, no. 332 (1984): 321–43.

————. "Capital Crimes, Colonial Law, and Human Rights: The Mau Mau Trials, Kenya, 1952–1958." Paper presented at the 6th Stanford–Berkeley Symposium on Law and Colonialism in Africa, April 1999.

Armstrong, Alice, ed. *Women and Law in Southern Africa*. Harare: Zimbabwe Publishing House, 1987.

Arnell, H. M. "Correspondence: Administration of Quinine during Pregnancy." *Kenya Medical Journal* 1, no. 6 (1924): 189.

Arnold, David. "Medical Priorities and Practice in Nineteenth-Century British India." *South Asia Research* 5, no. 2 (1985): 167–83.

————. *Colonizing the Body: State Medicine and Epidemic Disease in Nineteenth-Century India*. Los Angeles: University of California Press, 1993.

————. "Public Health and Public Power: Medicine and Hegemony in Colonial India." In *Contesting Colonial Hegemony: State and Society in Africa and India*, edited by Dagmar Engels and Shula Marks, 131–51. New York: British Academic Press, 1994.

Ashforth, Adam. *The Politics of Official Discourse in Twentieth-Century South Africa*. Oxford: Oxford University Press, 1990.

Asiyo, Phoebe M. "Legislative Process and Gender Issues in Kenya." In *Women and Law in Kenya: Perspectives and Emerging Issues*, edited by Mary Adhiambo Mbeo and Oki Ooko-Ombaka, 41–49. Nairobi: Public Law Institute, 1989.

Askwith, Tom. *From Mau Mau to Harambee*. Edited by Joanna Lewis. Cambridge: African Studies Centre, 1995.

Atieno-Odhiambo, E. S. "The Formative Years, 1945–55." In *Decolonization and Independence in Kenya, 1940–1993*, edited by B. A. Ogot and W. R. Ochieng', 25–47. London: James Currey, 1995.

Balmer, D. H., E. Gikundi, M. Kanyotu, and R. Waithaka. "The Negotiating Strategies Determining Coitus in Stable Heterosexual Relationships." *Health Transition Review* 5, no. 1 (1995): 85–95.

Baltazar, G. M., J. Stover, T. M. Okeyo, B. O. N. Hagembe, R. Mutemi, and C. H. O. Olola, eds. *AIDS in Kenya: Background, Projections, Impact and Interventions*. 5th ed. Nairobi: National AIDS/STDs Control Programme, Ministry of Health, 1999.

Barker, Gary Knaul, and Susan Rich. "Influences on Adolescent Sexuality in

Nigeria and Kenya: Findings from Recent Focus-Group Discussions." *Studies in Family Planning* 23, no. 3 (1992): 199–210.

Bartholomew, Lilian. "In Kenya, East Africa." *Women's Work* 9, no. 1 (1933): 3–5.

Baur, John. *The Catholic Church in Kenya: A Centenary History.* Nairobi: St. Paul Publication—Africa, 1990.

Bayart, Jean-François. *The State in Africa: The Politics of the Belly.* New York: Longman, 1993. Originally published as *L'Etat en Afrique: La politique du ventre* (Paris: Librairie Arthème Fayard, 1989).

Baylies, Carolyn. "Overview: HIV/AIDS in Africa: Global and Local Inequalities and Responsibilities." *Review of African Political Economy* 86 (2000): 487–500.

Beck, Ann. *A History of the British Medical Administration of East Africa, 1900–1950.* Cambridge: Cambridge University Press, 1970.

Beinart, Jennifer. "Darkly Through a Lens: Changing Perceptions of the African Child in Sickness and Health, 1900–1945." In *In the Name of the Child: Health and Welfare, 1880–1940*, edited by Roger Cooter, 220–43. New York: Routledge, 1992.

Bell, Heather. "Midwifery Training and Female Circumcision in the Inter-War Anglo-Egyptian Sudan." *Journal of African History* 39, no. 2 (1998): 293–312.

———. *Frontiers of Medicine in the Anglo-Egyptian Sudan, 1899–1940.* Oxford: Clarendon Press, 1999.

Bell, Stanley. "The Ameru People of Kenya: A Medical and Social Study," part 1, "Geographical and Ethnological Background." *Journal of Tropical Medicine and Hygiene* 58, no. 10 (1955): 233.

Bella, Hassan. "Sudanese Village Midwives: Six Decades of Experience with Part-Time Health." In *Advances in International Maternal and Child Health*, vol. 4, edited by D. B. Jelliffe and E. F. P. Jelliffe, 124–48. Oxford: Clarendon Press, 1984.

Bennett, George, and Carl G. Rosberg. *The Kenyatta Election: Kenya, 1960–1961.* Oxford: Oxford University Press, 1961.

Bennett, George, and Alison Smith. "Kenya: From 'White Man's Country' to Kenyatta's State, 1945–1963." In *History of East Africa*, vol. 3, edited by D. A. and Alison Smith, 109–53. Oxford: Clarendon Press, 1976.

Berman, Bruce. *Control and Crisis in Colonial Kenya: The Dialectic of Domination.* Athens: Ohio University Press, 1990.

———. "Bureaucracy and Incumbent Violence: Colonial Administration and the Origins of the 'Mau Mau' Emergency." In *Unhappy Valley: Conflict in Kenya and Africa*, by Bruce Berman and John Lonsdale, 227–64. Athens: Ohio University Press, 1992.

Berman, Bruce, and John Lonsdale. "Coping with the Contradictions: The Development of the Colonial State in Kenya, 1895–1914." *Journal of African History* 20, no. 4 (1979): 487–505.

———. *Unhappy Valley: Conflict in Kenya and Africa*. Books One and Two. Athens: Ohio University Press, 1992.

Bernard, Frank E. "Meru District in the Kenyan Spatial Economy, 1890–1950." In *The Spatial Structure of Development: A Study of Kenya*, edited by R. A. Obudho and D. R. F. Taylor, 264–90. Boulder, Colo.: Westview Press, 1979.

Bernardi, Bernardo. *The Mugwe: A Failing Prophet*. London: Published for the International African Institute by the Oxford University Press, 1959.

———. *Age Class Systems: Social Institutions and Polities Based on Age*. New York: Cambridge University Press, 1985.

———. "An Anthropological Odyssey." *Annual Review of Anthropology* 19 (1990): 1–15.

Berry, Sara. *No Condition is Permanent: The Social Dynamics of Agrarian Change in Sub-Saharan Africa*. Madison: University of Wisconsin Press, 1993.

Bhabha, Homi. "Of Mimicry and Man." *October* 28 (spring 1984): 125–33.

———. "Signs Taken for Wonders: Questions of Ambivalence and Authority under a Tree Outside Delhi, May 1817." In *Europe and Its Others*, vol. 1, edited by Francis Barker et al. Colchester, U.K.: University of Essex, 1985.

Bianco, Barbara. "The Historical Anthropology of a Mission Hospital in Northwestern Kenya." Ph.D. diss., New York University, 1992.

Bledsoe, Caroline H. *Women and Marriage in Kpelle Society*. Palo Alto, Calif.: Stanford University Press, 1980.

———. "The Political Use of Sande Ideology and Symbolism." *American Ethnologist* 11, no. 13 (1984): 455–72.

———. "Side-stepping the Postpartum Sex Taboo: Mende Cultural Perceptions of Tinned Milk in Sierra Leone." *The Cultural Roots of African Fertility Regimes*, 101–24. Proceedings of the Ife Conference, Department of Demography and Social Statistics, Obafemi Awolowo University, and Population Studies Center, University of Pennsylvania, February.–March 1987.

———. "The Politics of AIDS, Condoms, and Heterosexual Relations in Africa: Recent Evidence from the Local Print Media." In *Births and Power: Social Change and the Politics of Reproduction*, edited by in Penn Handwerker, 197–224. Boulder, Colo.: Westview Press, 1990.

———. "School Girls and the Marriage Process for Mende Girls in Sierra Leone." In *Beyond the Second Sex: New Directions in the Anthropology of Gender*, edited by Peggy Sanday and Ruth Goodenough, 283 -309. Philadelphia: University of Pennsylvania Press, 1990.

———. "Marginal Members: Children of Previous Unions in Mende Households in Sierra Leone." In *Situating Fertility: Anthropology and Demographic Inquiry*, edited by Susan Greenhalgh, 130–53. Cambridge: Cambridge University Press, 1995.

———. "Numerators and Denominators in the Study of High Fertility Populations: Past and Potential Contributions from Cultural Anthropology."

Paper presented at the Seminar in Honour of John C. Caldwell, "The Continuing Transition," Australian National University, August 1995.

Bledsoe, Caroline H., and Barney Cohen, eds. *Social Dynamics of Adolescent Fertility in Sub-Saharan Africa*. Washington, D.C.: National Academy Press, 1993.

Bledsoe, Caroline H., Allan Hill, Patricia D'Alessandro, and Umberto D'Alessandro. "Local Cultural Interpretations of Western Contraceptive Technologies in Rural Gambia." Paper presented at the Institute on Health and Demography, Northwestern University, 5 February 1993.

Bledsoe, Caroline H., and Gilles Pison, eds. *Nuptiality in Sub-Saharan Africa: Contemporary Anthropological and Demographic Perspectives*. Oxford: Clarendon Press, 1994.

Bock, Gisela, and Pat Thane, eds. *Maternity and Gender Policies: Women and the Rise of the European Welfare States, 1880s–1950s*. London: Routledge, 1991.

Boddy, Janice. *Wombs and Alien Spirits: Women, Men, and the Zar Cult in Northern Sudan*. Madison: University of Wisconsin Press, 1989.

———. "Body Politics: Continuing the Anticircumcision Crusade." *Medical Anthropology Quarterly* 5, no. 1 (1991): 15–17.

Bondestam, Lars. "The Foreign Control of Kenyan Population." In *Poverty and Population Control*, edited by Lars Bondestam and Staffan Bergstrom, 157–77. New York: Academic Press, 1980.

Booker, Salih, and William Minter. "Global Apartheid." *The Nation* 273, no. 2 (2001): 11–17.

Bozzoli, Belinda. "Marxism, Feminism, and South African Studies." *Journal of Southern African Studies* 9, no. 2 (1983): 139–71.

Brass, William, and Carole L. Jolly, eds. *Population Dynamics of Kenya*. Washington, D.C.: National Academy Press, 1993.

Brassington, E. " 'Go Ye Therefore and Teach.' " *Women's Work* 9, no. 14 (1936): 321–22.

Bravman, Bill. *Making Ethnic Ways: Communities and Their Transformations in Taita, Kenya, 1800–1950*. Portsmouth, N.H.: Heinemann, 1998.

Brett, E. A. *Colonialism and Underdevelopment in East Africa: The Politics of Economic Change, 1919–1939*. New York: Nok Publishers, 1973.

Brett-Smith, Sarah. *The Making of Bamana Sculpture*. Cambridge: Cambridge University Press, 1994.

Brookes, Barbara. *Abortion in England, 1900–1967*. London: Croom Helm, 1988.

Brown, Barbara A. "Facing the 'Black Peril': The Politics of Population Control in South Africa." *Journal of Southern African Studies* 13, no. 3 (1987): 256–73.

Browne, Dallas L. "Christian Missionaries, Western Feminists, and the Kikuyu Clitoridectomy Controversy." In *The Politics of Culture*, edited by Brett Williams, 243–72. Washington, D.C.: Smithsonian, 1991.

Buell, Raymond Leslie. *The Native Problem in Africa*. 2 vols. 1928; reprint, London: Frank Cass, 1965.

Bujra, Janet. "Women 'Entrepreneurs' of Early Nairobi." *Canadian Journal of African Studies* 9, no. 2 (1975): 213–34.

Burke, Timothy. *Lifebuoy Men, Lux Women: Commodification, Consumption, and Cleanliness in Modern Zimbabwe.* Durham: Duke University Press, 1996.

Burns, Catherine. "Reproductive Labors: The Politics of Women's Health in South Africa, 1900 to 1960." Ph.D. diss., Northwestern University, 1995.

———. "Louisa Mvemve: A Woman's Advice to the Public on the Cure of Various Diseases." *KRONOS* 23, no. 1 (1996): 108–34.

Burton, Antoinette. *Burdens of History: British Feminists, Indian Women, and Imperial Culture, 1865–1915.* Chapel Hill: University of North Carolina Press, 1994.

Butchart, Alexander. *The Anatomy of Power: European Constructions of the African Body.* New York: Zed Books, 1998.

Byfield, Judith. "Women, Marriage, Divorce, and the Emerging Colonial State in Abeokuta (Nigeria), 1892–1904." *Canadian Journal of African Studies* 30, no. 1 (1996): 32–51.

Carlebach, Julius. *Juvenile Prostitutes in Nairobi.* Kampala: East African Institute of Social Research, 1962.

Carton, Ben. *Blood from Your Children: The Colonial Origins of Generational Conflict in South Africa.* Charlottesville: University of Virginia Press, 2000.

Cashmore, T. H. R. "A Random Factor in British Imperialism: District Administration in Colonial Kenya." In *Imperialism, the State, and the Third World,* edited by Michael Twaddle, 124–35. London: British Academic Press, 1992.

Chakrabarty, Dipesh. "Postcoloniality and the Artifice of History: Who Speaks for 'Indian' Pasts?" *Representations* 37 (winter 1992): 1–26.

———. "The Difference-Deferral of (A) Colonial Modernity: Public Debates on Domesticity in British Bengal." *History Workshop* 36 (autumn 1993): 1–34.

Chanock, Martin. "Making Customary Law: Men, Women, and Courts in Colonial Northern Rhodesia." In *African Women and the Law: Historical Perspectives,* edited by Margaret J. Hay and Marcia Wright, 53–67. Boston: Boston University Press, 1982.

———. *Law, Custom, and Social Order: The Colonial Experience in Malawi and Zambia.* Cambridge: Cambridge University Press, 1985.

Chatterjee, Partha. *The Nation and Its Fragments: Colonial and Postcolonial Histories.* Princeton, N.J.: Princeton University Press, 1993.

Chauncey, George. "The Locus of Reproduction: Women's Labor in the Zambian Copperbelt, 1927–1953." *Journal of Southern African Studies* 7, no. 2 (1981): 135–64.

Chege, Jane. "Dynamics of the Regulation of Sexuality, Gender Relations, and Demographic Trends in Kenya: The Igembe Socio-Cultural Context." Paper presented at the Institute on Health and Demography, Northwestern University, 1993.

Chitere, Preston O. "The Women's Self-Help Movement in Kenya: A Historical Perspective, 1940–1980." *Transafrican Journal of History* 17 (1988): 50–68.

Ciancanelli, Penelope. "Exchange, Reproduction, and Sex Subordination among the Kikuyu of East Africa." *Review of Radical Political Economics* 12, no. 2 (1980): 25–36.

Clark, Carolyn. "Land and Food, Women and Power in Nineteenth Century Kikuyu." *Africa* 50, no. 4 (1980): 357–70.

Clauson, Gerard L. M. "Some Uses of Statistics in Colonial Administration." *Journal of the Royal African Society* 36 (supplement to October 1937): 1–16.

Clayton, Anthony. *Counter-Insurgency in Kenya: A Study of Military Operations against Mau Mau.* Manhattan, Kans.: Sunflower University Press, 1984.

Clayton, Anthony, and Donald Savage. *Government and Labour in Kenya, 1895–1963.* London: Frank Cass, 1974.

Clough, Marshall S. *Fighting Two Sides: Kenyan Chiefs and Politicians, 1918–1940.* Niwot: University Press of Colorado, 1990.

Cohen, David William. "Doing Social History from Pim's Doorway." In *Reliving the Past: The Worlds of Social History,* edited by Olivier Zunz, 191–232. Chapel Hill: University of North Carolina Press, 1985.

———. " 'A Case for the Basoga': Lloyd Fallers and the Construction of an African Legal System." In *Law in Colonial Africa,* edited by Kristin Mann and Richard Roberts, 239–54. Portsmouth, N.H.: Heinemann, 1991.

Cohen, David William, and E. S. Atieno Odhiambo. *Siaya: The Historical Anthropology of an African Landscape.* Portsmouth, N.H.: Heinemann, 1989.

———. *Burying SM: The Politics of Knowledge and the Sociology of Power in Africa.* Portsmouth, N.H.: Heinemann, 1992.

Cohn, Bernard S., and Nicholas B. Dirks. "Beyond The Fringe: The Nation State, Colonialism, and The Technologies of Power." *Journal of Historical Sociology* 1, no. 2 (1988): 224–29.

Collier, Jane, and Sylvia Junko Yanagisako, eds. *Gender and Kinship: Essays toward a Unified Analysis.* Stanford, Calif.: Stanford University Press, 1987.

Comaroff, Jean. "Medicine, Colonialism, and the Black Body." In *Ethnography and the Historical Imagination,* by John L. Comaroff and Jean Comaroff, 215–33. Boulder, Colo.: Westview Press, 1992.

Comaroff, Jean, and John L. Comaroff. *Of Revelation and Revolution: Christianity, Colonialism, and Consciousness in South Africa.* Vol. 1. Chicago: University of Chicago Press, 1991.

———. *Ethnography and the Historical Imagination.* Boulder, Colo.: Westview Press, 1992.

———. "Home-Made Hegemony: Modernity, Domesticity, and Colonialism in South Africa." In *African Encounters with Domesticity,* edited by Karen Tranberg Hansen, 37–74. New Brunswick, N.J.: Rutgers University Press, 1992.

———. *Of Revelation and Revolution: The Dialectics of Modernity on a South African Frontier.* Vol. 2. Chicago: University of Chicago Press, 1996.

Comaroff, John L. "Images of Empire, Contests of Conscience: Models of Colonial Domination in South Africa." *American Ethnologist* 16, no. 4 (1989): 661–85.

Comaroff, John L., and Simon Roberts. "Marriage and Extra-Marital Sexuality: The Dialectics of Legal Change among the Kgatla." *Journal of African Law* 21, no. 1 (1977): 97–123.

Constantine, Stephen. *The Making of British Development Policy, 1914–1940.* London: Frank Cass, 1984.

Cook, Albert R. "Obstetrics in Uganda." *The Practitioner* 134 (1935): 748–61.

———. *Uganda Memories (1897–1940).* Kampala: The Uganda Society, 1945.

Cook, Rebecca J., and Bernard M. Dickens. "Abortion Laws in African Commonwealth Countries." *Journal of African Law* 25, no. 2 (1981): 60–79.

Cooper, Barbara. *Marriage in Maradi: Gender and Culture in a Hausa Society in Niger, 1900–1989.* Portsmouth, N.H.: Heinemann, 1997.

Cooper, Frederick. *From Slaves to Squatters: Plantation Labor and Agriculture in Zanzibar and Coastal Kenya, 1890–1925.* New Haven, Conn.: Yale University Press, 1980.

———. "Introduction: Urban Space, Industrial Time, and Wage Labor in Africa." In *Struggle for the City: Migrant Labor, Capital, and the State in Urban Africa,* edited by Frederick Cooper, 7–50. Beverly Hills: Sage, 1983.

———. *On the African Waterfront: Urban Disorder and the Transformation of Work in Colonial Mombasa.* New Haven, Conn.: Yale University Press, 1987.

———. "From Free Labor to Family Allowances: Labor and African Society in Colonial Discourse." *American Ethnologist* 16, no. 4 (1989): 745–65.

———. "Conflict and Connection: Rethinking Colonial African History." *American Historical Review* 99, no. 5 (1994): 1516–45.

———. *Decolonization and African Society: The Labor Question in French and British Africa.* Cambridge: Cambridge University Press, 1996.

Cooper, Frederick, and Randall M. Packard, eds. *International Development and the Social Sciences: Essays on the History and Politics of Knowledge.* Berkeley and Los Angeles: University of California Press, 1997.

Cooper, Frederick, and Ann Laura Stoler, eds. *Tensions of Empire: Colonial Cultures in a Bourgeois World.* Berkeley and Los Angeles: University of California Press, 1997.

Corfield, F. D. *The Origins and Growth of Mau Mau: An Historical Survey.* Command Paper, no. 1030. London: HMSO, 1960.

Corrigan, Philip, and Derek Sayer. *The Great Arch: English State Formation as Cultural Revolution.* Oxford: Oxford University Press, 1985.

Cotran, Eugene. *Report on Customary Criminal Offenses in Kenya.* Nairobi: Government Printer, 1963.

———. *Restatement of African Law, Kenya.* Vol. 1, *The Law of Marriage and Divorce.* London: Sweet and Maxwell, 1968.

Cruce, Ashley P. "Meru Women's Self-Help Movement: Problems and Possibilities." Bloomington, Indiana, August 1996. Manuscript.

Culwick, A. T. "The Population Trend." *Tanganyika Notes and Records* 11 (1941): 13–17.

Culwick, A. T., and G. M. Culwick. "A Study of Population in Ulanga, Tanganyika." *Sociological Review* 30, no. 40 (1938): 365–79.

Daly, Mary. "African Genital Mutilation: The Unspeakable Atrocities." In *Gyn/Ecology: The Metaethics of Radical Feminism*, 153–77. 2d ed. Boston: Beacon Press, 1978.

Das, Veena. *Critical Events: An Anthropological Perspective on Contemporary India*. Delhi: Oxford University Press, 1995.

Davin, Anna. "Imperialism and Motherhood." *History Workshop* 5 (spring 1978): 9–65.

Davis, Angela Y. *Women, Race, and Class*. New York: Random House, 1981.

Davison, Jean, with the women of Mutira. *Voices from Mutira: Change in the Lives of Rural Gikuyu Women, 1910–1995*. 2d ed. Boulder, Colo.: Lynne Rienner, 1996.

Dawson, Marc H. "The 1920s Anti-Yaws Campaigns and Colonial Medical Policy in Kenya." *International Journal of African Historical Studies* 20, no. 3 (1987): 417–35.

———. "Health, Nutrition, and Population in Central Kenya, 1890–1945." In *African Population and Capitalism: Historical Perspectives*, edited by D. D. Cordell and J. W. Gregory, 187–200. 1987; reprint, Madison: University of Wisconsin Press, 1994.

Deacon, Desley. "Political Arithmetic: The Nineteenth-Century Australian Census and the Construction of the Dependent Woman." *Signs* 11, no. 1 (1985): 27–47.

D'Emilio, John, and Estelle Freedman. Introduction to *Intimate Matters: The History of Sexuality in America*, edited by John D'Emilio and Estelle Freedman, 9–47. New York: Harper and Row, 1988.

Dickens, Bernard M., and Rebecca J. Cook. "Development of Commonwealth Abortion Laws." *International and Comparative Law Quarterly* 28 (July 1979): 424–57.

Dirks, Nicholas. "Castes of Mind." *Representations* 37 (winter 1992): 56–78.

———, ed. *Colonialism and Culture*. Ann Arbor: University of Michigan Press, 1992.

Donham, Donald L. *Marxist Modern: An Ethnographic History of the Ethiopian Revolution*. Berkeley and Los Angeles: University of California Press, 1999.

Dorkenoo, Efua. *Cutting the Rose: Female Genital Mutilation, The Practice and Its Prevention*. London: Minority Rights Publications, 1994.

Duden, Barbara. "Population." In *The Development Dictionary: A Guide to Knowledge as Power*, edited by Wolfgang Sachs, 146–57. London: Zed Books, 1992.

East African Women's League. *They Made It Their Home*. Nairobi: East African Standard Limited, 1962.

Edholm, Felicity, Olivia Harris, and Kate Young. "Conceptualizing Women." *Critique of Anthropology* 3, no. 9/10 (1977): 101–30.

Editorial. "The Pax Britannica and the Population." *East African Medical Journal* 24, no. 2 (1947): 77–80.

Egero, Bertil, and Edward Mburugu. "Kenya: Reproductive Change under Strain." In *Understanding Reproductive Change: Kenya, Tamil Nadu, Punjab, Costa Rica,* edited by Bertil Egero and Mikael Hammarskjold, 31–64. Lund, Sweden: Lund University Press, 1994.

Ehrlich, Paul R. *The Population Bomb.* New York: Ballantine Books, 1968.

El Dareer, Asma. *Women, Why Do You Weep?* London: Zed Books, 1982.

Eliot, Charles. *The East Africa Protectorate.* London: Cass, 1905.

Elkins, Caroline. "Forest War No More: Detention, Villagization, and the Mau Mau Emergency." Working paper no. 227, African Studies Center, Boston University, 2000.

———. "The Struggle for Mau Mau Rehabilitation in Late Colonial Kenya." *International Journal of African Historical Studies* 33, no. 1 (2000): 25–57.

El Saadawi, Nawal. *The Hidden Face of Eve.* Boston: Beacon Press, 1980.

Engels, Dagmar. "The Age of Consent Act of 1891: Colonial Ideology in Bengal." *South Asia Research* 3, no. 2 (1983): 107–34.

Engels, Dagmar, and Shula Marks, eds. *Contesting Colonial Hegemony: State and Society in Africa and India.* New York: British Academic Press, 1994.

Engels, Frederick. *The Origin of the Family, Private Property, and the State.* London: Lawrence and Wishart, 1972.

Engelstein, Laura. *The Keys to Happiness: Sex and the Search for Modernity in Fin-de-Siècle Russia.* Ithaca, N.Y.: Cornell University Press, 1992.

Etienne, Mona, and Eleanor Leacock, eds. *Women and Colonization: Anthropological Perspectives.* New York: J. F. Bergin/Praeger, 1980.

Evans-Pritchard, Edward E. *Kinship and Marriage Among the Nuer.* Oxford: Clarendon Press, 1951.

Fabian, Johannes. "Religious and Secular Colonization: Common Ground." *History and Anthropology* 4, no. 2 (1990): 339–55.

Fadiman, Jeffrey A. "Early History of the Meru of Mount Kenya." *Journal of African History* 14, no. 1 (1973): 9–27.

———. "The Meru Peoples." In *Kenya before 1900: Eight Regional Studies,* edited by B. A. Ogot, 153–73. Nairobi: East African Publishing House, 1976.

———. *The Moment of Conquest: Meru, Kenya, 1907.* Athens: Ohio University Center for International Studies, 1979.

———. *An Oral History of Tribal Warfare: The Meru of Mount Kenya.* Athens: Ohio University Press, 1982.

———. *When We Began, There Were Witchmen: An Oral History from Mount Kenya.* Berkeley and Los Angeles: University of California Press, 1993.

Favazza, Armando. *Bodies Under Siege: Self Mutilation in Culture and Psychiatry.* Baltimore, Md.: Johns Hopkins University Press, 1987.

Feeley-Harnik, Gillian. "Dying Gods and Queen Mothers: The International Politics of Social Reproduction in Africa and Europe." In *Gendered*

Encounters: Challenging Cultural Boundaries and Social Hierarchies in Africa, edited by Maria Grosz-Ngate and Omari H. Kokole, 153–81. New York: Routledge, 1997.

Feierman, Steven. "African Histories and the Dissolution of World History." In *Africa and the Disciplines: The Contribution of Research in Africa to the Social Sciences and Humanities,* edited by Robert H. Bates, V. Y. Mudimbe, and Jean O'Barr, 167–212. Chicago: University of Chicago Press, 1993.

Feierman, Steven, and John M. Janzen. Introduction to *The Social Basis of Health and Healing in Africa,* edited by Steven Feierman and John M. Janzen, 1–23. Berkeley and Los Angeles: University of California Press, 1992.

Ferguson, Alan, Jane Gitonga, and Daniel Kabira. *Family Planning Needs in Colleges of Education: Report of a Study of Twenty Colleges in Kenya.* Nairobi: Ministry of Health, Division of Family Health/GTZ Support Unit, 1988.

Ferguson, James. *Expectations of Modernity: Myths and Meanings of Urban Life on the Zambia Copperbelt.* Berkeley and Los Angeles: University of California Press, 1999.

Ferguson, Moira. *Subject to Others: British Women Writers and Colonial Slavery, 1670–1834.* New York: Routledge, 1992.

Fetter, Bruce, ed. *Demography from Scanty Evidence: Central Africa in the Colonial Era.* Boulder, Colo.: Lynne Reinner, 1990.

FIDA–Kenya. *A Kenyan Woman's Guide to the Law.* Nairobi: Kaibi, 1990.

Fields, Karen. *Revival and Rebellion in Colonial Central Africa.* Princeton, N.J.: Princeton University Press, 1985.

Fineman, Martha Albertson. *The Neutered Mother, the Sexual Family, and Other Twentieth-Century Tragedies.* New York: Routledge, 1994.

Finer, Morris and O. R. McGregor. *See* U.K., House of Commons, "Appendix V: The History of the Obligation to Maintain."

Fleming, Bruce E. "African Perceptions of AIDS: Another Way of Dying." *The Nation* 250 (2 April 1990): 446–500.

Forbes, Geraldine. "Managing Midwifery in India." In *Contesting Colonial Hegemony: State and Society in Africa and India,* edited by Dagmar Engels and Shula Marks, 152–72. New York: British Academic Press, 1994.

Forrester, Jay W. *World Dynamics.* Cambridge: Wright-Allen Press, 1971.

Fortin, Alfred. "The Politics of AIDS in Kenya." *Third World Quarterly* 9, no. 3 (1987): 906–19.

Foster, W. D. *The Church Missionary Society and Modern Medicine in Uganda: The Life of Sir Albert Cook, K.C.M.G., 1870–1951.* Newhaven, East Sussex, U.K.: Newhaven Press, 1978.

Foucault, Michel. *The History of Sexuality.* Vol. 1, *An Introduction.* Translated by Robert Hurley. New York: Vintage Books, 1980.

———. "Governmentality." In *The Foucault Effect: Studies in Governmentality with Two Lectures by and an Interview with Michel Foucault,* edited by Graham Burchell, Colin Gordon, and Peter Miller, 87–104. Chicago: University of Chicago Press, 1991.

Gachihi, Margaret W. "The Role of Kikuyu Women in Mau Mau." Master's thesis, University of Nairobi, 1986.

Gaitskell, Deborah. "Housewives, Maids, or Mothers: Some Contradictions of Domesticity for Christian Women in Johannesburg, 1903–1939." *Journal of African History* 24, no. 2 (1983): 241–56.

———. " 'Getting Close to the Hearts of Mothers': Medical Missionaries among African Women and Children in Johannesburg between the Wars." In *Women and Children First: International Maternal and Infant Welfare, 1870–1945,* edited by Valerie Fildes, Lara Marks, and Hilary Marland, 178–202. New York: Routledge, 1992.

Gelfand, Michael. *Midwifery in Tropical Africa: The Growth of Maternity Services in Rhodesia.* Salisbury: University of Rhodesia, 1978.

Gervais, Raymond R. "État colonial et savoir démographique en AOF, 1904–1960" (The colonial state and demographic knowledge in French West Africa, 1904–1960). *Cahiers québécois de démographie* 25, no. 1 (1996): 101–31.

Ghai, Y. P., and J. P. W. B. McAuslan. *Public Law and Political Change in Kenya: A Study of the Legal Framework of Government from Colonial Times to the Present.* London: Oxford University Press, 1970.

Giblin, James L. *The Politics of Environmental Control in Northeastern Tanzania, 1840–1940.* Philadelphia: University of Pennsylvania Press, 1992.

Gilks, J. L. "The Incidence and Character of Syphilis and Yaws in Kenya." *Kenya and East African Medical Journal* 8, no. 2 (1931): 131–42.

Gillan, Robert U. "Notes on the Kikuyu Custom of Female Circumcision." *Kenya and East African Medical Journal* 6, no. 7 (1929): 199–203.

Gillman, Clement. "The Population Map of Tanganyika Territory." *The Geographical Review* 26, no. 3 (1936): 353–76.

Gilman, Sander L. "Black Bodies, White Bodies: Toward an Iconography of Female Sexuality in Late Nineteenth-Century Art, Medicine, and Literature." *Critical Inquiry* 12, no. 1 (1985): 204–42.

Gilroy, Paul. *Against Race: Imagining Political Culture Beyond the Color Line.* Cambridge: The Belknap Press of Harvard University Press, 2000.

Ginsburg, Faye, and Rayna Rapp. "The Politics of Reproduction." *Annual Review of Anthropology* 20 (1991): 311–43.

———, eds. *Conceiving the New World Order: The Global Politics of Reproduction.* Berkeley and Los Angeles: University of California Press, 1995.

Goldsmith, Paul. "The Production and Marketing of Miraa in Kenya." In *Satisfying Africa's Food Needs: Food Production and Commercialization in African Agriculture,* edited by Ronald Cohen, 121–52. Boulder, Colo.: Lynne Rienner, 1988.

———. "Symbiosis and Transformation in Kenya's Meru District (Agriculture)." Ph.D. diss., University of Florida–Gainsville, 1994.

Goldsworthy, David. *Tom Mboya: The Man Kenya Wanted to Forget.* London: Heinemann, 1982.

Goldthorpe, J. E. "Attitudes to the Census and Vital Registration in East Africa." *Population Studies* 6, no. 2 (1952): 163–71.

———. "Appendix 7: The African Population of East Africa." In *Report of the East African Royal Commission, 1953–55*, 462–73. London: HMSO, 1955.

Good, Mary-Jo DelVecchio, Esther Mwaikambo, Erastus Amayo, and James M'Imunya Machoki. "Clinical Realities and Moral Dilemmas: Contrasting Perspectives from Academic Medicine in Kenya, Tanzania, and America." *Daedalus* 128, no. 4 (1999): 167–95.

Gordon, April. "Gender, Ethnicity, and Class in Kenya: 'Burying Otieno' Revisited." *Signs* 20, no. 4 (1995): 883–912.

Gordon, Colin. "Governmental Rationality: An Introduction." In *The Foucault Effect: Studies in Governmentality*, edited by Graham Burchell, Gordon, and Peter Miller, 1–51. Chicago: University of Chicago Press, 1991.

Gordon, Linda, ed. *Women, the State, and Welfare*. Madison: University of Wisconsin Press, 1990.

Gosselin, Claudie. "Handing Over the Knife: *Numu* Women and the Campaign Against Excision in Mali." In *Female "Circumcision" in Africa: Culture, Controversy, and Change*, edited by Bettina Shell-Duncan and Ylva Hernlund, 193–214. Boulder, Colo.: Lynne Rienner, 2000.

Greeley, Edward H. "Men and Fertility Regulation in Southern Meru: A Case Study from the Kenya Highlands." Ph.D. diss., Catholic University of America, 1977.

———. "Planning for Population Change in Kenya: An Anthropological Perspective." In *Anthropology of Development and Change in East Africa*, edited by D. W. Brokensha and P. D. Little, 201–16. London: Westview Press, 1988.

Greenhalgh, Susan. "The Social Construction of Population Science: An Intellectual, Institutional, and Political History of Twentieth-Century Demography." *Comparative Studies in Society and History* 38, no. 1 (1996): 26–66.

———, ed. *Situating Fertility: Anthropology and Demographic Inquiry*. Cambridge: Cambridge University Press, 1995.

Griffiths, Anne. "Support for Women with Dependent Children: Customary, Common, and Statutory Law in Botswana." In *Women and Law in Southern Africa*, edited by Alice Armstrong, 164–92. Harare: Zimbabwe Publishing House, 1987.

Gruenbaum, Ellen. "The Cultural Debate Over Female Circumcision: The Sudanese Are Arguing This One Out for Themselves." *Medical Anthropology Quarterly* 10, no. 4 (1996): 455–75.

Gulliver, P. H. "Counting with the Fingers by Two East African Tribes." *Tanganyika Notes and Records* 51 (December 1958): 259–62.

Guy, Jeff. "Gender Oppression in Southern Africa's Precapitalist Societies." In *Women and Gender in Southern Africa to 1945*, edited by Cherryl Walker, 33–47. London: James Currey, 1990.

Guyer, Jane. "Wealth in People and Self-Realization in Equatorial Africa." *Man*, n.s., 28 (1993): 243–65.

———. "Wealth in People, Wealth in Things—Introduction," *Journal of African History* 36, no. 1 (1995): 83–90.

Guyer, Jane, and Samuel M. Eno Belinga. "Wealth in People as Wealth in Knowledge: Accumulation and Composition in Equatorial Africa." *Journal of African History* 36, no. 1 (1995): 91–120.

Gwako, Edwins Laban Moogi. "Continuity and Change in the Practice of Clitoridectomy in Kenya: A Case-Study of the Abagusii." *Journal of Modern African Studies* 33, no. 2 (1995): 333–37.

Hailey. *An African Survey.* London: Oxford University Press, 1938.

———. *An African Survey.* Rev. ed. London: Oxford University Press, 1945.

Hale, Sondra. "A Question of Subjects: The 'Female Circumcision' Controversy and the Politics of Knowledge." *Ufahamu* 22, no. 3 (1994): 26–35.

Hamilton, Carolyn. *Terrific Majesty: The Powers of Shaka Zulu and the Limits of Historical Invention.* Cambridge, Mass.: Harvard Universtiy Press, 1998.

Handwerker, W. Penn, ed. *Births and Power: Social Change and the Politics of Reproduction.* Boulder, Colo.: Westview Press, 1990

Hansen, Karen Tranberg. *Distant Companions: Servants and Employers in Zambia, 1900–1985.* Ithaca, N.Y.: Cornell University Press, 1989.

———, ed. *African Encounters with Domesticity.* New Brunswick, N.J.: Rutgers University Press, 1992.

Hardinge, Arthur. *Report on the East Africa Protectorate to July 1897.* London: Harrison and Sons, 1899.

Harris, Olivia, and Kate Young. "Engendered Structures: Some Problems in the Analysis of Reproduction." In *The Anthropology of Pre-Capitalist Societies,* edited by Joel S. Kahn and Josep R. Llobera, 109–47. Atlantic Highlands, N.J.: Humanities Press, 1981.

Hartmann, Betsy. *Reproductive Rights and Wrongs: The Global Politics of Population Control and Contraceptive Choice.* New York: Harper and Row, 1987.

Haugerud, Angelique. *The Culture of Politics in Modern Kenya.* Cambridge: Cambridge University Press, 1995.

Havinden, Michael, and David Meredith. *Colonialism and Development: Britain and its Tropical Colonies, 1950–1960.* London: Routledge, 1993.

Hay, Margaret J. "Luo Women and Economic Change During the Colonial Period." In *Women in Africa: Studies in Social and Economic Change,* edited by Nancy J. Hafkin and Edna G. Bay, 87–109. Stanford, Calif.: Stanford University Press, 1976.

———. "Women as Owners, Occupants, and Managers of Property in Colonial Western Kenya." In *African Women and the Law: Historical Persepctives,* edited by Margaret J. Hay and Marcia Wright, 110–23. Boston: Boston University Press, 1982.

Hay, Margaret J., and Marcia Wright, eds. *African Women and the Law: Historical Perspectives.* Boston: Boston University Press, 1982.

Hayes, Patricia. " 'Cocky' Hahn and the 'Black Venus': The Making of a Native Commissioner in South West Africa, 1915–1946." *Gender and History* 8, no. 3 (1996): 364–92.

Heald, Suzette. "The Making of Men: The Relevance of Vernacular Psychology to the Interpretation of a Gisu Ritual." *Africa* 52, no. 1 (1982): 15–35.

———. *Manhood and Morality: Sex, Violence and Ritual in Gisu Society.* London: Routledge, 1999.

Henriques, U. R. Q. "Bastardy and the New Poor Law." *Past and Present* 37 (July 1967): 103–29.

Herbert, Eugenia W. *Iron, Gender, and Power: Rituals of Transformation in African Societies.* Bloomington: Indiana University Press, 1993.

Herbst, Jeffrey. *States and Power in Africa: Comparative Lessons in Authority and Control.* Princeton, N.J.: Princeton University Press, 2000.

Hernlund, Ylva. "Cutting Without Ritual and Ritual Without Cutting: Female 'Circumcision' and the Re-ritualization of Initiation in the Gambia." In *Female "Circumcision" in Africa: Culture, Controversy, and Change,* edited by Bettina Shell-Duncan and Ylva Hernlund, 235–52. Boulder, Colo.: Lynne Rienner, 2000.

Herskovits, M. J. *Dahomey, an Ancient West African Kingdom.* Evanston, Ill.: Northwestern University Press, 1967.

Hetherington, Penelope. "The Politics of Female Circumcision in the Central Province of Colonial Kenya, 1920–1930." *Journal of Imperial and Commonwealth History* 26, no. 1 (1998): 93–126.

Hirsch, Susan F. *Pronouncing and Persevering: Gender and the Discourses of Disputing in an African Islamic Court.* Chicago: University of Chicago Press, 1998.

Hobsbawm, Eric, and Terence Ranger, eds. *The Invention of Tradition.* Cambridge: Cambridge University Press, 1983.

Hodgson, Dorothy L., and Sheryl McCurdy. "Wayward Wives, Misfit Mothers, and Disobedient Daughters: 'Wicked' Women and the Reconfiguration of Gender in Africa." *Canadian Journal of African Studies* 30, no. 1 (1996): 1–9.

Hofmeyer, Isabel. *"We Spend Our Years as a Tale that is Told": Oral Historical Narrative in a South African Chiefdom.* Portsmouth, N.H.: Heinemann, 1993.

Holden, Pat. "Colonial Sisters: Nurses in Uganda." In *Anthropology and Nursing,* edited by Pat Holden and Jenny Littlewood, 67–83. New York: Routledge, 1991.

Holding, E. Mary. "Winding Ways." *Women's Work* 14, no. 3 (1941): 4–5.

———. "Some Preliminary Notes on Meru Age Grades." *Man,* n.s. 30–31 (1942): 58–65.

———. "Women's Institutions and the African Church." *International Review of Missions* 31 (August 1942): 291–300.

———. "The Woman Who Was Too Old." *Women's Work* 17, no. 3 (1944): 7–10.

———. *Utheru bwa Mucii* (Cleanliness of the home). Nairobi: Eagle Press, 1950.

———. *Kamincuria Metho* (The little one that opens eyes). Nairobi: East African Literature Bureau, 1951.

———. *Mucii Jumwega* (The good village). Nairobi: Eagle Press, n.d.

———. *Ngono cia Afya* (Hygiene games and stories). Nairobi: Eagle Press, n.d.

———. *Uria Maari Jaatigire na Gukira* (How the cooking stones broke their silence). Translated by Philip M'Inoti. Nairobi: East African Literature Bureau, n.d.

Homan, F. Derek. "Land Consolidation and Redistribution of Population in the Imenti Sub-Tribe of the Meru (Kenya)." In *African Agrarian Systems*, edited by Daniel Biebuyck, 224–44. London: Published for the International African Institute by the Oxford University Press, 1963.

Horn, David G. *Social Bodies: Science, Reproduction, and Italian Modernity*. Princeton, N.J.: Princeton University Press, 1994.

Hosken, Fran P. "The Epidemiology of Female Genital Mutilations." *Tropical Doctor* 8, no. 3 (1978): 150–56.

———. *The Hosken Report: Genital and Sexual Mutilation of Females*. 3d rev. ed. Lexington, Mass.: Women's International Network News, 1982.

Howes, R. J. C. "A Kenya Experiment in Training for Local Government." *Journal of African Administration* 3, no. 2 (April 1951): 87–90.

Humphrey, Norman. *The Kikuyu Lands: The Relation of Population to the Land in South Nyeri*. Nairobi: Government Printer, 1945.

———. *The Liguru and the Land: Sociological Aspects of Some Agricultural Problems of North Kavirondo*. Nairobi: Government Printer, 1947.

Hunt, Nancy Rose. " 'Le bébé en brousse': European Women, African Birth Spacing, and Colonial Intervention in Breastfeeding in the Belgian Congo." *International Journal of African Historical Studies* 21, no. 3 (1988): 401–32.

———. "Placing African Women's History and Locating Gender." *Social History* 14, no. 3 (1989): 359–79.

———. "Domesticity and Colonialism in Belgian Africa: Usumbura's *Foyer Social*, 1946–1960." *Signs* 15, no. 3 (1990): 447–74.

———. "Noise over Camouflaged Polygamy, Colonial Morality Taxation, and a Woman-Naming Crisis in Belgian Africa." *Journal of African History* 32, no. 3 (1991): 471–94.

———. "Colonial Fairy Tales and the Knife and Fork Doctrine in the Heart of Africa." In *African Encounters with Domesticity*, edited by Karen Hansen, 143–71. New Brunswick, N.J.: Rutgers University Press, 1992.

———. "Negotiated Colonialism: Domesticity, Hygiene, and Birth Work in the Belgian Congo." Ph.D. diss., University of Wisconsin, 1992.

———. Introduction to *Gendered Colonialisms in African History*, edited by Tessie P. Liu Hunt and Jean Quataert, 1–15. Oxford: Blackwell Publishers, 1997.

———. *A Colonial Lexicon of Birth Ritual, Medicalization, and Mobility in the Congo*. Durham, N.C.: Duke University Press, 1999.

Hunter, Monica. *Reaction to Conquest.* Oxford: Oxford University Press, 1936.

Hutchinson, Sharon. *Nuer Dilemmas: Coping with Money, War, and the State.* Berkeley and Los Angeles: University of California Press, 1996.

Hyam, Ronald. *Empire and Sexuality: The British Experience.* New York: Manchester University Press, 1990.

Ifeka-Moller, Caroline. "Female Militancy and Colonial Revolt: The Women's War of 1929, Eastern Nigeria." In *Perceiving Women,* edited by Shirley Ardener, 127–57. New York: John Wiley and Sons, 1975.

Iliffe, John. *A Modern History of Tanganyika.* Cambridge: Cambridge University Press, 1979.

———. *Africans: The History of a Continent.* Cambridge: Cambridge University Press, 1995.

———. *East African Doctors: A History of the Modern Profession.* Cambridge: Cambridge University Press, 1998.

Irvine, Clive. *Chogoria, 1930.* Chogoria: Church of Scotland Mission, 1930.

Ivaska, Andrew M. " 'Anti–Mini Militants Meet Modern Misses': A Debate Over Dress in 1960s Tanzania." Ann Arbor, Michigan, April 1999. Manuscript.

Jalland, Pat, and John Hooper, eds. *Women from Birth to Death: The Female Life Cycle in Britain, 1830–1914.* Sussex: Harvester Press, 1986.

Janzen, John M. *The Quest for Therapy in Lower Zaire.* Berkeley and Los Angeles: University of California Press, 1978.

Jeannerat, Caroline F. "Invoking the Female *Vhusha* Ceremony and the Struggle for Identity and Security in Tshiendeulu, Venda." *Journal of Contemporary African Studies* 15, no. 1 (1997): 87–106.

Jeater, Diana. *Marriage, Perversion, and Power: The Construction of Moral Discourse in Southern Rhodesia, 1894–1930.* Oxford: Clarendon Press, 1993.

Jenson, Jane. "Gender and Reproduction: Or, Babies and the State." *Studies in Political Economy* 20 (summer 1986): 9–46.

Jochelson, Karen. "The Color of Disease: Syphilis and Racism in South Africa, 1910–1950." Ph.D. diss., Oxford University, 1993.

Johnson, Frederick. *A Standard Swahili–English Dictionary.* 1939; reprint, Oxford: Oxford University Press, 1991.

Jones, Bertha. *Kaaga Girls.* Nairobi: Uzima Press, 1985.

———. *Kenya Kaleidoscope: The Story of Bertha Jones, for Ttwenty-eight Years a Servant of the Church in Kenya.* Devon: Brightsea Press, 1995.

Jordan, Winthrop. *White Over Black: American Attitudes Toward the Negro, 1550–1812.* New York: Norton, 1968.

Kaler, Amy. "Fertility, Gender, and War: The 'Culture of Contraception' in Zimbabwe, 1957–1980." Ph.D. diss., University of Minnesota, 1998.

———. " 'Who Has Told You to Do This Thing?' Toward a Feminist Interpretation of Contraceptive Diffusion in Rhodesia, 1970–1980." *Signs* 25, no. 3 (2000): 677–708.

Kaler, Amy, and Susan Cotts Watkins. "Disobedient Distributors: Street-level Bureaucrats and Would-be Patrons in Community-based Family Planning

Programs in Rural Kenya." *Studies in Family Planning* 32, no. 3 (2001): 254–69.

Kamunchuluh, J. T. Samuel. "The Meru Participation in Mau Mau." *Kenya Historical Review* 3, no. 2 (1975): 193–216.

Kanogo, Tabitha. "Kikuyu Women and the Politics of Protest: Mau Mau." In *Images of Women in Peace and War,* edited by Sharon Macdonald, Pat Holden, and Shirley Ardner, 78–96. Madison: University of Wisconsin Press, 1987.

———. *Squatters and the Roots of Mau Mau, 1905–1963.* London: James Currey, 1987.

———. "The Medicalization of Maternity in Colonial Kenya." In *African Historians and African Voices: Essays Presented to Professor Bethwell Allan Ogot on His Seventieth Birthday,* edited by E. S. Atieno Odhiambo, 75–111. Basel: P. Schlettwein Publishing, 2001.

Karani, Florida A. "Educational Policies and Women's Education." In *Women and Law in Kenya: Perspectives and Emerging Issues,* edited by Mary Adhiambo Mbeo and Oki Ooko-Ombaka, 23–28. Nairobi: Public Law Institute, 1989.

Karanja, J. K. *Founding an African Faith: Kikuyu Anglican Christianity, 1900–1945.* Nairobi: Uzima Press, 1999.

Kangoi, B. M. I. "A History of the Tigania of the Meru to about 1908." Bachelor's thesis, University of Nairobi, 1972.

Kazembe, Joyce. "Methodological Perspectives on Research and Maintenance Law in Zimbabwe." Paper presented at the Women and Law in Southern Africa Research Project Seminar on Research Methodology, Harare, Zimbabwe, March 1990.

Kennedy, Dane. *Islands of White: Settler Society and Culture in Kenya and Southern Rhodesia, 1890–1939.* Durham, N.C.: Duke University Press, 1987.

Kenya. "The Children Act, 2001, No. 8 of 2001." In *Kenya Gazette Supplement Acts, 2001.* Nairobi: Government Printer, 2002.

———. *Commission on the Law of Marriage and Divorce Report.* Nairobi: Government Printer, 1968.

———. *House of Representatives Debates.* 1963–75.

———. *National Assembly Debates.* 1964, 1966–69.

———. Bureau of Statistics. *Kenya Population Census 1989.* Vol. 1. Nairobi: Government Printer, 1994.

———. Bureau of Statistics. *The 1999 Population and Housing Census: Counting Our People for Development.* Vol. 1. Nairobi: Government Printer, 2001.

———. Ministry of Finance and Economic Planning. Statistics Division. *Kenya Population Census, 1962.* Vol. 3, *African Population.* Nairobi: Government Printer, 1966.

Kenya, Colony and Protectorate. "The Affiliation Ordinance, 1959, No. 12 of 1959." In *Ordinances Enacted during the Year 1959.* Nairobi: Government Printer, 1960.

————. *Legislative Council Debates, 1925–60.*

————. *Official Gazette.* 1946.

————. *The Pattern of Income, Expenditure, and Consumption of African Middle Income Workers in Nairobi, July 1963.* Nairobi: Government Printer, 1964.

————. *Report of the Committee on the Utilization of the Services of Medical Missions, February and March 1926.* Nairobi: Government Printer, 1926.

————. *Report of the Committee on Young Persons and Children.* Nairobi: Government Printer, 1953.

————. *Report on Native Tribunals. See* Phillips, Arthur.

————. African (Native) Affairs Department. *Annual Reports, 1927–40.*

————. Medical Department. *Annual Reports, 1920–58.*

Kenyatta, Jomo. *Facing Mount Kenya: The Tribal Life of the Gikuyu.* 1938; reprint, New York: Vintage Books, 1965.

Kershaw, Greet. "The Changing Roles of Men and Women in the Kikuyu Family by Socioeconomic Strata." *Rural Africana* 29 (winter 1975–76): 173–94.

————. *Mau Mau from Below.* Athens: Ohio University Press, 1997.

Khasiani, Shanyisa A., and E. I. Njiro, eds. *The Women's Movement in Kenya.* Nairobi: Association of African Women for Research and Development, 1993.

Kielmann, Karina. " 'Prostitution,' 'Risk,' and 'Responsibility': Paradigms of AIDS Prevention and Women's Identities in Thika, Kenya." In *The Anthropology of Infectious Disease: International Health Perspectives,* edited by Marcia C. Inhorn and Peter J. Brown, 375–411. Amsterdam: Gordon and Breach Publishers, 1997.

Kinyua, Joseph I. "A History of the *Njuri* in Meru, 1910–1963." Bachelor's thesis, University of Nairobi, c. 1969–70.

Kirby, Vicki. "On the Cutting Edge: Feminism and Clitoridectomy." *Australian Feminist Studies* 5 (summer 1987): 35–55.

Kitching, Gavin. *Class and Economic Change in Kenya: The Making of an African Petite-Bourgeoisie.* New Haven, Conn.: Yale University Press, 1980.

Klugman, Barbara. "Population Policy in South Africa: A Critical Perspective." *Development Southern Africa* 8, no. 1 (1991): 19–34.

Korir, Kipkoech Motonik arap. "An Outline Biography of Simeon Kiplang'at arap Baliach: A 'Colonial African Chief' from Kipsigis." *Kenya Historical Review* 2, no. 2 (1974): 163–73.

Koronya, Charity Kinya. "Female Circumcision and Family Life Education in Kenya." Research paper submitted in partial fulfillment for the Postgraduate Diploma in Population and Sustainable Development, University of Botswana, June 1998.

Koso-Thomas, Olayinka. *The Circumcision of Women: A Strategy for Eradication.* London: Zed Books, 1987.

Koven, Seth, and Sonya Michel. "Womanly Duties: Maternalist Politics and the Origins of Welfare States in France, Germany, Great Britain, and the United

States, 1880–1920." *American Historical Review* 95, no. 4 (1990): 1076–1108.

———. *Mothers of a New World: Maternalist Politics and the Origins of Welfare States.* London: Routledge, 1993.

Kratz, Corinne. *Affecting Performance: Meaning, Movement, and Experience in Okiek Women's Initiation.* Washington, D.C.: Smithsonian Institution, 1994.

Kreiss, Joan K., Davy Koech, Francis A. Plummer, et al. "AIDS Virus Infection in Nairobi Prostitutes: Spread of the Epidemic to East Africa." *New England Journal of Medicine* 314, no. 7 (1986): 414–18.

Kuczynski, R. R. *Colonial Populations.* London: Oxford University Press, 1937.

———. *Demographic Survey of the British Colonial Empire.* 3 vols. 1949; reprint, Sussex: Harvester Press, 1977.

Kuklick, Henrika. *The Savage Within: The Social History of British Anthropology, 1885–1945.* Cambridge: Cambridge University Press, 1992.

Kulczycki, Andrzej. "Abortion in Kenya: The Tyranny of Silence." In *The Abortion Debate in the World Arena*, 41–75. New York: Routledge, 1999.

Lambert, H. E. *The Use of Indigenous Authorities in Tribal Administration: Studies of the Meru in Kenya Colony.* Communications from the School of African Studies, no. 16. Cape Town: University of Cape Town, 1947.

———. "History of the Tribal Occupation of the Land." Pt. 1 of *The Systems of Land Tenure in the Kikuyu Land Unit.* Communications from the School of African Studies, no. 16. Cape Town: University of Cape Town, 1950.

———. *Kikuyu Social and Political Institutions.* London: Published for the International African Institute by the Oxford University Press, 1956.

Landau, Paul. *The Realm of the Word: Language, Gender, and Christianity in a Southern African Kingdom.* Portsmouth, N.H.: Heinemann, 1995.

———. "Explaining Surgical Evangelism in Colonial Southern Africa: Teeth, Pain, and Faith." *Journal of African History* 37, no. 2 (1996): 261–81.

Laughton, W. H. "An Introductory Study of the Meru People." Master's thesis, Cambridge University, 1938.

———. *The Meru.* Nairobi: Ndia Kuu Press, 1944.

———. "A Meru Text." *Man*, n.s., 64, no. 9 (1964): 17–18.

Launay, Robert. "The Power of Names: Illegitimacy in a Muslim Community in Côte d'Ivoire." In *Situating Fertility: Anthropology and Demographic Inquiry*, edited by Susan Greenhalgh, 108–29. Cambridge: Cambridge University Press, 1995.

Leakey, L. S. B. "The Kikuyu Problem of the Initiation of Girls." *Journal of the Royal Anthropological Institute of Great Britain and Ireland* 61 (1931): 277–85.

———. *The Southern Kikuyu before 1903.* 3 vols. New York: Academic Press, 1977.

Lema, Valentino M., and Janet Kabeberi-Macharia. *A Review of Abortion in Kenya.* Nairobi: Centre for the Study of Adolescence, 1992.

Lema, Valentino M., and Wangoi P. Njau. "Abortion in Kenya: Traditional

Approach to Unwanted Pregnancy." The Centre for the Study of Adolescence, Nairobi, 1991. Manuscript.

Leo, Christopher. *Land and Class in Kenya.* Toronto: University of Toronto Press, 1984.

Leonard, David K. *African Successes: Four Public Managers of Kenyan Rural Development.* Berkeley and Los Angeles: University of California Press, 1991.

Lerner, Gerda. *The Creation of Patriarchy.* Oxford: Oxford University Press, 1986.

Levasseur, Alain A. "The Modernization of Law in Africa with Particular Reference to Family Law in the Ivory Coast." In *Ghana and the Ivory Coast: Perspectives on Modernization,* edited by Philip Foster and Aristide R. Zolberg, 151–66. Chicago: University of Chicago Press, 1971.

Lewis, Jane. *The Politics of Motherhood: Child and Maternal Welfare in England, 1900–1939.* London: Croom Helm, 1980.

Lewis, Joanna. *Empire State-Building: War and Welfare in Kenya, 1925–52.* Athens: Ohio University Press, 2000.

Leys, Colin. *Underdevelopment in Kenya: The Political Economy of Neo-Colonialism, 1964–1971.* Berkeley and Los Angeles: University of California Press, 1975.

Leys, Norman. *Kenya.* London: Hogarth Press, 1924.

Lindemann, Mary. "Confessions of an Archive Junkie." In *Theory, Method, and Practice in Social and Cultural History,* edited by Peter Korsten and John Modell, 152–80. New York: New York University, 1991.

Lindsay, Jenny. "The Politics of Population Control in Namibia." In *Women and Health in Africa,* edited by Meredith Turshen, 143–67. Trenton, N.J.: Africa World Press, 1991.

Lindsay, Lisa A. " 'No Need . . . To Think of Home'? Masculinity and Domestic Life on the Nigerian Railway, c. 1940–1961." *Journal of African History* 39, no. 3 (1998): 439–66.

Lohrentz, Kenneth. "The Campaign to Depose Chief Mulama in Marama Location: A Case Study in Politics of Kinship." *Kenya Historical Review* 4, no. 2 (1976): 245–63.

Lonsdale, John. "When Did the Gusii (or Any Other Group) Become a 'Tribe'?" *Kenya Historical Review* 5, no. 1 (1977): 123–33.

———. "States and Social Processes in Africa: A Historiographical Survey." *African Studies Review* 24, no. 2/3 (1981): 139–225.

———. "The Moral Economy of Mau Mau: Wealth, Poverty, and Civic Virtue in Kikuyu Political Thought." In *Unhappy Valley: Conflict in Kenya and Africa,* bk. 2, *Violence and Ethnicity,*" edited by Bruce Bermann and John Lonsdale, 315–504. Athens: Ohio University Press, 1992.

Lorimer, Frank. "Chapter III: East Africa." In *Demographic Information on Tropical Africa,* edited by Frank Lorimer. Boston: Boston University Press, 1961.

Lovett, Margot. "Gender Relations, Class Formation, and the Colonial State in Africa." In *Women and the State in Africa,* edited by Jane Parpart and Kathleen Staudt, 23–46. Boulder, Colo.: Lynne Reinner, 1989.

Low, D. A., and John Lonsdale. "Introduction: Towards the New Order, 1945–1963." In *History of East Africa,* vol. 3, edited by D. A. Low and Alison Smith, 1–63. Oxford: Clarendon Press, 1976.

Low, D. A., and Alison Smith, eds. *History of East Africa.* Vol. 3. Oxford: Clarendon Press, 1976.

Lugard, Frederick. *The Dual Mandate in British Tropical Africa.* London: William Blackwood and Sons, 1922.

Lyons, Harriet. "Anthropologists, Moralities, and Relativities: The Problem of Genital Mutilations." *Canadian Review of Society and Anthropology* 18, no. 4 (1981): 499–518.

Maathuis, J. B. "To Teach or Not to Teach Family Planning in Kenyan Primary Schools." *East African Medical Journal* 47, no. 11 (1970): 545–49.

Maboreke, Mary. "The Love of a Mother: Problems of Custody in Zimbabwe." In *Women and Law in Southern Africa,* edited by Alice Armstrong, 137–63. Harare: Zimbabwe Publishing House, 1987.

Mackenzie, A. Fiona. *Land, Ecology and Resistance in Kenya, 1880–1952.* Portsmouth, N.H.: Heinemann, 1998.

Macmillan, Hugh. "The East Africa Royal Commission, 1953–1955." In *History of East Africa,* vol. 3, edited by D. A. Low and Alison Smith, 544–57. Oxford: Oxford University Press, 1979.

Macpherson, Robert. *The Presbyterian Church in Kenya.* Nairobi: The Presbyterian Church, 1970.

Madan, A. C. and Frederick Johnson. *A Standard English–Swahili Dictionary.* London: Oxford University Press, 1939.

———. *A Standard Swahili–English Dictionary.* London: Oxford University Press, 1939.

Maendelo ya Wanawake. "Harmful Traditional Practices that Affect the Health of Women and Children in Kenya." Nairobi, 1992. Manuscript.

Mager, Anne Kelk. *Gender and the Making of a South African Bantustan: A Social History of the Ciskei, 1945–1959.* Portsmouth, N.H.: Heinemann, 1999.

Mahner, J. "Outsider-Insider in Tigania-Meru." *Africa* 45, no. 4 (1975): 400–409.

Majeed, Javed. *Ungoverned Imaginings: James Mill's "The History of British India and Orientalism."* Oxford: Clarendon Press, 1992.

Maloba, Wunyabari O. *Mau Mau and Kenya: An Analysis of a Peasant Revolt.* Bloomington: Indiana University Press, 1997.

Mamdani, Mahmood. *Citizen and Subject: Contemporary Africa and the Legacy of Late Colonialism.* Princeton, N.J.: Princeton University Press, 1996.

Mani, Lata. "Contentious Traditions: The Debate on Sati in Colonial India." *Cultural Critique* 7 (fall 1987): 119–56.

———. *Contentious Traditions: The Debate on Sati in Colonial India.* Berkeley and Los Angeles: University of California Press, 1998.

Manicom, Linzi. "Ruling Relations: Rethinking State and Gender in South African History." *Journal of African History* 33, no. 3 (1992): 441–65.

Mann, Kristin. *Marrying Well: Marriage, Status, and Social Change among the Educated Elite in Colonial Lagos.* Cambridge: Cambridge University Press, 1985.

Mann, Kristin, and Richard Roberts. "Law in Colonial Africa." In *Law in Colonial Africa,* edited by Kristin Mann and Richard Roberts, 3–58. Portsmouth, N.H.: Heinemann, 1991.

———, eds. *Law in Colonial Africa.* Portsmouth, N.H.: Heinemann, 1991.

Marks, Lara. "Mothers, Babies, and Hospitals: 'The London' and the Provision of Maternity Care in East London, 1870–1939." In *Women and Children First: International Maternal and Infant Welfare, 1870–1945,* edited by Valerie Fildes, Lara Marks, and Hilary Marland, 48–73. New York: Routledge, 1992.

Marks, Shula. *Divided Sisterhood: Race, Class, and Gender in the South African Nursing Profession.* New York: St. Martin's Press, 1994.

Martin, C. J. "The East African Census, 1948: Planning and Enumeration." *Population Studies* 3, no. 3 (1949): 303–20.

———. "Demographic Study of an Immigrant Community: The Indian Population of British East Africa." *Population Studies* 6, no. 3 (1953): 223–47.

———. "Some Estimates of the General Age Distribution, Fertility, and Rate of Natural Increase of the African Population of British East Africa." *Population Studies* 7, no. 2 (1953): 181–99.

Masson, Jeffrey Moussaieff. *A Dark Science: Women, Sexuality, and Psychiatry in the Nineteenth Century.* New York: Farrar, Straus, and Giroux, 1986.

Maupeu, Hervé. *L'Administration indirecte, les methodistes et la formation de l'identité Meru (Kenya, 1933–63).* Recueils est-Africains, no. 1. Paris: Centre d'Études Africaines, Ecole des Hautes Études en Sciences Sociales, 1990.

Mavisi, Violet, and Anne Kyalo. "The Affiliation Act: A Case for Its Reinstatement." In *Women and Autonomy in Kenya: Law Reform and the Quest for Gender Equality,* edited by Kivutha Kibwana, 89–137. Centre for Law and Research International (CLARION) Monograph, no. 1. Nairobi: CLARION, 1994.

Maxon, Robert. "Social and Cultural Changes." In *Decolonization and Independence in Kenya, 1940–1993,* edited by B. A. Ogot and W. R. Ochieng', 110–47. London: James Currey, 1995.

Maxon, Robert, and Peter Ndege. "The Economics of Structural Adjustment." In *Decolonization and Independence in Kenya,* edited by B. A. Ogot and W. R. Ochieng', 151–86. London: James Currey, 1995.

May, Joan. *Changing People, Changing Laws.* Gweru: Mambo Press, 1987.

Mbembe, Achille. "Provisional Notes on the Postcolony." *Africa* 62, no. 1 (1992): 3–37.

———. *On the Postcolony.* Berkeley and Los Angeles: University of California Press, 2001.

Mbeo, Mary Adhiambo, and Oki Ooko-Ombaka, eds. *Women and Law in Kenya: Perspectives and Emerging Issues.* Nairobi: Public Law Institute, 1989.

Mbiti, John S. *African Religions and Philosophy.* Oxford: Heinemann International, 1969.

Mburu, F. M. "The Social Production of Health in Kenya." In *The Social Basis of Health and Healing in Africa,* edited by Steven Feierman and John M. Janzen, 409–25. Berkeley and Los Angeles: University of California Press, 1992.

McClendon, Thomas V. "Tradition and Domestic Struggle in the Courtroom: Customary Law and the Control of Women in Segregation-Era Natal." *International Journal of African Historical Studies* 28, no. 3 (1995): 527–61.

McClintock, Ann. *Imperial Leather: Race, Gender, and Sexuality in the Colonial Contest.* New York: Routledge, 1995.

McCulloch, Jock. *Black Peril, White Virtue: Sexual Crime in Southern Rhodesia, 1902–1935.* Bloomington: Indiana University Press, 2000.

McKittrick, Meredith. "The 'Burden' of Young Men: Property and Generational Conflict in Namibia, 1880–1945." *African Economic History* 24 (1996): 115–29.

———. "Faithful Daughter, Murdering Mother: Transgression and Social Control in Colonial Namibia." *Journal of African History* 40, no. 2 (1999): 265–83.

McLaren, Angus. *A History of Contraception: From Antiquity to the Present Day.* Cambridge: Blackwell, 1987.

McLean, Scilla. *Female Circumcision, Excision, and Infibulation: The Facts and Proposals for Change.* London: Minority Rights Group, 1980.

Meadows, Donella H., D. L. Meadows, J. Randers, and W. W. Brehrens III. *The Limits to Growth: A Report for the Club of Rome's Project on the Predicament of Mankind.* New York: Universe Books, 1972.

Mehta, Uday. "Liberal Strategies of Exclusion." *Politics and Society* 18, no. 4 (1990): 427–54.

Meillassoux, Claude. "From Reproduction to Production: A Marxist Approach to Economic Anthropology." *Economy and Society* 1, no. 1 (1972): 93–105.

———. *Maidens, Meal, and Money: Capitalism and the Domestic Community.* Cambridge: Cambridge University Press, 1981.

———. *The Anthropology of Slavery: The Womb of Iron and Gold.* Translated by Alide Dasnois. Chicago: University of Chicago Press; London: Athlone Press, 1991.

Middleton, Nigel. *When Family Failed: The Treatment of Children in the Care of the Community during the First Half of the Twentieth Century.* London: Gollancz, 1971.

Midgley, Clare. "Anti-Slavery and the Roots of 'Imperial Feminism.' " In *Gender and Imperialism,* edited by Clare Midgley, 161–79. Manchester: Manchester University Press, 1998.

————. *Women against Slavery: The British Campaigns, 1780–1870.* New York: Routledge, 1992.

Miers, Suzanne, and Igor Kopytoff, eds. *Slavery in Africa: Historical and Anthropological Perspectives.* Madison: University of Wisconsin Press, 1977.

Mikell, Gwendolyn. "Pleas for Domestic Relief: Akan Women and Family Courts." In *African Feminism: The Politics of Survival in Sub-Saharan Africa,* edited by Gwendolyn Mikell, 96–123. Philadelphia: University of Pennsylvania Press, 1997.

————, ed. *African Feminism: The Politics of Survival in Sub-Saharan Africa.* Philadelphia: University of Pennsylvania Press, 1997.

Miller, Joseph. *Way of Death: Merchant Capitalism and the Angolan Slave Trade, 1730–1830.* Madison: University of Wisconsin Press, 1988.

Miller, Robert A., Lewis Ndhlovu, Margaret M. Gachara, and Andrew A. Fisher. "The Situation Analysis Study of the Family Planning Program in Kenya." *Studies in Family Planning* 22, no. 3 (1991): 131–43.

M'Imanyara, Alfred M. *The Restatement of Bantu Origin and Meru History.* Nairobi: Longman Kenya, 1992.

Mink, Gwendolyn. *Welfare's End.* Ithaca, N.Y.: Cornell University Press, 1998.

M'Inoti, Philip. "Asili ya Wameru na tabia zao" (The origin of the Meru and their customs). Boston University Library, c. 1930. Manuscript.

————. *Mwari Uri Muuno Utinda* (Moral and sex teaching for girls in the form of a story). Nariobi: East African Literature Bureau, 1955.

————. *Murungu Naimenyithanagia Kiri Ameru na Njira ya Ngono Ciao* (God showed himself to the Meru people by the way of stories). Meru: Methodist Bookshop, n.d.

Mitchell, Timothy. *Colonising Egypt.* 1988; reprint, Cambridge: Cambridge University Press, 1991.

Mizra, Sarah, and Margaret Strobel. *Three Swahili Women.* Bloomington: Indiana University Press, 1991.

Moffett, J. P. "The Need for Anthropological Research." *Tanganyika Notes and Records* 25 (December 1945): 39–47.

Mohanty, Chandra. " 'Under Western Eyes': Feminist Scholarship and Colonial Discourse." *Feminist Review* 30 (autumn 1988): 61–88.

Molokomme, Athaliah. *"Children of the Fence": The Maintenance of Extra-Marital Children under Law and Practice in Botswana.* Research Reports, no. 46. Leiden: African Studies Centre, 1991.

Moore, Sally Falk. *Social Facts and Fabrications: "Customary" Law on Kilimanjaro, 1880–1980.* Cambridge: Cambridge University Press, 1986.

More, Adelyne. *Uncontrolled Breeding or Fecundity versus Civilization: A Contribution to the Study of Over-Population as the Cause of War and the Chief Obstacle to the Emancipation of Women.* New York: Critic and Guide Company, 1917.

Morgan, Jennifer Lyle. "Women in Slavery and the Transatlantic Slave Trade." In *Transatlantic Slavery: Against Human Dignity,* edited by Anthony Tibbles, 60–69. London: HMSO, 1994.

————. " 'Some Could Suckle over Their Shoulder': Male Travelers, Female Bodies, and the Gendering of Racial Ideology, 1500–1770." *William and Mary Quarterly* 54, no. 2 (1997): 167–92.

Morris, H. F., and James S. Read. *Indirect Rule and the Search for Justice.* Oxford: Oxford University Press, 1972.

Mungeam, G. H. *British Rule in Kenya, 1895–1912: The Establishment of Administration in the East African Protectorate.* Oxford: Oxford University Press, 1966.

Munro, J. Forbes. "Migrations of the Bantu-Speaking Peoples of the Eastern Kenya Highlands: A Reappraisal." *Journal of African History* 8, no. 1 (1967): 25–28.

————. *Colonial Rule and the Kamba: Social Change in the Kenya Highlands, 1889–1939.* Oxford: Clarendon Press, 1975.

Muriuki, Godfrey. *A History of the Kikuyu, 1500–1900.* New York: Oxford University Press, 1974.

Murray, Jocelyn. "The Kikuyu Female Circumcision Controversy, with Special Reference to the Church Missionary Society's 'Sphere of Influence.' " Ph.D. diss., University of California at Los Angeles, 1974.

————. "The Church Missionary Society and the 'Female Circumcision Issue' Issue in Kenya." *Journal of Religion in Africa* 8, no. 2 (1976): 92–104.

Murray-Brown, Jeremy. *Kenyatta.* London: Allen and Unwin, 1972.

Muthamia, E. "A Study of Political Development among the Meru of Kenya." Bachelor's thesis, University of Nairobi, 1973.

Mutongi, Kenda. "Generations of Grief and Grievances: A History of Widows and Widowhood in Maragoli, Western Kenya, 1900 to the Present." Ph.D. diss., University of Virginia, 1996.

————. " 'Worries of the Heart': Widowed Mothers, Daughters, and Masculinities in Maragoli, Western Kenya, 1940–1960." *Journal of African History* 40, no. 1 (1999): 67–86.

————. " 'Dear Dolly's' Advice: Representations of Youth, Courtship, and Sexulaties in Africa, 1960–1980." *International Journal of African Historical Studies* 33, no. 1 (2000): 1–23.

Mwangi, Meja. *Striving for the Wind.* Portsmouth, N.H.: Heinemann, 1992.

Mwaniki, H. S. K. "The Chuka Struggle for Survival in the Traditional Days to 1908." *Mila* 3, no. 2 (1972): 13–21.

————. "A History of Circumcision in Mount Kenya Zone." Paper presented to the Department of History, Kenyatta University, November 1985.

National Council for Population and Development, Central Bureau of Statistics (Office of the Vice President and the Ministry of Planning and National Development) [Kenya], and Macro International, Inc. *Kenya Demographic and Health Survey 1998.* Calverton, Md.: NCPD, CBS, and MI, 1999.

Ndeti, Kivuto, and Cecilia Ndeti. *Cultural Values and Population Policy in Kenya.* Nairobi: Kenya Literature Bureau, 1980.

Ndirangu, Simon. *A History of Nursing in Kenya.* Nairobi: Kenya Literature Bureau, 1982.

Ndumbu, Abel. *Out of My Rib: A View of Women in Development.* Nairobi: Development Horizons, 1985.

Needham, Ronald. "The Left Hand of the Mugwe: An Analytical Note on the Structure of Meru Symbolism." *Africa* 30, no. 1 (1960): 20–33.

Nelson, Nici. " 'Selling Her Kiosk': Kikuyu Notions of Sexuality and Sex for Sale in Mathare Valley, Kenya." In *The Cultural Construction of Sexuality,* edited by Pat Caplan, 217–39. London: Tavistock Publications, 1987.

Nicholson, Linda. *Gender and History: The Limits of Social Theory in the Age of the Family.* New York: Columbia University Press, 1986.

Niehaus, Isak. "Towards a Dubious Liberation: Masculinity, Sexuality, and Power in South African Lowveld Schools, 1953–1999." *Journal of Southern African Studies* 26, no. 3 (2000): 387–407.

Njau, Rebeka, and Gideon Mulaki. *Kenya Women Heroes and Their Mystical Power.* Nairobi: Risk Publications, 1984.

Njonjo, Charles. Foreward to *Restatement of African Law: Kenya.* Vol. 1, *The Law of Marriage and Divorce,* by Eugene Cotran, v–vi. London: Sweet and Maxwell, 1968.

Nthamburi, Zablon John. *A History of the Methodist Church in Kenya.* Nairobi: Uzima Press, 1982.

Nyaga, Daniel. *Mĩkarĩre na Mĩtũũrĩre ya Amĩĩrũ: Nteto chia bajũũjũ beetũ* (Customs and traditions of the Meru: The words of our grandparents). Nairobi: Heinemann Kenya, 1986.

———. *Customs and Traditions of the Meru.* Nairobi: East African Educational Publishers, 1997.

Nzioka, Charles. "Policies in Kenya: Critical Perspective on Prevention." In *AIDS*: Foundations for the Future, edited by Peter Aggleton, Peter Davies, and Graham Hart, 159–75. London: Taylor and Francis, 1994.

Nzomo, Maria. "Kenyan Women in Politics and Public Decision Making." In *African Feminism: The Politics of Survival in Sub-Saharan Africa,* edited by Gwendolyn Mikell, 232–54. Philadelphia: University of Pennsylvania Press, 1997.

Nzomo, Maria, and Kathleen Staudt. "Man-Made Political Machinery in Kenya: Political Space for Women?" In *Women and Politics Worldwide,* edited by Barbara J. Nelson and Najma Chowdhury, 415–35. New Haven, Conn.: Yale University Press, 1994.

"Obituary: Robert René Kuczynski, 1876–1947." *Journal of Royal Statistical Society* 110, pt. 4 (1947): 383–84.

Ochieng', William R. "Colonial African Chiefs—Were They Primarily Self-Seeking Scoundrels?" In *Hadith: Politics and Nationalism in Colonial Kenya,* edited by B. A. Ogot, 46–69. Nairobi: East African Publishing House, 1972.

———. "Structural and Political Changes." In *Decolonization and Independence in Kenya, 1950–1993,* edited by B. A. Ogot and William R. Ochieng, 98–100. Athens: Ohio University Press, 1995.

Odinga, Agnes. "Criminalizing the Sick: Women and the Anti-VD Campaigns in South Nyanza, 1920–1945." Minneapolis, 1997. Manuscript.

Ogden, Jessica. "Producing Respect: The 'Proper Woman' in Postcolonial Kampala." In *Postcolonial Identities in Africa,* edited by Richard Werbner and Terence Ranger, 165–92. London: Zed Books, 1996.

Ogot, B. A. "Revolt of the Elders: An Anatomy of the Loyalist Crowd in the Mau Mau Uprising." In *Hadith: Politics and Nationalism in Colonial Kenya,* edited by B. A. Ogot, 134–48. Nairobi: East African Publishing House, 1972.

———. "The Decisive Years, 1956–1963." In *Decolonization and Independence in Kenya, 1940–1993,* edited by B. A. Ogot and W. R. Ochieng', 48–79. London: James Currey, 1995.

———. "The Construction of Luo Identity and History." Paper presented at the workshop on "Words and Voices: Critical Practices of Orality in Africa and in African Studies," Bellagio Study and Conference Center, Bellagio, Italy, 24–28 February 1997.

———, ed. *Politics and Nationalism in Colonial Kenya.* Nairobi: East African Publishing House, 1972.

Ogot, B. A., and W. R. Ochieng', eds. *Decolonization and Independence in Kenya, 1940–1993.* London: James Currey, 1995.

Okeyo, Achola Pala. "Daughters of the Lake and Rivers: Colonization and the Land Rights of Luo Women in Kenya." In *Women and Colonization: Anthropological Perspectives,* edited by Monica Etienne and Eleanor Leacock, 186–213. New York: Academic Press, 1980.

Omolade, Barbara. "Hearts of Darkness." In *Words of Fire: An Anthology of African-American Feminist Thought,* edited by Beverly Guy-Sheftall, 362–78. New York: The New Press, 1995.

Oppong, Christine, ed. *Domestic Rights and Duties in Southern Ghana.* Legon: Institute of African Studies, University of Ghana, 1974.

Orde Browne, G. St. J. "Circumcision Ceremonies among the Amwimbe." *Man* 13 (1913): 137–40.

———. "Circumcision Ceremony in Chuka." *Man* 15 (1915): 65–68.

Owino, Rosemarie. *Sugar Daddy's Lover.* Nairobi: Spear, 1975.

Oyewùmí, Oyèrónké. *The Invention of Women: Making an African Sense of Western Gender Discourses.* Minneapolis: University of Minnesota Press, 1997.

Packard, Randall M. *Epidemiologists, Social Scientists, and the Structure of Medical Research on AIDS in Africa.* Working Papers in African Studies, no. 137. Boston: African Studies Center, Boston University, 1989.

———. *White Plague, Black Labor: Tuberculosis and the Political Economy of Health and Disease in South Africa.* Berkeley and Los Angeles: University of California Press, 1989.

Page, Hilary J., and Ron Lesthaeghe, eds. *Child-Spacing in Tropical Africa: Traditions and Change.* New York: Academic Press, 1981.

Parpart, Jane, and Kathleen Staudt, eds. *Women and the State in Africa.* Boulder, Colo.: Lynne Reinner, 1989.

Parsons, Timothy. *The African Rank-and-File: Social Implications of Colonial*

Military Service in the King's African Rifles, 1902–1964. Portsmouth, N.H.: Heinemann, 1999.

Pateman, Carole. *The Sexual Contract.* Stanford, Calif.: Stanford University, 1988.

Paterson, A. R. "Venereal Disease Work in Kenya." *Kenya Medical Journal* 1, no. 12 (1925): 368–70.

———. "Population in Kenya." *Kenya Medical Journal* 2 (1925–26): 301–8.

———. "The Human Situation in East Africa—Part I: On the Increase of the People." *East African Medical Journal* 24, no. 2 (1947): 81–97.

———. "The Human Situation in East Africa—Part II: Towards a Population Policy." *East African Medical Journal* 24, no. 4 (1947): 144–51.

Pearce, Tola Olu. "Women's Reproductive Practices and Biomedicine: Cultural Conflicts and Transformations in Nigeria." In *Conceiving the New World Order: The Global Politics of Reproduction,* edited by Faye Ginsburg and Rayna Rapp, 195–208. Berkeley and Los Angeles: University of California Press, 1995.

Peatrik, Anne-Marie. "Age, generation et temps: Chez les Meru tigania-igembe du Kenya." *Africa* 63, no. 2 (1993): 241–60.

———. *La Vie à pas contés: Génération, âge et société dans les Haute Terres du Kénya (Meru Tigania-Igembe).* (Life in Steps Recounted: Generation, Age, and Society in the Highlands of Kenya [Meru Tigania-Igembe]). Nanterre: Société D'Ethnologie, 1999.

Pedersen, Susan. "National Bodies, Unspeakable Acts: The Sexual Politics of Colonial Policy-Making." *Journal of Modern History* 63 (December 1991): 647–80.

Penwill, D. J. *Kamba Customary Law: Notes Taken in the Machakos District of Kenya Colony.* London: Macmillan, 1951.

Peretz, Elizabeth. "A Maternity Service for England and Wales: Local Authority Maternity Care in the Inter-War Period in Oxfordshire and Tottenham." In *The Politics of Maternity Care: Services for Childbearing Women in Twentieth-Century Britain,* edited by Jo Garcia, Robert Kilpatrick, and Martin Richards, 30–45. Oxford: Clarendon Press, 1990.

Perkin, Harold. *The Rise of Professional Society: England Since 1880.* London: Routledge, 1989.

Perrott, D. V. *The E.U.P. Concise Swahili and English Dictionary.* London: The English Universities Press, Ltd., 1965.

Petchesky, Rosalind. Introduction to *Negotiating Reproduction Rights: Women's Perspectives Across Countries and Cultures,* edited by Rosalind Petchesky and Karen Judd, 1–30. New York: Zed Books, 1998.

Phillips, Arthur. *Report on Native Tribunals.* A special report prepared at the request of the Kenya Colony and Protectorate, Legal Department. Nairobi: Government Printer, 1945.

Philp, H. R. A. "Native Gynecology." *Journal of the Kenya Medical Service* 1 (1924): 3–4.

———. "Artificial Atresia in Kikuyu Women." *Kenya Medical Journal* 2 (1925): 86–87.

———. "Vescical Fistula Complicating Labor." *Kenya and East African Medical Journal* 4, no. 4 (1927): 126–28.

Piot, Charles. *Remotely Global: Village Modernity in West Africa.* Chicago: University of Chicago Press, 1999.

Pitshandenge, Iman Ngondo a. "Marriage Law in Sub-Saharan Africa." In *Nuptiality in Sub-Saharan Africa: Contemporary Anthropological and Demographic Perspectives,* edited by Caroline Bledsoe and Gilles Pison, 117–129. Oxford: Clarendon Press, 1994.

Presley, Cora Ann. *Kikuyu Women, the Mau Mau Rebellion, and Social Change in Kenya.* Boulder, Colo.: Westview Press, 1992.

Program for Appropriate Technology in Health (PATH). "Qualitative Research Report on Female Circumcision in Four Districts in Kenya." Nairobi, 1993. Manuscript.

Puja, Grace Khwaya, and Tuli Kassimoto. "Girls in Education—And Pregnancy at School." In *Chelewa, Chelewa: The Dilemma of Teenage Girls,* edited by Zubeida Tumbo-Masabo and Rita Liljeström, 54–75. Östersund, Sweden: Scandinavian Institute of African Studies, 1994.

Purseglove, J. W. "Land Use in the Over-Populated Areas of Kabale, Kigezi District, Uganda." *East African Agricultural Journal* 12, no. 1 (1946): 3–10.

Quine, Maria Sophia. *Population Politics in Twentieth-Century Europe.* New York: Routledge, 1996.

Radcliffe-Brown, A. R., and Daryll Forde, eds. *African Systems of Kinship and Marriage.* 1950; reprint, New York: KPI, 1987.

Radel, David. "Kenya's Population and Family Planning Policy: A Challenge to Developmental Communication." In *The Politics of Family Planning in the Third World,* edited by T. E. Smith, 67–121. London: Allen and Unwin, 1973.

Ram, Kalpana, and Margaret Jolly, eds. *Maternities and Modernities: Colonial and Postcolonial Experiences in Asia and the Pacific.* Cambridge: Cambridge University Press, 1998.

Ramazanoglu, Caroline, ed. *Up Against Foucault: Explorations of Some Tensions between Foucault and Feminism.* New York: Routledge, 1993.

Ranger, Terence. "Godly Medicine: The Ambiguities of Medical Mission in Southeastern Tanzania, 1900–1945." *Social Science and Medicine* 15B, no. 3 (1981): 261–77.

———. "The Invention of Tradition in Colonial Africa." In *The Invention of Tradition,* edited by Eric Hobsbawm and Terence Ranger, 211–62. Cambridge: Cambridge University Press, 1983.

Read, James S. "Patterns of Indirect Rule in East Africa." In *Indirect Rule and the Search for Justice,* edited by H. F. Morris and James S. Read, 253–86. Oxford: Oxford University Press, 1972.

Rechenbach, Charles W. *Swahili–English Dictionary.* Washington, D.C.: The Catholic University of America Press, 1967.

Redding, Sean. "Legal Minors and Social Children: Rural African Women and Taxation in the Transkei, South Africa." *African Studies Review* 36, no. 3 (1993): 49–74.

Reining, Priscilla, et al. *Village Women, Their Changing Lives and Fertility: Studies in Kenya, Mexico, and the Philippines.* Washington, D.C.: American Association for the Advancement of Science, 1977.

Retel-Laurentin, Anne. *Infécondité en Afrique noire: Maladies et conséquences sociales* (Infertility in Black Africa: Illnesses and Social Consequences). Paris: Masson, 1974.

Richards, Audrey. *Chisungu: A Girl's Initiation Ceremony among the Bemba of Zambia.* 1956; reprint, New York: Routledge, 1982.

Riesman, Paul. "The Person and the Life Cycle in African Social Life and Thought." *African Studies Review* 29, no. 2 (1986): 71–138.

Riley, Denise. *"Am I that Name?": Feminism and the Category of 'Women' in History.* Minneapolis: University of Minnesota Press, 1988.

Rimita, David Maitai. *The Njuri-Ncheke of Meru.* Meru: David Maitai Rimita, 1988.

Riungu, M. W. "Political History of Imenti." Bachelor's thesis, University of Nairobi, 1975.

Robertson, Claire. "Grassroots in Kenya: Women, Genital Mutilation, and Collective Action, 1920–1990." *Signs* 21, no. 3 (1996): 615–42.

———. *Trouble Showed the Way: Women, Men, and Trade in the Nairobi Area, 1890–1990.* Bloomington: Indiana University Press, 1997.

Robinson, Warren C. "Kenya Enters the Fertility Transition." *Population Studies* 46, no. 3 (1992): 445–57.

Rogo, K. O., L. Bohmer, and C. Ombaka. "Developing Community-based Strategies to Decrease Maternal Morbidity and Mortality Due to Unsafe Abortion: Pre-Intervention Research Report." *East African Medical Journal* 76, no. 1 (1999; supplement): S1–S71.

Rogo, Khama. "Induced Abortion in Kenya." Paper presented at the International Planned Parenthood Federation and the Centre for the Study of Adolescence, Nairobi, October 1993.

Rogo, Khama, and Wangoi Njau. "Newspaper Articles on Family Life Education/Sex Education in Kenya." Centre for the Study of Adolescence, Nairobi, December 1994. Manuscript.

Rosberg, Carl G., and John Nottingham. *The Myth of "Mau Mau": Nationalism in Kenya.* 1966; reprint, New York: Meridian Books, 1970.

Rutenberg, Naomi, and Susan Cotts Watkins. "The Buzz Outside the Clinics: Conversations and Contraception in Nyanza Province, Kenya." *Studies in Family Planning* 28, no. 4 (1997): 290–307.

Rwebangira, Magdalena K. "What Has the Law Got To Do With It?" In *Chelewa, Chelewa: The Dilemma of Teenage Girls,* edited by Zubeida Tumbo-Masabo and Rita Liljeström, 187–210. Östersund, Sweden: Scandinavian Institute of African Studies, 1994.

———. "Maintenance and Care in Law and Practice." In *Haraka, Haraka . . . Look Before You Leap: Youth at the Crossroad of Custom and Modernity,* edited by Magdalena K. Rwebangira and Rita Liljeström, 165–202. Stockholm: Nordiska Afrikainstitutet, 1998.

Rwebangira, Magdelena K., and Rita Liljeström, eds. *Haraka, Haraka . . . Look Before You Leap: Youth at the Crossroad of Custom and Modernity.* Stockholm: Nordiska Afrikainstitutet, 1998.

Rwezaura, B. A. "Tanzania: More Protection for Children." *Journal of Family Law* 25 (1986–87): 261–67.

Saberwal, Satish C. "Historical Notes on the Embu of Central Kenya." *Journal of African History* 8, no. 1 (1967): 29–38.

Sacks, Karen. *Sisters and Wives: The Past and Future of Sexuality Equality.* Urbana: University of Illinois Press, 1976.

Sadowsky, Jonathon. *Imperial Bedlam: Institutions of Madness in Colonial Southwest Nigeria.* Berkeley and Los Angeles: University of California Press, 1999.

Sanderson, Lilian Passmore. *Against the Mutilation of Women: The Struggle to End Unnecessary Suffering.* London: Ithaca Press, 1981.

Sandgren, David. *Christianity and the Kikuyu: Religious Divisions and Social Conflict.* New York: Peter Lang, 1989.

Santilli, Kathy. "Kikuyu Women in the Mau Mau Revolt: A Closer Look." *Ufahamu* 8, no. 1 (1977): 143–59.

Sargent, Carolyn Fisher. *Maternity, Medicine, and Power: Reproductive Decisions in Urban Benin.* Berkeley and Los Angeles: University of California Press, 1989.

———. "Confronting Patriarchy: The Potential for Advocacy in Medical Anthropology." *Medical Anthropology Quarterly* 5, no. 1 (1991): 24–25.

Scarnecchia, Timothy. "Poor Women and Nationalist Politics: Alliances and Fissures in the Formation of a Nationalist Political Movement in Salisbury Rhodesia, 1950–1956." *Journal of African History* 37, no. 2 (1996): 283–310.

Schapera, Isaac. "Premarital Pregnancy and Native Opinion: A Note on Social Change." *Africa* 6, no. 1 (1933): 59–89.

———. *Married Life in an African Tribe.* New York: Sheridan House, 1941.

Schmidt, Elizabeth. "Patriarchy, Capitalism, and the Colonial State in Zimbabwe." *Signs* 26, no. 4 (1991): 732–56.

———. *Peasants, Traders, and Wives: Shona Women in the History of Zimbabwe, 1870–1939.* Portsmouth, N.H.: Heinemann, 1992.

Schoenbrun, David Lee. *A Green Place, A Good Place: Agrarian Change, Gender, and Social Identity in the Great Lakes Region to the Fifteenth Century.* Portsmouth, N.H.: Heinemann, 1998.

Schoepf, Brooke Grundfest. "AIDS, Gender, and Sexuality during Africa's Economic Crisis." In *African Feminism: The Politics of Survival in Sub-Saharan Africa,* edited by Gwendolyn Mikell, 310–32. Philadelphia: University of Pennsylvania Press, 1997.

Scott, David. "Colonial Governmentality." *Social Text* 43 (fall 1995): 191–220.

Scott, Guy. "Political Will, Political Economy, and the AIDS Industry in Zambia." *Review of African Political Economy* 86 (2000): 577–82.

Scott, Joan. *Gender and the Politics of History.* New York: Columbia University Press, 1988.

Scully, Pamela. "Rape, Race, and Colonial Culture: The Sexual Politics of Identity in the Nineteenth-Century Cape Colony, South Africa." *American Historical Review* 100, no. 2 (1995): 335–59.

———. "Narratives of Infanticide in the Aftermath of Slave Emancipation in the Nineteenth-Century Cape Colony, South Africa." *Canadian Journal of African Studies* 30, no. 1 (1996): 89–105.

Searle, W. F., E. J. Phillips, and C. J. Martin. "Colonial Statistics: A Discussion before the Royal Statistical Society held on March 22, 1950." *Journal of the Royal Statistical Society* 113, pt. 3 (1950): 271–97.

Seeley, Janet. "Social Welfare in a Kenyan Town: Policy and Practice, 1902–1985." *African Affairs* 86, no. 345 (1987): 541–66.

Shadle, Brett L. " 'Changing Traditions to Meet Current Altering Conditions': Customary Law, African Courts, and the Rejection of Codification in Kenya, 1930–1960." *Journal of African History* 40, no. 3 (1999): 411–31.

———. "Rape and Justice in Kenya, c. 1940–1970." Paper presented at the Stanford Conference on Colonialism, Law, and Human Rights in Africa, May 1999.

———. " 'Girl Cases': Runaway Wives, Eloped Daughters, and Abducted Women in Gusiiland, Kenya, c. 1900–c. 1965." Ph.D. diss., Northwestern University, 2000.

Sharpless, John. "Population Science, Private Foundations, and Development Aid: The Transformation of Demographic Knowledge in the United States, 1945–1965." In *International Development and the Social Sciences: Essays on the History and Politics of Knowledge*, edited by Frederick Cooper and Randall M. Packard, 176–200. Berkeley and Los Angeles: University of California Press, 1997.

Shaw, Carolyn Martin. *Colonial Inscriptions: Race, Sex, and Class in Kenya*. Minneapolis: University of Minnesota Press, 1995.

Shear, Keith. " 'Not Welfare or Uplift Work': White Women, Masculinity, and Policing in South Africa." *Gender and History* 8, no. 3 (1996): 393–415.

Sheehan, Elizabeth. "Victorian Clitoridectomy." *Medical Anthropology Newsletter* 12 (1981): 9–15.

Shell-Duncan, Bettina, and Ylva Hernlund. "Female 'Circumcision" in Africa: Emerging Perspectives." In *Female "Circumcision" in Africa: Culture, Controversy, and Change*, edited by Bettina Shell-Duncan and Ylva Hernlund, 1–40. Boulder, Colo.: Lynne Reinner, 2000.

———, eds. *Female "Circumcision" in Africa: Culture, Controversy, and Change*. Boulder, Colo.: Lynne Reinner, 2000.

Shell-Duncan, Bettina, Walter Obungu Obiero, and Leunita Auko Muruli. "Women Without Choices: The Debate over Medicalization of Female Genital Cutting and Its Impact on a Northern Kenyan Community." In *Female "Circumcision" in Africa: Culture, Controversy, and Change*, edited by Bettina Shell-Duncan and Ylva Hernlund, 109–28. Boulder, Colo.: Lynne Reinner, 2000.

Scheper-Hughes, Nancy. "Virgin Territory: The Male Discovery of the Clitoris." *Medical Anthropology Quarterly* 5, no. 1 (1991): 25–28.

Shuma, Mary. "The Case of the Matrilineal Mwera of Lindi." In *Chelewa, Chelewa: The Dilemma of Teenage Girls,* edited by Zubeida Tumbo-Masabo and Rita Liljeström, 120–32. Östersund, Sweden: Scandinavian Institute of African Studies, 1994.

Silberschmidt, Margrethe. *"Women Forget that Men are the Masters": Gender Antagonism and Socio-Economic Change in Kisii District, Kenya.* Stockholm: Nordiska Afrikainstitutet, 1999.

Silla, Eric. *People Are Not the Same: Leprosy and Identity in Twentieth-Century Mali.* Portsmouth, N.H.: Heinemann, 1998.

Silverblatt, Irene. "Women in States." *Annual Review of Anthropology* 17 (1988): 427–60.

———. "Interpreting Women in States: New Feminist Ethnohistories." In *Gender at the Crossroads of Knowledge: Feminist Anthropology in the Postmodern Era,* edited by Micaela di Leonardo, 140–71. Berkeley and Los Angeles: University of California, 1991.

Smith, James H. "Njama's Supper: The Consumption and Use of Literary Potency by Mau Mau Insurgents in Colonial Kenya." *Comparative Studies in Society and History* 40, no. 3 (1998): 524–48.

Smith, Richard Saumarez. "Rule-by-records and Rule-by-reports: Complementary Aspects of the British Imperial Rule of Law." *Contributions to Indian Sociology* 19, no. 1 (1985): 153–76.

Snoxall, R. A. *A Concise English–Swahili Dictionary.* Nairobi: Oxford University Press, 1958.

Soja, Edward. *The Geography of Modernization in Kenya: A Spatial Analysis of Social, Economic, and Political Change.* Syracuse, N.Y.: Syracuse University Press, 1968.

Soloway, Richard A. *Demography and Degeneration: Eugenics and the Declining Birthrate in Twentieth-Century Britain.* Chapel Hill: University of North Carolina Press, 1990.

Spear, Thomas. *Kenya's Past: An Introduction to Historical Method in Africa.* Essex: Longman, 1981.

Spencer, John. *The Kenya African Union.* London: KPI, 1985.

Spivak, Gayatri Chakravorty. "Can the Subaltern Speak?" In *Marxism and the Interpretation of Culture,* edited by Cary Nelson and Lawrence Grossberg, 271–313. Urbana: University of Illinois Press, 1988.

Stambach, Amy. "Curl Up and Dye: Civil Society and the Fashion-Minded Citizen." In *Civil Society and the Political Imagination in Africa: Critical Perspectives,* edited by John L. Comaroff and Jean Comaroff, 251–66. Chicago: University of Chicago Press, 1999.

Stamp, Patricia. "Kikuyu Women's Self-Help Groups: Toward an Understanding of the Relation between Sex-Gender System and Mode of Production in Africa." In *Women and Class in Africa,* edited by Claire Robertson and Iris Berger, 27–46. New York: Africana Publishing Company, 1986.

———. "Local Government in Kenya: Ideology and Political Practice, 1895–1974." *African Studies Review* 29, no. 4 (1986): 17–42 .

———. "Burying Otieno: The Politics of Gender and Ethnicity in Kenya." *Signs* 16, no. 4 (1991): 808–45.

———. "Mothers of Invention: Women's Agency in the Kenyan State." In *Provoking Agents: Gender and Agency in Theory and Practice,* edited by Judith Kegan Gardiner, 69–92. Chicago: University of Illinois Press, 1995.

Stein, Karen, Beverly Winikoff, and Virginia Kallianes. "Abortion: Expanding Access and Improving Quality." Robert H. Exert Program on Critical Issues in Reproductive Health. New York: Population Control, 1998.

Stevens, Jacqueline. *Reproducing the State.* Princeton, N.J.: Princeton University Press, 1999.

Stewart, Kearsley A. "Toward a Historical Perspective on Sexuality in Uganda: The Reproductive Lifeline Technique for Grandmothers and their Daughters." *Africa Today* 47, no. 3/4 (2000): 122–48.

———. "Unprecedented Millions in U.S. Aid to Fight HIV/AIDS in Africa: Why Now?" *PAS News and Events* 11, no. 1 (2000): 2–3

Stichter, Sharon. "Women and the Labor Force in Kenya, 1895–1964." *Rural Africana* 29 (winter 1975–76): 45–67.

———. *Migrant Labour in Kenya: Capitalism and African Response, 1895–1975.* London: Longman, 1982.

Stoler, Ann Laura. "Making Empire Respectable: The Politics of Race and Sexual Morality in Twentieth-Century Colonial Cultures." *American Ethnologist* 16, no. 4 (1989): 634–60.

———. "Rethinking Colonial Categories: European Communities and the Boundaries of Rule." *Comparative Studies in Society and History* 13, no. 1 (1989): 134–61.

———. "Carnal Knowledge and Imperial Power: Gender, Race, and Morality in Colonial Asia." In *Gender at the Crossroads of Knowledge: Feminist Anthropology in the Postmodern Era,* edited by Micaela di Leonardo, 55–101. Berkeley and Los Angeles: University of California Press, 1991.

———. "Sexual Affronts and Racial Frontiers: European Identities and the Cultural Politics of Exclusion in Colonial Southeast Asia." *Comparative Studies in Society and History* 34, no. 2 (1992): 514–51.

———. *Race and the Education of Desire: Foucault's 'History of Sexuality' and the Colonial Order of Things.* Durham, N.C.: Duke University Press, 1995.

Stoler, Ann Laura, and Frederick Cooper. "Between Metropole and Colony: Rethinking a Research Agenda." In *Tensions of Empire: Colonial Cultures in a Bourgeois World,* edited by Frederick Cooper and Ann Laura Stoler, 1–56. Berkeley and Los Angeles: University of California Press, 1997.

Stone, Jeffrey C. "Recollections of the Annual Population Count in Late Colonial Zambia." In *Demography from Scanty Evidence: Central Africa in the Colonial Era,* edited by Bruce Fetter, 77–79. Boulder, Colo.: Lynne Rienner, 1990.

Strobel, Margaret. *Muslim Women in Mombasa, 1890–1957.* New Haven, Conn.: Yale University Press, 1979.

―――. *European Women and the Second British Empire.* Bloomington: Indiana University Press, 1991.

Strobel, Margaret, and Nupur Chaudhuri, eds. *Western Women and Imperialism: Complicity and Resistance.* Bloomington: Indiana University Press, 1992.

Summers, Carol. "Intimate Colonialism: The Imperial Production of Reproduction in Uganda, 1907–1925." *Signs* 16, no. 4 (1991): 787–807.

Tanganyika Territory. "An Ordinance to Provide for the Maintenance of Illegitimate Children. 1949, No. 42 of 1949." In *Ordinances Enacted During the Year 1949.* Dar es Salaam: Government Printer, 1950.

Teitelbaum, Michael, and Jay M. Winter, eds. *Population and Resources in Western Intellectual Traditions.* Cambridge: Cambridge University Press, 1989.

Tetelman, Michael S. "In Search of Discipline: Generational Control, Political Protest, and Everyday Violence in Cradock, South Africa, 1984–1985." In *The Politics of Age and Gerontocracy in Africa: Ethnographies of the Past and Memories of the Present,* edited by Mario Aguilar, 177–210. Trenton, N.J.: Africa World Press, 1998.

Thane, Pat. "Women and the Poor Law in Victorian Edwardian England." *History Workshop* 6 (autumn 1978): 29–51.

Thomas, Lynn M. "Contestation, Construction, and Reconstitution: Public Debates over Marriage Law and Women's Status in Kenya, 1964–1979." Bachelor's and Master's thesis, Johns Hopkins University, 1989.

―――. "Regulating Reproduction: State Interventions into Fertility and Sexuality in Rural Kenya, c. 1920–1970." Ph.D. diss., University of Michigan, 1997.

Thomas, Nicholas. "Sanitation and Seeing: The Creation of State Power in Early Colonial Fiji." *Comparative Studies in Society and History* 32, no. 1 (1990): 149–70.

―――. *Entangled Objects: Exchange, Material Culture, and Colonialism in the Pacific.* Cambridge, Mass.: Harvard University Press, 1991.

Thomas, Samuel Price. "Old Age in Meru, Kenya: Adoptive Reciprocity in a Changing Rural Community." Ph.D. diss., University of Florida, 1992.

Thompson, Warren S. *Danger Spots in World Population.* New York: Alfred A. Knopf, 1930.

―――. *Plenty of People.* Lancaster, Pa.: Jaques Cattell Press, 1944.

Throup, David W. *Economic and Social Origins of Mau Mau, 1945–1953.* London: James Currey, 1988.

Tignor, Robert L. *The Colonial Transformation of Kenya: The Kamba, Kikuyu, and Maasai from 1900 to 1939.* Princeton, N.J.: Princeton University Press, 1976.

Treichler, Paula A. "AIDS and HIV Infection in the Third World: A First World

Chronicle." In *Remaking History,* edited by Barbara Kruger and Phil Mariani, 31–86. Seattle: Bay Press, 1989.

Tumbo-Masabo, Zubeida, and Rita Liljeström, eds. *Chelewa, Chelewa: The Dilemma of Teenage Girls.* Östersund, Sweden: Scandinavian Institute of African Studies, 1994.

Turshen, Meredeth. *The Political Ecology of Disease in Tanzania.* New Brunswick, N.J.: Rutgers University Press, 1984.

———. "Population Growth and the Deterioration of Health: Mainland Tanzania, 1920–1960." In *African Population and Capitalism: Historical Perspectives,* edited by Dennis D. Cordell and Joel W. Gregory, 187–200. 1987; reprint, Madison: University of Wisconsin Press, 1994.

———. *Privatizing Health Services in Africa.* New Brunswick: Rutgers University Press, 1999.

Udvardy, Monica. "Women's Groups Near the Kenyan Coast: Patron–Clientship in the Development Arena." In *Anthropology of Development and Change in East Africa,* edited by David Brokensha and Peter Little, 217–35. Boulder, Colo.: Westview Press, 1988.

U.K. *Parliamentary Debates,* Commons, 5th ser., vol. 233 (1928–31).

U.K. Colonial Office. *Health and Progress of Native Populations in Certain Parts of the Empire.* 1931.

———. *Despatches from the Governors of Kenya, Uganda and Tanganyika, and from the Administrator of the Eat African High Commission concerning the East Africa Royal Commission, 1953–55.* Cmd. 9801. 1955.

———. *East African Royal Commission, 1953–55.* Cmd. 9475. 1955.

———. *Historical Survey of the Origins and Growth of Mau Mau.* Cmd. 1030. 1960.

———. *Report on the Colony and Protectorate of Kenya for the Year 1959.* 1960.

U.K. House of Commons. "Report of the Commission on One-Parent Families." *Sessional Papers, 1974, Department of Health and Social Security.* July 1974. Vol. 1.

———. "Appendix V: The History of the Obligation to Maintain," by Morris Finer and O. R. McGregor. In "Report of the Commission on One-Parent Families," presented to the Parliament by the Secretary of State for Social Services. *Sessional Papers, 1974, Department of Health and Social Security.* July 1974. Vol. 16, pp. 85–149.

United States Agency for International Development, AIDSCAP, and Family Health International. *AIDS in Kenya: Socioeconomic Impact and Policy Implications.* Arlington, Va.: AIDSCAP, Family Health International, 1996.

Vail, Leroy, ed. *The Creation of Tribalism in Southern Africa.* Berkeley and Los Angeles: University of California Press, 1989.

van Beusekom, Monica M. "From Underpopulation to Overpopulation: French Perceptions of Population, Environment, and Agricultural Development in

French Soudan (Mali), 1900–1960." *Environmental History* 4, no. 2 (1999): 198–219.

van der Vliet, Virginia. "AIDS: Losing 'The New Struggle'?" *Daedalus* 130, no. 1 (2001): 151–84.

van Onselen, Charles. "The Witches of Suburbia: Domestic Service on the Witwatersrand, 1890–1914." In *Studies in the Social and Economic History of the Witwatersrand, 1886–1914*, vol. 2, *New Nineveh*, by Charles van Onselen, 1–73. London: Longman, 1982.

van Zwanenberg, R.M.A., with Anne King. *An Economic History of Kenya and Uganda, 1800–1970*. London: Macmillan, 1975.

Vance, Carole S. "Anthropology Rediscovers Sexuality: A Theoretical Comment." *Social Science and Medicine* 33, no. 8 (1991): 875–84.

Vansina, Jan. *Paths in the Rainforests: Toward a History of Political Tradition in Equatorial Africa*. Madison: University of Wisconsin Press, 1990.

———. "Some Perceptions on the Writing of African History: 1948–1992." *Itinerario* 16, no. 1 (1992): 77–91.

Vaughan, Megan. "Measuring Crisis in Maternal and Child Health: An Historical Perspective." In *Women's Health and Apartheid: The Health of Women and Children and the Future of Progressive Primary Health Care in Southern Africa*, edited by Marcia Wright, Zena Stein, and Jean Scandlyn, 130–42. 3rd Workshop of the Project on Poverty, Health, and the State in Southern Africa. New York: Columbia University, 1988.

———. *Curing Their Ills: Colonial Power and African Illness*. Stanford, Calif.: Stanford University Press, 1991.

———. "Health and Hegemony: Representation of Disease and the Creation of the Colonial Subject in Nyasaland." In *Contesting Colonial Hegemony: State and Society in Africa and India*, edited by Dagmar Engels and Shula Marks, 173–201. London: British Academic Press, 1994.

Vaughan, Megan, and Henrietta Moore. *Cutting Down Trees: Gender, Nutrition, and Agricultural Change in the Northern Province of Zambia, 1890–1990*. Portsmouth, N.H.: Heinemann, 1994.

Vellenga, Dorothy Dee. "Attempts to Change the Marriage Laws in Ghana and the Ivory Coast." In *Ghana and the Ivory Coast: Perspectives on Modernization*, edited by Philip Foster and Aristide R. Zolberg, 125–50. Chicago: University of Chicago Press, 1971.

———. "Arenas of Judgement." In *Domestic Rights and Duties in Southern Ghana*, edited by Christine Oppong, 77–101. Legon: Institute of African Studies, University of Ghana, 1974.

Waciuma, Charity. *Daughter of Mumbi*. Nairobi: East African Publishing House, 1969.

Walker, Alice. *Possessing the Secret of Joy*. New York: Harcourt Brace Jovanovich, 1992.

Walker, Alice, and Pratibha Pramar. *Warrior Marks: Female Genital Mutilation and the Sexual Binding of Women*. New York: Harcourt Brace, 1993.

Walker, Cherryl, ed. *Women and Gender in Southern Africa to 1945.* Cape Town: David Philip, 1990.

Walker, Liz. " 'My work is to help the woman who wants to have a child, not the woman who wants to have an abortion': Discourses of Patriarchy and Power among African Nurses in South Africa." *African Studies* 55, no. 2 (1996): 43–67.

Walley, Christine. "Searching for 'Voices': Feminism, Anthropology, and the Global Debate over Female Genital Operations." *Cultural Anthropology* 12, no. 3 (1997): 405–38.

Waruhiu, S. N. *Affiliation Law in Kenya.* Nairobi: East African Literature Bureau, 1962.

Warwick, Donald P. *Bitter Pills: Population Policies and Their Implementation in Eight Developing Countries.* Cambridge: Cambridge University Press, 1982.

Watkins, Susan Cotts, and Dennis Hodgson. "Feminists and Neo-Malthusians: Past and Present Alliances." *Population and Development Review* 23, no. 3 (1997): 469–523.

———. "From Mercantalists to Neo-Malthusians: The International Population Movement and the Transformation of Population Ideology in Kenya." Paper presented at the Workshop on Social Processes Underlying Fertility Change in Developing Countries, Committee on Population, National Academy of Sciences, Washington, D.C., January 1998.

Watkins, Susan Cotts, Naomi Rutenberg, and Steven Green. "Diffusion and Debate: Controversy about Reproductive Change in Nyanza Province, Kenya." Paper presented at the Annual Meeting of the Population Association of America, San Francisco, California, 6–8 April 1995.

Weeks, Jeffrey. *Sex, Politics, and Society: The Regulation of Sexuality since 1800.* New York: Longman, 1981.

Weindling, Paul. "Facism and Population in Comparative European Perspective." In *Population and Resources in Western Intellectual Traditions,* edited by Michael Teitelbaum and Jay M. Winter, 102–21. Cambridge: Cambridge University Press, 1989.

Weiss, Brad. " 'Buying Her Grave': Money, Movement, and AIDS in North-West Tanzania." *Africa* 63, no. 1 (1993): 19–35.

Werbner, Richard. "Introduction: Multiple Identities, Plural Arenas." In *Postcolonial Identities in Africa,* edited by Richard Werbner and Terence Ranger, 1–25. London: Zed Books, 1996.

Were, Gideon S., ed. *Meru District, Socio-Cultural Profile.* Nairobi: Ministry of Planning and National Development and Institute of African Studies, University of Nairobi, 1988.

West, Michael O. "Nationalism, Race, and Gender: The Politics of Family Planning in Zimbabwe, 1957–1990." *Social History of Medicine* 7, no. 3 (1994): 447–71.

White, Luise *The Comforts of Home: Prostitution in Colonial Nairobi* Chicago: University of Chicago Press, 1990.

————. "Separating the Men from the Boys: Constructions of Gender, Sexuality, and Terrorism in Central Kenya, 1939–1959." *International Journal of African Historical Studies* 23, no. 1 (1990): 1–26.

————. "Between Gluckman and Foucault: Historicizing Rumour and Gossip." *Social Dynamics* 20, no. 1 (1994): 75–92.

————. " 'They Could Make Their Victims Dull': Genders and Genres, Fantasies and Cures in Colonial Southern Uganda." *American Historical Review* 100, no. 5 (1995): 1379–1402.

————. *Speaking with Vampires: Rumor and History in Colonial Africa.* Berkeley and Los Angeles: University of California Press, 2000.

Wilkinson, G. S. *Affiliation Law and Practice.* 3d ed. London: Oyez Publications, 1971.

Willis, Justin. *Mombasa, the Swahili, and the Making of the Mijikenda.* Oxford: Clarendon Press, 1993.

————. " 'Men on the Spot,' Labor, and the Colonial State in British East Africa: The Mombasa Water Supply, 1911–1927." *International Journal of African Historical Studies* 28, no. 1 (1995): 25–48.

Winter, Jay M. "Socialism, Social Democracy, and Population Questions in Western Europe: 1870–1950." In *Population and Resources in Western Intellectual Traditions,* edited by Michael Teitelbaum and Jay M. Winter, 122–46. Cambridge: Cambridge University Press, 1989.

Wipper, Audrey. "Equal Rights for Women in Kenya?" *Journal of Modern African Studies* 9, no. 3 (1971): 429–42.

————. "The Politics of Sex: Some Strategies Employed by the Kenyan Power Elite to Handle a Normative-Existential Discrepancy." *African Studies Review* 14, no. 3 (1971): 463–82.

————. "African Women, Fashion, and Scapegoating." *Canadian Journal of African Studies* 6, no. 2 (1972): 329–49.

————. "The Maendeleo ya Wanawake Organization: The Co-optation of Leadership." *African Studies Review* 18, no. 3 (1975): 99–119.

————. "The Maendeleo ya Wanawake Movement in the Colonial Period: The Canadian Connection, Mau Mau, Embroidery, and Agriculture." *Rural Africana* 29 (winter 1975–76): 195–214.

————. "Kikuyu Women and the Harry Thuku Disturbances: Some Uniformities of Female Militancy." *Africa* 59, no. 3 (1989): 300–37.

Wolff, Richard. *The Economics of Colonialism: Britain and Kenya, 1870–1930.* New Haven, Conn.: Yale University Press, 1974.

Working Group on Demographic Effects of Economic and Social Reversals. *Demographic Effects of Economic Reversals in Sub-Saharan Africa.* Washington, D.C.: National Academy Press, 1993.

World Health Organization. *Kenya Epidemiological Fact Sheet on HIV/AIDS and Sexually Transmitted Infections,* 2000 Update. Geneva: UNAIDS / WHO Working Group on Global HIV/AIDS and STI Surveillance, 2000. http://www.who.int/emc-hiv/fact_sheets/pdfs/africa.html

————. Department of Women's Health, Health Systems, and Community Health. "Female Genital Mutilation Programmes to Date: What Works and What Doesn't." 1999. http://www.who.int/frh-whd/PDFfiles/Programmes%20to%20Date.pdf

Wylie, Diana. "Confrontation over Kenya: The Colonial Office and Its Critics, 1918–1940." *Journal of African History* 18, no. 3 (1977): 427–47.

Zambia. *Report on Affiliation and Maintenance Orders Project.* Lusaka: Government Printer, 1988.

Index

Compositor: Binghamton Valley Composition
Text: 10/13 Aldus
Display: Aldus
Printer and Binder: Maple-Vail Manufacturing Group